Global History and Migrations

Global History

Bruce Mazlish, Carol Gluck, and Raymond Grew,
Series Editors

Global History and Migrations,
edited by Wang Gungwu

Conceptualizing Global History,
edited by Bruce Mazlish and Ralph Buultjens

FORTHCOMING

The Global Imperative: An Interpretive History of the Spread of Mankind,
edited by Ronald P. Clark

Global Civilization and Local Cultures,
edited by Wolf Schäfer

Global History and Migrations

edited by
Wang Gungwu

WestviewPress
A Division of HarperCollins*Publishers*

Global History

Published in 1997 in the United States of America by Westview Press, 5500 Central Avenue, Boulder, Colorado 80301-2877, and in the United Kingdom by Westview Press, 12 Hid's Copse Road, Cumnor Hill, Oxford OX2 9JJ

Library of Congress Cataloging-in-Publication Data
Global history and migrations / edited by Wang Gungwu.
p. cm. — (Global history)
Includes bibliographical references.
ISBN 0-8133-3123-4. — ISBN 0-8133-3124-2 (pbk.)
1. History, Modern—20th century. 2. Emigration and immigration—History. I. Wang, Gungwu. II. Series.
D445.G55 1997
909.82—dc20 96-34282
CIP

The paper used in this publication meets the requirements of the American National Standard for Permanence of Paper for Printed Library Materials Z39.48-1984.

10 9 8 7 6 5 4 3 2

Contents

1

Migration History: Some Patterns Revisited

Wang Gungwu

When Bruce Mazlish invited me to join his global history enterprise, he gave me an opportunity to bring my work on Chinese migrations to a larger canvas. The invitation led me to write "Migration and Its Enemies", which appeared in the volume of essays, *Conceptualizing Global History* (Mazlish and Buultjens 1994). It also led to the theme of migrations becoming the focus for further exploration of the scope and significance of global history. I was stimulated to bring some migration specialists from various disciplines and a small group of historians together in Hong Kong to test the usefulness of a global historical perspective on the subject of migration. That this approach might be different from world history has been argued eloquently by Bruce Mazlish, and I do not propose to open that subject here (see Mazlish 1994; Grew 1994; and *Journal of World History*, essays by McNeil [1990] and Frank [1991]). Following that meeting, we agreed that a book such as this one would help to extend the debate about the relationship between globalisation and the history of migrations.

The book would not be just another collection of writings about migration. The authors were asked to focus on what migration history had contributed to our understanding, and possibly the actual shaping, of global history. If such explorations should deepen interpretations of contemporary migration issues and perhaps also influence future thinking about migration patterns, so much the better. But that is not what we sought to do. The primary purpose was to take a few steps forward in grasping some features of globalisation and apply a global history approach to one of its most important manifestations. For myself, the starting point would be patterns of migration in history.

It is important that I set down why I am predisposed to link global history with migrations and why, throughout this chapter, I shall often use examples from the history of the two contrasting regions of China and Southeast Asia to illustrate some broader observations. I grew up as the son of a sojourner from China who decided to become an immigrant because it was time to acquire a new nationality. (Sojourning is a distinct form of temporary and experimental migration. See Wang G. 1992c and 1994.) The year was 1949 in the Federation of Malaya, eight years before it became an independent state. Immigrants were enjoined to take part in something quite profound, the noble task of nation-building. This was a common experience around me, and I took this to be the norm in the unfolding of modern history. Chinese sojourners were observing the emergence of a postcolonial state, a new nation in the making (Ongkili 1985; Horowitz 1985). The decision whether to become new citizens or to remain sojourners and aliens and forgo the chance to be the future nationals of an independent nation had to be faced. For all kinds of reasons, most of the Chinese chose to become citizens of Malaya.

In varying forms, this experience, following the end of empires around the world, could be replicated all over Southeast Asia for peoples of very different origins. The situation was seen as the inevitable sorting out of miscellaneous communities created by the great Western powers within newly drawn-up borders. It had the added characteristic of being a colonial experience in the special sense that it was the product of long-distance maritime empires in which the rulers were physically departing but leaving legal and administrative structures behind for indigenous elites to either maintain or dismantle. It was not obvious to me at the time that the phenomenon was anything more than historic long-distance empires running out of steam and recognising that it was time for the imperialists to leave. It was only when I came to study history that I became aware of a more global perspective (McNeill and Adams 1978; Kritz et al. 1981). My own family's story of migration was merely one of the many that reached back to the beginnings of time. It was a universal story that had undergone great changes and had been intensified during the past 500 years of modernisation that had enveloped every part of the globe.

Where migration patterns were concerned, each region had its exceptional features (Contrast R. King 1993 with Emmer and Murner 1992 and Chan 1991). Three broad categories, however, may be recognised, each appearing at different periods of history. The first was migration within kingdoms, principalities, and empires of the three Old World continents, which shared similar cultures, religions, and languages. The second was emigration to distant lands that were conquered or colonised, which led to the formation of migrant states, notably in the Americas and Australasia. The third centered on immigration to states with fully developed or nascent historical identities. To the citizens of these states, the immigrants were of different racial or cultural backgrounds and therefore would have to be treated as foreigners or aliens. The study of history enables us to trace the different stories of settlement and mobility and distinguish among the three distinctive experiences. When it became clear that the modern world was being defined in terms of nationalities, nation-building stages, and nation-states, the many types of migration stories began to converge. It is this that has led me to global history as an approach that could capture the meaning of such a significant convergence of human experience. Attempting such an approach would not merely serve to narrate and explain the new terms of reference for new and aspiring nations and analyse their significance but would also project a kind of focus on pervasive global developments that uncover new connections and open up fresh areas of concern.

Let me return to the most exceptional example, Southeast Asia. This region, unlike its neighbours in east and south Asia, clearly belongs to the third category of migration (Pryor 1979). Before the in-migration of Indians, Persians, Arabs, Chinese, and Europeans, the region had its own migratory traditions within its many kingdoms and tribal groupings, each at different stages of state formation. The arrival from outside of new faiths, ideas, and peoples played an important part in the shaping of what was eventually to become nascent national states. But there was no conscious record of migratory forces playing any part in the origins of its various political entities, or of what was indigenous and what was not. Only those who came from outside the region, especially the Europeans after the sixteenth century, were fascinated by the early influences of Hinduism and Buddhism and by the later power of Islam in the archipelago and Theravada Buddhism on the mainland (Coedes 1948, 1968). In modern times, this interest was further extended to studies of the Christian (especially Catholic) enterprise, of the usefulness of foreign traders, and of the economic value of imported Chinese and Indian labour.

It was the modern Western historians of the nineteenth century who began to present a picture that appeared to indicate that everyone except for a small number of aboriginal tribes—and there was a rigid definition of aborigines—had come from outside the region. Some suggested that the region might have been a larger one that began further north and west on the continental mainland and embraced a larger area than simply the lands between China and India. The Malay peoples were vividly portrayed to have been the earliest of the non-Chinese peoples to migrate from Yunnan some centuries before the Christian era and settle down in the various islands of the archipelago, which carried the name Malay (Winstedt 1947, 1961). What is more, the ancestors of the present Malays traveled even further—eastward toward the Pacific and beyond to people all the islands from Hawaii in the north to Tahiti in the south; and westward across the Indian Ocean to the island of Madagascar. Furthermore, as these ancestors of the Malays came down the mountains of mainland southeast Asia to the plains and the seas, they were followed by later migrating races, originally from even further north and west of Yunnan. The most notable of these were the various Tai (including Shan, Lao, and Thai peoples today), Vietnamese, and Burmese peoples. Finally, the smaller groups of latecomers bearing trading goods, challenging ideas, and other cultural artifacts from India, China, the Perso-Arab world, and including various kinds of Franks from Europe, simply confirmed the long-term pattern of migratory forces that helped to determine the region's history.

The most striking of the modern perspectives on past migrations was the ready acceptance by the historians of Thailand that not only had their peoples come from Yunnan Province in southwest China, but their rulers had been the founders of the Nan Chao kingdom, once an empire that had ruled over southwestern China. It was speculated that its ruling house and the leading tribal leaders had brought their people south because their armies had been defeated by the Mongols in the thirteenth century (Hall 1964: 134–136). The picture of Thai southward migration matched that of the Malays and other Malay-Polynesian speakers as one that resulted from northern military and political pressures forcing people to move further south. However, this was presented by the modern historians in a very positive way. To such historians of expanding global empires, migrations were, like the process of colonisation and settlement, not only normal but also progressive and ultimately beneficial to the extension of civilisation.

A similar picture could be presented of Vietnamese southward expansion down the coast at the expense of the ancient kingdoms of Champa and Cambodia and of the Burmans pushing south into the territories of, among others, the Shan, the Kachin, the Karen, and finally the territories of the Mon peoples of the Irrawaddy delta. It was easy to see the whole movement as coming from further north, and the migration southward as responding to the population pressures of the Han peoples of the Chinese Empire (Wiens 1954; Lee 1978). Thus when Southeast Asia was brought into world history by the end of the nineteenth century as fragmented parts of the Portuguese, Spanish, Dutch, British, French, and American Empires, the context was one in which migration from land and sea, and from almost every direction, had for a long while been seen as an integral part of historical development. What was misleading in the history-writing thus produced, even though probably unintended, was the failure to recognise the native contributions to the dominant cultures of the region (Wolters 1982).

The migration bias in Southeast Asian history-writing lasted until the process of decolonisation began to lead to the era of new national consciousness in the 1950s. Strenuous efforts after that were made to restore the past to the indigenous peoples. As this seemed to have happened in all former colonies, my generation began to assume that our region's history had always been like that of every other region and that the patterns of migration described for Southeast Asia would also have been similar to those everywhere else. Certain historical norms were identified, and the new historians of the region began to see the region's growth and development as having always conformed to those norms. We joined the world only to find that we had always been part of it (Wallerstein 1974, 1980, 1989).

The advent of the new globalisation should have strengthened that perception even further. But a contrary awareness slowly emerged. My own studies of the British Empire and Commonwealth led me to the whole course of modern western expansion into the Americas, with the Europeans seeking "Christians and gold" and, ultimately, territory in Asia and Africa, for the better pursuit of maritime trade. It was their historians who had projected a picture of Southeast Asia as an open region of active migrations. My studies, however, also led me back to the full length of Chinese history. The east Asian region gave me a totally different perspective on trade and travel. On the one hand, there was the dominance of a unitary and authoritarian civilisation that insisted on conformity of behaviour from ancient times. On the other, there were agreed-upon imperial policies against voluntary migration and, in particular, against emigration. The contrast to what I was used to in Southeast Asia and what I knew of the West was so great that I could not help reshaping some of my previous conceptions. I became more inclined to believe in the discreteness of regional history.

This inclination was reinforced by my undergraduate studies in Nanjing after World War II. In succession, the Japanese were driven out of China, followed by Europeans and Americans and by foreign migrants of all kinds (Hooper 1986). Furthermore, there was a systematic welcoming home of overseas Chinese and new walls were steadily built to keep all Chinese inside (FitzGerald 1972). This was nothing new. It conformed to at least a thousand years of Chinese history and was the very opposite of my Southeast Asian experience. Thus, when I returned to the familiar open world of migrants on my return to Malaya, the sense of contrast at the time was never greater.

My own migratory life continued for the next forty years. I went on to more studies in colonial Singapore and cosmopolitan London and then returned to teach in multiracial, multicultural, and multilingual Kuala Lumpur. Twelve years later, I moved again. First, I was drawn to the research environment and facilities of Canberra, the capital of a successful migrant state that was just beginning to regret its racist past. It was most enlightening to see firsthand the truly long-distance efforts to strengthen global links through the reform of immigration policies, changing from allowing European immigration exclusively to opening the country to peoples from Asia, Africa, and the Americas (Jupp 1988). Then came the temptation, which I could not resist, for me to live in one of the great migrant centers of Asia—the yet un-decolonised metropolis of Hong Kong. Whether it is the Vietnamese refugees; the 50,000 to 60,000-per-year rate of emigration; the 100-per-day officially approved immigrants from the Chinese mainland; the foreign maids, labourers, or multinational executives; the Hong Kong migrants returning with foreign passports; the ubiquitous I.I.'s (illegal immigrants); or those being smuggled intercontinentally to more distant shores—not a day passes without a headline or two about subjects that tie migrations to the process of globalisation (Skeldon 1994).

In each place that I have lived, the growing force of globalisation was first slightly discernible and then became unmistakable. In contrast to the closed nationalism of Nanjing and the artificial internationalism of Beijing, much of the noncommunist world outside was advancing along the modernising capitalist road. These advances were led, for better or for worse, by individuals and companies who commanded the technology and skills to cross communal and national boundaries with relative ease. The insidious marketing networks of financial and labour mobility penetrated increasingly into the social and political systems of the postcolonial world (Cohen 1987).

All this time, I was introduced to the experience of being, like so many others of my generation who were educated abroad, 'globalised'. This was happening while an increasingly more dynamic and intensive globalisation was transforming the rest of the world. There was also a growing sense that migrant peoples everywhere were being overwhelmed by the rapidity of political and economic change (Kritz et al. 1981). Among these migrant people were many whose identity was threatened by globalisation. Many would be stimulated by the excitement; yet others by fear and uncertainty at what lay ahead. The more they became aware of what could be learnt about global history and of the different migration patterns that could be found worldwide, the more difficult it was to distance themselves from the agonies of isolation, loneliness, and alienation that most migrants shared. The more their manifold struggles for community became widely known, the more unclear it was that the desire to lose one's original identity by becoming assimilated was a positive value (Hall 1991). Some came to wonder if assimilation would turn out to be desperately unfulfilling and possibly futile.

In short, using global history as a response to globalisation would seem to point away from accepting the normative features of modernisation.

For example, instead of confirming that the history of Southeast Asian migration has always shown how much it had in common with migrations in other regions, this approach stirred some opposite images. It brought forth the realisation that the prominence of migrations as a regular and continuous phenomenon in historical times made Southeast Asia's ancient and early modern past quite exceptional. A region with the longest coastlines and the largest number of islands was more open than the largely land-based civilisations like China and India that had built their wealth on agrarian triumphs (Reid 1988, 1993). With the exception of the Caribbean, no other region had the natural land-sea formations that would create the same geographical condition. And before the age of Columbus, that area was so far from the spectacular developments of the Eurasian world that they were simply out of range of the migratory flows and culture contacts. Furthermore, the Caribbean did not have as neighbours the thrusting dynamic forces of south and west Asia on the one side and those of east Asia on the other. Indeed, for Southeast Asia to have been situated between two of the oldest and richest civilisations for thousands of years and still to have kept its unique features of maritime ebbs and flows makes its survival a truly astounding phenomenon (Wolters 1982).

In short, modern and contemporary world history has tended to show that the region was like all others in wanting to build its new nations and in choosing to link in firmly with the international marketing system. A global history approach, however, would lead us to discern how uncertain the earlier state formations of the archipelago world were and to distinguish the real migratory challenges that the region actually had to endure before it eventually became, in modern terms, 'globalised'. Thus by placing the migration patterns of the past in a longer perspective, the more recent changes that demonstrate how the region conforms to the global condition can now be better understood.

Having said that, it is not clear how the global history that shows the region to have been exceptional in the past can illuminate present trends and point to future directions. Far from confirming the 'global village', the longer perspective will always be there to remind us that the roots of difference are still with us underneath the surface similarities. Southeast Asia remains essentially distinct from the massiveness of China and the special complexities of multinational India (Reid 1988, 1993). In sharp contrast to its early history of in-migrations, the region now exports more emigrants to other parts of the world than it receives new immigrants from outside (Castles and Miller 1993). Indeed, quite extraordinarily, once the new nations of Southeast Asia were established, they virtually stopped immigration from outside the region, and this at about the same time that Europe, the Americas, and Australasia began to accept immigrants from Asia in unprecedented numbers. No doubt, other characteristics in which the region conforms to the global norms have to be taken into account. For example, the nation-building practice of integrating and assimilating minorities (especially migrant minorities) was learnt directly from the Europeans, and the varieties of 'brain drain' emigrations and the more recent remigrant patterns do resemble the patterns evolving all over the world (for remigration, see Wang G. 1991b and 1994). The patterns all suggest that global history is not a teacher of the directions of change. Instead, it focuses and sharpens our awareness of variation and flux by turning more lights on to the past and opening more windows to a possible global future.

Many scholars have argued and, in some cases, demonstrated that globalisation turns people back to the particular, the regional, and the local. Indeed, the second volume in this series, entitled *Global Civilisation and Local Cultures* (Schafer forthcoming) focuses on this theme. The subject of migrations is no exception to this observation. I have already reflected this by pointing to the uniqueness of the local phenomena in Southeast Asia. Three chapters in this volume juxtapose the global and the regional in illuminating ways. Certainly Philip Curtin's study of the larger continental and intercontinental migrations into and out of the African region is no less global than similar studies of movements in and out of various Asian regions. What he highlights is how the total past of migration patterns for one part of the world could be drawn on to delineate the complex configurations of global history. Similarly, over a much shorter span of time and through the interactions of the more- and the less-developed subregions of a smaller area, that of Europe, Ewa Morawska and Willfried Spohn bring out the varieties and complexities of population movements. Their chapter emphasises how recent events in the era of globalisation can have strong and distinctive local characteristic and how particular changes carry universal features that have to be recognised in global history. Indeed, one cannot help but feel that what transpired in the moving of Europeans over the past two centuries is but an intensification of the pain and agony that one might expect among migrants in one of the most concentrated, developed, and warlike corners of the globe (Moch 1992). Aristide Zolberg brings us down to earth even more determinedly by focusing on forty years (1885–1925) of wall-building against human movement at the point when globalisation by the Western industrial powers could be triumphantly proclaimed.

Three patterns of migration that emerge from these chapters deserve revisiting. Of these, let me first consider slavery. The prominence of slavery in the Euro-African and Eurasian economic relationships is closely linked to the value of land and labour in the evolution of technology. Work that no individual or single family can perform without help can be priced and commercialised. Both voluntary and nonvoluntary movements of people depend on the sophistication of the marketing system for labour. No less important are the further divisions of labour that occur in response to developments of the economy. The need for poorer or weaker nonkin neighbours, or better still, strangers, to carry the burdens of distasteful functions grows with wealth and discrepancies of wealth. New industries that require large numbers of workers differ only in scale. At heart, they are but variants of the same phenomena. Of course, when the new industries stimulate large-scale migrations, the norm would be that of rural to urban movements. And where the imbalance of demand and supply is too great, industries resort to long-distance migrations to satisfy the need (Curtin 1984). Transportation costs are then added to the value and price of the labour and they tend to rise significantly in the short run.

That the general features underlying labour migrations were universal long before they took on global forms is now understood. It is global history, however, that confirms the universality. Yet all the previously mentioned elements can be found without the need for slavery. I am reminded of the elaborate efforts of hundreds of historians and thousands of ideologues in the People's Republic of China, who struggled to find slavery in premodern Chinese history. Did not Marx and Engels say that slavery was a key mode of production before the arrival of feudalism? Once it was established that there was *fengjian,* which most historians equated with a form of feudalism, the search for a *nuli* (slavery) system of the Greco-Roman variety began. The debates over the dates for the institution ranged from roughly the eleventh century B.C. to the fourth century A.D. (Feuerwerker 1968; Wang G. 1991a). In the end, no final conclusion was reached. Today, slavery as an issue has simply faded back into the obscurity in which it had lain for 2,000 years. Throughout the debate in China, there was no serious attempt to deal with the large-scale market for, and long-distance transportation of, slaves that Philip Curtin writes about. And certainly there was an uncomfortable silence about the possibility of that form of migration playing a direct part in the rise of capitalism. Here at least there was no claim to a global history approach.

Indeed, in China, India, and Southeast Asia, as in the Middle East and in Europe, privately owned slaves (or various kinds of serfs) were extensively used in farm and domestic service (Phillips 1985). For the purpose of war and public works, however, rulers, tribal leaders, and the various bureaucratic regimes used corvée labour, a precursor of conscription rather than a variety of slavery. This often entailed moving large numbers of people over long distances, but there was no association of slavery with new technologies or industries like plantations and mines. In China, mines were normally officially controlled, and forms of contract or corvée labour were used. Privately sponsored mines, however, had to develop other alternatives. Instead of corvée labour or slavery, what developed was the *kongsi,* a kind of working brotherhood that resorted to the language of male-dominated kinship to bind workers to a crude form of profit sharing built on the idea of male relatives sharing the family heritage (Wang T.P. 1994). It is not clear whether a global history approach that recognises the expansion of the world-system economy should conclude that China's lack of certain forms of enforced labour migration proves that China is a late developer, a latecomer into the age of globalisation.

The second pattern is the state-sponsored moving of people. What is telling is that the official moving of people was common throughout Chinese history, and there appear to be echoes of this practice in the modern moving of Europeans that Ewa Morawska and Willfried Spohn describe. Of special relevance is the origin of the Chinese word, *yimin,* which today translates to migrant and literally means 'moving people'. It comes from two phrases, both of which imply official decisions to have people moved—either to strengthen defences on the border or to respond to changing economic demands (Wang G. 1992c). The striking difference is that, whereas *yimin* had always taken place *within* China, official transportation of peoples in Europe involved moving people *across* national borders, either outward to get rid of them or inward because other nations had evicted their aliens or undesirable 'ethnics'. The new developments arose logically from the sacrosanct nation-state structures that were invented in Europe as the epitome of modernisation, sometimes touted to the rest of the world as the prelude to the most advanced state of globalisation. Can global history play a part here, by exposing the false progress represented by the tendency toward 'ethnic cleansing' that national moving of peoples implies?

China continues to move people, millions of them at a time, whether to relieve the cities and learn from the peasantry, as happened during the Cultural Revolution decade, or to clear the space needed to build the Three Gorges Dam. There are human rights issues involved here, because modern governments do not force such movements on their own peoples. Forced movement of nonnationals, however, would be different; it could be explained. Nonnationals are often considered lesser humans in terms of national ideology. A global history perspective on the varieties of migration would lead us to understand that this is the new norm. What happens in European nations can be made to justify what may have to happen in other nations, wherever they may be. If this is the price of globalisation, the global history approach can help to determine the roots of the competing value systems that led one to win over the others in the name of modernity and progress. With a clearer idea of the worldwide changes over a long period of time, it might both curb the rush to judgment and sharpen the criteria for future permissible migrations. But the authors, Morawska and Spohn, end their chapter with wise words, derived from their larger global perspective of migration history, which leaders in regions outside Europe should heed. They ask that the enduring inequalities in the migration experience not be forgotten; that the strong link with political and administrative interests be constantly kept in mind; and that greater attention be paid to the growth of extensive social networks. This last may yet humanise the wretched history of moving people, of which Europe and Africa have most recently borne the brunt.

Let us move on to the third pattern of migration. Nation-states have walls in a way that porous imperial frontiers and remote and distant tribal territories rarely had. Aristide Zolberg notes that it was when "the globalisation of the economic, strategic, and cultural spheres" was visible that the barriers against immigration began to go up, and "the receivers quickly came to see themselves as victims of an alien invasion". The tensions between free-trade capitalism, or what Zolberg calls "mature capitalist society", and sovereign nation-states led to the building of bureaucratic walls against human movements in unprecedented ways. Walls went up only to be lowered and were then built even higher so that the next lowering still left the immigration officials in control and ever ready to push them higher again.

Turning to global history in depth is of little help here. This pattern of migration manipulation is a sophisticated product of nationalism and modernity. Only the reference to walls rings a bell. Did the Chinese not have the greatest walls ever built? The noted Chinese historian Fang Chaoying asked in one of his lectures if the walls were there to keep the barbarians out or really to keep the Chinese in. His answer was inconclusive where migrations were concerned. Nevertheless, the question confirms the Chinese norm that moving people to or from the borders was an imperial prerogative. The walls could have served both functions, particularly during the Ming dynasty (1368–1644) when there were elaborate trading walls as well (Waldron 1990).

Yet the Chinese experience may be relevant, if only as a contrast to the region to its south, that of Southeast Asia. To have physical walls to protect all levels of administration is normal for the Chinese. Their strategic and political value was always appreciated. Southeast Asians, on the other hand, depended on natural barriers like the highlands and the jungles that effectively divided rivers and valley systems from one another and made migrations across them very difficult. And the Malay peoples sought their best defence from the very seas that enabled their adventurous sons to migrate extensively and often. Globalisation today has brought the Southeast Asians to new forms of wall-building within their emerging nation-states. The question is whether a global history that enhances the quality of comparisons and contrasts over long periods of time and wide expanses of space can modify the extreme effects that modern wall-building against human movements can bring.

The sharp contrast between having walls against the movement of people but none that inhibit trade leads me to the chapters by Yash Ghai and Ronald Skeldon. They both have pointed to the deep relationship that migrations of most kinds have with markets and, more recently, with the remarkable successes of capitalism. They have both examined their subjects globally, that is, they have recognised the global expansion of markets as being a single process that has largely been linear and continuous. Yet, regional and local variations are significant, and neither variation is ignored in their chapters. Two unequal features in the patterns of historical change, however, deserve special attention.

Yash Ghai was quick to identify the first. The laws of the market had never been equal. Labour never enjoyed what capital enjoyed according to the laws of the market. But law as applied to migrant labour has seen improvements. A global approach can show that conditions for labour are likely to go on improving as they have improved since the days of slavery. Ghai identifies three stages of change in the legal status of workers who move away from their home environment, especially if they are transported long distances from their countries of origin. The experience of slaves in New World plantations was a specific one confined to one part of the world (Curtin 1990). When slavery came to an end, its replacement was more universal. This was the indentured labour system, which was probably the first kind of cross-cultural migration to be acknowledged by statutory law. As the practice spread to every continent, it marked "the beginnings of the formalisation of global migrations". Statutory law, however, was inadequate protection for such migrants (Tinker 1974 and Emmer 1986). The inequality of the law for capital as compared to the law for labour ensured that indentured labourers would remain severely handicapped in the eyes of the law as long as they were subject to predetermined terms of work and livelihood drawn up in the interest of trade and investment. It will not be until migrant labourers have access to freely negotiated contracts that they can hope to enjoy some of the fruits of struggle that some of their local native counterparts have begun to take as given and sacred.

Global history confirms that, even for free labour, there is a further obvious inequality that will not disappear, that between the developed and the underdeveloped regions, that between rich and poor nations

(Appleyard 1988). The profound differences between workers' rights in the former as compared with those in the latter are there for all to see. It is instructive to learn that there is no legal system that protects migrants as such. They remain at best in a transitional state until they either become full citizens and enjoy full rights or they leave. What is significant is that the protection for the working class in the rich and developed countries is much greater than that in the poorer countries. The difference is so marked that, if and when they become citizens, the great leap forward that migrant workers would make is a very large jump indeed. The size of this gap puts immense pressure on all concerned. It drives local leaders to keep migrant numbers down to a minimum. The migrants want to stay as long as they can in order to achieve equality in some form or other. Their families back home want them to stay longer in order to maximise their benefits. The capitalists will do their utmost to bring cheaper labour to reduce the power of the local trade unions. And the regions that send the migrant labour work to ensure that the volume of remittances does not fall (Castles and Miller 1993).

Thus, the rights of free labour that global organisations began to work for after the end of World War I continue to improve on paper. These rights have been upgraded into the stratosphere of universal human rights, and the highest claims are now being made for the sacred right to work. But the inequalities where migrants are concerned remain more real, and they are still justified and remarkably well supported by the legal system in each country. In the wider context of increasing globalisation, regional differences increase as steadily and stubbornly as ever. It is no wonder that Yash Ghai feels that the market is failing migrant workers. His global history approach has helped him identify the contradictory conditions that have made the market less responsive today than it was a century or two ago.

Let me now turn to the second and even more obvious inequality, that of the market conditions in the capitalist system. Ron Skeldon's chapter brings this out fully in the migration patterns pertaining to the great cities. The correlation between supply and demand may not be perfect for the periods surveyed, but there is little doubt that globally, the market is poised for a fundamental shift in emphasis. The historic migrations in response to labour-intensive needs are diminishing, and the capital- or skill-related migrations are better placed to meet global demands. This may appear to be contrary to the point Yash Ghai made about migrations being less market-based today than in the past. But Ron Skeldon's view refers to the more permanent migrations of skilled personnel who are capable of moving from the periphery to the centre as well as from the centre to the periphery if the market requires them to do so (Skeldon

1994). They have noticeably different behaviour patterns to those of the more traditional migrant workers inevitably drawn to the great cities from the rural hinterlands.

Here too the globalisation of open market systems does not diminish regional distinctiveness. Let me take the neighbouring regions of China and Southeast Asia again as examples. Unlike the Chinese mandarins, Southeast Asian rulers never erected walls against trade. Throughout the centuries, their openness, especially with regard to the freedom of the seas, was only restricted by the boldness and ferocity of the pirates that infected those seas. It has been suggested that that openness might have influenced Grotius in his "Mare Liberum" after he learned through the Dutch East India Company about the maritime codes prevalent in the Malay archipelago. Among the Malays, in particular, there was an established respect for the merchant. The tradition of princes and kings partaking directly of the fruits of trade has left its mark on contemporary politics and industry (van Leur 1955).

In contrast, the traditions of bureaucratic wall-building in China applied strongly where migrations and foreign trade were concerned. Thus, when a major shift in migration pattern began to occur, that openness in Southeast Asia enabled the region to adjust with relative ease. A China loyal to either its closed imperial or communist past will find it difficult to adapt to such changes. The real tests are yet to come as to whether China has really discarded the shackles with which it bound itself for thirty years after 1949. Policies toward internal migrations were the first to change and have changed decisively, and economic developments since reforms began in 1978 have reflected that success (Siu and Li 1993; Wu 1994). No less important will be the policies toward emigration and immigration. The shock the Chinese experienced when they discovered how far behind their country had become in technology, management, and living conditions did have extraordinarily beneficial effects. For the first ten years, their speed in response to manifold challenges has been almost unbelievable. Is China on the verge of openness in ways that would make its Southeast Asian neighbours comfortable? Or will they continue to resist freeing themselves to allow more capitalist penetration and opt instead for the route of controlled importation of ideas and people? A global history approach would caution that the tensions between globalisation and the local defence against its broader ramifications will continue. What is more likely is that, behind the warm handshakes at the gates, China's deep-rooted traditions of wall-building and repairing will be carefully protected.

There are indeed many ramifications following a period of rapid and intensive globalisation in this century. The chapters in the second half of this book tackle that subject with an eye on more recent changes. The chapters by Robin Cohen, Mike Featherstone, and Astri Suhrke take a broader historical perspective on some of the ramifications. Myron Weiner's chapter offers an analysis of the migration crisis position today and provides an appropriate conclusion to the range of issues raised in the book. The variety of approaches challenges us to ask if the study of global history can contain the proliferation of larger historical and contemporary questions that the migration experience poses. The chapters in this book, using different starting points, offer a rich collection of possible answers. I shall select only those issues that allow me to revisit some migration patterns that I believe to be particularly important.

The first I have already discussed in part earlier in this chapter, that is, the role of the nation-state in determining patterns of migration. This, it would appear to me, is at the heart of Myron Weiner's analysis of the global migration crisis. But Robin Cohen traces the story back to its roots, to the deep tradition of exile and dispersal that underlies the idea of the diaspora and points to the extraordinary revival of that concept just at the point when the nation-state seemed to have made it irrelevant and little more than a powerful historical image. It is too early to say if diasporas will survive in the interstices of successful globalisation, or if the process of globalisation itself will be reinforced by the growing numbers of identifiable diasporas around the world. There is certainly no doubt that modern, large-scale migrations have led to the formation of strong ethnic identities (Featherstone 1990). What is still unclear is whether the reestablishment of communal structures has revitalised the diaspora as a political and economic force in a large number of countries.

What strikes me most in Robin Cohen's mention of the three choices migrants had to choose among in ancient Israel—Zealotism, Herodianism, and the in-between position of accepting difference—is how close that experience was to that of the Chinese sojourner in twentieth-century Southeast Asia. My study of Chinese politics in Malaya (now Malaysia) identified a small group that I called Group A (although the context was vastly different, this was roughly comparable to the Zealots), another small group called Group C (similar to the Herodianists), and a sizable majority, Group B, who believed in "the positive acceptance of difference" (Wang G. 1992a). I was reluctant to say that these Group B Chinese would form the diaspora, because the word was then used only for the Jews. A direct comparison of the Chinese and the Jews would be misleading. In addition, to suggest that the Chinese were like the Jews at a time of nation-building in a Muslim state that fully supported the Palestinian cause would have been offensive and unacceptable.

Globalisation has now made the diaspora phenomenon more 'universal' than anyone could have expected only a decade ago. Suddenly, the assimilationist ideal of modern nationalism has lost its credibility (Connor 1994; Smith 1991). In the long term, assimilation or the migrants' return to their home country may be unavoidable choices. The current resurfacing of the idea of diaspora reminds us how shallow the roots of nationalism are in comparison with the long history of diasporas. But, at the same time, we should not underestimate the unprecedented power of the modern nation-state (Greenfeld 1993; Anderson 1983). What Robin Cohen's long perspective of history has done is to expose the deep tensions between global migrations and the sovereign borders of the 190 members of the United Nations. A testing time awaits all those leaders who face these rising tensions in their own backyards.

The second issue comes from Mike Featherstone's idea of mobility and travel, a basic factor in migration history. But, unlike a decision to migrate, the urge to move and travel around is not much troubled by boundaries and procedures (Clifford 1992). It appears to be related to an early kind of sojourning, what I have called experimental migration, but it is less focused and purposeful. Mike Featherstone has found much in sociological literature to support this concern with mobility and has noted the limitations of some of the static studies of villages and communities. What is significant is that the rapid globalisation process in recent years has loosened the study of societies from its positivist origins and its Eurocentric backgrounds (Said 1973; Prakash 1990). Without necessarily labeling it postcolonial or postmodernist, the enhancement of cultural sensitivity has pushed at the frontiers of inquiry to such an extent that we now do have fresh perspectives on the acts and consequences of migration as well as on the ramifications of globalisation itself. Without this new sensitivity, the interest in travel and mobility (as with Ewa Morawska and Willfried Spohn's concern with the potential links between tourism and migration) would not have surfaced so readily.

Given that the urge to be mobile and to travel is associated with the desire for openness and freedom, I would like to introduce a word from the Malay world that captures the spirit of this deep-seated drive. It is the inclusive word *merantau* (or *pergi merantau*) used most often by the Minangkabau people of Sumatra, but in common use for centuries among other Malays (Wang G. 1992b). The word carries ambivalence and can be stretched to cover many nuances. It means to leave one's home village or country; it could imply that the move is only temporary, or that it could be for a very long time, or even that it could turn out to be permanent. Its wide usage reminds us of what anthropologists have always claimed, that in the simplest social and cultural structures can be found concrete examples of what we know to be true for all of us. Global history today can provide many similar ways of reaching out to such experiences and drawing them into the wider context in order to infuse new meaning to the concept of globalisation.

The third concern comes from the chapters written by Astri Suhrke and Myron Weiner. The recent aggravations in refugee problems led to Astri Suhrke's doubts about globalisation; and Myron Weiner frankly talks about a global migration crisis. What they have in common is a return to moral considerations, the lack of which becomes apparent when the numbers of refugees pass easy comprehension. The moral is the emphatic point with which Myron Weiner concludes his chapter. It is not something that global history can comfortably handle in the context of a modern globalisation that exults in the advances in standards of living, in science and technology, and in the oneness of civilisation (Zolberg et al. 1989). The rational agenda for the conquest of nature and the universe has left us weakened when our morality is questioned. Conventional responses are inadequate in the face of radical global challenges demanding ever stronger, bolder, and more imaginative solutions to the problems of humanity.

Yet there is no avoiding what must be central to the practice of global history, the role and fate of humans and their societies. Indeed there are so many areas in which civilisation has advanced that to quibble about what would be seen as a traditional issue of morality might seem small-minded and ungrateful to the pioneers, creators, and discoverers who made the new worlds for us all. Are we not now the bearers of the one single civilisation that religious leaders and theologians had long predicted would come about, or what the great scientific minds of the nineteenth century dreamed of (Beyer 1994)? Perhaps material progress will produce a superior morality. The hardheaded Chinese thinkers believed that bellies had to be filled first before one could talk about virtue, but they also warned about the corruption of wealth and plenty and the dangers of great inequalities.

Today there is want and deprivation (and not only among the refugees). There are inequalities not only among citizens, especially in the treatment of ethnic minorities and between men and women, but also wealth and power inequalities between countries and between large geographic regions. Globalisation has improved knowledge and communications generally but has also revealed the full extent of areas of moral discontent and despair. The reaction against the dominance of victorious nations who claimed to be the only people who could be called civilised has led to the conscious revival of traditional values, especially among the economic and military pygmies among the new nations. There has been much conjuring up of defensive cultural barriers against the encroachments of modernity. When grouped together under labels besides nationality, there is a new awareness that other claims to civilisation as the symbol of a superior moral system must be heard.

In addition, through the history of migrations from the earliest times, it could be claimed that other civilisations are now no less globalised. The use of Ayatollah Khomeini's cassettes among Iranian migrants in Europe and America was a powerful call to global action that has had many imitators since and will have many more. So much so that Samuel Huntington has conceded the single civilisation hypothesis and speaks of the clash of several civilisations (Huntington 1993). By this concession, he would appear to recognise that groups of peoples who reject the supremacy of Western civilisation and who question the adequacy of nation-states could seek allegiance to other civilisations as larger and stronger vehicles on which to base their alternatives to the idea of one global morality.

At the other end of the moral spectrum, migration history offers a more positive vista. Increasingly sophisticated studies of long-distance migration as a global phenomenon has distinguished between the macroaggregations of statistical significance and the microdecisions of individuals and families who migrate. There is better appreciation today that the cumulative impact of such decisions, especially those made by the skilled and the educated, has added new layers to migration history. These layers are qualitative features in the spatial linkages that bind more and more people around the world. The following changes are particularly significant:

1. Migrants are more important today to both the host and the home countries. Host countries, however reluctant and defensive, have learnt a great deal about migrants. The methods host countries employ to choose whom to accept reflect a willingness to take a long view of the migrants' value to their new home.
2. Much more is now known about the background of those who decide to migrate.
3. New communications technology and social networks enable the migrants to keep in touch with their original homes and share experiences with other migrants.
4. The three factors just listed have increased the migrants' impact on political affairs; and there is both greater multicultural enrichment and tenser ethnic relations that require delicate handling. Most of all, there is a keener sense of the nuances of multiple identities and an enhancement of individual self-consciousness (King, A.D. 1991 and Nandy 1995).

A global history approach toward the study of migrations would show that there has never before been such a degree of understanding of migrants as people. Parallel to the macromigrations that dealt in numbers, the movements of craftspeople, artisans, and those offering a wide range of other technical or skilled services have rarely been noticed. The recent shift in emphasis from migrants with rare skills to those who are trained and educated in interchangeable skills have changed that (Klein 1987). The advent of modern mass education and the universal transmission of common basic skills distinguishes this era of migration as one in which migrants have risen from anonymity. The future of macromigrations may be grim: It may rest on the continuous supply of desperate refugees rather than on the orderly movements of peoples. If nation-states continue to behave according to form, perhaps only micromigrations of the more enterprising products of schools, colleges, and universities, whether vocational, commercial, technical, or academic, would be permitted if and when nation-states encourage any migration at all. This does not face the larger moral considerations, but it may be all the moral gain we can hope for.

References

Anderson, Benedict. (1983) *Imagined Communities: Reflections on the Origin and Spread of Nationalism.* London: Verso.

Appleyard, Reginald, ed. (1988) *The Impact of International Migration on Developing Countries.* Paris: OECD.

Beyer, Peter. (1994) *Religion and Globalization.* London: SAGE Publications.

Castles, Stephen, and Mark J. Miller. (1993) *The Age of Migration: International Population Movements in the Modern World.* Basingstoke, Engl.: Macmillan.

Chan Sucheng. (1990) *Asian Americans: An Interpretative History.* Boston: Twayne Publishers.

Clifford, James. (1992) "Traveling Cultures", in Lawrence Grossberg, Cary Nelson, and Paula Treichler, eds., *Cultural Studies,* pp. 96–112.

Coedes, Georges. (1948, 1968) *Les Etats Hindouises d'Indochine et d'Indonesie.* Translated as *The Indianized States of Southeast Asia* by Susan Brown Cowing (edited by Walter F. Vella). Honolulu: East-West Center Press.

Cohen, Robin. (1987) *The New Helots: Migrants in the International Division of Labour.* Aldershot, Engl.: Gower.

Connor, Walker. (1994) *Ethnonationalism: The Quest for Understanding.* Princeton: Princeton University Press.

Curtin, Philip D. (1984) *Cross-Cultural Trade in World History.* Cambridge: Cambridge University Press.

Curtin, Philip D. (1990) *The Rise and Fall of the Plantation Complex.* Cambridge: Cambridge University Press.

Emmer, P. C., ed. (1986) *Colonialism and Migration: Indentured Labour Before and After Slavery.* Dordrecht, Netherlands: Nijhoff.

Emmer, P. C., and M. Murner, eds. (1992) *European Expansion and Migration: Essays on the Intercontinental Migration from Africa, Asia, and Europe.* Oxford: Berg.

Featherstone, Mike, ed. (1990) *Global Culture: Nationalism, Globalization and Modernity.* London: SAGE Publications.

Feuerwerker, Albert, ed. (1968) *History in Communist China.* Cambridge, Mass.: MIT Press.

FitzGerald, Stephen. (1972) *China and the Overseas Chinese: A Study of Peking's Changing Policy, 1949–1970.* Cambridge: Cambridge University Press.

Greenfeld, Liah. (1993) *Nationalism: Five Roads to Modernity.* Cambridge, Mass.: Harvard University Press.

Grew, Raymond. (1994) "On the Prospect of Global History", in Mazlish and Buultjens, *Conceptualizing Global History,* pp. 227–249.

Grossberg, Lawrence, Cary Nelson, and Paula Treichler, eds. (1992) *Cultural Studies.* New York: Routledge.

Hall, Stuart. (1991) "The Local and the Global: Globalization and Ethnicity", and "Old and New Identities, Old and New Ethnicities", in Anthony King, ed., *Culture, Globalisation and the World-System,* pp. 19–39 and 41–68.

Hooper, Beverley. (1986) *China Stands Up: Ending the Western Presence, 1948–1950.* Sydney: Allen & Unwin.

Horowitz, Donald L. (1985) *Ethnic Groups in Conflict.* Berkeley: University of California Press.

Huntington, Samuel. (1993) "The Clash of Civilisations", *1993 Summer Foreign Affairs Reader.* New York: Foreign Affairs.

Journal of World History. Essays by William McNeil 1/1 (1990), pp. 1–21 and Andre Gunther Frank 2/1 (1991), pp. 1–28.

Jupp, James. (1988) *The Australian People: An Encyclopedia of the Nation, Its People and Their Origins.* Sydney: Angus and Robertson.

King, Anthony D., ed. (1991) *Culture, Globalisation and the World-System: Contemporary Conditions for the Representation of Identity.* Basingstoke, Engl.: Macmillan.

King, Russell, ed. (1993) *Mass Migrations in Europe: The Legacy and the Future.* London: Belhaven Press.

Klein, Sidney, ed. (1987) *The Economics of Mass Migration in the Twentieth Century.* New York: Paragon House Publishers.

Kritz, Mary M., Charles B. Keely, and Silvano M. Tomasi, eds. (1981) *Global Trends in Migration: Theory and Research on International Population Movements.* New York: The Center for Migration Studies.

Lee, James. (1978) "Migration and Expansion in Chinese History", in McNeil and Adams, *Human Migration,* pp. 20–47.

Mazlish, Bruce. (1994) "An Introduction to Global History", in Mazlish and Buultjens, *Conceptualizing Global History,* pp. 1–24.

Mazlish, Bruce, and Ralph Buultjens, eds. (1994) *Conceptualizing Global History.* Boulder: Westview Press.

McNeill, William H., and Ruth S. Adams, eds. (1978) *Human Migration: Patterns and Policies.* Bloomington: Indiana University Press.

Moch, Leslie Page. (1992) *Moving Europeans: Migration in Western Europe Since 1650.* Bloomington: Indiana University Press.

Nandy, Ashis. (1995) "History's Forgotten Doubles", in *History and Theory 1995,* pp. 44–66.

Ongkili, James P. (1985) *Nation-Building in Malaysia, 1946–1974.* Singapore: Oxford University Press.

Philips, William D., Jr. (1985) *Slavery from Roman Times to the Early Transatlantic Trade.* Minneapolis: University of Minnesota Press.

Pomper, Philip, et al., eds. (1995) *History and Theory 1995. Theme Issue 34. World Historians and Their Critics.* Middletown, Conn.: Wesleyan University.

Prakash, Gyan. (1990) "Writing Post-Orientalist Histories of the Third World: Perspective from Indian Historiography", *Comparative Studies in Society and History* 32:383–408.

Pryor, Robin J., ed. (1979) *Migration and Development in South-East Asia: A Demographic Perspective.* Kuala Lumpur: Oxford University Press.

Reid, Anthony. (1988) *Southeast Asia in the Age of Commerce, 1450–1680. Volume One: The Lands Below the Winds.* New Haven: Yale University Press.

Reid, Anthony. (1993) *Southeast Asia in the Age of Commerce, 1450–1680. Volume Two: Expansion and Crisis.* New Haven: Yale University Press.

Reid, Anthony, ed. (1983) *Slavery, Bondage, and Dependency in Southeast Asia.* St. Lucia: Queensland University Press.

Said, Edward W. (1973) *Orientalism.* New York: Pantheon Books.

Schafer, Wolf, ed. (forthcoming) *Global Civilisation and Local Cultures.* Boulder: Westview Press.

Siu Yat-ming and Li Si-ming. (1993) "Population Mobility in the 1980s: China on the Road to an Open Society", in Joseph Cheng and Maurice Brosseau, eds., *China Review 1993.* Hong Kong: Chinese University Press, pp. 19.1–31.

Skeldon, Ronald, ed. (1994) *Reluctant Exiles? Migration from Hong Kong and the New Overseas Chinese.* Armonk, N.Y.: M. E. Sharpe.

Smith, Anthony D. (1991) *National Identity.* Reno: University of Nevada Press.

Tinker, Hugh. (1974) *A New System of Slavery: The Export of Indian Labour Oveseas, 1830–1920.* London: Oxford University Press.

van Leur, J. C. (1955) *Indonesian Trade and Society.* The Hague: van Hoeve.

Waldron, Arthur. (1990) *The Great Wall of China: From History to Myth.* Cambridge: Cambridge University Press.

Wallerstein, Immanuel. (1974) *The Modern World-System: Capitalist Agriculture and the Origins of the European World Economy in the Sixteenth Century.* New York: Academic Press.

Wallerstein, Immanuel. (1980) *The Modern World-System II: Mercantilism and the Consolidation of the European World Economy, 1600–1750.* New York: Academic Press.

Wallerstein, Immanuel. (1989) *The Modern World-System III: The Second Era of Great Expansion of the Capitalist World-Economy, 1730–1840s.* San Diego: Academic Press.

Wang Gungwu. (1991a) "Juxtaposing Past and Present in China Today", in Wang Gungwu, *The Chineseness of China: Selected Essays.* Hong Kong: Oxford University Press, pp. 209–229 and 327–331. First published in *The China Quarterly* 61 (1975).

Wang Gungwu. (1991b) "Patterns of Chinese Migration in Historical Perspective", in Wang Gungwu, *China and the Chinese Overseas.* Singapore: Times Academic Press, pp. 3–21. First published in 1989.

Wang Gungwu. (1992a) "Chinese Politics in Malaya", in Wang Gungwu, *Community and Nation: China, Southeast Asia and Australia.* Sydney: Allen & Unwin, pp. 251–280. First Published in *The China Quarterly* 43 (1970).

Wang Gungwu. (1992b) "Migration Patterns in History: Malaysia and the Region", in *Community and Nation*, pp. 168–186. First published in *Journal of the Malaysian Branch of the Royal Asiatic Society* 58 (1985).

Wang Gungwu. (1992c) "Sojourning: The Chinese Experience in Southeast Asia", Jennifer Cushman Memorial Lecture. To be published in Anthony Reid, *Migrants and Sojourners* (forthcoming).

Wang Gungwu. (1994) "Migration and Its Enemies", in Mazlish and Buultjens, *Conceptualizing Global History*, pp. 131–151.

Wang Tai Peng. (1994) *The Origins of Chinese Kongsi.* Petaling Jaya: Pelanduk Publications.

Wiens, Harold J. (1954) *China's March Towards the Tropics: A Discussion of the Southward Penetration of Chinese Culture, Peoples, and Political Control in Relation to the Non-Han Peoples in South China and in the Perspective of Historical and Cultural Geography.* Hamden, Conn.

Winstedt, Richard. (1947) *The Malays: A Cultural History.* Singapore: Kelly and Walsh. (Also 6th ed. (1961) London: Routledge & Kegan Paul.)

Wolters, O. W. (1982) *History, Culture, and Region in Southeast Asian Perspectives.* Singapore: Institute of Southeast Asian Studies.

Wong, Linda. (1994) "China's Urban Migrants—The Public Policy Challenge", *Pacific Affairs* 335–355.

Xiaoying Wu, Harry. (1994) "Rural to Urban Migration in the People's Republic of China", *The China Quarterly* 139:669–698.

Zolberg, Aristide, Astri Suhrke, and Sergio Aguayo. (1989) *Escape from Violence—Conflict and the Refugee Crisis in the Developing World.* New York: Oxford University Press.

2

Moving Europeans in the Globalizing World: Contemporary Migrations in a Historical-Comparative Perspective (1955–1994 v. 1870–1914)

Ewa Morawska and Willfried Spohn

The purpose of this chapter is twofold. On the one hand, we illuminate the main mechanisms, forms, and patterns, at macro and micro levels, of post–World War II mass migrations of the Europeans in the context of quickening globalization. On the other hand and simultanously, we compare and contrast those mechanisms, forms, and patterns with those of the earlier high wave of population flows across and beyond the European Continent that occurred at the time of the "densification" of long-distance interconnections in the so-called Atlantic world-system, between 1870 and 1914, so as to identify and elucidate the continuities and discontinuities between these two movements. As a brief synthesis of an extensive and complex subject, our discussion unavoidably simplifies the matters dealt with; we have been careful to formulate the generalizations that, in our judgment, "stand" despite the existence of nonsupportive cases and justified reservations regarding aggregation of nonidentical territorial or social units.[1]

Our understanding of the major concepts used in this chapter should be briefly explained before we move on. First, the concept of *migration* denotes one-way as well as repeated movements across nation-state boundaries or within the multinational community (such as the now-borderless EC) for permanent or shorter- and longer-term sojourns. In order not to expand further an already unwieldy subject, we have considered only migration of Europeans (from all regions of the Continent) but excluded post–World War II migrations arrivals from outside the Continent.

The concepts of *globalization* and the *world-system* have been used in the literature in several different ways.[2] We understand globalization as a historical process of the increasing "systemness" or interconnectedness of various dimensions (technological, economic, sociocultural, political-military) of social life and, in consequence, of different regions of the world; the latter stipulates the necessity to consider the positioning and interrelations of other dimensions or parts of the emerging system in order to understand the location and attributes of a particular fragment of this system. We view globalization as an uneven, long-lasting development whose roots reach deep into the nineteenth century and even earlier, and the pace of movement (forward or in reverse) is contingent on time and place. The notion of the world-system as used in this chapter relates to transnational structures characterized by considerable but variable levels of systemness, large but flexible scopes of coverage, and different degrees of openness or closure; we speak about the Atlantic world-system, the Soviet world-system, and the global world-system (or just global system). Finally, we take globalization and regionalism, or the world-system and localism, to be noncontradictory, empirically as well as theoretically. The latter assumption derives from the representation of social life as an ongoing mutually constitutive relationship, or "structuration" in Anthony Giddens' renowned coinage, between the micro-, meso-, and macrolevels or contexts of social life, that is, individual and collective human agencies and their proximate, intermediate, and distant environments. Large-scale human migrations that are a component part of the globalization process actually take place in the micro-to-intermediate environments constituting the social world: The configuration and pressure of forces at the upper structural layers set the limits of the possible and the impossible within which people move, but it is at the level of the more proximate surroundings that individuals and groups evaluate their situations, define purposes, and undertake actions.[3]

The chapter consists of three sections. The first section outlines the macrostructural—specifically, world-system, framework, and main parameters of European international migrations at the turn of the twentieth century and, against this comparative background, in the post–World War I era, and points out elements of continuity and change in the latter. In the next section, we identify, and discuss in the macrostructural (global and regional) context, the major categories of European international migrants as well as their origins, destinations, and occupational and legal status in the home and/or host countries. We argue, and demonstrate, that in the interplay with globalizing forces and their countercurrents, the migratory types have become increasingly diversified. The last section deals with micro-level social support networks, informal and institutional, relied on by migrants as they plan their travels and come to sojourn or remain permanently in a host country; as in the preceding section, we have tried to identify the regional, occupational, and political status correlates of the specific forms of assistance networks used by migrants and to assess the enduring and new elements in these micro-facilitators. The separation of macro and micro contexts of migration is unfortunate, since the social world is really a "continuous" phenomenon, but there is too much material for us to combine them in a legible way.

European International Migrations in Macrostructural Contexts (Past and Present)

We begin by identifying large-scope structures and processes as contexts of long-distance population movements inside and out of Europe. Contemporary European migrations as a component part of globalization have roots in the era known as the "long turn of the century" (1870–1914) that witnessed the maturation of modern Western capitalism and the emergence of the Atlantic world-system through the accelerated urbanization-industrialization of social life patterns in Europe as well as the Americas, intercontinental expansion of commerce and capital flows, and significant improvements in long-distance transport and communication. We will sketch out the major features of the turn-of-the-twentieth-century Atlantic world-system and, in this framework, of the population flows across and out of Europe, in order to better assess contemporary migrations of the Europeans: their volume, destinations, composition, and purposes, as shaped by the configurations of the longer lasting and more recent processes and mechanisms.

Triggered by the disintegration of the rural socioeconomic order that uprooted millions of people ("push") on the one hand and, on the other, by the expansion of cities and factories ("pull"), and facilitated by improved transportation and communication systems, immense population movements across and, increasingly with time, outside the European Continent—probably 60–70 million of "comings" and "goings" (rather than persons, since repeated journeys were common) between 1870 and 1914—were the integrative part of these transformations and an important element in the formation of the world-system linking two sides of the Atlantic.[4]

Inherent in the emergent Atlantic world-system was a profound inequality in the developmental impetus and in the resulting techno/economic prowess between its component parts, divided roughly along the west-east and north-south axes, into the more- (core) and less- ([semi-]periphery) modernized/powerful regions, respectively. The general pattern of the European population movement at once reflected and contributed to this regional imbalance. At the turn of the twentieth century, it flowed, increasingly, in the form of labor-seeking migration, from the still largely rural, poor, and overpopulated southern and eastern corners of the Continent as they were incorporated into the capitalist world-system, toward the urbanized-industrialized western parts (especially England and France where modern-capitalist transformation, started two centuries earlier, was already well advanced), the central regions (especially Germany whose economy was forcefully modernized "from above" during that period), and then beyond it across the Atlantic (mainly to the United States where the urbanization-industrialization progressed at an even much faster speed than the west European leaders in this development).[5]

The specific demands of the industrial economies of the N/W core receivers, combined with the limited human capital, in terms of modern skills, of the majority of labor migrants from S/E (semi-)peripheries, channeled those arrivals into the low(er)-level occupational positions that offered little job security and advancement opportunities. (Another factor in this placement, migrants' group support networks, will be discussed later in this chapter.) In this way, the macrostructural inequality between the E/S-W/N parts of the world-system was replicated or, as it were, domesticated, at the meso-level in the regional/national distribution of the resident workforce in the socioeconomic structures of the receiver societies. (For example, in the United States and Germany, the two most dynamically growing industrial powers in the Atlantic world-economy that by the last quarter of the 1870–1914 period became the most preferred destinations for European migrants [about 25 million and 15 million gross inflows, respectively], over 90 percent of the South and East European migrants occupied such lowly positions, as compared with about 50 percent [in the United States] and 70 percent [in Germany] of those from western parts of Europe.[6])

Against this comparative background, we now consider post-1945 world-system and the European migrations as one of its multiple interconnecting structures. The most outstanding feature of the contemporary world-system has been its globalization in scope and complexity of interconnections, dwarfing all predecessors. Forces that generate this global system have become more pervasive and also more diversified than the ones that gave shape to the Atlantic world-system at the turn of the twentieth century. They include progressive transnationalization of production, capital, and exchange and unprecedented acceleration in technological advancement, particularly innovations in (air) transportation and (tele)communication. Related to these are two major developments: the restructuring of regional and national-state economies and social structures toward high-tech production and services easily relocated in space; and the unprecedented intensification of global cultural diffusion through actual and, in particular, virtual contact. Finally and important, in part reflecting the "unifying" trends noted previously and in part in reaction to the atrocities of World War II and to the pervasiveness of human misery and oppression in the world perceived at close range or from a (tele)distance, is a recognition of humankind as both global condition and shared identity spread across regions, accompanied by a proliferation of world organizations and informal forums founded to improve worldwide cooperation on common concerns, such as human rights, environmental protection, trade, and economic development. The disintegration of the colonial system during the 1950s and 1960s, and, more recently, of the Soviet bloc, can also be included in this category of generative factors—as developments with globalizing effects on political culture.

Like the more encompassing system of which they are part, migrations in and out of Europe have in the course of the last fifty years greatly expanded in scope and complexity. Although only a fraction, between 12 percent and 15 percent, of the global movements (more than 60 million migrants in 1992 alone, not counting six to seven times larger numbers of international tourists), the number of Europeans on the move in that year was two to three times bigger than the number of European migrants in 1914, the peak year of the earlier wave. Also, for the first time in history, the number of foreign-born residents in all European countries combined (20-odd million) has about reached the number in the United States, the traditional leader in this regard.[7]

Although it has become much more global or interlinked, the contemporary world-system—in fact, expanded to include practically the entire globe—has retained three major structural characteristics of its turn-of-the-twentieth-century Atlantic predecessor (the fourth characteristic, of the micro-social nature, will be discussed in the last section of this chapter).

First, it continues to function in the context of the enduring inequality along the NW-SE divide in access to and control over techno/economic resources and political/military power.[8] This disequilibrium, pronounced on the world map, has also retained, basically, a similar geographical layout on the European Continent, although not without some important modifications. Whereas the position of the southern countries, included one after another into the economic and political structures of the European Community dominated by its western members, has gradually improved over the last forty years, that of the eastern countries, incorporated by force into the Soviet system, has decidedly weakened. (Measured by the per capita GDP, shortly before World War II, in 1938, the economic performance of southern and eastern Europe reached about 40 percent of the west European level. Twenty-five years later, this proportion increased by a few points in both of the less-developed regions, with eastern Europe somewhat ahead. By the end of the 1980s, southern Europe, although still considerably behind the western core with 55 percent of the latter's per capita GNP, had distanced itself by more than 30 percentage points from its eastern counterpart, where inefficient and outdated Soviet-style economies were rapidly deteriorating across the region.[9])

Second and relatedly, the continuing NW-SE division of resources and power in the contemporary world-system has also sustained the basic geographic pattern of migrations that continue to flow from the less-techno/economically developed southern and eastern (semi-) peripheries toward the northern and western core parts of the globe. The European Continent, itself divided into core and (semi-)periphery regions, since 1955 has witnessed continuous interregional migration along the SE-NW axes, which have been "stretching out" in southern and eastern directions, including, with progressive globalization, increased flows of migrants from even more peripheral parts of the world, such as Africa, the Middle East, and all corners of Asia. It may be noted here that this growing inflow of migrants from less-developed countries (LDCs) in southern and, more recently, eastern corners of Europe has relativized the notion of the "European core": Once exclusively denoting northwestern Europe, with the globalization of migrations, the concept has expanded depending on the standpoint of prospective migrants. It includes southwestern Europe from the perspective of East Europeans, North Africans, and inhabitants of the Middle East and envelops the westernmost countries of Eastern Europe when approached by migrants from the "far East" of the Continent and from Asia.

And third, the entrenched SE-NW division of the contemporary world-system and the resulting pattern of the population flows toward its more developed regions have contributed to the re-creation of a similar cleavage inside the socioeconomic structures of the receiver countries, with the upper positions dominated by the NW national/ethnic groups and the lower positions dominated by the SE ethnic groups. Some commentators have called this phenomenon "the (semi-)periphery of the core." In this regard, the recent influx into the European Continent of migrants from the remote southern and eastern LDCs relativizes the notions of "core" and "periphery" in the previous concept by elevating SE migrants—white, better-skilled, and more culturally acceptable in comparison with the LDC arrivals—somewhat in the socioeconomic structures of NW receiver societies.

Although they bear recognizable similarities to the patterns of population movements in the Atlantic world-system, contemporary long-distance migrations of the Europeans are not a straightforward continuation of Atlantic-system population movements, modified somewhat by the shifted parameters of the global system. Significant new factors have become involved in shaping the volume, forms, and directions of postwar international travels of the Europeans (and, for that matter, of other peoples as well), whose interaction with the enduring patterns makes for a familiar yet quite distinctive picture of the migratory flows. We will point out these new developments and their meaning for international population movements and characterize the general tendency in migrations they produce.

The development of great consequence for international population movements has been the politicization of the issue of international migration, that is, the questions of whether, where, and which migrants are able to travel. In the Atlantic world-system these decisions were by and large the prerogative of the migrants themselves and their local communities, contingent on the general and local economic conditions in the sending and the receiving societies and on availability of transportation. (Two European governments in that era, precursors, one might say, of the forthcoming "etatization" of international migrations—Russian on the sending side and German on the receiving—intervened in migratory movements to a considerable extent, the former by withholding exit passports for the undesirable petitioners and the latter by limiting the length of stay of the migrant sojourners, particularly those from southern and eastern Europe.) Today, international migrations are intricately entangled in politics and ideology and are negotiated at the "upper stories" of the contemporary global system way above the heads of those personally interested. The involvement of political (denoting actual policies) and ideological (declared doctrines) interests in deciding the size, composition, and directions of population movements in the postwar world creates considerable tensions and contradictions that have been the subject of public debate and a substantial literature in the field of international migration studies. For the purposes of this discussion, it will suffice to point out the locus classicus of the problem—the continual tension between the reality of profound economic inequalities in the world and the resulting SE-NW migratory thrust and, reflecting it, restrictive/selective immigration policies of particular nation-states on the one hand and, on the other, the ideological declarations of universal human rights, including the freedom of movement as the superior principle, used in defense of specific cases by international and regional bodies. (In postwar history, this principle was first formulated in the UN declaration in 1948 and has since been amended and expanded in nearly fifty proclamations, more than one-fourth of which concern migrants and refugees, issued by international agencies at worldwide and regional levels, including the European Community.)[10] A tension resulting from this discrepancy is further increased by the acknowledgment of the legitimacy of national security (particular) interests in some international treaties obliging state signatories to respect (universal or global) human rights.

A profound economic restructuring of the NW core societies, and with them of the global economy, triggered by the international oil crisis of

1973 and the subsequent industrial slowdown, is another important development to be noted. It has comprised three related processes: an accelerated shift from industrial to high-tech production and to services, as the driving forces of economic development; increasing automation of production in the existing industries; and, under the umbrella of transnational enterprises, a gradual transfer of labor-intensive production to less-developed, low-wage countries in Asia, South America, and, clandestinely, the Soviet bloc. These transformations were soon to alter—with the aid of the appropriate policies instituted by the receiver countries—the (semi-)periphery-to-core migration pattern, by decreasing the demand for low-skilled labor migrants and increasing the demand for highly skilled personnel. (This latter category, minuscule in the turn-of-the-twentieth-century industrial migration, has grown with alacrity since the mid-1970s; we shall discuss its subtypes and their trajectories across and outside of Europe in the following section.)

Finally, cultural diffusion via global media and the availability of quick and comfortable long-distance travel, has contributed to the unprecedented numerical growth and global spread of what we may call entertainment migration, of which the lion's share is taken by international tourism. Like other forms of population movements considered here, international tourism fosters and is fostered by the globalizing processes. As we shall see, however, its main routes and actors are significantly different.

The most striking effect of the previously mentioned developments, progressive over the postwar era, has been heterogenization of the types of international population movements of the Europeans in terms of purposes of migrations, ways of exit and entry, and socioeconomic and political status of migrants. This diversification, in turn, has complicated migratory paths of the travelers. In the following section we take a closer look at the main genres of postwar European migrations and, specifically, at their socioeconomic, political, and cultural contexts, fluctuating volumes, and specific subtypes, as they have been shaped by the longer duration and more recent factors and processes over the last four decades.

Major Types of European International Migration Since the 1950s

Whereas assessing the causes and purposes of turn-of-the-twentieth-century long-distance travels across and beyond the European Continent is pretty straightforward: They were primarily economic or employment-related (East European Jews, whose mass exodus had a combined economic-political character, were the most outstanding exception), because of a significant blurring of boundaries between distinguishable genres accompanying the progressive differentiation of contemporary international migration of the Europeans, constructing a self-explanatory and clear-cut typology appears to be impossible. Aware of other possible classifications, we have settled for four major categories of the population flows in postwar Europe, three of which have arguably more akin, and one evidently disparate, "contents": (1) The largest of all, *economic or employment-related migration,* including, besides labor migration, job-related travels of highly skilled or professional/managerial personnel (although their mechanisms are not solely economic, but involve as well cognitive and emotive needs and rewards) and educational journeys of youth for professional training abroad; (2) *political migration,* including resettlers, refugees, and political asylum-seekers; (3) *entertainment migration,* including, besides the already mentioned international tourism, globe-trotting artists, and sportsmen and women, and their followings; and (4) *mixed-type migration,* including various configurations of the previous three categories and their subtypes.

We shall discuss these major types of international population movement in the order they were mentioned. Since in comparison with the characteristics of the European economic migrants during the period between the 1950s and the international oil crisis of 1973, the regional origins, skill level, and political status of the travelers in the subsequent two decades have become significantly more differentiated, they will be discussed in two (pre- and post-oil crisis) consecutive subgroups.

Economic or Employment-Related Migration

In the precrisis era, international economic or employment-related migration of the Europeans was characterized, first, by the domination of only one sender in the traditional double-track SE-NW axis, that is, the southern part of the Continent. During the 1950s and 1960s, residents of the Mediterranean region, which entered the postwar era industrially underdeveloped, with a large rural proletariat, and still "emigration unsaturated," constituted 70–75 percent of foreign job-seekers in the developed countries of northwestern Europe.[11] Incorporated into the Soviet bloc, eastern Europe became separated from the rest of the world by the Iron Curtain, through which only political refugees passed at that time. (The "migration thirst" of eastern European rural proletariat was slaked during the early postwar era by large-scale internal population movements from the countryside to the rapidly developing cities and industries during the accelerated economic perestroikas centrally planned and administered by Communist Party authorities.[12])

The receiver, or NW, side of the international exchange also became reduced—the second distinctive feature of the discussed category in the early postwar period—to a truncated version of the turn-of-the-twentieth-century Atlantic world-economy, because of a great diminution of the role of North America, particularly the United States, as the receiver of job-related migration. At the beginning of the twentieth century nearly two-thirds of all European international migrants traveled overseas, but after an upsurge of resettlement travels during the first post–World War II decade, this proportion dropped to 25 to 30 percent. Viewed "from the other side," the figures show the same trend: Whereas during the first post–World War II decade arrivals from Europe made up over 70 percent of the total (down by 15 percent in comparison with 1914), by the end of the 1960s this share was only 34 percent.[13] The main reasons for the drop were two: On the one hand, the continuation by the U.S. government of the modified quota system restricting immigration (the national origins system introduced in the 1920s was replaced in 1965 by a system of preferences, privileging family reunions and specific occupational categories[14]) and, on the other, vigorous recruitment of wage-seeking migrants in southern parts of Europe sponsored by governments of west and north European countries.

Which brings us to a set of related characteristics of the international migration of the Europeans in the period preceding the international oil crisis of 1973: its predominantly (75–85 percent) low-skill industrial character, limited expected duration abroad, and disproportionately male composition. Interesting to note is the apparent resemblance of this profile of post–World War II economic migrants to the characteristics of their turn-of-the-twentieth-century predecessors.[15] But whereas the latter had been the outcome of the demands of the host economies negotiated through migrants' social networks and cultural norms and expectations, the former had been primarily shaped by a new and powerful force in the migration process: political decisions made at the state level.

Postwar reconstruction of western Europe, generously supported by the Marshall Plan, soon created shortages of industrial labor that became more acute as the recovering economies picked up steam. Attracting workers from the less-developed Mediterranean region seemed a perfect solution to the insufficiency of the indigeneous supply, and two mechanisms for labor migration were institutionalized. First, groups of nation-states established shared labor markets within which member nationals could move without restrictions: The two largest organizations have been EFTA (founded in 1954), the association of four Scandinavian countries, and the EEC (founded by the Treaty of Rome in 1957), composed of six members: five developed West European countries, including Germany and Italy. Second, governments made bilateral treaties: Rapidly developing Germany, for example, first concluded a treaty with Italy, its traditional labor supplier, in 1955 (before Italy joined the EC) and then, in the

1960s, in rapid succession, with Spain, Greece, Portugal, Turkey, and Yugoslavia.[16] The main purpose of these agreements was not acquiring a permanent foreign-born workforce, but securing for West and North European countries a flexible labor pool easily adjustable to short-term economic fluctuations.

Initiated and controlled in this way by state interests, a population flow from southern to northwestern parts of the Continent created in the latter a large population of a predominantly male (65–75 percent) sojourner workforce. The number of first-time work permits issued to migrants arriving in five EC member countries grew from 300,000 in 1958 to 700,000 in 1968 and over 800,000 in 1973. In the period 1870–1914, Germany, the most dynamically developing country in the EC, attracted the largest numbers of *Gastarbeiter,* or guest workers (their number, increased four-fold in a decade, was 2.6 million in 1973, making up over 40 percent of the total for the EEC and the EFTA countries combined).[17]

This profile of European job-related international migration has been significantly complicated during the two decades following the 1973 energy crisis, as a consequence of a new configuration of economic-political developments: the accelerated restructuring of global economy, the "softening" and subsequent collapse of Communist regimes in Eastern Europe, and the new immigration policies of the highly developed EC/EFTA countries implemented in a "joint response" to the collapse of communism and to humanitarian obligations implied in international agreements.

As the demand for traditional industrial labor decreased in the highly developed EEC/EFTA countries, large populations of low-skilled foreign workers imported from southern Europe in the previous decades became superfluous. The reaction of German, French, Swiss, and Dutch governments was so-called *Anwerbestopp,* or stoppage of foreign labor recruitment, followed by a series of various material incentives, "return bonuses" and "reintegration assistance" programs aimed at persuading resident guest workers to return home. Between 1974 and 1976 the foreign stock population in these countries indeed decreased somewhat, in part because of the reduction of inflows (more than halved in that period) and in part as a result of departures of those taking advantage of the return incentives (e.g., in Germany, the number of the employed foreign workers dropped during these two years from 2.4 million to 1.9 million).[18]

But the decrease of guest worker population in northwestern Europe was much smaller than the employer states hoped for. Besides the higher standard of living in the host societies as compared with their native countries, there were other reasons for the guest workers' reluctance to return home. One was that a large number of them had already lived abroad for a long time (by the late 1970s about 40 percent of the South

European population in the highly developed EC countries had resided there, on the average, for more than ten years, and—an even stronger indication of putting down roots—one-fifth of the total foreign stock were second-generation youth under fifteen.[19] Another factor related to increased length of stay was the improvement of the occupational position of the guest worker population; although the majority of them, over 60 percent, were still employed in manual occupations, by the beginning of the 1980s nearly one-fourth worked in trade and services and nearly one-tenth held higher-level jobs in banking and insurance.[20] Last but not least, a circumstance enhancing the migrants' sense of permanence was the establishment of ethnic communities in the cities where they worked. As they continued to delay their return, the once sojourners (more accurately, state policies of the receiver countries) created a new subcategory of economic (im)migrants: illegal overstayers of the expired work permits. Unable to continue their former government-sponsored employment, such *indocumentados* occupied themselves, instead, in petty entrepreneurship or in the unofficial/underground economy.[21]

When it became clear that there were no anxious *Gastarbeiter* crowds waiting to return to their homelands, under the pressure of the Council of Europe, the receiver nation-states implemented family reunion policies, creating in this way yet another subtype, or, perhaps more accurately, supplement, of the economic migration. As a consequence of these policies, Southern European populations in the northwestern EC member-countries continued to grow, primarily now through the influx of women and children related to the former soujourner guest workers (by the mid-1980s the average proportion of females among South European residents in the EC reached about parity). Family reunions have constituted yet another very important factor in turning migrant workers into immigrant residents.[22]

An outcome of another constellation of political-economic developments and another contributing element in the internal differentiation of European economic migration during the period considered here has been the reappearance in northwestern parts of the Continent of growing numbers of job-seeking migrants from its eastern regions. This renewed inflow results from a combination of a long-time "hungry" awareness among East Europeans of much higher wages in northwestern Europe,[23] increased facility of westward travel from the Soviet bloc countries (especially Poland, Hungary, and Czechoslovakia) in the last decade of Communist regime, and, after its collapse, a significant lessening of border controls in this region. The largest group among these arrivals has formed two more varieties of the expanding category of illegal economic migrants: tourists who overstay their short-term visitor visas and those who enter the receiver countries without the appropriate documents. (On a more limited scale, clandestine border crossing was practiced in the 1960s by residents of the Iberian countries who were interested in performing seasonal agricultural labor in France but who would not have received exit permission from their authoritarian governments.[24]) The majority of East European illegal job-seekers in the EC/EFTA countries apparently find lower-skill employment in personal services and petty entrepreneurship and in the underground economy where they are often reported to work for their better-established Mediterranean (usually Italian) predeccessors.[25] Most recently, a widening stream of illegal economic migrants of the two varieties just discussed is flowing to former Soviet satellite countries in the higher developed northwestern tier of Eastern Europe, from Russia and other member states of the NIS southwest of the Urals. Their employment pattern seems to resemble that of their westernmore fellow East Europeans—illegal sojourners in the EC/EFTA countries.

No statistics exist of present-day illegal European migrants, only estimates for particular countries. In 1990/1991 they added up to a minimum of 2 to 2.5 million *indocumentados* across Europe (all categories of illegal stay and all regions combined, including the increased influx into Europe of African and Asian livelihood-seeking migrants from the LDCs since the 1980s). Germany, again, has reveived the largest proportion—35 to 40 percent of the total. Italy, Spain, Portugal, and Greece combined have received 20 to 25 percent; and Poland, the Czech Republic, and Hungary combined have received 15 to 20 percent.[26] So far, various punitive means of stemming this unwanted influx, such as renewed border checks, police raids on workplaces, or fines imposed on airlines and ground transportation companies for carrying undocumented foreigners, have proven largely unsuccessful. More successful have been legalization programs implemented, for instance, by the French and Italian governments. More recently, the German government has instituted another preventive measure against the swelling flow from the east: a series of bilateral agreements with individual East European countries granting them annual quotas of work permits valid from 12 to 24 months, depending on job category.[27]

Increased demand for a highly skilled workforce during the last two decades—the other corollary of the technological revolution and economic restructuring with major impact on global and national job markets—has triggered a rapid expansion of international movement of managerial/professional personnel. Between 1978 and 1989, this kind of employment-related long-distance migration of Europeans grew by a factor of 2.5. Unlike the international movement of low-skill job-seekers discussed earlier, the flows of professional/managerial manpower (the label is sexist regardless of the fact that men constitute the decided majority, about 2:1 on the average, of the migrants in this category) reach again across the Atlantic, primarily to the United States. As the acceleration of globalization processes since the late 1970s strengthened the economic, scientific, and cultural exchange links between Europe and the United States, the volume of trans-Atlantic migration has also considerably increased (although, because of a rapid growth of Latin American and Asian immigrants in the United States, by the 1980s the proportion of the European foreign population dropped to about 10 percent. After tourism, inflow of professional/managerial/educational migrants, as measured by the number of L-1, H-1, and J-1 visas issued to Europeans, has been the second largest contributor to this growth.[28]

As it is channeled in certain directions by long-lasting inequalities in the techno/economic development between European regions and "adjusted" by shorter-term economic fluctuations and immigration policies of particular nation-states, the international high-skill migration takes on different forms. We have classified them in two subtypes of "brain flows." (Unfortunately, data on managerial/professional migration, even within the EC, are scanty, and those that do exist have often been formulated by use of unclarified concepts and rules of aggregation.[29] Our typology is, therefore, a tentative and rather crude proposition.)

We distinguish between *"brain exchange,"* involving mostly temporary transfers of managerial/professional workforce and high-skill trainees/students between countries/regions at about equal levels of economic development; and *"brain drain,"* involving primarily, although, as we shall see, not exclusively, permanent or longitudinal migration of managerial/professional workforce and high-skill trainees/students from less to more developed countries (to avoid offense to postcolonial countries, from which most such transfers have come since the 1950s, UN recommended usage is the "reverse transfer of technology"). A subvariety of the latter type (because characteristic mainly of movements from less to more developed countries) that involves particularly high social and personal costs is what we have termed *"brain waste,"* that is, high-skill migration resulting in occupational skidding.

The most common species of brain exchange are medium-term transfers of personnel of large corporations (including transnationals or TNCs) and short-term international travels of business managers and entrepreneurs. In both categories EC-core member nationals have on the average the largest share numerically, and their movement occurs primarily within the EC and to/from the United States. (Examples: Nearly two-thirds of international business visits made by Europeans took place during the 1980s within the European Community; EC member nationals, largely from the northwestern part of the community, constituted the bulk the European-origin employees of multinationals stationed in the United States during that period and nearly 40 percent of the total foreign workforce.[30]

The third largest subcategory of international brain exchange, that is, back and forth transfers of scholars, artists/entertainers, and other professionals and college students, has similarly been dominated by flows of EC member nationals and by travels within the core (northwestern) parts of the European Community and across the Atlantic to the United States. (Examples: Among German scholarly/professional out-migrants in 1991, 60 percent followed this double-track pattern; over 80 percent of postsecondary European students in the United States in 1989 were from the EC.[31] Although contemporary high-skill transfers in this category have had primarily the "brain exchange" character, it should be noted that some of the core/EC-to-USA migration has displayed as well certain features of brain drain, that is, longer-term or even permanent relocation abroad of highly skilled workforce resulting from un- or underemployment in the home country. (For example, economic superpower that it is, Germany has a large amount of such underused highly skilled manpower among younger-generation residents of the former FRG—a combined product of the "rationalization" or shrinkage of employment in several high-tech industries and overproduction of college graduates in such fields as economics and engineering, not to mention the notorious political and social sciences. As a result, many such superfluous professionals move abroad for several years in order to make a living there, often assisted in this project by the German state.[32]

Although it occurs as well in northwestern parts of Europe, the brain drain phenomenon is much more typical of eastern European high-skill (westward) migration.[33] During the 1950s and 1960s this brain drain took place primarily as the result of politically motivated emigration. In the last two decades and, especially, since the fall of Communism, increasing state- and other institutionally sponsored professional and educational exchanges as well as international production and trade agreements have become first the alternative and then the main channels of high-skill outmigration from eastern Europe. But unlike the largely unrestricted movement of their Western counterparts, and reflecting eastern Europe's inferior position in the Continental as well as global economic/political power structures, contemporary westward migration of East European "brains" has also been much more and more directly dependent on immigration policies of the receiving countries. The largest volumes of this politically regulated (read: constrained) high-skill migration are flowing, like turn-of-the-twentieth-century international labor transfers, to Germany and the United States, the traditional top-ranking receivers of population movement from eastern Europe.[34]

The brain hemorrhage from Poland after the imposition of martial law in 1981 (and since) can be viewed as a precursor of a movement that set on across the entire region following the collapse of Communist regimes in 1989/1990 and a radical reduction of state subsidies for research, science, and the arts. Among nearly a million Polish emigrants to the West (including overstayers—the "brain" equivalent of *indocumentado* South European industrial workers from the earlier period) between 1981 and 1991, university graduates constituted about 15 percent, their number almost identical to the average annual number of university graduates in the 1980s. (According to a different report, during the same period, 25 percent of Polish scholars, most frequently computer scientists, physicists, and biologists, either permanently emigrated or left the country for long-term contracts abroad.) Among a quarter million recent (post-1991) emigres from the former Soviet Union, university graduates make about 15 percent of the total, and 15 to 20 percent of the Bulgarians who left their country between 1989 and 1991 were university graduates.[35]

As the few existing follow-up studies suggest, however, only a minority of these migrants find jobs in their own or related specialties; for example, a 1991 survey found only about 30 percent (average) of highly skilled Poles who left their country in the early to mid-1980s to have held such jobs; the remaining experienced occupational skidding, falling into the "brain waste" subcategory.[36]

Political Migration

We now move to the next major type of international migrants to be considered here: resettlers, refugees, and asylum-seekers, that is, people pushed out of their home countries by natural and human-caused disasters or relocations associated with sudden unsettlings of sociopolitical orders. The distinctiveness of contemporary political migration in comparison with turn-of-the-twentieth-century flight of people from national/ethnic or religious oppression by the authoritarian regimes in their home countries (although dwarfed by the employment-seeking movement of the Europeans in that period, it was nevertheless the continuous trickle) is not just its immense volume but also its politicization, or contingency on state-national and international political decisions (re)defining its very existence qua political migration and regulating its flow.

In this case, too, the 1970s can be treated as a watershed period during which (to be accurate: at its end rather than the beginning) new developments in global and state-national environments modified the origins, composition, and fates of political migrants.

While East-to-North/West has remained the primary direction of political migration flows of the Europeans throughout the postwar era, during the last two decades this type of international population movement has assumed several new features. First, there has occured a dramatic general increase in the volume of movement. The global number of resettlers, refugees, and asylum-seekers has grown from about 2.5 million in 1970 to nearly 20 million in 1993; to the latter figure should be added about 24 million people forced into exile within their own countries. (Over three-quarters of the present-day total are refugees flowing, or fleeing, rather, from South to South, or S-S, in the so-called Third World.)[37] In Europe, after massive resettlements of displaced persons during the first decade following World War II, the number of refugees and asylum-seekers had remained more or less stable for a quarter of a century, by 1981 totaling 2.2 to 2.4 million (including, in the order of size, German *Ubersiedler* from DDR to GDR [about 75 percent of this total]; Soviet bloc Jews; other East European nationals [mainly Hungarians, Poles, and Czechs]; and, from southern parts of the Continent, Greek, Spanish, and Portuguese escapees from the right-wing autocratic regimes in their homelands).[38]

During the 1980s, political migration of Europeans rapidly accelerated, and, as democratic governments were established in the previously mentioned Mediterranean countries, its sources became practically exclusively eastern European. Between 1983 and 1991, or within only one-third of the time span of the previously considered period, the total number of European resettlers, refugees, and asylum-seekers in all corners of the Continent exceeded the figure for the 1955–1981 period, totaling nearly 2.7 million. Over 40 percent of this number were most recent, 1990–1991, flows. (As before, German *Aussiedler*, primarily from Russia and Poland, and *Ubersiedler*, resettlers from pre- and postcollapse DDR, have held the largest numerical share in this movement, the Yugoslavs fleeing "ethnic cleansings" in their homelands were second, and relocating in various directions, residents of the former Soviet Union, third.)[39]

The next two interrelated features characteristic of post-1980 European political migration are the eastward/southeastward geographic extension of political migratory flows and the involvement of more and different ethnic/national groups that had until recently remained largely outside of the contemporary world-system's orbit. A larger part of this movement has thus far occurred within the territories of the former USSR following the dismantling of the Soviet Union, but rising flows have also been moving beyond its old western borders into the countries traditionally known as senders rather than receivers of larger-scale international migration: ex-Soviet satellites (Hungary, Poland, Slovak, and Czech Republics) and, more to the South, the Mediterranean region (Greece, Italy, Spain, and Portugal). (The latter for a longer time, and the former in most recent years, have also become receivers of political migrants from Asian and African LDCs.)[40]

Fourth, restrictive policies on the admission of political refugees and asylum-seekers, implemented in 1990–1993 by several EC member countries in response to the massive influx of migrants from all over the world and skyrocketing costs involved in taking care of this population, have replaced the open-door policy of the earlier period. The asylum system in core NW regions has been created to deal with the political/military and ideological conflict with world and, specifically, Soviet Communism, and with refugee flows from Soviet-dominated regions. Provisions of this system, based on the 1951 Geneva Convention, the mandates of UNHCR and IOM, and national legislation introduced between the 1950 and 1975, almost automatically granted asylum to the petitioners.[41] In the 1990s, a shared sense has emerged among policymakers and public opinion in northwestern Europe that the old system has gotten out of control and that restrictions had to be introduced that would eliminate petitioners whose claims of political persecution or insufficient civil liberties in their homelands could not be substantiated. Several measures were introduced by individual countries and jointly by the EC in 1990–1991, such as tighter checks at the borders and during stays and, based on a list of countries that according the EC Commission on Migration do not meet refugee criteria (e.g., former member states of the Soviet bloc), much higher rejection rates for asylum applications. Last to follow among NW core countries, two years later and after a prolonged national debate, Germany abandoned its exceptionally lenient law of unconditional asylum. Germany has been the leading European receiver of resettlers and refugee asylum-seekers, in part because of its geographic proximity to East European senders, but more importantly, as a result of explicit inducement directed at German diaspora as well as by implicit invitation, through their unconditional-asylum law, instituted as a "reparation" of sorts for the genocidal nationalism of the Nazi period, directed particularly against Eastern Europe. A new policy, for the most part conforming to the earlier policy agreed on by the EC, went into effect in 1993, and within twelve months the number of applicants was half that of the previous year.[42] At present, more than 80 percent of petitions in northwestern Europe are rejected, compared with less than half in the late 1970s.

New receiver countries in the Mediterranean region that have so far experienced a stream, or perhaps a river, but not a flood of refugees, continue "migrant-friendly" policies for now, whereas countries in eastern Europe, where the inflows that started a few years ago are still only a trickle turning into a stream, have not yet formulated consistent refugee policies either at nation-state or regional levels.[43]

Fifth and last, redefinition by NW states of the political situation (treated en bloc) in post-1989 eastern Europe as satisfactory and the implementation of this blanket assessment in the "negative" asylum policy toward migrants from the former Soviet bloc created a new, and growing, subcategory of "illegal refugees" from that region. These are primarily petitioners (also from other parts of the world) from the prerestriction period remaining in the host country after formal rejection of their petition for asylum (approximately 75 to 80 percent of such turned-down applicants apparently stay on). Such *indocumentado* persisters, not qualified anymore for shelter, food, and medical assistance from the receiver welfare states, undertake some "unofficial" employment in order to make a living, thus enlarging the army of the already discussed illegal economic migrants. Mixed types will be discussed later.

Entertainment Migration

Because its gigantic volume—a staggering 395 million arrivals in 1993, projected to be 641 million in 1995—dwarfs not only other kinds of entertainment migration (such as, for example, popular art- and sports-related travels) but also all other types of long-distance human movement combined, international tourism will be the focus of this overview. A privilege of the elite in the past, by the middle of the third quarter of the twentieth century, domestic and international tourism was quickly becoming a mass phenomenon in European societies, facilitated by the institutionalization of "the right to rest and leisure," a provision in the 1948 UN Universal Declaration of Human Rights, in the form of paid holidays offered by employers in the signatory countries, and by the improvement in transportation. In the developed northwestern European countries, vacation travel, especially international tourism, was further fostered as a mass phenomenon by postwar economic prosperity and the resulting growth of the middle class and by the rapid expansion of tourist industry. In much poorer eastern Europe, mass-scale tourism was made possible by the financial and organizational assistance of Communist welfare states that enabled large numbers of working people to travel on vacations—mostly domestic, but also in other Soviet-bloc countries.[44]

The growth rate of international tourism in Europe (all regions) since the late 1970s has been exceeded only by the East Asia/Pacific region. Some 180 million arrivals in 1978 increased to more than 250 million in 1988, or by nearly 40 percent, and the projected volume for 1995 is 376 million, an increase of another 50 percent. In the 1990s Europe has generated 57 percent of international tourism and has received about 63 percent (the latter figure has been gradually decreasing, from 73 percent in the mid-1970s; the difference has been taken over mostly by the East Asia/Pacific region).[45]

As already noted, the dominant pattern of international tourism has differed in important aspects from that characteristic of the migration types considered thus far. Therefore, instead of comparing this case with itself over time (as was done with the previously discussed types), we thought it would be more interesting to compare the main features of international tourist travels of Europeans with the main characteristics of their economic and political movement.

We will start with the two most clearly distinguishing features. First, rather than following "compass," or SE-NW, flows like the bulk of economic and political movement, most international tourism moves between the highly developed countries. This pattern obtains globally as well as on the European Continent (nearly three-quarters of the total volume of both international tourism in general and travels of Europeans in specific falls into this category). To core-NW countries, too, accrue about 80 percent (or US$220 billion) of all tourism-related revenues.

Second, within this dominant pattern, one of the most frequented tourist routes reverses the accustomed direction of economic and political migratory flows, so that instead of S-to-N, there is a mass movement from northwestern Europe to the Mediterranean region; the latter, especially Italy and Spain, have regularly received about one-third of all tourist arrivals in Europe, whereas Germany, the leading receiver of two other forms of migration, has received only 5 percent.[46]

Of the two remaining traits of European international tourism to be noted here, one differs (although not entirely) and the other resembles the specific patterns of the economic and political migration considered earlier. The former feature has been a comparatively lesser politicization of international tourism. Only comparatively, however, because a closer look at its mechanisms reveals reflections of both long-lasting world political order and shorter-term political developments. (Two examples, general and specific: Political turbulence, to which the volume and directions of international tourism are highly sensitive, is much less likely to occur in the affluent and well-established liberal democracies in the NW than in the SE parts of the world. There is a necessity to petition for entry visas and to comply with requirements regarding the length of stay imposed on tourists from the eastern part of Europe by their prospective hosts in the West.) International tourism in Europe shares the latter characteristic with the evolving patterns of refugee and illegal migratory flows, and, more recently, it shares a new guest worker trek: eastward expansion that sweeps a swelling flow of tourists from faraway corners of Europe toward the West. (To Poland alone came 2 million Russian tourists in 1989, 4 million in 1990, and 9 million in 1991.)[47]

Mixed Types of Migration

Whereas turn-of-the-twentieth-century migrations in the Atlantic world-system represented basically one "pure" type: economic (except for the already mentioned case of East European Jews, whose mass exodus had a combined economic-political character), in the post–World War II era there first appeared just a few mixed varieties (by the mid-1970s we identified illegal entrants/labor migrants, *indocumentado* ex-guestworkers, and tourists/business travelers) and, accompanying accelerated diversification of migration types since the 1980s, more "blurring of genres" has occurred.

Two related factors seem to have been of particular importance in triggering this "polymerization." Progressive globalization opens before our eyes new and more options and possibilities (material possessions, lifestyles, adventure), and new and more ways to pursue them. At the same time, those whose opportunities to realize these promises are constrained by restrictive policies of admission to the core regions where these possibilities can be best realized, and/or by their peripheral location in the structure of world economy, are inclined to "play against the system," or, to borrow from Robert Merton's classic anomie model, "innovate" by using (socially, politically) illegitimate means in order to achieve the (culturally approved) objectives otherwise unavailable.[48] In what follows we note only the most common varieties of such blurred genres of migration in present-day Europe: first, combinations encountered among migrant-members in the core, northwestern parts of the Continent, and, next, those—more numerous—found among migrants from its (semi-)peripheral regions, namely, eastern Europe, and, in this case, southern Italy.

Among the former, the most common blend is a combination of business and tourism (over one-third of west European travelers to Poland in 1993 declared this double purpose for their visit). A short-distance variant of this combination is represented by travels of tourist-shoppers in frontier areas, who weekly or monthly shop for food and household items in the neighboring country. The direction of such escapades is usually the reverse of compass migration: After cheaper prices, they flow N-to-S and W-to-E (according to one report, over 40 percent of German tourists arriving in western Poland do their regular shopping in local towns).[49]

A combination of tourism with business has also been common among East European migrants. However, although the number of Western-style international tourist businesspeople, such as investors, bankers, commercial agents, and so on, has been growing since the 1990s, the most popular forms of this variety are particular to the (semi-)peripheral position of the region. Blending business with tourism in eastern Europe dates back to the early 1970s, when Communist welfare state-sponsored international vacation travels inside the Soviet bloc became a mass phenomenon. In a spontaneous adjustment to Soviet-style shortage economies that intra-bloc tourism was used as an opportunity for a huge-scale unofficial, in fact illegal, commercial traffic between the vacationing member nationals of Soviet-bloc countries (the volume of this exchange was estimated at 25 to 30 percent of the entire COMECON trade).[50] Since the collapse of Communism, this commercial tourism has expanded in volume and scope and diversified. The most popular form is international tourist travels combined with bazaar or street vending of little items from clothing to hardware (routinely practiced by hundreds of thousands of Poles in Germany, Austria, and Turkey and by Russians and Ukrainians in Poland and Hungary).

Over and above this popular (legal) traffic in small things, there is a large-scale, intercontinental crime that criminologists refer to as "Global Mafia" to underscore its greatly enlarged scope and increased mobility within the last decade or so.[51] Although global mafia has not been commonly considered in the purview of migration studies (except, perhaps, in Italian-American history), we believe that its recent employs and ways of operation make such an inclusion sensible. It engages an army of international envoys traveling under various disguises as tourists, businesspeople, scientists, and so on, and controls thousands of middle-size entrepreneur contrabandists of various kinds.

In present-day Europe, southern Italian and Russian Mafias represent the major organized structures of "global crime." The former, an old player, has reportedly been heavily involved in the smuggling of illegal aliens from Africa and the Middle East into western Europe (this function alone qualifies it as a relevant subject for international migration studies); intracontinental contraband of alcohol and cigarettes; and, of course, intercontinental trafficking in drugs (the "African" and "South American" routes). The latter is a newcomer on the European scene. Apparently composed largely of the former Soviet *nomenklatura,* or holders of higher-level positions in the bureaucractic structure of the Communist system that were reserved for party members, including a strong representation of the military, it has a loyal personnel well-trained in secretive dealings (the operation of the higher-level Communist *apparat* was often compared to the Mafia) and a huge capital accumulated during several decades of feudal-style corrupt rule over a large empire. At present, the Russian Mafia and its affiliates across the NIS (i.e., deep into Asia) and in the former satellites (including former East Germany) seem to control to a significant extent the market for gold and art objects (smuggled to the West); the contraband of Western, mostly German, cars (to Eastern Europe); selling of Soviet and East German military equipment (mostly to the Middle East, but also to Asia and Africa); and, increasingly and apparently in a ruthless war with its Italian competitor, the "Asian route" in the smuggling of drugs through Eastern Europe to Germany and further west.[52]

Another mixed type of migration very common among East Europeans, mentioned already in a different context, is illegal work on a tourist (or other nonemployment) visa. In a mail survey conducted in the mid-1980s in Poland, nearly half of 137,000 respondents who had overstayed their tourist visas in the West and eventually returned admitted that they had worked abroad illegally. Illegal work by tourists or other visitors without work permits has been practiced by both low-skill and high-skill East European migrants. In the former category, we may mention about a quarter of a million Russian and Ukrainian tourists in Poland in 1991 who took up illegal employment (primarily in agriculture and the private construction industry). Highly educated migrants—for example, Polish biologists and chemists on short- to medium-term visits in the West—have been found performing laboratory jobs in hospitals and research institutes (exploitative by Western standards at $12 per hour, such occupations earned them ten times more in a month than their professional salaries in Poland in 1992). Russian students and researchers on short-term fellowships in Berlin and Vienna have been reported to supplement their stipends by window and office cleaning (such jobs are apparently considered beneath their more "Westernized" Polish colleagues).[53]

Last to note is a blend of political and economic migration. It exists in three varieties. One is a "simple" (actually often torturous to the bearer) mix of political and economic motivations in the migrant's decision to leave his/her country, and later to remain (or return) home. It is probably the most common kind in this category, but practically uninvestigated by the sociologists of contemporary European migrations. The other two forms are distinguished not by the motivations of the travelers ("pure" or mixed) but, rather, by the sequencing of these two identities in the migrants' experience: political-to-economic, or economic-to-political, each of which has different consequences for migrants' status in the receiver society.

The former kind, already mentioned, is created by a change in the immigration policy of the receiver country that refuses asylum to migrant-petitioners from certain regions/countries, thus forcing them to find work without permit; the position of such migrants becomes, then, doubly precarious: They are illegal stayers illegally employed. (Nota bene, although it may be partially accurate, the EC political authorities' perception of present-day asylum-seekers from peripheral regions as "really" economic migrants, is blind to the fact that a significant proportion of the earlier refugees from the Soviet bloc was also motivated, in part or mostly, by economic dissatisfaction. But in the Cold War era the motivations of such escapees were automatically assumed to be political.) The latter variety, economic-to-political sequence, is usually much less punitive for the migrants: It occurs when they shift their status from the employment-related sojourn (or tourist visit) to that of political refugees/asylum-seekers as the result of a sudden deterioration of the political situation in their home country. The legal/legal position of such migrants (assuming, to simplify, that the asylum is granted by the receiver society) gives them a security their reverse-sequence counterparts do not have.

Micro-Contexts of Migration: Information and Assistance Networks

More than once in the preceding sections, we have referred to ground-level or local social structures in the sending and the receiving societies that within broader economic and political contexts shape the decisions migrants make and actions they pursue. We now look at this matter more directly by considering—in a comparative perspective of microlevel networks of information and assistance relied on by the turn-of-the-twentieth-century European travelers—social support arrangements relied on by their contemporary successors.[54] Not to expand further this already lengthy chapter, we shall focus on the (low- and high-skilled) employment-related migration. The general conclusions from our comparative investigation have been the following.

Although individual or self-supported long-distance travels have definitely increased in the contemporary world, other-dependent and chain migration patterns have remained very much in use. In the Atlantic world-economy as well as in the contemporary world-system these networks of information and assistance have played an important role in the decisions made by prospective migrants about whether, where, and how to go. Like other features of contemporary international migration, however, patterns of local social support networks have over time become more complex and polymorphic; in this case, as the result of interpenetration of microlevel, informal social networks and larger political and other organizational structures in influencing processes of migration. In the remainder of this section we briefly look at the functioning and regional patterning of these support networks that have assisted European migrants. We specified four main types: informal, institutional, and two mixed categories distinguished by their primary assisting structure—informal/institutional and institutional/informal. The popularity of particular types has varied, however, by the migrants' region of origin and skill level.

Informal social networks had been, expectedly, the major source of assistance for turn-of-the-twentieth-century migrants, regardless of regional origin: They furnished information regarding possible directions of migration (between 1900 and 1906, over 8 million letters circulated between the United States and Europe), provided aid in organizing transport (50 to 60 percent of overseas ship tickets were prepaid by family or friends, and intra-Continental seasonal workers traveled in groups sharing costs), and, after arrival, assisted in obtaining initial housing and employment. (An exception were East European Jews, whose migration was also assisted by emigration agencies organized by their Western coreligionists.)[55]

European international migrants in the post–WW II era have also relied on informal social networks for information and assistance regarding their projects, although reliance on personal social resources as the only or main source of support has been generally more common among travelers from (semi-)peripheral regions of the Continent (unless the process of relocation is managed by the core employers with or without the cooperation of the sending states) and among lower-skilled migrants. (But a recent study of highly skilled migrants from Ireland—viewed as periphery by the authors—showed them to rely mostly on the informal ways of assistance in moving.[56]

Expectedly, it has also been the main channel of assistance to migrants who either before or after arrival in a host country as tourists, visiting family members, or students/researchers, decide to undertake illegal employment. (As we have seen, present-day illegal migrant workers—that is, European ones—are usually from the eastern parts of the Continent, and they represent both low- and high-skill occupations.) A considerable amount of these international kin and primary social relations used for assistance, we may point out, was established, and has endured since, five to eight decades ago, during the periods of earlier mass migrations (post–World War II and the beginning of the twentieth century). (These networks are quite extensive: For example, every third Polish family today reportedly has either family or friends living outside of Poland, and about 18 million members of national minorities in the European part of the NIS have family or ethnic ties abroad.[57])

A contemporary innovation in the composition of primary social contacts as the source of assistance in organizing migrants' international travel and sojourn abroad in comparison with turn-of-the-twentieth-century personal networks, has been the appearance, usually in the case of highly skilled travelers, of Western (besides or rather than coethnic) friends as the facilitators. The jobs they arrange for their acquaintances range from legitimate (through wavers, exemptions, etc., often requiring quite a bit of know-how in legal maneuvering on the part of the assisting native) to semilegitimate (migrant visitors as laboratory workers or field-workers assigned special tasks, paid from private grants of the native researchers).

Primary reliance on institutional networks in assisting the process of migration and settling down in a host country is by and large a contemporary development and has been practiced primarily in the highly developed (EC/AFTA) countries. The most common among these formal assistance structures are corporations (including multinationals), scientific and research institutes (sponsored by governments or public foundations), and recruitment agencies (state- or employer-sponsored); the first two assist in transfers of highly skilled workers, and the last one in moving labor (specifically, Mediterranean guestworkers to northwestern

Europe between 1955 and the early 1970s).[58] In Eastern Europe during the Communist period, formal institutional channels were used to organize an exodus of Jews and ethnic Germans to the West, agreed on by bilateral government treaties and in intra-COMECON transfers of workers. They may assume a new importance after recent treaties on annual *Gastarbeiter* quotas between Germany and East European states.

We tend to believe that two hybrid types of migration assistance networks—informal/institutional and institutional/informal—may actually represent the most common forms of contemporary migration assistance networks. There are no solid empirical data to substantiate this belief (i.e., not in the migration studies; the inherent presence of personal networks, whether "weak" or "strong ties," in all forms of social relations, including formal organizations, has been long recognized by the sociologists[59]), but our personal experience and observations, occasional reports in the media, and the results of some informal interviews we conducted among our friends and acquaintances from NW and SE regions of Europe all seem to support it.

The informal/institutional hybrid is certainly common in Eastern Europe (and all that we know about South European societies and cultures suggests this type should also be popular there). It involves using informal networks to initiate or "hook up" to the institutional connection. This tactic was customarily used, for example, by East European workers in the Soviet bloc to "hook up" to well-paid labor exchange programs between COMECON countries and has endured in the post-Communist era in all urban classes. It is, for instance, common knowledge among that region's academics that this is the most effective way for scholars to obtain fellowships at West European or North American institutes.

The institutional/informal combination differs from the previous form in the primary agency that initiates or (if travel is to be clandestine or its real purpose hidden) "covers up" for the process of assisted migration. This variety seems to have been common in all regions of Europe and at all skill levels. In the eastern part, the cover-up form was routinely used by Communist *nomenklatura* members to arrange lucrative foreign appointments or other short-to-medium-term sojourns abroad for themselves or their relatives. Another illustration can be found in informal networks of information and assistance created by South European guest workers even while their migration was organized and monitored by the employer-state recruitment agencies. Forged in the course of migration "processed" by the institutional channels, these group support networks were subsequently used to create ethnic entrepreneurial niches in tertiary and "quaternary," or underground, sectors of the economies of the receiving countries. The organization of and assistance in illegal crossing into the receiving country by organized criminal groups, such as the Mafia, could perhaps also be included in this category. Finally, perhaps the most intangible variety of the institutional/informal migration assistance networks is the encroachment of personal networks and potlatch obligations on the decisions regarding the assignments of foreign fellowships, appointments, and transfers made by the boards of scientific and research institutions.

Before concluding, let us make two more observations. One concerns the controlling "power" of accustomed outlooks and customs in the local social environment over individual decisions of migrants regarding their destinations. Turn-of-the-twentieth-century local sanctions in these matters were strong and binding, and, as contemporary enthnographic studies report, only the marginal members of the group or newcomers did not follow the accepted routes (the pioneer migrants from East European villages to North America were just such marginal residents).[60] Although local views and customs influence contemporary international migrations as well, generally this control has become less direct; it operates through "trends" and "fashions" rather than straightforward prohibitions and prescriptions. (Two specific exceptions come to mind, one in a *Gemeinschaft* and the other *Gesellschaft* social environment: First, in the staunchly anti-Communist micro-milieu of the Warsaw intelligentsia, traveling to the Soviet Union on vacation or for any other purpose was so thoroughly condemned by the social code of the group that even contemplating such a voyage was prohibited; and second, in the highly formalized structures of large corporations, it has been prescriptions rather than prohibitions, in the form of dispositions from above, that largely determine the destinations of transferred individuals.)

The other observation has to do with the existence of the previously established community of fellow nationals in the receiving country as a determining factor in choosing the destination by prospective migrants. For turn-of-the-twentieth-century wage-seeking migrants (excepting social marginals and, of course, seasonal workers) it was of crucial importance, because of their multiple dependence on the social net: for economic survival, communication, companionship, religious practice, and a sense of identity. For the same reasons it was also of great significance for a small group of better-educated migrants at that time: Organized communities of fellow nationals were practically the only place where these people could find jobs as teachers in ethnic parochial schools, clergy in parishes, or journalists in the foreign-language press.

As studies indicate, the existence abroad of an established ethnic community has been an important, often decisive, factor in choosing (if choice is possible) the destination by contemporary wage-seeking migrants: For tourists planning illegal work, unless, like domestics, they have already secured a steady position for the entire stay, at stake are, besides social and cultural needs, economic survival and "political security," because it is easier to stay out of view of the immigration authorities in a large crowd. Contract workers have secure jobs, but for all other needs just mentioned they turn to a local ethnic community. Present-day highly skilled migrants are usually employed by mainstream institutions, they have greater familiarity with the language and culture of the receiving society, and their primary social relations tend to be more "supralocal." Unless they are political refugees who want to return to their countries as soon as the circumstances change and, while waiting, form close-knit residential, economic, and cultural niches abroad (there exist, for example, thriving little communities of East European intelligentsia occupied in publishing, fund-raising, and political lobbying in Paris, London, and New York), such professional migrants seek, rather, such "supralocal," residentially dispersed, networks of friends with whom they can occasionally meet to discuss current events in their home countries, go out, and regularly talk on the telephone.[61]

Conclusion

We have argued that both "great migrations," the 1870–1914 wave and that since the mid-1950s to the present, can be seen at once as outcomes and contributors to globalization processes, and as the latter progress, international movements of the Europeans become increasingly more complex. Specifically, migration has become increasingly diversified in kind; and the act of it, once dependent primarily on the individual decision and the local community's priorities and controls, has become increasingly enmeshed in various, not always congruous, macro- and mesolevel institutional purposes and concerns (political/ideological, organizational/bureaucratic). Three major factors structuring population movements in Europe: economy, politics (including pragmatically and ideologically motivated actions and policies), and social relations have informed our discussion of the differentiation and growing institution-dependence of migration. Here are, in brief, its main points.

First, contemporary population movements—global as well as European—occur in the context of the enduring economic inequalities between parts of the world. Specifically, the division NW(core)-SE ([semi-] periphery), present already in the Atlantic world-economy, has been responsible for the persistence of so-called compass migration (S-to-N; E-to-W) that is stretching outward, as new regions are incorporated into the global system. At the same time, in consequence of the restructuring of global economy, there have emerged new and different types of employment-related migration.

Second, "hooking up" (the Polish idiom is again useful) of migration to political/ideological and organizational/bureaucratic interests and concerns—a development absent in turn-of-the-twentieth-century population movements—reflects two discordant tendencies in the contemporary world. One promotes globalization: universalist declarations of international organizations relevant to migration issues; expansion of multinationals fostering movement of high-skill personnel; and international tourist industry that organizes "migration" abroad for millions of tourists each year. The other tendency, itself a product of globalization, runs counter to it, in no small measure as a reaction to swelling compass migration: restrictive immigration policies of the receiver countries confronted with a deluge of foreign residents; *Gastarbeiter*-like agreements between receiver and sender companies, limiting the number of entering migrants and the duration of their sojourns.

Third and last, social networks of information and assistance in migration have significantly diversified in comparison with the earlier period, mainly as the result of increased penetration of formal organizations into group and individual lives. Distinct patterns indirectly reflecting macro-level divisions between world's core and (semi-)periphery can be detected also in this realm: Whereas travelers from the former rely primarily on institutional and institutional-informal supports, migrants from the latter, who have to "beat the system" in order to move effectively in pursuit of their purposes, use, rather, informal and institutional-informal supports.

Notes

1. The main simplifications should be pointed out in advance so that readers are aware of them as we move on. Thus, we combine and counterpose at several occasions NW or northwestern (used interchangeably with "core"), and SE or southeastern ("[semi-]periphery") European regions/countries; then S or South, and E or East European migrants; finally "eastern eastern" Europeans, i.e., residents of the former Soviet Union, each of which could be justifiably fragmented into smaller pieces. (E.g., there is a notorious Ireland, NW for sure, but certainly not core; there is in "eastern Europe" a more highly developed northern tier [Poland, the Czech Republic, Hungary] as well as a less-developed South [Romania, Bulgaria]; Germany, NW and a "giant core," has absorbed five years ago, and cannot quite digest still, East European semi-periphery called GDR, and so on.) We may also explain here that in order to make our historical comparison more straightforward, we decided to omit the period of mass resettlements resulting from World War II, 1945–1955.

2. For cogent and well-informed critical overviews of different conceptualizations of globalism and world-system(s), see, for example, Christopher Chase-Dunn, *Global Formation: Structures of the World-Economy,* New York: Basil Black-

well, 1989; and Bruce Mazlish and Ralph Buultjens, eds., *Conceptualizing Global History,* Boulder: Westview Press, 1993. On migration in the global framework, see Mary Kritz et al., *Global Trends in Migration: Theory and Research on International Population Movements,* New York: The Center for Migration Studies, 1983.

3. We would like to clarify a little further our position in this regard. We view the technological/economic and political/military dimensions, and regions of the world where these forces display greater dynamism and effectiveness, as usually (although not universally) "mightier" than other factors in shaping the general power relations and, relatedly, the main directions of flows (capital, labor, and ideas) in the supraregional system. At the same time, however, we consider the existing power arrangements and processes of globalization, like all historical situations and processes, as inherently *under*determined and containing plural possibilities. It is in this sphere of undetermination and "plural potential" ever-present in social life, that the microlevel, agentic interests, values, and purposes play out, with or against the pressures of macrostructural forces.

4. Estimations of the total volume of longer-distance migrations within and outside Europe between 1870 and 1914 differ quite considerably because of different methods used by the recording agencies (state, transport, employment) in various countries and because not all migratory movements were recorded. The range quoted here, the total of 60–70 million "moves," including intra- and intercontinental travels, seems to us most convincing. Information and estimates concerning European migrations in the period considered here can be found in Imre Ferenczi and Walter Willcox, *International Migrations,* Geneva: International Labor Office, 1929, 2 vols; CNRS, *Les migrations internationales de la fin du XVIII siecle a nos jours.* Paris: CNRS, 1980; Ulrich Herbert, *Geschichte der Auslanderbeschaftigung in Deutschland 1880–1980: Saisonarbeiter, Gastarbeiter, Zwangsarbeiter,* Berlin: Dietz, 1986; J. D. Gould, "European Inter-Continental Emigration 1815–1914: Patterns and Causes," *The Journal of European Economic History* 8 (1979), pp. 593–980 and "European Inter-Continental Emigration: The Role of 'Diffusion' and 'Feedback'," *Journal of European Economic History* 9(1980), pp. 41–112; Leslie Page Moch, "Migration in an Age of Urbanization and Industrialization," *Moving Europeans: Migration in Western Europe Since 1650,* pt. 4; and Walter Nugent, *The Great Transatlantic Migrations, 1870–1914,* Bloomington: Indiana University Press, 1992. These estimates, it should be noted, still undercount the actual movements during the period considered here: Omitted are traditional short-distance labor migrations, which, even if diminished in frequency relative to more remote destinations, were by no means eliminated. We have also excluded, because it escaped, as it were, the forces incorporating eastern Europe into the Atlantic world-system, a multimillion-person emigration during the same era of central Russian peasantry to Siberia and Central Asia (see e.g., V. Obolensky-Ossinsky, "Emigration from and Immigration to Russia," in Ferenczi and Willcox, *International Migrations* II, pp. 523–565).

5. Information compiled from Alexander Gerschenkorn, *Economic Backwardness in Historical Perspective.* Cambridge, Mass.: Belknap Press of Harvard University Press, 1962; Sidney Pollard, "Industrialization and the European Economy," *The Economic History Review* (2nd series) 26(1973), pp. 636–649; Clive Trebilcock, *The Industrialization of the Continental Powers, 1780–1914,* New York: Longman, 1981;

Ivan Berend and Gyorgi Ranki, *Economic Development in East-Central Europe in the 19th and 20th Centuries,* New York: Columbia University Press, 1974 and *The European Periphery and Industrialization, 1780–1914,* Cambridge: Cambridge University Press, 1982; Boris F. Brandt, *Innostrannye kapitaly, ikh vlijanye na ekonomicheskoye razvite stravy.* St. Petersburg: V. Kirpbayma, 1901, 2 vols.; and Willfried Spohn, *Weltmarktkonkurrenz und Industrialisierung Deutsch Lands 1870–1914,* Berlin: Olle & Wolter, 1977.

6. Data compiled from Ferenczi and Willcox, *International Migrations,* I, pp. 167–186, 384–389, and 294–296; II, pp. 219–230 and 387; Nugent, *Crossings,* p. 15; Gould, "European Inter-Continental Emigration: The Road Home," pp. 108–110; Karl M. Bolte, Dieter Kappe, and Josef Schmid, *Bevolkerung: Statistik, Theorie, Geschichte und Politik des Bevolkerungsprozesses,* Opladen: Leske, 1980; Herbert, *Geschichte der Auslanderbeschaftigung,* pp. 15–55; and Moch, *Moving Europeans,* chapter 4.

7. The European and global figures have been estimated from data found in Aaron Segal, *An Atlas of International Migration,* London: Hans Zell Publishers, 1993, pp. 20–25, 40, 56–62, and 72; Anthony King, "European International Migration 1945–1990: A Statistical and Geographical Overview," in Russell King, ed., *Mass Migrations in Europe: The Legacy and the Future,* London: Belhaven Press, 1993, pp. 19–39; *Trends in International Migration,* pp. 131–145; current press reports. Considering that data from the NIS are incomplete and most likely underestimate the number of Russian residents in the former Soviet republics (a considerable proportion of whom were born in Russia and are now considered as "foreigners" by the authorities of new independent states), the total number of foreign-born residents in Europe is likely to be higher than 20-odd million.

8. In a powerful metaphor, these divisions have also been called "global apartheid"—see R. Falk, "Democratizing, Internationalizing, and Globalizing: A Collage of Blurred Images," paper presented at the International Conference of Changing World Order and the United Nations System, Yokohama, March 24–27, 1992—as quoted in Stephen Gill, "Economic Globalization and the Internationalization of Authority: Limits and Contradictions," *Geoforum* 23(1992), p. 280.

9. West European data do not include Scandinavian countries, and for east Europe, we averaged only data for Soviet-bloc countries (i.e., without Yugoslavia and Albania). It should be reiterated, however, that there were, and remain to this day, considerable differences between countries in the level of economic development within both southern and eastern Europe (with Italy in the former and Czechoslovakia in the latter showing the highest indices, and, respectively, Romania and Portugal, the lowest. The data were compiled from F. E. Ian Hamilton, "A Global Region in the Melting-pot?" *Geoforum* 21(1990), pp. 151–153; Paul Bairoch, "International Industrialization Levels from 1750 to 1980," *Journal of European Economic History* 11(1982), esp. pp. 280–300; Ralf Rytlewski and M. Opp de Hipt, *Die Bundesrepublik Deutschland in Zahlen 1945/49–1980,* Beck: Munchen, 1987, p. 106.

10. On world-level international organizations and proclamations regarding human rights and international policy on migrants and refugees, see, e.g., Aristide Zolberg, "International Migrations in Political Perspective," in Mary Kritz et al., *Global Trends in Migration,* pp. 3–28; Guy Goodwin-Gill, "International Law and

Human Rights: Trends Concerning Migrants and Refugees," in Bruce Mazlish and Ralph Buultjens, eds., *Conceptualizing Global History,* pp. 526–546; and David Martin, "Effects of International Law on Migration Policy and Practice: The Uses of Hypocrisy," in Mazlish and Buultjens, *Conceptualizing Global History,* pp. 547–578. Specifically on human rights declarations and (im)migration and refugee policies in the European Community, see Anthony Fielding, "Migrants, Institutions, and Politics: The Evolution of European Migration Policies," in Russell King, ed., *Mass Migrations in Europe: The Legacy and Future,* London: Belhaven Press, 1993, pp. 40–64; *Trends in International Migration,* Paris: OECD Sopemi, 1992, Pt. 1B, "Panorama of Migration Policies"; Gary Freeman, "Migration Policy and Politics in the Receiving States," *International Migration Review* 26:4(1992) 1154–1163; "European Immigration Policy," special issue of *Contemporary European Affairs* 3, 1990.

11. J. D. Gould, a historian of late nineteenth-/early twentieth-century European migrations, has argued that by the outbreak of World War I West Europeans were already "emigration saturated," but that their southern (and eastern) counterparts, still far behind in the urban-industrial transformation, remained acutely migration-thirsty or "on the go" ("European International Emigration: The Role of 'Diffusion' and 'Feedback'," p. 294 and throughout). During the two interwar decades opportunities for international migration in the Atlantic world-economy became significantly reduced. In the 1920s the United States, the main overseas destination, discontinued its open-door immigration policy and established annual entry quotas, and war reparations and hyperinflation turned Germany, formerly the primary European receiver, into a sending country, which it remained for primarily political reasons after Hitler's National-Socialist Party came to power in the 1930s. The Great Depression on both sides of the Atlantic further diminished the volume of international migration. The statistical figures quoted in text are from Anthony King, "European International Migration, 1945–1990: A Statistical and Geographical Overview," in Russell King, ed., *Mass Migrations in Europe: The Legacy and the Future,* London: Belhaven Press, 1993, pp. 19–39.

12. For a summary discussion of mass migrations related with the forced urbanization-industrialization of the Soviet bloc countries during the first decade and a half following the conclusion of World War II, see, e.g., Daniel Chirot, *The Origins of Backwardness in Eastern Europe,* Berkeley: University of California Press, 1989.

13. Calculated from *Historical Statistics of the United States: Colonial Times to 1970,* Washington, D. C.: U.S. Department of Commerce, 1972, pt. 1, pp. 105–109 and 119; *Statistical Abstract of the United States: 1980,* Washington, D.C.: U.S. Department of Commerce, 1982, pp. 93–99; *Continuous Reporting System on Migration,* Paris: OECD Sopemi, 1990, p. 163.

14. See Charles Keely and Patricia Elwell, "International Migration: Canada and the United States," in Kritz, *Global Trends in Migration,* pp. 182–188.

15. On the demographic and socioeconomic characteristics of turn-of-the-twentieth-century European international migrants, see Moch, *Moving Europeans,* Pt. 4.

16. After Hans Heinrich Blotevogel et al., "From Itinerant Worker to Immigrant? The Geography of Guestworkers in Germany," in King, *Mass Migrations in*

Europe, pp. 83–89. Generally on the guest worker experience, see W. R. Bohning, *Studies in International Migration,* New York: St. Martin's, 1984.

17. Data compiled from John Salt, "International Labor Migration in Western Europe: A Geographical Review," in Kritz, *Global Trends in Migration,* pp. 138–139, and Blotevogel et al., "From Itinerant Worker to Immigrant?" pp. 85–88.

18. Data compiled from King, "European International Migration, 1945–1990," p. 30 and Blotevogel et al., "From Itinerant Worker to Immigrant?" p. 87. On the return incentives policies of West European governments in the second half of the 1970s, see Rosemarie Rogers, "Incentives to Return: Patterns of Policies and Migrants' Responses," in Kritz, *Global Trends in Migration,* pp. 338–364 and Goran Rystad, "Immigration History and the Future of International Migration," *International Migration Review* 26:4 (1992) 1178–1184.

19. As reported in *The Future of Migration,* Paris: OECD, 1987, pp. 49 and 190–194; Anthony Fielding, "Migrants, Institutions, and Politics: The Evolution of European Migration Policies," p. 46; and Blotevogel et al., "From Itinerant Worker to Immigrant?" p. 89.

20. Data compiled from *The Future of Migration,* pp. 190–194; Kritz, *Global Trends in Migration,* pp. 153–154; *Trends in International Migration,* pp. 131–145.

21. On overstaying former guest workers and their employment in the underground economy, see *The Future of Migration,* pp. 277–278.

22. Data compiled from King, "European International Migration, 1945–1990," pp. 32–35. On the process of transition "from migrant workers to immigrants," see John Murray, "Migration and European Society: A View from the Council of Europe," *International Review of Comparative Public Policy,* vol. 1, 1989, pp. 181–185 and throughout.

23. For example, in Germany, Polish economic migrants earn six to ten times the wages paid in their home country. We were puzzled and dismayed to realize that, in comparison, turn-of-the-twentieth-century average wages of Polish migrant laborers in Germany were "only" about 50–60 percent higher than they could have earned for the same work at home. Present date/wage ratio as reported in Marek Okolski, "La nouvelle donne migratoire en Europe de l'Est," *Revue Europeenne des Migrations Internationales,* vol. 7, no. 2, 1991, p. 25; turn-of-the-twentieth-century figure is from Ewa Morawska, "Labor Migrations of Poles in the Atlantic World-Economy, 1870–1914," *Comparative Studies in Society and History* 31 (April 1989), esp. pp. 257–258.

24. Perfectly legal seasonal and frontier migrations of agricultural workers continue today in the EC at a stable rate of about 400,000 annually. For the Iberian illegal migration in the 1960s, see Stephen Castles, "The Guest Worker in Western Europe: An Obituary," *International Migration Review* 4 (1986), p. 763 and elsewhere.

25. See, for example, Piotr Korcelli, "International Migrations in Europe: Polish Perspectives for the 1990s," *International Migration Review* 26, 2(1992), p. 302; Okolski, "La nouvelle donne migratoire," pp. 7–39, and post-1989 Polish and German press reports inspected, respectively, by Ewa Morawska and Willfried Spohn. The same sources also suggest that in contrast to the backgrounds of their turn-of-the-twentieth-century fellow nationals seeking wages in that country, the majority of the East European illegal job-seekers come from highly urbanized areas. But no systematic sociological data yet apparently exist regarding the socioeconomic ori-

gins and occupational placement in the receiver countries of present-day illegal economic migrants from Eastern Europe.

26. Estimates compiled from *Mass Migration in Europe,* p. 290; *The Future of Migration,* pp. 308 and 317–318; Claudio Calvaruso, "Illegal Immigration to Italy," in *The Future of Migration,* pp. 306–314; Sotiris Soulis, "Illegal Immigration to Greece," in *The Future of Migration,* pp. 315–319; *Continuous Reporting System on Migration,* pp. 21–23 and 50–52; Korcelli, "International Migrations in Europe," pp. 302–303; Laszlo Szoke, "Hungarian Perspectives on Emigration and Immigration, in the New European Architecture," *International Migration Review* 26, 2(1992), pp. 306–308 and 312–317; and Joseph Blaschke, "Les travailleurs immigres dans l'Allemagne reunifie," *Revue Europeenne des Migrations Internationales* 7(2), 1991, p. 78.

27. On the "regularization" programs in France and Italy, see *Continuous Reporting System on Migration, SOPEMI,* 1989, pp. 77–84. On the details of these bilateral agreements, see *The Changing Course of International Migration,* pp. 100–101; *Trends in International Migration,* pp. 108 and 114. The similarity of recent bilateral agreements between German and East European governments to the former's importation of South European labor during the 1960s has been pointed to by a number of commentators, who refer to the East European contract workers as "new *Gastarbeiter.*"

28. Proportion of Europeans among immigrants to the United States from *Continuous Reporting System on Migration SOPEMI,* Paris: OECD, 1990, p. 173; on the surge in L-1 and H-1 visas, see *Continuous Reporting System on Migration SOPEMI,* Paris: OECD, 1987, p. 25; see also John Salt and Allan Findlay, "International Migration of Highly Skilled Manpower: Theoretical and Developmental Issues," in Reginald Appleyard, ed., *The Impact of International Migration on Developing Countries,* Paris: OECD, 1988, pp. 160–162.

29. Aggregate data and interpretations published in *Eurostats* and the *Continuous Reporting System on Migration SOPEMI* reports. The best available sources on contemporary EC migration still focus primarily, as in the 1960s and 1970s, on labor and family-reunion flows from the Mediterranean member-countries to northwestern Europe. In addition, most EC member nationals do not need work permits anymore (and therefore their employment is not recorded by ILO and IMO), and individual country data are often incompatible. On these and related difficulties of conducting research on contemporary intra-EC migrations, see John Salt, "High Level Manpower Movements in Northwest Europe and the Role of Careers: An Explanatory Framework," *International Migration Review* 17, 4(1983), pp. 634–637 and Allan Findlay, "New Technology, High-Level Labour Movements and the Concept of the Brain Drain," *Continuous Reporting System on Migration SOPEMI,* Paris: OECD, 1991, pp. 150–151.

30. It should be noted, however, that in intracompany transfers within the EC, the proportion of EC member nationals varies, depending on the type of form, from a mere 20 to 25 percent to a high 75 to 80 percent. Information compiled from Allan Findlay, "A Migration Channels Approach to the Study of High Level Manpower Movements: A Theoretical Perspective," *International Migration,* vol. 28, no. 1, March 1990, pp. 16–17; Salt and Ford, "Skilled International Migration in Europe," pp. 298–302; John Salt, "Highly Skilled International Migrants, Careers and International Labour Markets," *Geoforum,* vol. 19, no. 4, 1988, pp. 392–393.

31. Data compiled from Paul Bailey and Aurelio Parisotto, "Multinational Enterprises: What Role Can They Play in Employment Generation in Developing Countries?" in *The Changing Course of International Migration*, p. 140; John Salt et al., "Skilled International Migration in Europe: The Shape of Things to Come?" in *Mass Migration in Europe*, p. 299. The number of European students in the United States grew from about 18,500 to over 46,000, or by 150 percent, between 1970 and 1990 (after *Annual Open Doors Report on Foreign Students in the U.S.A.*, New York: Institute of International Education, 1990, pp. 16 and 19).

32. Compiled from *Statistisches Jahrbuch* 1993, p. 92 and *From Higher Education to Employment*, Paris: OECD, 1990, vol. 1, pp. 27–28. It may be of interest to note in this context that the term *brain drain* was first used in Great Britain in the 1960s to describe such outflows (on high-skill emigration from Great Britain, see David Manasian, "The Exodus of the Elite," *International Management*, vol. 43, no. 2, February 1988, pp. 54–56; Ronald Bailey, "Science and Technology: Brain Drain," *Forbes*, vol. 144, no. 12, November 27, 1989, pp. 262–263; and Katrin Klinger, "Britain Running Out of Young Blood?" *Director*, vol. 40, no. 4, November 1986, pp. 4 and 9–52). This in-between kind of brain outflows from EC should be distinguished from what international migration analysts refer to as "high likelihood of permanent leave," such as, for example, those from Ireland, which chronically loses, most likely permanently, about 40 percent of its electronic engineering and 26 percent of its computer science graduates annually. In the Irish case, it is apparently not only underemployment that pushes out the country's young professionals but also what many of them perceive as the oppressiveness of cultural parochialism. On the Irish graduates' motivations to emigrate, see Ian Shuttleworth, "Irish Graduate Emigration: The Mobility of Qualified Manpower in the Context of Peripherality," in *Mass Migrations in Europe*, pp. 318–320.

33. Considering that Eastern Europe usually appears in western literature of the subject as "immobile" except for its westbound migrants, we would like to comment (the information is insufficient for more than that) on intra-COMECON transfers of this kind. Routine intra-(state)company transfers existed between COMECON-member countries, particularly in construction and industrial production. International business travel also took place within the Soviet bloc, largely by Communist Party card-carrying member-managers of state firms—about 1 million arrivals in 1988–1989. (It is not entirely clear whether the "business" conducted was economic, political, a mixture of both, or simply a cover name for sunny vacations the COMECON *aparatchiks* spent in the Crimea or at Varna resorts on the Black Sea.) Finally, there was a regular, even ideologically prescribed, educational and cultural exchange for adults and youth between countries in the "socialist family." On intra-Soviet bloc "brain exchange," see, e.g., *Tourism in Eastern Europe and the Soviet Union*, pp. 27, 41–44, 78–79, 97–99, and 131; John Salt, "Migration Processes among the Highly Skilled in Europe," *International Migration Review*, vol. 26, no. 2, 1992, pp. 493–495 (and notes).

34. After Norbert Ropers, *Tourismus zwischen West und Ost: Ein Beitrag zum Frieden?* Frankfurt: Campus, 1985; Jean-Claude Chesnais, "Soviet Emigration: Past, Present, and Future," in *The Changing Course of International Migration*, pp. 108–109; Janusz Hryniewicz et al., *The Brain Drain in Poland*, Warsaw: UW European Institute for Regional and Local Development, 1992, p. 52.

35. Information compiled from *An Atlas of International Migration,* p. 153; Lilia Shevtsova, "Post-Soviet Emigration Today and Tomorrow," *International Migration Review* 26, 2(1992), pp. 241–257; Okolski, "La nouvelle donne migratoire," pp. 7–39; Hryniewicz, *The Brain Drain in Poland,* pp. 35 and 46–47; *Kultura,* Paris, March 1994, p. 157 (editorial); and *Trends in International Migration,* p. 107. Exodus of Poles to the West after the crushing of "Solidarity" in December of 1981 and, since the late 1970s, exodus of Soviet Jews, have contained a considerable proportion of highly skilled emigrants, and this is why these two East-to-West population waves are included in our discussion. As political (or partially political) migrations they will also be considered in this category.

36. Compiled from Okolski, "La donne migratoire inconnue," pp. 27–28. Polish emigre biologists, chemists, physicists, and computer scientists were found to hold equivalent jobs in the West considerably more often than the social scientists, lawyers, and economists (after Hryniewicz, *The Brain Drain in Poland,* pp. 56–58). Most recent (1994) press reports and personal information from Poland suggest that in the social sciences and humanities high-skilled migration is becoming more circular (as opposed to one-way transfer; the latter continues to be the prevalent form of out-migration for natural scientists). It may be of interest to readers that a still larger brain waste associated with internal migration is taking place inside post-Communist countries as they restructure from state-subsidized to free-market economies: In Poland, for example, during the three years between 1989 and 1991 the number of university teachers leaving their occupations for extra-academic employment elsewhere in the country has grown by 209 percent relative to three years earlier (after *Kultura,* Paris, November 1993, p. 153).

37. As reported in the *New York Times,* November 10, 1993, A4.

38. Data compiled from King, "European International Migration 1945–1990," pp. 23–28; Chesnais, "Soviet Emigration," pp. 105–112; Marschalck, *Bevolkerungsgeschichte Deutschlands,* p. 154.

39. Data compiled from *Trends in International Migration,* pp. 19–20; Jonas Widgren, "Movements of Refugees and Asylum Seekers: Recent Trends in a Comparative Perspective," in *The Changing Course of International Migration,* pp. 87–93 and 100–101; Rogers, "The Future of Refugee Flows and Policies," pp. 1120–1121; "Stoked by Ethnic Conflict, Refugee Numbers Swell," *New York Times,* November 10, 1993, A3; and Blaschke, "Les travailleurs immigres dans l'Allemagne reunifie," pp. 76–77. There is no readily available, reliable data on the actual volume of population flows within the former Soviet Union, but in all likelihood it significantly exceeds Western estimates; see Sture Oberg and Helena Boubnova, "Ethnicity, Nationality, and Migration Potentials in Eastern Europe," in *Mass Migration in Europe,* pp. 234–256 and Chesnais, "Soviet Emigration," pp. 105–112.

40. On the population movement inside and out of the former Soviet Union, see, e.g., Lilia Shevtsova, "Central and Eastern Europe: The Twin Specters of Mass Unwanted Migration and Mass Involuntary Migration," *International Migration Review* 26, 2(1992), pp. 241–257; and Anatoli Vichnevski and Jeanne Zayontchkovskaia, "L'emigration de l'ex-Union sovietique: premices et inconnues," *Revue Europeenne des Migrations Internationales,* vol. 7, no. 3, 1991, pp. 5–30. Regarding four new Mediterranean receivers, information about their immigration policies, and the numbers and status of political migrants (mostly from North

Africa; in 1991 East European refugees constituted about one-fifth of the total) can be found in *Trends in International Migration,* pp. 64–67 and 75–77 and *Continuous Reporting System in Migration,* pp. 21–22 and 50–51. On political refugees in East European countries, see *Trends in International Migration,* pp. 100–101, 110–111, and 115; Korcelli, "International Migrations in Europe," pp. 292–304; and Laszlo Szoke, "Hungarian Perspectives on Emigration and Immigration in the New European Architecture," *International Migration Review,* 26, 2(1992), pp. 305–324.

41. See note 9 in this chapter for the bibliographic references on this and related issues.

42. It may be noted in this context that in view of the difficulties of incorporating the *Ubersiedler,* Germans from and still in the former DDR, into mainstream German society, from 1991/1992 on, the *Aussiedler,* or ethnic Germans, from Eastern Europe have also been discouraged from coming. As a result of this "discouragement policy," the number of the latter arrivals decreased between 1992 and 1993 from about 240,000 to 150,000, or by almost 40 percent.

43. For a review of specific measures adopted by EC member countries, see bibliographic references in note 10 in this chapter.

44. On the history of tourism, see John Towner, "History and Tourism," *Annals of Tourism Research* 18(1990), pp. 71–84. In the Western world the international tourism began to accelerate in the late 1960s, but because of the energy crisis, slowed down or even declined, to resurge in the late 1970s; see *Summary of Developments in the Fields of World Economy, Demography, and Energy: Prospects for Tourism,* Madrid: World Tourism Organization, 1983. On tourism in the Soviet bloc, see Eva Kerpel, *Tourism in Eastern Europe and the Soviet Union: Prospects for Growth and New Market Opportunities,* Special Report no. 2042, London: The Economist Intelligence Unit, October 1990, pp. 14f; also "Tourism in Centrally Planned Economies," special issue of the *Annals of Tourism Research* 17, 1(1990).

45. Data compiled from *Tourism to the Year 2000. Qualitative Aspects Affecting Global Growth,* Geneva: World Tourism Organization, 1991, p. 27; *Tourism Development Report,* Geneva: World Tourism Organization, 1987, pp. 32–33; *Tourism Development Report,* Geneva: World Tourism Organization, 1990, pp. 376–385; and *Annuaire des statistiques du tourisme,* Geneva: World Tourism Organization, 1988, 1989. See also George Caves, *Le Tourisme International,* Paris: Hatier, 1989.

46. Data from *Tourism Development Report,* 1990, pp. 376–385 and *Annuaire des statistiques du tourisme,* 1989.

47. *Trends of International Migration,* pp. 109–110; Oleg Shamshur, "Ukraine in the Context of New European Migrations," *International Migration Review* 26, no. 2, 1992, pp. 264–267; Polish press reports, 1991–1994.

48. Robert K. Merton, "Social Structure and Anomie," in Robert K. Merton, *Social Theory and Social Structure.* Glencoe, Ill.: Free Press, 1968, pp. 195–223.

49. Joanna Solska, "Do Polski Jak do Sklepu," *Polityka,* August 20, 1994, p. iv.

50. To the extent that "playing against the system" had been the routine tactic of negotiating the regime of all-pervasive constraints and prohibitions for citizens of the Soviet bloc countries, present-day East European migrants may be particularly well prepared to brave the obstacles of EC immigration policies.

51. Richard Clutterbuck, *Terrorism, Drugs, and Crime in Europe After 1992,* New York: Routledge, 1992; Hans Leyendecker et al., *Mafia im Staat: Deutschland fallt*

unter die Rauber, Gottingen: Steidl Verlag, 1992; Fabrizio Calvi, *L'Europe des Parrains: La Mafia a l'assaut de l'Europe,* Paris: Bernard Grasset, 1993; Frances Heidensohn and Martin Farrell, eds., *Crime in Europe,* London: Routledge, 1992; and "Global Mafia," *Newsweek,* December 13, 1993, pp. 18–27.

52. Information compiled from Calvi, *L'Europe des Parrains;* Heidsohn and Farrell, *Crime in Europe;* Leyendecker, *Mafia im Staat;* Arkady Vaksberg, *The Soviet Mafia,* New York: St. Martin's Press, 1991; Oleg Shamshur, "Ukraine in the Context of New European Migrations," *International Migration Review* 26, no. 2, 1992, pp. 264–267.

53. Compiled from Oberg and Boubnova, "Ethnicity, Nationality, and Migration," p. 254; *Trends in International Migration,* pp. 109–110; Blaschke, "Les travailleurs etrangers," p. 78; Okolski, "La nouvelle donne migratoire," p. 15; Hryniewicz, *Brain Drain in Poland,* pp. 15–18; and personal observations of Ewa Morawska.

54. Historians of long-distance migration seem to have concerned themselves with these issues more often and more thoroughly than have the social scientists studying contemporary population movements, probably because the latter's approach to international migration has been largely dominated either by macrostructural concerns of the world-system theories or by rational-choice models derived from large samples of aggregate data.

55. On the significance of informal support networks in stimulating and assisting mass labor migration of Europeans at the turn of the twentieth century (and earlier in the nineteenth century as well), see, e.g., Moch's *Moving Europeans* and Nugent's *Crossings.* Although the recruiting agents (not agencies) visited villages looking for agricultural workers in Germany and, until the procedure was delegalized in 1885, for industrial workers in the United States, this was not the main form of labor recruitment.

56. Shuttleworth, "Irish Graduate Emigration," pp. 319–320.

57. See *Continuous Reporting System on Migration SOPEMI,* 1989; pp. 78–79; A. Pohjola, "Social Networks—Help or Hindrance to the Migrant?" *International Migration* 29, 3(1991), pp. 435–441; *The Future of Migration,* pp. 276–277; Korcelli, "International Migrations in Europe," pp. 300–302; *The Changing Course of International Migration,* p. 109; Oberg and Boubnova, "Ethnicity, Nationality, and Migration Potentials," p. 251; and *Tourism in Eastern Europe and the Soviet Union,* p. 97.

58. On assistance in obtaining or provision of housing to highly skilled workers by the employer companies and on different residential patterns of the former, see Paul White, "Skilled International Migrants and Urban Structure in Western Europe," *Geoforum,* vol. 19, 4(1988), pp. 411–422; on the Mediterranean guestworkers' housing and living conditions in western Europe, see King, "European International Migration 1945–1990," pp. 26–27; Fielding, "Migrants, Institutions, and Politics," p. 54; Paul White, "Immigrants and Social Geography of European Cities," in *Mass Migrations in Europe,* pp. 65–82; Blotevogel, "From Itinerant Worker to Immigrant?" pp. 92–96; and Salt, "International Labor Migration in Europe," p. 145.

59. For the classic formulation of the penetration of informal social networks into formal organizations, see Mark Granovetter, "Economic Action and Social Structure: The Problem of Embeddedness," *American Journal of Sociology,* vol. 91, 3(1985), pp. 481–510.

60. See Morawska, "Labor Migrations of Poles," pp. 255–266.

61. Information based on our personal experience and observations and on informal interviews with our expatriate and emigre colleagues. See also White, "Skilled International Migrants and Urban Structure in Western Europe," pp. 411–421.

3

Africa and Global Patterns of Migration

*Philip D. Curtin**

Africa has a special place in the world history of migration in several respects. It was the place from which all modern humans derived. It was in this sense the origin of all human migrations. About 300,000 years ago, *Homo sapiens sapiens* first evolved in Africa, differentiated from a variety of other hominids.[1] All of this happened too long ago to be easily understood or understandable. Over such a long time, many people left Africa to populate the rest of the world, and others certainly returned—part of an enormous, if unrecorded, population movement that must have taken place through many millennia of alternating ice ages and interglacial warm periods.

Much later, only a few centuries ago, Africa was also the center of the first massive population movement between continents. The Atlantic slave trade was the greatest intercontinental migration that is known up to the eighteenth century. It was followed in the nineteenth century by the even more massive movement of Europeans to the many Neo-Europes overseas and overland into Siberia. These two movements together were among the first steps toward the globalization of world populations.

Africa is also an important laboratory for migration studies from the point of view of movement in Africa itself. Historians, linguists, and archaeologists in recent decades have been concerned with explaining the patterns of language and culture that exist today. This search for an explanation of present distribution has led to studies about why people move.

Finally, and within the Africa continental limits, some authorities believe that Africa is the continent with the most mobile population in the

---

*Portions of this chapter were presented at Baylor University in conjunction with the 1994 Charles Edmonson Historical Lecture and are reproduced here with permission of the copyright holder, Baylor University Press.

world today. That is, a higher proportion of its population lives at some distance from its place of birth or follows a pattern of seasonal or semiannual migration than do populations on any other continent. Whether this estimate is measurably the case is uncertain. No one to my knowledge has made a careful quantitative comparison, and demographic data from Africa are so scarce and inaccurate that it would be hard to place much faith in comparative data, even if they were assembled. In any event, Africans in the late twentieth century are among the most mobile people in the world.

Early Migration and the Positioning of Languages

Linguistic evidence tells something about the probable course of early movements within Africa. Studies on early migration based on patterns of biological evolution, and on genetic mapping, also contribute to an emerging pattern.[2] Whether based on biology, genetics, or linguistics, these studies suggest that most early human movement came from the success of a local population in achieving some technological breakthrough that made population growth and expansion possible. The invention of agriculture in the Middle East and the domestication of the horse on the Ukrainian steppe are examples from outside of Africa.

Some early migrations in Africa, and with similar origins, began even before the invention of agriculture. About 15,000 years ago, people in Nubia or perhaps the Red Sea hills discovered techniques for the intensive collection of wild grains. The technique and the language of these people spread north into the Middle East and west across North Africa. This movement was not necessarily blanket or tidal, but it is safe to assume that the superior technology made possible population growth and migration into more sparsely settled territory—where the local people may well have picked up both the language and the technical skills of the immigrants.[3]

The evidence for this migration is both archaeological and linguistic, associated with the spread of Afro-Asiatic languages. That language family includes Arabic and Hebrew along with other, closely related Semitic languages of Ethiopia, like the classical Geez and the later Amharic and Tigrinya. It also includes Ancient Egyptian, Berber, and the Chadic languages spoken in West Africa south of the Sahara. Linguists today believe that this language family originated in Africa, probably somewhere in northern Ethiopian highlands or the Red Sea hills.

This hypothesis rests on reasoning sometimes called "the rule of least moves." If a large number of similar languages, about equally distant linguistically from one another, exist in a fairly confined region—as many different Afro-Asiatic languages do in the Horn of Africa—and if only a few of them are spoken today in distant places, it is logical to assume that an extensive language group, like the Semitic languages, which touch that cluster, spread outward from that point. We know that Arabic moved into Africa only after the eighth century A.D., but the earlier, preagricultural migration is the one that carried the Berber languages into the northwest corner of Africa. Similar reasoning is used in biology to determine the origin and diffusion of plant or animal species.[4]

Another major influence on early migration is changing climate. Until recently, the climatic record depended on indicators like the Nile floods or changes in the size of glaciers in Europe; but the pollen deposited in lakes and estuaries is an even better record going further back in time. Paleobotanists can now study these deposits through drilled core samples.

Historians have long known that the present aridity of the Sahara came into existence at about 2500 B.C., isolating sub-Saharan Africa from the main lines of change in the intercommunicating zones of Egypt and Mesopotamia—and later on from the Hellenic zone and world of classical antiquity.

Recent research confirms that date for the desiccation of the present Sahara, but the climatic past is now known to have been far more complex, so complex that climatologists now set their studies in several different time scales. Change at one level took place within a century or so; at another level, over a millennium. Still other changes have to be plotted over several millennia. Northern Africa passed through a period of comparatively humid conditions from about 22,000 to 19,000 years ago, followed by extreme aridity about 16,000 to 13,000 years ago, with new periods of even greater humidity about 10,000 to 8,000 years ago and again at 6,000 years ago.[5] These changes have obvious long-term consequences for human migration, even when the patterns of migration are not yet clear in the archaeological record. People must have moved north into the present desert region during humid periods, only to retreat when the arid millennia returned.

One population movement beginning about 10,000 years ago can be traced to a combination of newly humid conditions and new techniques to deal with them. The new technology was a complex of fishing and forms of land use for people living near water. Some archaeologists have called this an "aquatic civilization." This aquatic culture can be related to the present distribution of Nilo-Saharan languages, a movement westward from a place of origin in the Sudan Republic to the upper Benue Valley in present-day Nigeria and into the Sahara north of Lake Chad—with the related Songhai even further west at the northern bend of the Niger, isolated from the main body of Nilo-Saharan languages.[6]

Still another and far larger population movement in early Africa can be traced mainly through linguistic evidence. This is the movement of the

Bantu-speaking people, who originally lived in the grasslands of Cameroon and neighboring parts of Nigeria, but who moved to occupy almost all of the great southern bulge of Africa. This was, again, a movement made possible by the technical superiority of Bantu-speakers over the dominantly hunting and gathering people who already occupied most of the great southern bulge of Africa. It is thought to have begun no earlier than about 3000 B.C., based at first on the cultivation of cereals and yams, along with hunting and fishing. The Proto-Bantu-speakers also kept goats and made ceramics.

The first phase of Bantu expansion took place along the border between forest and savanna, keeping to the same ecological zone their forefathers had occupied, the zone where their agricultural practices had been invented and worked best. Further advance to the south was slow, because it required an adaptation to the new conditions of the tropical forest, then to the forest-savanna mosaic south of the equator, still later to the dry woodland found still further south. It can be assumed that the advance of the language was mainly a migration of people, but it is also certain that the Bantu-speaking farmers assimilated many individuals from among the earlier, if sparser, populations.

With the introduction of iron smelting about 500 B.C., this slow expansion—first west to east and then southward—began to change drastically. The precise entrance point for the early use of iron is unclear. It could have come from North Africa by one of several routes, or it could have been developed independently south of the Sahara. With iron smelting and improved techniques for cattle-keeping among the eastern Bantu-speakers, their expansion became more rapid, reaching the upper Zambezi valley about 200 B.C. and the Indian Ocean coast about A.D. 100. From that point a final phase was still more rapid, carrying the Bantu languages as far as northern Natal in South Africa by about A.D. 250. This whole process must have been far more complex than we now know, and it certainly absorbed many of the pre-Bantu inhabitants. The Nguni subgroup of Bantu languages, now the most southerly of all Bantu languages, picked up some elements from the Khoisan languages already spoken there, including three of the click sounds so characteristic of Khoisan.[7]

Although the Bantu migration was the most spectacular in these millennia, other, similar migrations can be traced through linguistic evidence. In each case, the speakers of the expanding language also possessed a new technique for food production, which gave them an advantage over earlier inhabitants. Such an advanage made possible the eastward expansion of the Ubangian peoples from the vicinity of Lake Chad toward the Nile.[8] Or, in the first millennium of our era, innovations in pastoral technology helped others move south from the upper Nile into parts of present-day Uganda and Kenya.[9]

Early Movements into Africa

People also moved into Africa with a similar base in new technology. About 1000 B.C., seaborne migrations became more common in the world. The Inuit began their eastward movement from Siberia along the Arctic shores toward Greenland. The Polynesians also began their seaborne migration eastward into the Pacific in the first millennium B.C.[10] A little after the Polynesians began moving east, the Malagasy, who also spoke an Austronesian language, moved west across the Indian Ocean from Indonesia to Madagascar, using maritime technology similar to that of the Polynesians, including double-hulled sailing vessels, a form of celestial navigation, and (perhaps most important of all) the habit of seeking new land for settlement. These voyages were not simply trading expeditions with an all-male crew. They included women, plants, and domestic animals, so that newly discovered lands could be colonized.

Direct written evidence about the routes taken by these Malagasy voyages is missing, but two routes were possible, one was to sail directly west from Indonesia on the southeast trade winds. The other was to move north of the equator to catch the northeast trades, with the monsoon of the summer months providing an easy return. The northerly route was already known to mariners in Malaya and Sumatra, but, the lack of evidence of Malagasy settlement in East Africa makes the southerly route seem more probable.[11] In any event, the Malagasy were the original settlers of Madagascar, and the Malagasy language is the dominant language on that island today, both for those of Indonesian origin and for those whose ancestors migrated later from the African mainland.

Outsiders also moved into northern Africa. The Muslim conquest of North Africa, beginning in the seventh century, linked the Maghreb more closely to the Middle East, but conquest alone was no migration. It probably involved even fewer people than the estimated 80,000 or so Vandals who infiltrated the Roman empire and moved south through Spain to conquer Roman North Africa in the fifth century. The initial Arab armies and Arab garrisons were small compared to the existing urban populations in Egypt or the Maghreb. By the time the Muslim invaders reached Spain, indeed, the armies themselves were mainly Berber-speaking people from North Africa, not Arabs from Arabia.

The more significant movement of populations into North Africa had different causes and different consequences. It began with the infiltration of Bedouins out of Arabia into the sedentary societies of the Middle East, continuing the drift of pastoral, Semitic-speaking people into the fertile crescent that had been chronic during the last two millennia B.C. Its origins seem to lie in the recurrent tendency of nomadic peoples to move into better-watered lands when they had the opportunity. They moved whenever population growth bought pressure on grazing land and disruption in sedentary societies made infiltration easy. William McNeill has called this tendency a "geographic gradient," moving nomadic peoples outward over centuries from such unfavorable and fragile climatic regions as Arabia and Mongolia.[12]

Arabs had begun to infiltrate the desert east of the Nile even before the Muslim era, and the Bedouin movement continued afterward as a sideshow to the more spectacular conquests of the early Umayyads. The Bedouin with their camels moved into an ecological niche that had not been fully occupied by Egyptians from the Nile valley. They infiltrated along the fringes of the irrigated lands, sometimes crossing into the western desert, with a gradual movement southward parallel to the Nile. The nomadic Beja of the Red Sea hills converted to Islam, but they held their own in their own territory; and they kept their Cushitic language into the twentieth century, even though the sedentary population of the Nile valley shifted to Arabic.[13]

Another nomadic drift out of Arabia stayed north of the desert. A little before about A.D. 1000, the Banu Hilal and Banu Sulaym of central Arabia moved into the Egyptian desert east of the Nile. Beginning in about 1050, they moved west in force, not merely as nomads drifting on the fringe of sedentary civilization but also as raiders and occasional conquerors of sedentary states. Their westward drift continued for the next two centuries, until some of them reached the plains of Morocco. This Hilalian migration was not a truly massive movement of population. A common estimate is that about a hundred thousand people left Arabia, but its influence was enormous. Some historians once blamed the Hilali for the destruction of the North African civilization that had survived the decay of the Roman empire. Whereas this view is probably exaggerated, the Hilalian passage through the Maghreb helped to complete the Arabization of Tunisia and to encourage the shift to Arabic language among Berber-speakers in Algeria, Morocco, and the western Sahara.[14]

The cultural influence of any of these Arab migrations was far greater than the numbers involved might suggest. Present-day "Arabs" of the northern Sudan Republic speak Arabic, but the Arabian contribution to the gene pool of that region is usually estimated at 15 percent or less. In the Maghreb, it was probably less still. Few as they were, however, these Arabian immigrants carried the prestige of Arabic as the language of God, expressed through the Koran. Without such migrants, Arabic might have spread to North Africa and the Sudan as only the language of religion and high culture—as it did to Muslim Spain or Persia.

Once south of the desert, some of these desert nomads made an ecological switch and turned to a pattern of transhumant, seminomadic cattle-keeping along the southern desert edge. They came to be called *baqarra* in the Sudan. The opportunity was available because sedentary farmers south of the desert were tied to their fields during the three or four months of summer rain. Pastoral specialists, however, could take cattle north into the steppe where rainfall was enough to produce rich, if temporary, pasture from June into September. With the dry season, they could return to some base in the south with year-round water, where their cattle could live on dried grasses left from the rainy season. The Fulbe in West Africa filled a similar position of seminomadic transhumance, and they tended to drift eastward from the Senegal valley, just as the *baqarra* drifted west, until they met in the vicinity of Lake Chad.

These migrations were partly drawn forward by ecological opportunity, but they were also pushed by climatic variation. Periodic droughts lasting a few years, or as long as a decade, had been common along the desert fringe over recorded history. For transhumant pastoralists, these periodic droughts were like a demographic pump. A sequence of good years made for an increase in people and cattle alike. Then, when the rains failed, pastoralists were forced south away from the desert in search of a better dry-season base. Once the drought was over, they moved north again, but not necessarily to their old wet-season pasture.

Early Slave Migrations

Slavery and the slave trade entered into African migrations a little after the fifth century A.D., when camels first became available in the Sahara and North Africa. Camel caravans changed the Sahara from a barrier to trade and communication into a relatively easy north-south route, largely because camels were the most efficient form of land transportation available at the time.[15] The numbers are uncertain, but some flow of slaves from tropical Africa into the Mediterranean basin and Arabia had begun by the seventh century.[16]

Slavery, however, was much less important in Islamic North Africa than it had been in Roman times. Islamic social forms were a direct descendent of Roman patterns, but the Muslim societies no longer employed slaves as agricultural labor on a large scale, the most important exceptions being the use of black slaves—presumably from Africa—in irrigation and drainage works in southern Iraq in the eighth and ninth centuries. The more common institutional pattern, sometimes called Muslim service slavery, replaced the Roman pattern of latifundia. Slaves were valued less for their labor than for the fact that they were aliens, who could be placed most usefully in occupations better left to strangers. One of these was domestic service of a particularly intimate sort, including concubines, eunuchs as harem guards, and women held for prostitution.[17]

Another occupation best left to strangers was military service and certain administrative functions, even those of considerable importance. A ruler could better trust a slave, his own property, than members of the local society with kinship ties and personal interests different from his own. Slave armies were common in the Muslim world—in Ottoman Turkey, in Egypt, and in Morocco, where slave soldiers from across the Sahara were used extensively in the eighteenth century. Because these slaves were valued as strangers, that value declined after the first generation, and successors had to be recruited beyond the frontiers of Islam. Comparatively few of these recruits came from Africa. Byzantine Christians and other Christian war prisoners were one source. The Caucasus mountain region was another. Still another, perhaps the most important of all, was the plains of Ukraine and other Slavic regions north of the Black Sea.[18] That region had been a major source of slaves for the Roman world, and it once again became an important source for the Mediterranean between the twelfth century and the fifteenth. It was at this period that the Medieval Latin word, *sclavus,* identifying Slavs as slaves, came into common use, with cognates in several European languages and in Arabic.

In these same centuries, slaves from across the Sahara began to be important in North Africa, with some spillover into Mediterranean Europe. The traffic began in the first centuries of Islamic control over North Africa,[19] but the size of the movement is a continuing puzzle for historians. The contemporaneous estimates are far too large for the apparent present-day influence of sub-Saharan Africans in the North African gene pool, especially so because this traffic is reported to have included a large proportion of women.[20]

The importance of places like sub-Saharan Africa and Ukraine as sources of slaves over several centuries raises an important question for the world history of migration. Why did some societies seemingly serve as recurrent sources of slaves for export, whereas others were chronic importers? Among the exporting regions were tropical Africa, Ukraine, Circassia, and some regions in India and south China—at least for the quasi slave trade in indentured labor in the nineteenth century. Speculative explanations have sometimes stressed overpopulation, especially for India and China; but the slave-furnishing regions of tropical Africa were certainly not overpopulated to the same extent.

In now seems clear that warfare in much of western tropical Africa included the convention that the entire conquered population could be legitimately enslaved—not just the combatant war prisoners. This in turn made the capture of the opposing population a major military objective—in contrast to the more common European effort to defeat the enemy's army in the field or to seize enemy territory.[21]

In tropical Africa, this military objective encouraged an internal slave trade. Women and children could sometimes be reduced to servitude and kept within the victorious society, but young male adults were too dangerous to keep around. In later centuries, such captives were often sold to merchants who followed the armies. A hundred miles or more from the scene of capture, they might be sold to a new society more capable of absorbing them, and the chance of a successful escape would be reduced. Young men of military age could sometimes be fitted into the purchasers' own fighting force. The prevalence of these patterns of capture and commercialization of prisoners meant that slaves were available for an export trade as well, once North Africans appeared on the desert edge or Europeans appeared on the coast.[22]

These patterns of enslavement were related in turn to other aspects of society in west tropical Africa. Control over land was rarely transferable by purchase. Low levels of population density might have contributed to this pattern, in the sense that land, being plentiful, earned no rent.[23] John Thornton has recently pointed out that population densities were not nearly low enough to have that consequence in most of tropical Africa. In his view, slavery was prevalent because slaves were the most readily available form of revenue-producing property recognized by African law. In the traditions of medieval Europe, land was key to productive capability, and ownership of land often included the control over a labor force to work it. In contemporaneous Africa, land was owned, but it was owned corporatively by kinship groups or by the state. It was not always plentiful, but it was readily available at a low price or no price to those who could make use of it—that is, to those who owned the labor to work it.[24] In Europe, then, landownership tended to imply easy control over labor, whereas in Africa ownership of labor tended to make for easy control over land.[25]

Intercontinental Migration out of Africa: Maritime Technology

The slave trade from tropical Africa was relatively small before about 1450. It took on major dimensions in two important steps—both involving technological change. The first was the revolution in European maritime technology, centered toward the end of the fifteenth century. The second, beginning about the 1680s, was to be based on incipient industrialization—partly in Europe and partly in the plantation complex Europe had created overseas.

The earlier phase was perhaps the more important of the two, because it set the patterns of slavery and the slave trade within a plantation complex—patterns that would mold the massive intercontinental migration of the decades between 1680 and 1860.[26] The slave trade at this time and later grew out of three independent developments in world history. The first was the existing pattern of warfare and enslavement in tropical western Africa, which was to make slaves available for sale on the African coast once European buyers appeared. The other two were on the demand side. One was the ancient pattern of using the slave trade to concentrate people for new enterprises. The second was the demographic consequences of maritime contact across the Atlantic.

Before the industrial revolution, the vast majority of any human population had to work at food production and preparation. This need required an even distribution of human population, with the size of that population adjusted to the availability of land and technology. A new enterprise like a mine or a plantation needed new concentrations of people, since the people already present were necessarily busy with other, existing tasks. The newcomers had to be drawn in as migrants from a distance. In the absence of an organized labor market, the usual way to recruit migrants was by purchase. In Periclean Athens, for example, comparatively few slaves worked the land, but an estimated 15 to 30 percent of the slave population worked the silver mines at Laurium.[27] Early sugar plantations were equally labor-intensive and required people from a distance. As early as the eighth century, some sugar plantations in Mesopotamia had used African slaves.[28]

When Europeans borrowed Muslim sugar technology to create plantations in the Levant during the crusades, they too turned to the slave trade to meet their need for labor—although not yet mainly from Africa. Africans began to appear toward the end of the fifteenth century, imported to work new sugar plantations on the Atlantic islands like Madeira and the Canaries. After 1453, the Turkish capture of Constantinople reduced access to the old source of slaves at the Black Sea ports, and the west coast of Africa was much closer to the new plantations.

The Columbus quincentenary attracted public attention to the importance of "the encounter" between Europe and the Americas, but it also created a false emphasis. The maritime encounters of the fifteenth century involved three continents—Europe, tropical Africa, and the Americas, not just two of these. In fact, the main breakthrough in maritime technology took place on the coast of Africa, roughly a half-century before Columbus's voyage. European mariners who wanted to sail west faced a problem in the existing wind patterns. Prevailing winds in northern Europe blew from the west, whereas in southern Europe they blew still more strongly and regularly from the northeast—favorable for an outward passage but too strong for an easy return. In the European Middle Ages, it was safe enough in summer to explore at sea to the northwest—say to Iceland, or even Greenland—and the prevailing westerlies ensured the possibility of a return.

The northeast trades were different. They blew all year round, and they set up a southwesterly current along the Moroccan and Saharan coasts. With the ships available in the fifteenth century and earlier, it was hard enough to make way against an unfavorable wind by tacking. With an opposing current of a half-knot to a knot and a half, like that off the Saharan coast, it was nearly impossible. That was why sailors' talk sometimes told of ships that set out to the southwest and fell off the edge of the earth.

In about the 1440s, anonymous Portuguese mariners solved the problem of a return from the southwest. They first discovered that the winds along the Saharan coast were variable according to the time of day—more onshore in the daytime and more offshore at night. That discovery made it possible to tack laboriously back up the coast. The most important breakthrough, however, came when someone discovered that long tack to the northwest, sailing as close as possible to the northeast trades, would carry a ship north to the belt of prevailing westerlies that began just north of the Azores. A return to Portugal from that point would be simple.[29]

With that discovery, it was possible to reach any coastal point in west or west-central Africa and to return with comparative ease. The Portuguese began to build their castle at Elmina in 1481, established diplomatic relations with Congo and Benin, and began to establish sugar plantations as far away as São Tomé by 1493. What these Portuguese mariners had done was to discover the north Atlantic portion of the world wind system. Knowing how to return from West Africa meant that they also knew that a ship sailing west in the latitude of the Canaries could easily return to the east in latitudes north of the Azores. That is, of course, precisely what Columbus did, and he already had the experience of a voyage to the Gold Coast and back to learn the wind patterns.

From these beginnings, Africa continued as an important part of an Atlantic triangle. European mariners provided the technology, and European monarchs claimed the conquered territory in the New World, but it was African, more than European diseases that depopulated the American tropics, and, in any decade before the 1840s, it was Africans who provided the vast majority of migrants across the Atlantic.

The depopulation of the humid tropics in the Americas began with smallpox, carried by illicit African slave imports to Hispaniola in 1517. Falciparum malaria and yellow fever followed. These three depopulated the tropical lowlands of the Caribbean islands and mainland, northeast Brazil, and the Amazon basin—with an assist from other, European, diseases, although those played a more important role in North America and the South American highlands.[30] A few Indian survivors contributed to the gene pool of the later Caribbean, but, except for scattered mixed groups like the Caribs, Indian communities disappeared.

Ironically, the same diseases that killed off the American Indians made Africans the ideal population to take their place. Most people in West

Africa had acquired an apparent immunity to falciparum malaria. They usually had an acquired immunity to yellow fever, which is far less fatal to children than it is to adults. Africans were less immune to pneumonia than Europeans were at that period, but the death rate of newly arrived Africans in the American tropics was usually a quarter or less that of newly arrived Europeans.[31]

Epidemiological conditions thus set up conditions that might seem to make a massive migration across the tropical Atlantic a foregone conclusion. That was the outcome, but it was not automatic. Africans had no incentive to migrate, even if the full horrors of plantation slavery were hidden from them. The incentives that set the slave trade in motion operated on the rulers and mercantile elites in Africa and in Europe—not on the people who actually made the trip or manned the ships that carried them.

The Slave Trade at Its Apogee

In the decades centering in about 1680, migration out of Africa began to reach new levels of intensity. In the first half of the seventeenth century, slave imports from Africa into Europe and the Americas had stabilized at about 7,500 a year. By the last quarter of that century, the annual average had risen to more than 24,000, and it nearly doubled to reach 43,000 in the first two decades of the eighteenth century.[32]

The change in scale brought new participants and new centers of production. Even before 1492, the plantation complex had already moved to the Atlantic islands from its early home in the Levant. It moved on to Brazil in the second half of the sixteenth century, to the Lesser Antilles in the seventeenth, and on to the Greater Antilles and the Guianas in the eighteenth.[33] With these changes, English, Dutch, and French replaced the Portuguese as major carriers, and the plantation complex was more closely integrated with the centers of economic and technological change in Europe itself.

The change of scale reflected other changes in sugar technology. Cheap sugar was important because sugar had a high price-elasticity of demand. A slightly lower price led to even greater increases in production and consumption. The lower prices came partly from new economies of scale, partly from better machinery for grinding and refining cane, and partly from improved maritime technology that made it possible to move high-bulk, low-value cargoes of people and goods across thousands of miles. The sugar, the slaves, Indian textiles to pay for them on the African coast, and the salt fish to feed them were all carried by sailing ships—the most efficient and important source of nonhuman, nonanimal power before the invention of the steam engine. The technical innovations that counted most, however, were commercial practices that made possible the mature plantation complex—the first economic system anywhere in the world to import such a high proportion of its inputs—including labor—and to export such a large proportion of its outputs over intercontinental distances.

These changed commercial practices were not those of Europeans alone. The Indian textile industry responded with rising quantities of cloth for sale on the African coast. The west and west-central African trading partners built a sophisticated commercial system capable, by the eighteenth century, of delivering an annual average of more than 50,000 people for sale on the coast. In the peak year, it delivered more than 80,000.[34]

The forced migration grew through time. Around 42,000 people left Africa in the fifteenth century, bound almost entirely for Europe and the Atlantic islands. In the sixteenth century, 325,000 left Africa, mainly for Brazil and Spanish America. In the seventeenth century, the total rose to 1.9 million and in the eighteenth century and on to 1809, when the legal trade began to be cut off, it rose to 6.7 million, with the Caribbean now the most important destination. Between 1810 and the end of the trade about 1870, a further 2.6 million left, with Cuba and Brazil now the main destinations.[35]

The sheer size of this migration raises an important interpretive question for the study of global history. It seems clear that most aspects of globalization were a direct result of changing technology, more specifically the acceleration of technological change following the industrial revolution in early nineteenth-century Europe. Yet the massive migration of the Atlantic slave trade reached its peak a few decades before European industrialization was fully under way. How, then, was it related to the industrial revolution that was soon to mark such an important watershed in human history? In some ways, it was a clear extension of preindustrial patterns, like the earlier non-African slave trade that served to concentrate people for mining or plantations. It was partly an extension of African traditions of warfare and enslavement, and it contained some aspects of Muslim service slavery. With time, however, new levels of size and complexity made it a substantially different institution. Economic historians in recent decades have been pushing the earliest signs of the industrial revolution into the earlier eighteenth century and even into the seventeenth.[36] This change in timing weakens an older interpretation that considered the eighteenth-century apogee of the plantation complex to be a preindustrial phenomenon about to be swept away by the advance of capitalist industrialism in the nineteenth century. It is not necessary to include the plantation complex as *part of* the industrial revolution to see it as a dynamic aspect of the world economy in the eighteenth century and one closely related to the economic and technological changes leading toward industrialization.

The slave trade thus seems to be transitional. The early phases clearly belong to the preindustrial world, whereas the eighteenth-century trade was somehow a buildup toward the industrial age that was to come. By the nineteenth century, the industrial age was under way, and the African slave trade was phased out of existence. In its place came new global patterns of migration. Africa was to play a part, but no longer the central part, in intercontinental migration.

New Patterns in Nineteenth-Century Migration

The new players entered the scene progressively. European migration overseas began to increase from the second half of the eighteenth century. After the 1840s, it was larger than the movement out of Africa, and its total flow of people was soon larger than the whole of the past Atlantic slave trade. This migration created the neo-Europes of the Americas, Australia, and New Zealand, with important population movements across the Urals into Siberia.

In the tropical world, beginning with the nineteenth century and continuing to the 1920s, Indians and Chinese replaced Africans as the most important group of long-distance migrants. Some went to the Americas, to Cuba, Trinidad, and Guyana, but the plantation complex was globalized and expanded beyond its old center in the American tropics. Most of the new Asian migrants went to places as diverse as Malaysia, Thailand, Hawaii, Fiji, Peru, Cuba, and Australia.

Africans had some part in these movements, but for Africa the important fact was the end of the export slave trade.[37] The growing flow of more-or-less coerced, indentured, or shanghaied migrants from India and China replaced forced migration from Africa. It is not necessary here to be concerned with *how much* these new currents of labor migration were like the slave trade they replaced. *Some* coercion took place at the point of recruitment, but the terms of indenture normally stated that the contract could be sold to a third party without the worker's consent and that failure to work as directed in the country of destination was punishable by imprisonment at hard labor. That was coercion enough.[38]

These new sources and new destinations are at the core of world migration in the nineteenth century. In sheer numbers, this new migration far exceeded the size of the slave trade. In 1883 and 1884 alone, Singapore received an annual average of 112,000 immigrants from China, although not necessarily under indenture.[39] That alone was more than the whole of the Atlantic slave trade in its peak year. Africa, however, was only on the fringes of these new migrations, as a source or as a destination.

Migrants into Southern Africa

South Africa began to enter some of these new patterns in a small way as early as the seventeenth century. The earliest European immigrants were part of a worldwide pattern of trade diasporas—settlements by merchants who spread along the trade routes, where they could act as cross-cultural brokers. Trade diasporas were an ancient institution, with occurrences as early as 3000 B.C. in Mesopotamia. In the world history of globalization, they were a first and early step toward a process that was to accelerate greatly from the nineteenth century onward. The trade diaspora that first brought Europeans to South Africa was among those that spread along the sea lanes of the Indian Ocean and South China Sea beginning in the sixteenth century, although significant settlements in South Africa came only in the mid-seventeenth.[40]

The Cape of Good Hope was a natural way station for that trade. It had good harbors on either side of Table Mountain and a fertile, Mediterranean climate in the hinterland. The Portuguese had placed small settlements in southern Africa at various times, but the Khoikhoi had driven them off. The Dutch Vereenigte Oost-Indische Compagnie (VOC) established a new settlement in 1652 and fortified it with Cape Town Castle at the foot of Table Mountain.

Cape Town's intended function was like that of European posts serving the slave trade in West Africa. At the Cape settlement, no more than a thousand Europeans were present at any time before the 1680s—hardly enough to figure as significant immigration—but the disease environment of the Cape of Good Hope was unusually favorable to European residents, whereas that of tropical posts was remarkably unfavorable. Then, in 1679, the VOC decided to make the Cape more nearly self-supporting by encouraging settlers called free burghers. They were not on its payroll, but they might be called out for militia duty and they were encouraged to produce food for the garrison and for sale to passing ships. From 1679 to 1707, the VOC ran a program of assisted immigration by German, Dutch, and French Protestants. In all, it sent out some 1,630 people.

Although European settlers were few, their population growth was so rapid that the demographic consequences were *like* those of a stream of immigrants. By 1707, the European population consisted of about 700 VOC employees and 2,000 free burghers.[41] After that date, the VOC no longer encouraged immigration, and the flow died to a trickle; but the sex ratio soon became normal, and the population began to increase. In time, their descendants became the main constituents of a white Afrikaans-speaking population of nearly 3 million in South Africa today. (Much the same thing happened at the French trading base at the mouth of the Saint Lawrence, where an initial input of less than 10,000 settlers grew into the French Canadian population of more than 5 million.)

The recent racial domination of South Africa by overseas Europeans has tended to obscure the fact that the VOC brought far more migrants from Africa and Asia than it did from Europe. Slavery was common in the plantation sphere of the Americas and also on Java, where the Dutch had their principal Southeast Asian base. It was therefore logical for the company to import slaves, and the free burghers also used coercion to obtain labor from their Khoikhoi and San neighbors. The form of slavery at the Cape was like the plantation model common to the West Indies, with the difference that slaves were found in many different occupations, of which field labor was only one.

Through the whole period of legal slave imports, up to the early nineteenth century, the VOC brought in a total of 65,000 slaves, of whom 26 percent were from the African mainland, mostly from eastern Africa. Another 26 percent were from India. Twenty-three percent came from Indonesia, and 25 percent were from Madagascar. It is likely that each of these four segments was larger than the total emigration from Europe over this same period.[42]

The demographic results were different, however. A combination of unfavorable sex ratios, disease, and low standards of living kept the imported slaves from multiplying as rapidly as the European settlers did. Their descendants, with some genetic contribution from the Dutch and Khoikhoi, nevertheless are the "Coloured" population of South Africa today, a community only slightly larger than the Afrikaans-speaking whites.

The English-speaking segment of the present South African population is descended from later arrivals, part of the great European emigration of the nineteenth century. When Great Britain secured the Cape Colony in 1805, its objectives were much the same as those of the VOC—the colony was considered a way station on the route to India. A small flow of immigrants began to arrive as early as the 1820s, increasing greatly after the discovery of diamonds in the 1850s and of gold in the 1880s. At first, most came from Great Britain, but many came from continental Europe as well after the 1890s. Almost all of these later European immigrants joined the English rather than the Afrikaner community, to form the base for the white, English-home-language population of nearly 2 million in South Africa today.

Settler immigration was also important in Algeria, where the French conquest began in 1830 and ended about 1872. As in South Africa, the European immigrants and their descendants became a significant minority with dominant power and wealth, but the *colons*—coming from Spain and Malta as well as from France—rose to be only about 11 percent of the total before the war for Algerian independence.[43] After the war, the vast majority emigrated to Europe.

A final group of European settlers came from Portugal, which sponsored European emigration to its African colonies as a national policy during much of the period before the coup of 1975 brought independence to Lusophone Africa. As of 1956, Europeans made up 2.5 percent of the

Angolan population and 1.1 percent of the population of Mozambique. These are not enormous numbers, but the proportions were higher than they were in any British or French colony in tropical Africa, other than Southern Rhodesia.[44]

Nineteenth-Century Transitions in Southern Africa

Military innovation also entered the South African pattern of migration in the early nineteenth century, but it was not connected in any clear way to the pace of industrialization in Europe. In the first part of the century, two separate but parallel changes in military tactics led to widespread migration and demographic change. New productive technology had often supported earlier migrations, but destructive technology was the key in these cases. One was the creation of a new military system among the Nguni people of Natal. The other was the use of mounted infantry in the Boer expansion beyond the frontiers of British-held Cape Colony and Natal.

The Nguni military innovation consisted of disciplined infantry formations with some similarities to Roman legionaries or Swiss pikemen of sixteenth-century Italian wars. These units fought with a short stabbing spear and shield in a formation that kept the mass of the force in the center, with horn-like wings on either side to advance and surround an enemy.

These disciplined units, called *impi,* were based on the African institution of the age-grade, the social unit consisting of all young men initiated at the same time. By bringing an entire age-grade into a standing army as a unit, the Zulu achieved a high degree of discipline and esprit de corps. By the 1820s, the Zulu and others who used the new military system could usually win out against those who had not yet adopted it.

The new system thus gave an advantage only to those who directed aggression outward against more distant peoples to whom the new tactics were still unknown. This circumstance favored aggressive migration outward from the heartland of the Nguni culture in Natal. The whole movement is known in South African history as the Mfecane. Some of these military migrants were refugees, the defeated fleeing from the warfare in Natal, but taking the new military system with them. Others were organized by opportunists who saw an opening in which to build their own power or that of their group.

The movement and countermovement were complex, but the main lines can be simplified into a leapfrog pattern. One leader moved north into what is now Swaziland and founded the Swazi kingdom. Another passed still further north to found another kingdom in what is now southern Mozambique. Others went further still and founded a series of small kingdoms in central and southern Tanzania, where their descendants still live there as the Angoni, after the Nguni language of their original homeland.

Other offshoots of the Mfecane crossed the Drakensberg onto the high veld of what is now the Orange Free State and Transvaal. One leader in northern Transvaal attracted a following that was partly Nguni and partly local, creating the Ndebele, who moved further northwest into western Zimbabwe where their descendents still live. Another offshoot, the Kololo, moved out further still and conquered the Lozi kingdom on the upper Zambezi in present-day Zambia. There, the Lozi and Kololo cultures merged to form the political and cultural entity that became, in the colonial period, Barotseland in Northern Rhodesia.

The Boer migration north from Cape Colony was parallel and nearly simultaneous. It was an early example of the common nineteenth-century African phenomenon of secondary empire, a term used by historians of Africa to describe military aggression and political aggrandizement based in the new European weapons, in the hands of local people beyond European control. These empires were secondary in the sense that their power grew out of the technological achievements in Europe. The Cape Afrikaners in the early nineteenth century had developed their own new military system based on mounted infantry armed with muskets—a weapon that had been virtually unchanged since the end of the seventeenth century. This phase of secondary-empire building was therefore only vaguely related to the new industrial power of Europe. The Xhosa they confronted across their eastern frontier used the same military tactics, but the Mfecane made it possible for the Cape farmers using those methods to move west of the Xhosa and then north onto the high veld, where their tactics could usually defeat the impi. They established their own political and military dominance over the districts already disrupted by the Mfecane and founded a number of new political entities, of which the two Boer republics of the Orange Free State and Transvaal lasted longest. The overseas European migrants remained a minority among the African populations they came to dominate, but they maintained a troubled independence from Europe until the British conquest at the end of the century.

Slavery and Secondary Empire in Tropical Africa

By the early nineteenth century, the pattern of secondary empire began to emerge in tropical Africa as well, just when the Atlantic slave trade was drawing to an end. It was a confused period, when new leadership emerged and new state-building changed the political map across the Western Sudan from Senegambia to Lake Chad.

Some new political units, like the Sokoto Caliphate of northern Nigeria, had no apparent connection to major global events stemming from European industrialization. The main force was cavalry, and what muskets were used were in the older European style. Other religious revolutions that followed after the mid-century, however, include aspects of secondary-empire-building. In the 1850s and 1860s, Sheikh Umar Tal created a new empire with a Muslim ideological base. It stretched along the southern desert-edge and savanna country from the upper Senegal to the Niger. Samori Turé built another new empire, even more clearly based on European arms, along the forest-savanna fringe from the sources of the Niger across the present-day Côte d'Ivoire and ultimately into the northern part of present-day Ghana.

Extensive migration accompanied this secondary-empire-building, and it was not just the marching of armies. Umar Tal attracted a broad following from the Fulbe people of the Senegal valley, partly as military followers but also as settlers in the lands he conquered.[45] Samori's conquests also involved the movement of conquering migrants and of refugees who fled ahead of his armies.

All this military activity brought about an enormous increase in the number of slaves captured and sold into the trade—just at a time when the Atlantic slave trade was cut off. The result was a massive shift of population throughout West Africa, a shift that has only recently begun to be studied. The proportion of slaves in the population of the Western Sudan at the beginning of the nineteenth century is not known, but, at the moment of European conquest in the 1880s and later, it was commonly in the range of 50 to 70 percent.[46]

The pattern was similar in the eastern Sudan. In the 1820s, Muhammad 'Ali of Egypt created the first secondary empire with the conquest of the Nubia and the Nilotic Sudan down to the frontiers of Ethiopia. One incentive was his need for slave soldiers in the Egyptian army, and one result was an increase in the pace of enslavement across the savanna from Lake Chad to the Red Sea and up the Nile into the Bahr el Ghazal.[47] The resulting population movements were massive here as in West Africa, perhaps greater than the slave movements at any earlier period in African history, but the precise size and destinations of all these enslaved people may be beyond the possibility of accurate reconstruction.

The Slave and Coerced Labor in Eastern Africa

In East Africa, the nineteenth-century pattern of enslavement and slave trade was both different from and similar to the patterns just south of the desert edge. Historians of Africa sometimes draw a sharp distinction between the end of the export trade in slaves from West Africa and the continued slave exports from the east through most of the nineteenth century. In fact, the main difference was that the slaves moving in East Africa were often moved by sea up the coast to Kenya or Zanzibar, or offshore to islands like Madagascar or the Mascarenes, whereas slaves in West Africa moved overland.

One other striking difference, however, is that some parts of eastern and southern Africa and the offshore islands became receiving areas for coerced labor, as the Cape Colony had been since the eighteenth century. These changes stemmed in part from the globalization of the plantation complex, as it moved away from its earlier home in the tropical Americas. In the 1780s, the Mascarene Islands, then Isle de France and Bourbon (now Mauritius and Réunion) began a similar transition from way stations on the route to the east to full membership in the plantation complex. Slave imports began to grow, drawn mainly from the African coast around Mozambique and from the island of Madagascar.[48]

After 1808, the slave trade of the India Ocean began to taper off in some respects, but a trickle and sometimes more than a trickle of illicit slave trade continued.[49] If the Mascarenes, Madagascar, and Zanzibar are considered to be offshore Africa—and they should be so considered—these nineteenth-century slave movements were part of a complex pattern of African population movement, partly overland but partly by sea. The chief source of mainland slaves was the hinterland of the east coast from the mouth of the Zambezi to Dar es Salaam and inland to Lake Malawi and beyond. Madagascar was both a major source and a major destination in this intra-African slave trade. The other major destinations were the Mascarene sugar plantations along with the clove plantations on Zanzibar and Pemba and the food-producing plantations on the Kenya coast. A minor current in this trade also led further north to south Arabia and the Persian Gulf.[50]

By the 1830s and 1840s, the sugar industries on Réunion and Mauritius were growing rapidly, and legal slave exports from Africa were hard to find. Both turned to India as a new source of labor. This alternative was comparatively easy for Mauritius, now a British colony, but Réunion had been returned to France. It drew some indentured workers from French Indian posts like Pondicherry, but after 1860 an agreement with Britain permitted Réunion to import 6,000 indentured workers from British India each year.[51] The Réunionais population soon had an Indian majority—as Mauritius had done even earlier in the century.

Mauritius also served as a stepping-stone for the extension of Indian labor migration to South Africa. Britain annexed Natal in 1845. As early as 1847, would-be planters there introduced sugarcane from Mauritius, but they believed they had a labor problem. Local Africans could not be lured into estate labor—not, at least, for the wages planters were willing to pay.

After 1860, the government of Natal worked out an indentured-labor agreement with the Indian government. The normal contract stipulated that the workers could return to India free of charge when their time was up, but few actually did return. The result was a flow of coerced labor large enough to create an Indian community in coastal Natal. That community grew to just under a million people, or about 2 percent of the present South African population.[52]

Other Indians moved to the East African mainland. In the 1890s, the government of the East African Protectorate turned to India for contract labor to build the projected railway from Mombasa to Lake Victoria. In all, some 19,000 Indians worked on the railway, and about half of them returned to India. Many of the rest died, but the remainder settled in Kenya.[53]

The South African mining industry also toyed with the prospect of Asian labor. Between 1903 and 1907, mine owners on the Witwatersrand worked out a scheme to import Chinese miners on three-year contracts. They brought some 97,000 Chinese to South Africa under this arrangement, but it attracted such unfavorable notice in Britain that it had to be abandoned. In this case, almost all of those who survived were repatriated.[54]

Asian trade diasporas had brought Asian visitors to Africa for many centuries, but the numbers were too small to qualify as a migration until the nineteenth century, when Indian commercial activity in East Africa increased with the rising value of Indian-Ocean trade. Indian capital helped to finance the clove plantations of Zanzibar and Pemba and the Afro-Arab trade to the interior. Indian entrepreneurs came as individuals or small groups to participate in the growing trade of East Africa, Madagascar, and the Mascarene Islands. A Zanzibar Indian firm had, indeed, organized the trade in indentured workers to build the Uganda railway. At the end of the colonial period in eastern tropical Africa, Indians were more numerous than European colonizers almost everywhere. In Kenya at independence, Indians were 3 percent of the population, as against only 1 percent for settlers from Europe. Similar but somewhat smaller groups of Chinese were also active on all of the Indian-Ocean coasts.

African Migration in the Twentieth Century

With the consolidation of European colonial rule over Africa in the first decades of the twentieth century, the previous patterns of population movement—largely that of enslaved people being moved to new homes—began to change. With gradual emancipation, some people were able to return to their original homes, although most of them settled down where they already lived, often under pressure from the colonial governments not to move.[55]

At the same time, colonial governments wanted other population movement for the sake of economic development. The offer of wages was one incentive, but many colonial governments used forced labor for public employment, forced labor for private European firms, or less overt incentives like heavy direct taxation that could only be met with the proceeds of wage labor.

Together, these incentives drew workers toward the port towns like Lagos, Accra, Dakar, or Mombasa—or toward centers of development under European initiative in plantation agriculture, mining, or railway building. African initiative created other growth centers, like the Gold Coast cocoa farms, Senegalese and Nigerian peanuts, or Ugandan cotton farming.

Labor migration often began with the movement of young men on a short-term basis, often seasonal. This temporary or circulatory labor migration was common to most developing economies in recent centuries. It was an introductory phase that died out as workers settled down where jobs were, sent for their families, or married local women. Labor stabilization was slower in tropical Africa than it was elsewhere, partly because economic development there was comparatively weak.

Some circulatory labor existed throughout tropical Africa. In 1960, for example, more than 600,000 people in tropical Africa crossed international frontiers each year in search of work, a significant part of the total wage-labor force. In the savanna country of West Africa, many of these migrants moved back and forth in response to natural conditions. A dry season of six months or more meant that many were seasonally underemployed. It was easy and natural for people from Burkina Faso to move each dry season to the cocoa farms of Ghana or Côte d'Ivoire, where labor was needed at that time of the year, returning north when they could be useful again on their own farms.[56] Over recent decades, many of these circulatory migrants have tended to settle down as stabilized labor in cities and mining areas, although the pattern of continued drift toward centers of economic growth has by no means stopped.

Over the whole of the colonial and postcolonial periods, the drift of population in West Africa has been from north to south, out of the savanna country toward the forest and coastal regions, where economic development has been concentrated. Export agriculture was more important in the forest zone than in the savanna. Whatever industrial development took place tended to be located in or near the ports or other southern centers, and all important petroleum finds were near the coast.

The desert-edge drought that began in the 1960s and continued with only occasional remissions into the 1980s also pushed people southward.

As the chamber of the demographic pump had filled with people during the relatively humid years of the early century, drought now emptied it toward the south. Those forced south by a series of dry years, often found no incentive to return home when conditions improved. Similar considerations apply to flight from drought in the Horn of Africa, although the flight from drought in that part of the world is too intertwined with flight from oppression or fear of oppression to be easily disentangled.

North Africa also began the colonial period with patterns of circulatory labor gradually tending toward stabilization in major urban centers like Cairo, Tunis, Algiers, or Casablanca. In Egypt in particular, low-Nile cultivation was gradually introduced beginning in the nineteenth century with new systems of dams and canals. One result was a broad redistribution of people throughout the countryside. Agricultural change in the Maghreb also brought about redistribution of people, some of which was permanent. Some communities, however, like the Mozabites of certain oases in southern Algeria, made an important series of cultural adjustments so that they could send young men to the coastal cities for a few years at a time and still have them return to the home community.[57] Other Algerians began as early as the 1930s looking for work in France and elsewhere in Europe, beginning a drift that has continued and grown ever since.

Oscillating Labor in South Africa

South Africa was different. It had the fastest rate of industrialization and economic growth in Africa, but successive South African governments and industries tried to prevent labor stabilization, preferring a system of oscillating or circulatory labor.[58] South African gold mining firms began continuous recruiting of short-term workers as early as the 1890s. They set up a single labor-recruiting agency to attract labor from beyond the South African frontiers. By 1910, the annual number of recruits had already reached 100,000, almost all on short-term contracts, and non–South Africans were already more than half that number.

Between 1913 and 1923, the customary pattern got the support of law. The South African cities and the principal farming areas were declared to be "white man's country," where Africans were only permitted, in theory, under special circumstances and only as temporary sojourners. They were supposed to have permanent homes in the "reserves" set aside for them. In towns or near the mines, they were supposed to live in racially segregated "locations."

The reserves, however, were only 12 percent of South African territory, and that the least developed part. The reserves could not support the African population. South African workers had begun seeking urban employment even before the pattern of reserves was frozen by the Land Act of 1913, and population growth made labor migration even more necessary. Increasingly, men had to seek work in other parts of South Africa, often leaving their families behind. When the worker's contract expired, usually at the end of a year, he was no longer permitted to stay in the cities; and his family needed his labor in any case to help with chores that had gone undone during his absence. After a time, however, the need for cash income forced men to return to the mines or European-owned farms. By 1951, at any moment more than a half-million Africans from the reserves were absent on migratory labor in "white" South Africa, representing about 40 percent of all males between the ages of 15 and 65.[59]

Politics and Migration

Many recent patterns of African migration began in the early colonial period and continued with little change into the postcolonial. Political influence on migration, however, has changed drastically. The colonial powers paid comparatively little attention to Africans crossing colonial frontiers, even though they tried to control the movement of Europeans. Here and there, Africans would tend to leave a colonial state they thought was oppressive for better conditions elsewhere, if such conditions were available. People tended, for example, to drift from Mozambique into Nyasaland from time to time during the colonial period—or into the northern Gold Coast from adjacent regions of Upper Volta, if only because of French forced labor and forced military recruitment. But population movements of this kind were tiny compared to the massive displacement in search of employment. In 1960, the approximate end of the colonial period, the only sizable body of refugees was made up of a few hundred thousand Algerians who took refuge in Tunisia during the Algerian war for independence.

The number has been climbing ever since, whatever the basis of calculation. And refugees are notoriously difficult to define. It is hard to tell a political refugee from someone who believes economic conditions have become intolerable. Some authorities, like the United Nations High Commission on Refugees (UNHCR), count only refugees who cross national boundaries. Others also count those who are displaced within their home country. The UNHCR has kept track of refugees since the post–World War II years. Their count began with virtually none in the 1950s, rising to 400,000 refugees in all parts of Africa by 1964, to more than 1 million by 1970. After a small drop in the early 1970s, the United States Committee for refugees counted more than 3.5 million in 1981. The latest figures from the UNHCR are those for 1990, and they are on the order of 2 million for all of Africa,[60] but they are only for those who move across international frontiers. A recent issue of *The Economist* worked up some figures for the southern Sudan alone, estimating that 3 million southern Sudanese, or half the population, have been forced to leave their homes, whether for other countries or within the Sudan. About 2 million southerners had left for northern Sudan, 600,000 were displaced within southern Sudan, and 400,000 were in refugee camps in Uganda, Zaire, Kenya, Ethiopia, or the Central African Republic.[61] The *Washington Post* for March 6, 1994, estimated 2 million refugees from Liberia in neighboring countries and within Liberia itself. The civil wars just ending in Mozambique and still raging in Angola must have generated at least another million, and the fighting in Rwanda and Burundi in the spring of 1994 would add still more. The present total, therefore, appears to be in the range of 6 to 8 million people, and some estimates run as high as 12 million.

Ethnic conflict is the most general cause of the current African refugee problem, although ethnic conflict is probably no more serious in Africa than anywhere else. Beyond ethnic rivalries is the fact that postcolonial African states have not been strong enough to suppress these antagonisms. The parallel with Yugoslavia comes to mind. Ethnic conflict was there all along; it only appeared in the present disastrous form when the former Yugoslavia came apart, leaving no higher authority to settle differences. The Ethiopian state collapsed in a similar way beginning in 1974, and both superpowers were willing to arm whatever clients they could find to oppose the influence of the other. The collapse of Somalia followed, after the two superpowers had armed all and sundry. The fall of the Portuguese empire after 1975 released similar ethnic conflicts. This time, South Africa joined the superpowers in arming the potential antagonists, so as to turn ethnic conflict into major and disastrous civil wars in both Angola and Mozambique. The long-standing civil war in the Sudan has been exacerbated in the same way by the intervention of Iran and Libya.

It is still impossible to predict an outcome of these or similar conflicts, but it seems certain that the ethnic map (if not the political map) will be drastically changed. The longer refugees are forced to live abroad, the less likely they will be able to go "home." The earliest wave of the Tutsi and Hutu refugees from Rwanda and Burundi, respectively, occurred in 1962–1963. After thirty years, a predictable majority of the refugee communities in Kenya or Uganda were born in exile, and they have little incentive to return.

The Postwar Migration to the Most Developed World

Between the 1920s and the 1950s, new worldwide migration patterns began to appear as a part of the general globalization. Whereas people had earlier moved from one part of the tropical world to another in response to economic changes often directed from Europe, from the 1950s they moved from the less developed world to the more developed. This pattern included important migrations within the Soviet Union, from Mexico into the United States, from the less developed parts of Europe to the more developed, and from many parts of South Asia to the Persian Gulf.

In one sense, these movements were simply a new expression of the technological roots of human migration, but with differences. One was a decline in the element of coercion. In earlier centuries, people could be moved where economic conditions seemed to require them (in the minds of whose who had the power to decide such matters). After 1945, intercontinental migration from the tropical world was mainly voluntary and self-financed. People moved where economic opportunity promised a better life. A second change was demographic. Population growth rates in the developed world tended toward zero. Those in the tropical world were mainly higher than 2.5 percent per year. Economic growth rates in the two regions tended to be the reverse.

Africans were not the leading players in these new movements, but they were certainly participants. North Africans were among the most active, reversing the colonial flow of people across the Mediterranean. The Algerian population in the mid-1980s was about 22 million, but a million Algerians were temporary residents abroad, working mainly in France. Just before independence, the European settler population of Algeria had been about a million people, and nearly all left for France (even though a large minority of the settlers had come from somewhere else). The recent population of Morocco was about 23 million, of whom just over 60,000 were resident foreigners, but more than 1 million Moroccans were living abroad, mainly in Europe as migrant workers.[62] The Tunisian situation was similar.

By the late 1980s, African migration to other parts of Europe was also significant. In 1985, Africans made up more than 10 percent of all immigrants into Belgium and the Netherlands. Some of these were circulatory labor migrants, but not all. Many brought their families and settled in Europe. In the late 1980s, Belgium, West Germany, the Netherlands, and Switzerland reported the number of arrivals and departures by source and destination, and arrivals from Africa exceeded departures by about 50 percent.[63]

The United States has also shared in this new migration out of Africa. The U.S. Immigration and Naturalization Service reports, by country of origin, arrivals who intend to become U.S. residents. The annual number of immigrants from Africa rose tenfold between the 1960s and 1990. Although Africans were still only 2.3 percent of all immigrants, the total of 36,000 Africans arriving in 1990[64] was a good deal higher than the annual average arrivals from Africa in the era of the slave trade.

Summary

People migrated within Africa, into Africa, and out of Africa for many different reasons, but the oldest and most consistent was for some technological advantage—including the ability to use an occupational niche that was not already filled. We have seen this in the cases of Malagasy seafarers, the Arabian camel herders, and the early agricultural skills of the Bantu-speaking migrants.

Commercial skills also counted, like those of small groups who moved along the trade routes, although the numbers involved in early trade diasporas were probably too small to count as a real migration. In the nineteenth century, however, commercial opportunities increased with the industrialization of Japan and the West. Communities with developed commercial skills could move more freely into less-commercially developed regions like sub-Saharan Africa.

Military power was another kind of technological edge that led to migration in Africa. It lay behind some of the Arabian migrations across North Africa, behind the spread of the various offshoots of the Mfecane in southern Africa, behind the spread of the Afrikaners north from the Cape, and, in a more distant way, behind the smaller migrations that followed colonial conquest.

Another kind of migration was coerced in a different way, on the incentive of those who wanted the services of the migrants. The pull of the plantation complex expressed through the slave trade was a major factor in African history. Epidemiological factors reinforced the movement—on both sides of the tropical Atlantic—and sociopolitical conditions in Africa made recruitment of slaves there easier than it might have been in other societies.

By the eighteenth century and on into the nineteenth, Africa itself moved from the sending to the receiving end of this form of migration, with the movement of slaves from Indonesia, India, and Madagascar into the Cape Colony—and later of indentured Indian and Chinese workers into the sugar plantations of the Mascarene Islands and Natal, the Rand goldfields, and Kenyan railway construction.

A second kind of coerced migration was that of refugees. The initiative was often their own but only because fear for their safety led them to flee.

The final category is the migration of individuals, moving on their own initiative to seek their fortunes, not so much because they had skills to offer, but because they were willing to take work that members of more developed economies avoided. The movement out of Africa in the past forty years has been partly of this pattern, partly the brain-drain of the skilled and educated. In any event, the initiative was that of the migrants themselves, encouraged by lopsided economic growth centered in the north combined with lopsided population growth centered in the south.

Notes

1. For a recent review of the controversies over the evolution of early humans, see Roger Lewin, *The Origin of Modern Humans* (New York: W. H. Freeman, 1993).

2. Recent examples are Johathan Kingdon, *Self-Made Man: Human Evolution from Eden to Extinction* (New York: John Wiley, 1993) and Luigi Luca Cavalli-Sforza and others, *History and the Geography of Human Genes* (Princeton: Princeton University Press, 1994).

3. Christopher Ehret, "On the Antiquity of Agriculture in Ethiopia," *Journal of African History* 20:161–177 (1979).

4. For the application of the principle of least moves to African linguistic history, see Christopher Ehret and Merrick Posnansky, *The Archaeological and Linguistic Reconstruction of African History* (Berkeley: University of California Press, 1982), pp. 12–13.

5. Roderick J. Macintosh, "The Pulse Model: Genesis and Accommodation of Specialization in the Middle Niger," *Journal of African History* 34:181–220 (1993); George E. Brooks, "A Provisional Historical Schema for Western Africa Based on Seven Climate Periods (c. 9000 B.C. to the Nineteenth Century)," *Cahiers d'études africaines* 26:432–463 (1986); Alfred Muzzolini, "Les climats du Sahara et sur ses bordures, du Pleistocène final à l'aride actuel," *Empuries* 47:8–27 (1985).

6. J.E.G. Sutton, "The Aquatic Civilization of Middle Africa," *Journal of African History* 15:527–546 (1974); Ehret and Posnansky, *Archaeological and Linguistic Reconstruction,* esp. pp. 7–10.

7. For a recent summary of these movements, see Jan Vansina, chapter 1 in Philip D. Curtin, Steven Feierman, Leonard Thompson, and Jan Vansina, *African History,* 2nd ed. (London: Longman, 1995).

8. A.B.L. Stemler, J. R. Harland, and J.M.J. Dewet, "Caudatum Sorghums and Speakers of Chari-Nile Languages in Africa," *Journal of African History* 16:161–183 (1975); Douglas E. Saxon, "Linguistic Evidence for the Eastward Spread of Ubangian Peoples," in Ehret and Posnansky, *Archaeological and Linguistic Reconstrucion,* pp. 66–77.

9. Christopher Ehret, *Southern Nilotic History: Linguistic Approaches to the Study of the Past* (Evanston: Northwestern University Press, 1971).

10. Irving Rouse, *Migrations in Prehistory: Inferring Population Movements from Cultural Remains* (New Haven: Yale University Press, 1986).

11. F. Ramiandrasoa, *Atlas historique du peuplement de madagascar* (Antananarivo: Université de Madagascar, Académie Malgache, 1975); B. Domenichini-Ramiaramanana, "Madagascar," in UNESCO, *General History of Africa,* 8 vols. (London: Heinemann, 1988), 3:681–703.

12. William H. McNeill, *The Rise of the West: A History of the Human Community* (Chicago: University of Chicago Press, 1963), pp. 484–494; and "Human Migration in World Perspective," *Population and Development Review* 10:1–18 (1984), pp. 4–5.

13. Yusuf Fadl Hassan, *The Arabs and the Sudan from the Seventh to the Early Sixteenth Century* (Edinburgh: Edinburgh University Press, 1967); Richard W. Bulliet, *The Camel and the Wheel* (New York: Columbia University Press, 1975), pp. 114–124.

14. Humphrey J. Fisher, "The Eastern Maghrib and the Central Sudan," in Roland Oliver, ed., *Cambridge History of Africa* (Cambridge: Cambridge University Press, 1977), 3:232–330, pp. 243–245.

15. William H. McNeill, "The Eccentricity of Wheels, or Eurasian Transportation in Historical Perspective," *American Historical Review* 92:1111–1126 (1987); Bulliet, *The Camel and the Wheel,* pp. 111–140.

16. Ralph A. Austen, "The Trans-Saharan Slave Trade: A Tentative Census," in Henry A. Gemery and Jan S. Hogendorn, eds., *The Uncommon Market: Essays in the Economic History of the Atlantic Slave Trade* (New York: Acacemic Press, 1979), pp. 23–76.

17. Phillips, *Slavery,* pp. 66–87.

18. For Muslim military slavery, see Patricia Crone, *Slaves on Horses: The Evolution of an Islamic Polity* (New York: Cambridge University Press, 1980); Daniel Pipes, *Slave Soldiers and Islam: The Genesis of a Military System* (New Haven: Yale University Press, 1981).

19. Elizabeth Savage, "Berbers and Blacks: Ibadi Slave Traffic in Eighth-Century North Africa," *Journal of African History* 33:351–368 (1992).

20. J. O. Hunwick, "Black Africans in the Mediterranean," *Slavery & Abolition* 13:5–38 (1993), esp. pp. 25–27. Elizabeth Savage, ed., *The Human Commodity: Perspectives on the Trans-Saharan Slave Trade* (London: Frank Cass, 1992) reviews the recent scholarship concerning this trade. Also published as vol. 12, no. 1 of *Slavery & Abolition* (April 1992).

21. Geoffrey Parker makes the point that this contrast between the European objective to seize territory and the frequent non-European objective to seize people was an important contrast in the military history of the West and the non-West. ("Europe and the Wider World, 1500–1750: The Military Balance," in James E. Tracy, ed., *Political Economy of Merchant Empires: State Power and World Trade 1350–1750* (New York: Cambridge University Press, 1991), pp. 163–165.

22. John K. Thornton, *Africa and Africans in the Making of the Atlantic World, 1400–1680* (New York: Cambridge University Press, 1992), pp. 72–97.

23. Jack Goody, *Tradition, Technology, and the State* (London: Oxford University Press, 1971), pp. 21–38.

24. Thornton, *Africa and Africans,* pp. 74–79.

25. These conditions in Africa of the fifteenth and sixteenth centuries bear some resemblance to the evolution of slavery in Muscovy over those same centuries, leading in the Muscovite case to the changeover from slavery to a system of serfdom attached to the land. The major region of slave supply to the Mediterranean basin at that time was, however, south of Muscovy proper and drew to some degree on captured Muscovites. Richard Hellie, *Slavery in Russia: 1450–1725* (Cambridge, Mass.: Harvard University Press, 1982), pp. 1–26.

A long discussion of the relationship between land scarcity and labor control through slavery or other means goes back at least as far as Herman Merivale, *Lectures on Colonization and Colonies Delivered before the University of Oxford in 1839, 1840, and 1841,* 2nd ed. (London, 1861), and comes down through H. J. Nieboer,

Slavery as an Industrial System (The Hague: Martinus Nijhoff, 1910) to a variety of recent authorities.

26. For the role of the plantation complex in world history, see Philip D. Curtin, *The Rise and Fall of the Plantation Complex* (New York: Cambridge University Press, 1990).

27. Kingsley Davis, "The Migration of Human Populations," *Scientific American* 23:93–105 (1974), p. 95.

28. Phillips, *Slavery*, p. 79.

29. Raymond Mauny, *Les navigations médiévales sur les côtes sahariennes antérieures à la découverte portugaises (1434)* (Lisbon: 1960).

30. Philip D. Curtin, "Disease Exchange Across the Tropical Atlantic," *History and Philosophy of the Life Sciences* 15:169–196 (1993).

31. Philip D. Curtin, "Epidemiology and the Slave Trade," *Political Science Quarterly* 83:190–216 (1968).

32. Philip D. Curtin, *The Atlantic Slave Trade: A Census* (Madison: University of Wisconsin Press, 1969), pp. 119, 216, 266.

33. Curtin, *The Plantation Complex,* throughout.

34. Curtin, *Census.* For recent revision, see David Richardson, "Slave Exports from West and West-Central Africa, 1700–1810: New Estimates of Volume and Distribution," *Journal of African History* 30:1–22 (1989).

35. Paul Lovejoy, *Transformations in Slavery: A History of Slavery in Africa* (New York: Cambridge University Press, 1983); pp. 19, 47, and 141; Richardson, "Slave Exports," p. 10.

36. John Komlos, "Thinking About the Industrial Revolution," *Journal of European Economic History* 18:191–206 (1989).

37. The end of the Atlantic slave trade has been treated at enormous length and from many points of view. Some of these can be surveyed by consulting Eric Williams, *Capitalism and Slavery* (Chapel Hill: University of North Carolina Press, 1944); Seymour Drescher, *Econocide: British Slavery in the Era of Abolition* (Pittsburgh: University of Pittsburgh Press, 1977); and Barbara Solow and Stanley Engerman, *British Capitalism and Caribbean Slavery: The Legacy of Eric Williams* (New York: Cambridge University Press, 1988).

38. The literature about these migrations is large and increasing: Hugh Tinker, *A New System of Slavery: The Export of Indian Labour Overseas 1830–1920* (London: Oxford University Press, 1974); Peter C. Emmer, ed., *Colonialism and Migration: Indentured Labour Before and After Slavery* (Dordrecht: Nijhoff, 1986); Shula Marks and Peter Richardson, eds., *Studies in International Labour Migration: Historical Perspectives* (London: Macmillan, 1984); David Northrup, *Indentured Labor in the Age of Imperialism, 1838–1914* (New York: Cambridge University Press, 1995); Pieter C. Emmer, ed., *European Expansion and Migration: Essays on the Intercontinental Migration from Africa, Asia, and Europe* (Oxford: Berg, 1992).

39. David Northrup, *Indentured Labor,* Ch. 2, n. 2. See also P. D. Curtin, "Migration in the Tropical World," in Virginia Yans-McLaughlin, *Immigration Reconsidered: History, Sociology, and Politics* (New York, Oxford University Press, 1990), pp. 21–36.

40. Philip D. Curtin, *Cross-Cultural Trade in World History,* pp. 136–157.

41. Leonard Thompson, *A History of South Africa* (New Haven: Yale University Press, 1990), pp. 33–45.

42. Robert C. H. Shell, *Children of Bondage* (Middletown, Conn.: Wesleyan University Press, 1994), pp. 40–43.

43. United Nations, Department of Economic and Social Affairs, *Economic Survey of Africa Since 1950* (New York: 1959), p. 13.

44. UN, *Economic Survey of Africa Since 1950,* p. 13.

45. John H. Hanson, "Islam, Migration, and the Political Economy of Meaning: *Fergo Nioro* from the Senegal River Valley, 1862–1890," *Journal of African History* 35:37–60 (1994).

46. Richard L. Roberts, *Warriors, Merchants, and Slaves: The State and the Economy in the Middle Niger Valley, 1700–1914* (Stanford: Stanford University Press, 1987); Patrick Manning, "Slavery and the Slave Trade in Colonial Africa," *Journal of African History* 32:235–240 (1990); Paul E. Lovejoy, "The Impact of the Atlantic Slave Trade on Africa: A Review of the Literature," *Journal of African History* 30:365–394 (1989); and Suzanne Miers and Richard Roberts, eds., *The End of Slavery in Africa* (Madison: University of Wisconsin Press, 1989).

47. Janet J. Ewald, "The Nile Valley System and the Red Sea Slave Trade, 1820–1880," *Slavery & Abolition* 9:72–92 (1988), "Slavery in Africa and the Slave Trade from Africa," *American Historical Review* 97:465–485 (1992).

48. Burton Benedict, "Slavery and Indenture in Mauritius and Seychelles," in James L. Watson, ed., *Asian and African Systems of Slavery* (Berkeley: University of California Press, 1980), pp. 125–168.

49. Gwyn Campbell, "The East African Slave Trade, 1861–1895," *International Journal of African Historical Studies* 22:1–26 (1989).

50. Esmond Bradley Martin and T.C.I. Ryan, "Estimating Slave Imports to the Mascarenes: An Essay in Methodology," *Hekima: Journal of Humanities and Social Sciences* [Nairobi], no. 2, pp. 66–81 (December 1982); William Gervase Clarence-Smith, ed., *The Economics of the Indian Ocean Slave Trade in the Nineteenth Century* (London: Frank Cass, 1989); Gwyn Campbell, "The East African Slave Trade, 1861–1895" and "The State and Pre-Colonial Demographic History: The Case of Nineteenth-Century Madagascar," *Journal of African History* 32:415–445 (1991); and Abdul Sheriff, *Slaves, Spices, and Ivory in Zanzibar: Integration of an East African Commercial Empire into the World Economy, 1770–1873* (London: James Currey, 1987).

51. Tinker, *New System of Slavery,* pp. 65, 95, and 99.

52. Thompson, *History of South Africa,* p. 243.

53. Robet G. Gregory, *India and East Africa: A History of Race Relations Within the British Empire, 1890–1939* (Oxford: Clarendon Press, 1971); Tinker, *New System of Slavery,* p. 278.

54. Peter Richardson, "Chinese Indentured Labour in the Transvaal Gold Mining Industry, 1904–1910," in Kay Saunders, ed., *Indentured Labour in the British Empire 1834–1920* (London and Canberra: Croom Helm, 1984), pp. 260–290, esp. 266ff.

55. See, for example, Paul E. Lovejoy and Jan S. Hogendorn, *Slow Death for Slavery: The Course of Abolition in Northern Nigeria, 1897–1936* (Cambridge: Cambridge University Press, 1993) and Miers and Roberts, *End of Slavery in Africa.*

56. See, for example, Dennis D. Cordell, Joel Gregory, and Victor Piché, *Hoe and Wage: A Social History of a Circulatory Migration System in West Africa* (Boulder:

Westview, 1994) and John A. Arthur, "International Labor Migration Patterns in West Africa," *African Studies Review* 34:65–87 (1991).

57. Donald C. Holsinger, "Migration, Commerce, and Community: The Mizabis in Eighteenth- and Nineteenth-Century Algeria," *Journal of African History* 21:61–74 (1980).

58. Francis Wilson, *Labour in the South African Gold Mines, 1911–1969* (Cambridge: Cambridge University Press, 1972); Sharon Stichter, *Migrant Laborers* (New York: Cambridge University Press, 1985); and Philip D. Curtin, "Postwar Migrations in Sub-Saharan Africa," in William H. McNeill and Ruth Adams, *Human Migration: Patterns and Policies* (Bloomington: Indiana University Press, 1976), pp. 188–198.

59. Curtin, "Postwar Migrations," p. 191.

60. United Nations, General Assembly, 47th session, "Report of the United Nations High Commission for Refugees," Official Records, Supplement no. 12 (A/46/12), pp. 17–22. See also Aristide R. Zolberg, Astri Sulurke, and Serio Aguayo, *Escape from Violence: Conflict and the Refugee Crisis in the Developing World* (New York: Oxford University Press, 1989), pp. 37–40.

61. *The Economist* 330:39–40 (February 12, 1994).

62. Trevor Mostyn, ed., *Cambridge Encyclopedia of the Middle East and North Africa* (Cambridge: Cambridge University Press, 1988) pp. 302 and 388.

63. United Nations, *Demographic Yearbook 1989,* pp. 576–598.

64. *Statistical Abstract of the United States 1992,* p. 10.

4

The Global Migration Crisis

Myron Weiner

The migration of people is as old as recorded history. Moses led his persecuted people from Egypt across the Sinai to Canaan. The seafaring Greeks established colonies in Sicily and elsewhere in the Mediterranean. Jews in Palestine were dispersed into Mesopotamia, Persia, Greece, North Africa, and Europe following the Roman destruction of the second temple in A.D. 70. From Central Asia, the Turkish people migrated into Anatolia, where they founded the Turkish state. In China, the Han people colonized non-Han regions to the south and the west. The Vikings colonized Normandy and in 1066 invaded and settled Britain.

In the modern era there have been several distinctive waves of migration, starting in the seventeenth century with the emigration of Europeans to their overseas colonies, the forced migration of peoples under colonial domination, and the movement of peoples as a result of the breakup of empires and the devastation of two world wars. The globalization of migration has been accelerating since the end of World War II, the result of three major factors. The first is the growth of a more integrated global economy. A worldwide change in the price of oil, for example, led to a demand for foreign labor in the oil-rich countries of the Middle East and a decline in the demand in Western Europe. The second factor is the rapid increase in the number of states, some weak and divided, some autocratic and rapacious, but in either event sufficiently nasty so that many of their citizens prefer to move to another country. The third factor is the global communication and transportation systems, which enable individuals to learn of opportunities elsewhere and to move at low cost.[1] Distances have become less important as a barrier to migration. There has also emerged a migration "mafia," or labor recruiters who extract fees from would-be migrants (sometimes turning illegal migrants into bonded laborers), to arrange their transportation and employment abroad. Trafficking in migrants has become a major global business.

The number of people who want to leave their country, either to improve opportunities for themselves and their children or to escape intolerable conditions, is increasing. There has been a worldwide increase in virtually all categories of migrants—legal migrants, illegal migrants, refugees, asylum-seekers, and, in some countries, temporary guest workers. Indeed, the number of people who want to leave their country is now substantially greater than countries are willing to accept. The result is that in virtually every world capital the flow of people is regarded with alarm. In Bonn, Paris, Bern, Vienna, Brussels, and other European capitals, the major concerns are how to deal with a large-scale refugee influx from the Balkans, Eastern Europe, and the Third World, how to integrate millions of guest workers and their locally born children, what to do about illegal migration, and how to cope with the growth of antiforeign political parties. In the early 1990s, Germany became alarmed by the growing number of asylum-seekers who were fleeing not political persecution or violence but simply economic deprivation. Paris is now concerned with a potential flight of refugees from an Algeria threatened by Islamic fundamentalism. In Washington, the key concerns have been over Haitian, Cuban, and Chinese boat people, illegal migrants from Mexico and elsewhere, the burgeoning number of requests for asylum at U.S. airports, and the widespread violation of laws banning the employment of undocumented aliens. In Moscow, there is anxiety over the fate of Russian settlers in the Baltic states, the governments of which have established language and citizenship policies that may lead to a Russian exodus. In Japan, the primary concerns are the illegal population influx from China and Southeast Asia, the prospects of further refugee flows from Asia, and whether to formulate a guest-worker policy.

Concern is not confined to advanced industrial countries. In Islamabad the issues are how to induce Afghan refugees to return home and whether to respond to the demand of Urdu-speaking residents of Bangladesh who want to migrate to Pakistan. In Johannesburg hawkers complain of competition from illegal migrant traders from Mozambique, Zimbabwe, and China to the city center while the new government debates over whether to pursue a policy of Africanization or indigenization in high-skilled employment. In India there is an illegal influx of Bangladeshis into Assam and into Delhi, and Dhaka worries that India may expel them. The Thai government is concerned over the growing illegal influx of hundreds of thousands of Burmese in search of employment. In Egypt, the government has feared that UN sanctions against Libya might lead to the expulsion of thousands of Egyptian migrant workers from Libya to Egypt, adding to the country's unemployment and strengthening Islamic fundamentalist groups. Jordan remains concerned over the presence of large numbers of Palestinians who were forced to leave Kuwait after the Gulf

War. And in Africa, country after country has been overwhelmed with the influx of refugees from Rwanda, Angola, Liberia, Ethiopia, Somalia, and the Sudan.

The number of people fleeing to escape violence or persecution, to find employment, or to improve their own lives and those of their family members is greater than it has ever been. With the end of the cold war, the barriers to emigration have been removed from the successor states to the Soviet Union and from Eastern Europe and pressure for entry has consequently grown throughout Western Europe. Large numbers of migrants from Eastern Europe, North Africa, and Asia have obtained legal entry as permanent residents or guest workers in North America, Western Europe, and in the Persian Gulf. Other migrants languish in refugee camps in Africa, the Middle East, South Asia, and Hong Kong and along Cambodia's borders, victims of ethnic conflict, repressive and rapacious regimes, and civil wars. Many have fled their homes for other regions of their country. Still others have illegally crossed borders at night, crowded ramshackle ships, or landed at airports without papers, hoping to win legal asylum, or quietly and illegally slipped into the labor market to find employment in small businesses, shops, restaurants, households, and agriculture.

According to the United Nations Population Fund,[2] in 1993 there were 100 million migrants worldwide, including 15.5 million migrants to Western Europe, 20 million migrants in the United States, 8 million in Australia and Canada, several million migrant workers to the Gulf states, where they make up a majority of the workforce, and 19 million refugees. These figures do not include the growing number of illegal migrants who fail to appear in official census statistics: an estimated 280,000 in Japan in 1992, 1 million illegal migrants to Malaysia from Indonesia and Thailand,[3] several million Bangladeshis in India's northeastern state of Assam, over 3 million in the United States, and significant numbers in Spain, Portugal, and Italy. And these numbers do not include the many people who migrated within their own country—say, from Russia to Kazakhstan, Latvia, Estonia, and Ukraine, or across republic boundaries within Yugoslavia—who became international migrants when their country disintegrated.

The number of refugees worldwide has been growing at an alarming pace, from 2.8 million in 1976, to 8.2 million in 1980, 11.6 million in 1985, 17.2 million in 1990, 18.2 million in 1992, and 18.9 million in 1993.[4] In the 1970s, Indochina produced 2 million refugees; in the 1980s, Afghanistan produced 6 million refugees; and in the early 1990s, there was a large outpouring of refugees from the former Yugoslav republics. Another 24 to 25 million are displaced persons within the borders of their own countries, often looking for opportunities to leave.

In many countries, citizens have become fearful that they are now being invaded not by armies and tanks, but by migrants who speak other languages, worship other gods, belong to other cultures, and, they fear, will take their jobs, occupy their land, live off the welfare system, and threaten their way of life, their environment, and even their polity. Virtually every country in Western Europe now has a right-wing antiforeign political party or movement—the British National Party in the United Kingdom, the Northern League in Italy, Jean-Marie le Pen's Front National in France, the Liberal Party in Austria, the Republican Party in Germany, and the Vlaams Blok in Belgium. Many citizens feel that their governments have lost control of their borders, and in turn, governments are alarmed by the growing hostility of their citizens to the foreigners living and working in their midst.

The sense of crisis is not confined to advanced industrial societies.[5] The bulk of the world's refugees and immigrants is moving from one developing country to another. In portions of Pakistan, India, Bangladesh, Thailand, Mauritania, Senegal, Congo, Nigeria, and Libya local citizens or their governments have turned against foreigners. In many countries the burden of feeding and housing large numbers of refugees has placed acute strains upon society. The flow of illegal migrants in search of land or employment has often led to violence with local people fearful that they will lose their land and their jobs to people who are prepared to accept work at lower wages. International institutions, particularly the United Nations High Commissioner for Refugees and the International Red Cross, are overwhelmed with the costs of handling refugees and internally displaced people fleeing violence and repression.

Benign Phenomena or Growing Threat?

Not too many years ago, worldwide population movements were not regarded as particularly threatening. In the 1950s and 1960s to meet the labor demands of their growing economies Western European countries imported several million migrant guest workers from Turkey, North Africa, and Southern Europe. The United States expanded its intake, drawing migrants from Asia and Latin America. Australia ended its "White Only" policy and opened its borders to immigrants from Asia and the Middle East. In the mid-1970s the oil-producing countries of the Persian Gulf recruited migrant workers from other Arab countries and from Asia, so many in fact that in several countries there were more foreign workers than natives in the labor force.

So long as economies were growing, both industrial and oil-producing countries were willing and often eager to welcome migrants. Governments and economists regarded migration as beneficial to both sending and receiving countries; for sending countries it provided a way to reduce unemployment and earn remittances, and for receiving countries, it provided a way to satisfy labor shortages. Such positive views of migration were mitigated only by concerns of a "brain drain" of European scientists to the United States and of highly educated people from the Third World to the West.

In contrast, of course, refugee flows were regarded as a problem. At the end of World War II, 2 million displaced persons in Allied occupied zones were in need of repatriation. Some 12 million Germans were moved from Eastern Europe when Germany's eastern borders were redrawn. Starting in the late 1940s, with the establishment of new states in Africa, the Middle East, and South and Southeast Asia, the number of refugees again increased, primarily as people fled from one newly independent country to another. Many observers believed that the turmoil that led large numbers of people to become refugees was temporary—the result of revolutionary upheavals in some states (Cuba, China, Iran), violent rivalries or ethnic clashes among newly independent states, and conflicts exacerbated by super power rivalries. Although some of the flows were enormous—some 14 million people moved between India and Pakistan in 1947 and 1948—they were also perceived to be short-lived. Both sending and receiving countries often regarded migration as a necessary concomitant of the redrawing of boundaries, an "exchange" of populations, as it were, and of what was then euphemistically called "nation-building."

Many observers also regarded some of the refugee flows as the result of great power interventions—in Cambodia, Laos, Vietnam, Angola, Mozambique, the Horn of Africa, Central America, and Afghanistan. If only the great powers would remove themselves from these internal conflicts, it was said, in time the violence and the refugee flows would subside.

A less benign view of international migration emerged in Great Britain in the early 1960s and in the France and Germany in the early 1970s. The countries of Western Europe no longer needed imported labor. They also had large numbers of foreign guest workers who did not wish to return home and to whom governments were unwilling or reluctant to grant citizenship. As many observers have noted, governments had hoped to import migrants as labor but soon found that the migrants were people with wills of their own. Although foreign workers were no longer recruited, the wives and children of workers soon migrated into the country. Despite a worldwide recession the flow of migrants in search of employment continued. As governments became more restrictive on legal migration, illegal migration and claims for asylum increased.

The movement of people across borders has become less acceptable to developing countries as well. Already overburdened with large-scale rural-to-urban migration, many governments have become concerned with an influx of foreigners into their already congested urban centers. Local ethnic groups, increasingly self-conscious and organized, want to halt the influx of ethnic strangers, for both economic and cultural reasons. Nativist movements have begun to flourish in the Third World as they have in advanced industrial countries.

Worldwide refugee flows show no sign of abating.[6] To the contrary, there has been an increase in the numbers of people from the Third World fleeing across borders. Within Africa alone the number of refugees increased from 2.7 million in 1981 to 5.4 million in 1992, and in Asia it went from 4.6 million in 1981 to 7.2 million in 1992. Wars in Yugoslavia and in the former Soviet Union have also resulted in a massive increase in refugees in Europe, from 600,000 in 1981 to 3.6 million in 1992. Growing numbers of refugees have sought asylum in the United States and in Western Europe, over 400,000 alone in Germany in 1992. Although many are genuine refugees, others are economically motivated migrants using the asylum claim as a way of getting into countries that they cannot enter under migration laws. Furthermore, the war in the Persian Gulf generated still more new flows of refugees and displaced persons, most of whom were not classified as refugees since they were returning home from Saudi Arabia to Yemen and from Kuwait and Iraq to South and Southeast Asia. The list of countries now producing refugees is long: Afghanistan, former Yugoslavia, Rwanda, Mozambique, Somalia, Ethiopia, Eritrea, Liberia, Angola, Azerbaijan, Tajikistan, Burma, Sudan, Sierra Leone, Haiti, Burundi, Sri Lanka, and Armenia. Many of these countries also had large numbers of internally displaced persons. Since 1980, the number of refugees has been increasing by nearly 1 million a year. According to the World Refugee Survey, there was a decline in the number of refugees in 1993, but the number of internally displaced persons had grown, reflecting perhaps the growing capacity of governments and international agencies to confine people in flight within their own country. There are no signs that the end of the cold war has reduced violent conflicts within states and decreased the numbers of people in flight. Many of the conflicts were, no doubt, greatly exacerbated by great power interventions—in, for example, Afghanistan, Angola, Mozambique, and the Horn of Africa—but these conflicts have taken on lives of their own and are sustained by the ready availability of weapons. Moreover, many of the conflicts, such as in Rwanda, Sudan, and Liberia, are unrelated to direct great power interventions and there is a high potential for conflict in several other African states. The end of the cold war has not diminished (and has perhaps increased) the global flow of arms, now financially sustained by the drug traffic.

The breakup of the Soviet bloc has led to internal conflicts and massive flights similar to the breakup of the Ottoman and Hapsburg Empires at the end of World War I and the breakup of the colonial empires at the end of World War II. The disintegration of empires has been accompanied by the emergence of new ethnic identities, ethnic conflicts within states, and movements for autonomy and self-determination. As minorities feel threatened by an ethnic majority in control of the state, they look outside for support or, alternatively, for a place to flee. Three regions, hitherto relatively stable until the disintegration of the Soviet Union, are now rife with conflict and refugee flows: the Balkans, the Caucasus, and Central Asia.

Civil conflicts are also producing an increase in the number of internally displaced persons as well—an estimated 25 million worldwide in 1993. Sudan, with 4 million, had the largest number,[7] but there were also large numbers inside South Africa, Mozambique, Somalia, Angola, Bosnia-Herzegovina, Ethiopia, Eritrea, Liberia, Sri Lanka, Zaire, Afghanistan, Burma, Peru, Iraq, Lebanon, Tajikistan, Rwanda, Croatia, Colombia, India, Cyprus, and Azerbaijan.

Most troublesome to receiving countries was the increase in the number of illegal migrants. In the United States, a one-time amnesty program put in place in 1986 led 3.1 million people to come forth to regularize their status. The actual number of remaining illegal migrants in the country is probably higher. Despite a policy of penalizing employers for hiring illegal migrants, various studies reported that the flows across the U.S.-Mexican border continue to be large, adding perhaps 200,000 to 300,000 (some say more) to the stock of illegal migrants each year.[8] Europe also experienced a significant rise in the number of illegal migrants in the early 1990s. The total number of illegal migrants in Western Europe is estimated at about 3 million, many from eastern Europe and from Africa to Spain and Italy.[9] Japan too has reported an increase in illegal migrants from the Philippines, mainland China, and continental Southeast Asia. And the flows of illegal migrants are not confined to the advanced industrial countries. In Africa there have been substantial unauthorized or illegal flows into Côte d'Ivoire, South Africa, and Nigeria. Similarly, in Asia illegal labor flows from Indonesia to Malaysia, from Bangladesh to India, from Nepal to Bhutan, and from the People's Republic of China to Taiwan and Hong Kong.

Should we regard the population flows of workers with alarm? Is global labor migration, in combination with the flows of capital, technology, and trade, part of a developing global world community unfettered by national boundaries? Is international migration an economic burden and a threat to national identity and political stability, as some assert, or is the problem the result of the xenophobic reaction of some citizens and politicians and exaggerated fears of being overwhelmed by foreigners? If citizens were not xenophobic and governments not so obsessed with control could countries not live comfortably with open borders? In a more just world should people not freely choose where they want to live? Despite such reasoning, many governments and their citizens do believe that there is a crisis—although they do not always agree what the crisis is. It remains unclear as to whether the "crisis" is a matter of perceptions, exaggerated fears, and xenophobic reactions linked to the present global recession, or whether the global movement of peoples is a long-term threat to the security and the cultural and economic well-being of countries.

In the following pages I shall attempt to disaggregate the various dimensions of the crisis to ascertain what aspects of these flows have created anxieties among political leaders and their citizens. I shall examine five dimensions of the global migration crisis: (1) control over entry, (2) the absorption of migrants and refugees, (3) international relations, (4) international regimes and institutions, and (5) moral considerations.

Control over Entry

Since the development of the modern state from the fifteenth century onward, governments have regarded control over their borders as the core of sovereignty. It is axiomatic that states decide which people to admit, how many, and from where. But today many contemporary governments, and their citizens, fear that they can no longer control entry. Advanced industrial countries can protect their borders from invading armies, but not from countless individuals who slip into harbors, crawl under barbed wire fences, and wade across rivers. Tourists and students with visas stay on and disappear into the labor market. Airplanes bring in people with missing or false papers who then claim asylum. Asylum officers responsible for adjudicating claims are overwhelmed by the numbers. People whose asylum claims are pending may never appear in court, and those whose asylum requests have been rejected slip into the underground labor market to avoid repatriation.

The smuggling of migrants across boundaries has become an organized international business. "Businessmen," reports the *New York Times*,[10] "arrange each stage of a smuggling operation: finding passengers, arranging their travel documents, guiding them across borders, and extracting payment after arrival. Most immigrants borrow from relatives or loan sharks to pay the full amount almost immediately after they arrive, working for years to pay off the debt." When the United States halted ships at sea, smugglers moved larger numbers of immigrants by plane, providing passengers with forged passports and visas for check-in. The passports are then returned to the smugglers prior to departure so that upon arrival the passenger can request political asylum. Many illegal immigrants arrive with fake documents that are not readily detected by airport inspectors, who often spend less than a minute looking at the documents of each person entering the country. Many of the smugglers are Taiwanese businessmen moving illegal immigrants from Fujian Province in China to airports in Los Angeles, Miami, and Seattle. Most of the illegal migrants then join the Fujianese community in New York City. The migrant smuggling business has apparently become very lucrative. "No longer the 'mom and pop' operations that charged only a few thousand dollars in the 1980s," reports the *Far Eastern Economic Review*,[11] "they are now multinational, billion-dollar businesses that stretch from China to Hong Kong, Taiwan, Singapore, Thailand, Central America, and the U.S."

The smuggling business has become worldwide. Professional smugglers, working closely with shipping companies, are able to arrange the illegal movement of people from almost anyplace on the globe. For a fee, asylum-seekers can be smuggled into Germany or Canada or the United States and briefed as to what answers to give to officials to enable them to qualify under asylum laws. If the U.S. Coast Guard is particularly vigilant in interdicting boats from China, smugglers can divert the ships to Japan's west coast.

Almost every effort to control entry has run afoul of major obstacles. How can entry at borders be controlled when governments are trying to facilitate the flow of trade? Can every truck crossing an international border be inspected? Should all ships at sea be interdicted to ensure that no illegal immigrants are on board? Should travelers who arrive at airports without passports or visas be summarily repatriated without a hearing? How can employer sanctions be made to work when numerous small businesses and households find it advantageous to employ low-wage labor?

In the West, fears of uncontrollable entry are further fueled by anxieties that rapid population growth in developing countries will produce such vast numbers of unemployed young people in search of a livelihood that borders will not contain them. The world population has increased rapidly, from 2.5 billion in 1950 to 4.4 billion in 1980, to 5.3 billion in 1990. It is expected to reach 6.3 billion in the year 2000, and 8.5 billion by 2025. An estimated 90 to 100 million people are added to the world's population each year, mostly in low-income countries where the average annual population growth is 1.8 percent compared to 0.5 percent in high-income countries. Is the West, then, experiencing a population overflow from the Third World, as North and South America and Australia experienced an overflow from Europe in the nineteenth century during its period of rapid population growth?

To put the world's population growth in perspective it should be noted that world migration (including refugee flows) amounts to perhaps 4 million persons a year, or 4 percent of the world's annual population increase.[12] About half is to developed countries. Population growth in the

Third World has declined from 2.5 percent annually in the early 1960s to 1.8 percent in the 1990s, but emigration has increased. Moreover, some of the largest flows of migrant workers came from countries with low or modest population growth rates—Yugoslavia and Greece into Western Europe, for example. The outflow from mainland China is growing in spite of declining birthrates.

The relationship between rapid population growth and emigration is a complicated one, not easily encompassed by the simple notion that one necessarily leads to the other. Population growth is clearly an intervening variable, in itself rarely a cause, but in combination with other factors it can be a force for emigration. Where the number of young adults is increasing and incomes and employment are rising, many young people may acquire the financial means as well as the motivation to emigrate. Hence the emigration pressures in China's Fujian Province, notwithstanding its high rate of economic growth. After all, the great exodus from Europe in the nineteenth century—some 50 million people emigrated to the United States—took place during a time of rapid economic growth and population growth. A similar combination has existed in Korea, Taiwan, Italy, Turkey, Algeria, Mexico, and Puerto Rico, all of which have experienced high emigration rates, high economic growth rates and high population rates simultaneously.

And a long-term decline in population growth rates does not necessarily foreshadow a decline in emigration rates. The sharp decline in fertility rates throughout Eastern Europe and the former Soviet Union has not led to a decline in emigration pressures—a situation attributable to increased unemployment, declining wages, and deteriorating economic conditions.

There is no evidence of a direct relationship between rapid population growth rates, or even population density, and high emigration rates. Global migration appears to be more closely associated with rising expectations in many developing countries, differentials in wages and employment opportunities, knowledge about opportunities elsewhere, access to low-cost transportation, high levels of violence within countries, violations of human rights, persecution of minorities, and above all, growing knowledge about the ease of entering and remaining in another country. Nonetheless, fears that high population growth generates illegal migration, although unsupported by empirical evidence, has become an element in Western countries' anxieties about their inability to control their borders.

One explanation for these fears is not the high fertility rate of developing countries but the low fertility rate in industrial countries that receive migrants.[13] In countries with low population growth rates, migrants account for a very large proportion of the annual population increase. Although migrants add less than 0.5 percent to the U.S. population a year, immigrants and their offspring are expected to be responsible for almost two-thirds of the net population growth over the next fifty years.[14] Similarly, as the countries of central Europe move toward zero population growth, virtually all of the annual population increase is the result of immigration. Moreover, migrants tend to be in the high-fertility age group, 20 to 35, and fertility rates among migrants from the Third World tend to be higher than those of natives in developed countries. The children of migrants are therefore particularly visible in classrooms, especially in the large urban centers where migrants tend to concentrate. For countries with a low rate of natural population increase, the demographic impact of migration on population growth and on school attendance is highly visible even though rapid population growth in the Third World is not in itself a decisive element in international population movements.

Concern that political turmoil and violence within Third World countries or among the states of the former Soviet bloc will lead to population movements is, however, far more realistic. European governments have a legitimate reason to believe that conflicts over Islamic movements in North Africa and the Middle East could lead to an exodus or that ethnic conflicts in the successor states of the former Soviet Union might create large refugee flows. Similarly, the United States has had a legitimate concern that domestic conflicts within Cuba, Haiti, or elsewhere in the Caribbean or Latin America could lead to population flight.

Although most Western governments are prepared to accept limited numbers of individual refugees who are persecuted and whose lives are at risk, their humanitarian sentiments are much reduced when the volume of asylum-seekers is large and imposing a heavy burden on housing, employment, and the entitlement system. Governments are also reluctant to maintain a generous asylum system when so many asylum-seekers are would-be migrants, not individuals fearing persecution.

Governments want to be able to choose which people to admit, how many, for what purpose, and for how long. They do not want these decisions to be made by employers, other governments, or would-be migrants. So long as conditions in the Third World and in the former Soviet bloc continue to encourage the exodus of large numbers of people, anxiety will increase among governments and citizens that they are unable to control entry.

Absorption

International migration changes the ethnic composition of states. In the case of multiethnic states migration can change the ethnic balance and thereby precipitate a change in the balance of political power. For homogeneous countries a large influx of migrants raises the question of what the country should demand of its immigrants. Should the goal be total assimilation into the culture of the host society so that migrants and their children are no longer distinguishable? Or should migrants be allowed to retain their language, their religion, an attachment to their country of origin, and their distinctive identity? Among the nation-states of Western Europe there is the question of whether ethnic nationalism should give way to civic nationalism, that is whether citizenship implies a uniform cultural identity, or whether there can be cultural pluralism that is compatible with citizenship. This is a particularly vexing question for European countries that are coming to realize that their guest workers will remain. In advanced industrial societies much of the debate centers on educational policies—whether the educational system should be explicitly assimilationist or multicultural, whether children born of migrant parents should be permitted or encouraged to retain the language of their parents, and whether their religion has a place in the schools. Can and should traditional nation-states that have welcomed *political* pluralism come to accept and even welcome *cultural* pluralism? Should these differences be tolerated, respected, or even encouraged through government support, or should they be rooted out and eradicated? Almost every Western country is uncertain as to how to incorporate migrants and their children—whether to induce them to assimilate or to pursue a policy of multiculturalism.

What, in short, constitutes membership in the community and how should the community in turn define itself? Given the varied conceptions of community and citizenship prevailing in the Western world (from political definitions of citizenship to cultural norms, to notions of kinship and blood ties) it should not be surprising that countries vary in their responses to the issue of migrant absorption or to the contentious question of whether the locally born children of migrants should be granted automatic citizenship.

The issue of absorption, integration, or assimilation—the terms themselves are contentious—is as much a problem in the Third World as it is among the developed countries. The majority of the world's refugees and migrants move not from South to North but from one Third World country to another. Developing countries not only produce the largest number of migrants and refugees but are also the primary receivers. Third World governments and their citizens have often had a remarkable tolerance toward migrants and refugees from neighboring countries and a special generosity toward those with whom they share a common language, religion, or tribal identity. But many governments have been concerned that if the migrants and refugees belong to an alien ethnic group or add to the numbers of a minority community, the political, economic, social, and cultural dominance of the majority might be eroded. An influx of Indians to Fiji, Chinese or

Vietnamese to Malaysia, Nepalis to Bhutan, Bangladeshis to India's northeast, or Palestinians to Lebanon could jeopardize the precarious political balance among ethnic groups. Moreover, most countries in the Third World—indeed most countries in the world—are ethnically heterogeneous. How, many government officials ask, can a country manage ethnic conflicts when it is subjected to a continuous and substantial population influx?

Debates over cultural absorption are further complicated by the question of the absorption of migrants into the labor force. Some citizens want migrants to do the jobs that locals do not want. Members of the middle class want to hire domestics from abroad; owners of small businesses want low-wage foreign workers; and farmers want hardworking, nonunion foreign laborers. But citizens also worry that migrants may be taking jobs from other citizens, particularly that the country's own unskilled labor force may find it difficult to compete against foreign workers, and that wages will be pushed down if the immigrant influx is substantial. Among economists, the question of whether migrants depress wages and exacerbate unemployment among the native population is contentious, but whatever the reality, large numbers of citizens are fearful of losing their jobs when unemployment levels are high and economic growth is sluggish.

In much of the Third World, the fear of economic losses from immigration often have a solid basis in reality. In the Third World, there are few jobs that migrants take that locals do not want. Migrants from Central America to the Chiapas region in southern Mexico, from Bangladesh to the Indian state of Assam, and Haiti to the Bahamas compete against locals for jobs. Moreover, there are additional concerns when migrants and a rapidly growing local population compete for land and for dwindling forests.

The growth of antiforeign, antimigration political parties not only in Western Europe but in Third World countries as well has further complicated the task of absorbing foreigners. Governments are concerned that they will be weakened by right-wing, xenophobic parties appealing to the visceral anxieties of their citizens. The issues of absorption and border controls thus become linked as governments see a continued unwanted influx as fueling citizen anxieties, thereby making community acceptance of existing migrants and their children more difficult.

International Relations

Scholars of international relations have said that wars create refugees but refugees do not create wars. Although that is generally true, refugee flows have increasingly become the basis for conflict between sending and receiving countries.

Governments are concerned when the government of another country creates conditions that cause its citizens to flee. A government that violates the human rights of its citizens, persecutes its minorities, or is unable to halt a civil conflict creates a burden for others when its people flee across borders. If a country creates refugees, receiving countries generally believe that they have thereby acquired a right of "intervention"—a concept that encompasses a spectrum of actions, including conditionality in development assistance, restrictions on trade, sanctions, embargoes, and the threat and use of force.

How countries treat their own populations—once regarded as primarily an internal affair—has become an issue of international relations not simply because human rights are now a global matter but because governments may create refugee burdens for others. Thus the Russian government has been concerned over the citizenship rights in the Baltic states of Russians who migrated into the region when it was occupied by the Soviet Union, the Indian government has been concerned over ethnic conflicts in neighboring Sri Lanka, and the government of Turkey has been fearful that Iraq's Kurds might cross its borders. Russian policies toward many of the successor states to the Soviet Union will be greatly influenced by how the "near abroad" states treat Russians. The government of Turkey was influential in pressing the United Nations to protect the Kurdish population in Iraq by indicating that it would use force if necessary to prevent Kurds from crossing into Turkey.

Government strategies of deterrence and prevention may put countries on a collision course with one another, especially when states impose sanctions or threaten military intervention to change the internal behavior of another government that is inducing people to leave.

Moreover, migration policies themselves have become a matter for international negotiations and conflict between sending and receiving countries and among receiving countries. When the Soviet Union prevented the exodus of Jews to Israel and to the United States, emigration policy became an issue in U.S.-Soviet relations. Subsequently, Israel's policy of settling Russian immigrants in the West Bank was an issue in U.S.-Israeli relations. The British government's decision to repatriate forcibly Vietnamese refugees from Hong Kong was an issue in U.S.-British relations. Countries that border on states producing refugees call for a system of "burden sharing" with other countries, whereas distant countries often insist that the country of first asylum take responsibility. These two positions are particularly contentious in Europe.

The traditional obligations of states toward their own citizens living abroad have also become more complex not only as the numbers have increased but also as the migrant communities have become diasporas, communities whose members have citizenship in one country and ties of affection with another. Some 25 million people of Russian origin now live in the republics of the former Soviet Union; an estimated 30 million people of Chinese ancestry live outside of China, Hong Kong, and Taiwan, and millions of people of Indian, Turkish, and Arab origin live outside the countries of their birth. The relationship of diasporas to their host country and their country of origin has often become the basis for international and domestic conflict.[15]

Refugee and migrant flows have moved to the top of the foreign policy agenda. When a boatload of Chinese immigrants was spotted off the coast of California, the United States asked Mexico to intercept them. When Arab governments protested that Israelis were encouraging Russian immigrants to settle in occupied territories, the United States threatened to withhold loan guarantees from Israel as a means of getting Israel to change its settlement policies. When civil war in Pakistan led to a large-scale flight of East Pakistanis into India, India responded by going to war against Pakistan, declaring that the security of India's northeast region was threatened by the influx. When British authorities in Hong Kong forcibly repatriated Vietnamese, the United States formally protested to the British government. And when several countries of Western Europe declared that they would no longer accept refugees and asylum-seekers from countries of first asylum, there were protests from those European states that had previously accepted refugees on the understanding that they would provide transit to other countries. The migration and refugee decisions that countries make clearly have implications for others.

For these reasons, migration and refugee issues have become a matter of high international politics, engaging the attention of heads of state, cabinets, and key ministries involved in defense, internal security, and external relations.

International Regimes and Institutions

This issue has two closely related dimensions: the crisis for international regimes and the crisis for international institutions.

The international refugee regime is based on the 1951 United Nations Convention on Refugees. Under this Convention the definition of refugees is limited to individuals with a well-founded fear of persecution for reasons of race, religion, nationality, membership in a particular social group, or political opinion. In recent years, this definition has come under attack, both by advocates of extending the definition of refugees to include people fleeing from violence and by activists who seek to establish all violations of human rights as grounds for obtaining asylum. Some human rights activists argue that the new conceptions of persecution, such as gender-based oppression or coercive family planning, should be incorporated into asylum policies. However, many governments fear that such broader redefinitions would open their borders wide because only a minority of the world's peoples live in countries that respect human rights and are not torn by violence. Moreover, the international refugee regime is already threatened by large numbers of putative migrants who seek to use the asylum system to gain entry. As these numbers increase, governments have become less willing to follow the procedures put forth by the United Nations High Commissioner for Refugees. Instead of onshore adjudication procedures and rights of appeal, many governments have halted asylum claimants at the borders, interdicted them at sea, prevented them from flying on international flights without visas, or engaged in summary expulsions. The international refugee regime is thus under siege, both from those who would expand the definition of refugees to meet the burgeoning claims of people who live in repressive and violent societies and from those who find even the existing norms too difficult to enforce within UNHCR procedures in the face of growing claims for asylum.

International norms for the protection of migrant workers are no more satisfactory. Efforts by the International Labour Organization to generate global norms concerning the freedom of guest workers to change jobs, join unions, have access to the benefits of the welfare state, bring in families, and acquire the right to remain and become citizens of their host societies have received little support outside of Europe. Labor-importing Arab countries keep far tighter controls on migrant workers than European states by restricting their rights to change jobs or remain. During and shortly after the Gulf War, large numbers of noncitizens were summarily repatriated, especially from Kuwait and Saudi Arabia. Neither Third World countries nor international institutions have been in a position to protect the several million migrants residing in the oil-producing states.

International institutions are also in crisis as a result of the massive increase in migration and refugee flows. The United Nations High Commissioner for Refugees, the International Labour Organization, the International Organization for Migration, the International Committee of the Red Cross, and a host of other international agencies concerned with migrant workers and refugees no longer see their mission primarily as responding to the requests of receiving countries. According to the UNDP seventy-nine of the world's eighty-two armed conflicts from 1989 to 1992 took place within national borders. Most refugee flows are the result of internal violence, not wars between states. Now international agencies ponder how to "intervene" over the objections of states from which people are fleeing. Officials of international agencies increasingly regard conceptions of sovereignty as impediments to their tasks. Yet even as the budgets of these international institutions expand, professional staffs enlarge, and responsibilities grow, they are unable to intervene legally unless authorized by the state or by the UN Security Council. Furthermore, even when the Security Council gives international agencies responsibilities for providing humanitarian assistance to stem the exodus propelled by violence, this expanded role is generally not accompanied by the military support and collective sanctions against transgressors often required to make such efforts successful. Moreover, many international organizations do not have sufficient financial resources or adequate administrative capacity to take on these responsibilities worldwide. A crisis thus emerges as states that are unwilling or unable unilaterally to address the conditions inside countries that lead people to flee have turned to international institutions. Most of these institutions in turn lack adequate legal authority, military power, financial resources, and administrative capacity to satisfactorily take on such responsibilities.

Moral Considerations

Whenever policymakers engage in rationing there is a moral crisis over who should get the benefits and who should pay the costs. Global migration creates a moral crisis in receiving countries since, as we have noted, there are more people who want to permanently leave their country than other countries are willing to accept. Because not everyone can be admitted, countries prepared to admit migrants or refugees must establish criteria for choosing among a large pool of candidates. One dimension of the moral crisis in public policy, therefore, is the question of who should be admitted. Are some criteria for admission more moral than others? Should admissions be based on the needs and desires of the receiving country (which leads to a preference for migrants who are educated, know the local language, have ties to the local population, or are kinfolk of citizens—what some wags have called "designer" migrants) or should entry be based on the needs of those who seek admission?

The moral crisis has also become a conflict between people who emphasize global human rights and those who would give priority to the national interests of states and their current residents. In one industrial country after another, this moral debate has become intensely political. At one pole are right-wing political parties in virtually every European country that call for a halt to all immigration. These groups would bar asylum-seekers, deny citizenship to migrants and their children, and attempt to make life so unpleasant that migrants would be forced to return to their country of origin. At the other pole are human-rights activists concerned that all who seek asylum be freely admitted and given a full hearing and that illegal migrants be provided the entitlements of the welfare state and subsequently admitted into citizenship. They also argue that anyone in the world whose human rights are violated is entitled to asylum. Between these two poles are governments enmeshed in a moral quandary over how best to respond to people in other societies who want to migrate for jobs, decent incomes, and freedom from persecution and discrimination without imposing unacceptable costs on their own citizens.

To some observers, the claims of refugees evoke sympathy, moral concerns, and the image of a just and humane global order in which people whose human rights are violated can move to wherever it is safe and free. To others, refugee flows are a form of population dumping in which states cruelly relieve themselves of unwanted minorities, political dissidents, and the poor. Hence refugees generate in some people feelings of compassion and in others anger against the states that produce them.

A further moral quandary arises over the relationship between indigenous populations, on the one hand, and immigrants and their descendants, on the other, a relationship made complex by uncertainty over what constitutes indigenous status. Some analysts restrict such status to nondominant sectors of society with ancestral links to a precolonial past; that can be construed to include both the indigenous peoples of Canada, New Zealand, Australia, the United States, and Latin America and the titular peoples of Lithuania, Latvia, Estonia, Kazakhstan, and other newly independent republics recently freed from Soviet rule and Russian occupation. In these latter nations an alien people was imposed by imperial colonizers in territories that have now become sovereign states. Migrants and their descendants have committed no injustice, although an injustice may have been committed by the imperial powers that once forced or induced individuals to migrate. Some observers have therefore argued that the Russian settlers are illegitimate and must either return "home" or be given lesser rights than residents who have ancestral roots in the country. Similar arguments over the rights of settlers have shaped policies toward the Chinese in Malaysia and elsewhere in Southeast Asia and toward Indian settlers in East Africa. Contesting claims over group rights are increasingly being fought out in the political arena as each side asserts its own moral claims in a situation that is morally ambiguous.

As ethnic minorities come under siege, as failed states prove unable to protect their own citizens at home, as civil conflicts rage within many societies, and as authoritarian regimes continue to be oppressive, countries receiving people in flight face still another morally perplexing set of alternatives: Should they intervene to change the conditions that lead people to exit? Should they open their borders to people in distress? Should they create a wall around themselves to keep out most of the outsiders who wish to enter?

Intervention in any form is rarely cost-free for either side. Intervention, even when morally justifiable, can be expensive. To cut off trade to an offending country and impose sanctions may do damage to workers and farmers producing goods for export and inflict pain on the poor living under an autocratic regime rather than on the government, a dilemma made sharply clear when the United States imposed sanctions on Haiti. Military intervention may result in a loss of life for members of the armed forces of the attacking country and for innocent civilians in the country under attack. If anticipated costs are low, states may act out of moral concerns. But if the anticipated costs are high, states will intervene only if they believe that their national interests are at stake. When states are unable or unwilling to intervene to remedy conditions in source countries, the moral pressures increase for more generous entry policies, but if the number of asylum-seekers is high, governments may also conclude that domestic concerns require them to restrict entry. Governments may believe that there are conditions under which they are morally *justified* in intervening in the affairs of a sovereign state, but rarely do governments believe they are morally *obligated* to do so. Even the moral willingness to accommodate people in flight is ultimately constrained by what governments believe is in their national or political interests.

Global Migration and Global History

It is conceivable that by the beginning of the twenty-first century the global migration crisis will have subsided. Perhaps there will be fewer failed states in the Third World, fewer civil conflicts, fewer acts of ethnic violence, and fewer autocratic regimes. Perhaps minorities will feel more secure, employment and income levels will have significantly risen, and land pressures will have been reduced. Perhaps migration-receiving countries will want a larger labor force than they can provide themselves through domestic population growth. Perhaps, with the end of the recession, their tolerance for foreigners will have grown. But few of these developments are likely. On the contrary, as the pressure for emigration increases, states are more, rather than less, likely to become restrictive. What is uncertain is whether states will be effective at halting unwanted entries. As the pressures for international population movements increase, we can expect to live in a world in which the great global collisions are not only among states but among peoples, when the world outside a country's borders intrudes, and when global forces continue to erode states and the communities that live in them.

Global migration thus has a dual dimension. Migration can create opportunities for individuals, provide significant economic and social benefits to many countries, and enhance ties between peoples and among countries. But it can also create fears of unemployment, burden public expenditures, intensify conflicts among ethnic groups, threaten the stability of governments, and generate conflicts between states. The dual character of international migration has made it an object of intense national concern. At the same time, governments have begun to recognize that they cannot control international migration alone, for what one country does with its own citizens has an impact on others. For this reason governments find it necessary to intrude into what was traditionally regarded as another country's internal affairs. Global human rights has become more than a new moral standard but an important element in relations among states. It has also become clear that international migrants have become a transnational political, social, and economic force, much like the modern multinational corporation, playing a role in two or more societies and influencing relations among them.

For the historian, political scientist, sociologist, and economist, global migration presents a special challenge. None of these disciplines has an adequate intellectual framework for dealing with a phenomenon that is neither wholly national nor wholly international, neither shaped exclusively by the behavior of governments nor simply by the aggregate actions of individuals, and neither solely the result of impersonal global forces nor of intentional acts. What is apparent however, is that the unprecedented worldwide movement of millions of people across national boundaries, the reaction of governments and their citizens to these movements, and the consequences of both for the creation and expansion of international institutions and norms is an emerging field of scholarship.

Notes

1. For an overview of historical global migration trends, see Wang Gungwu, "Migration and Its Enemies," in Bruce Mazlish and Ralph Buultjens, *Conceptualizing Global History* (Boulder: Westview Press, 1993), pp. 131–151. Also see William H. McNeill and Ruth S. Adams, eds., *Human Migration Patterns and Policies* (Bloomington: Indiana University Press, 1978).

2. United Nations Population Fund, *The 1993 State of World Population Report* (New York: UNFPA, 1993).

3. Malaysian government officials have expressed concern over the security implications of a growing Indonesian population within the country. "It is a question of sovereignty," said Senator Mohamed Nasri Abdul Aziz, a member of the ruling United Malays National Organization. "We cannot simply become an extension of another country by allowing people to walk in." *Far Eastern Economic Review*, 6 August 1992, p. 21.

4. United Nations High Commissioner for Refugees, *The State of the World's Refugees: The Challenge of Protection* (New York: Penguin Books, 1994), p. 3.

5. Some people in the West do, however, see the migration crisis primarily in terms of the movement from South to North or, in racial terms, from nonwhite to white countries. For many Western countries, the central feature of the global migration crisis is that migration no longer flows from the core to the periphery, but

from the periphery to the core, resulting in changes in the racial, religious, and ethnic composition of advanced industrial societies.

6. United Nations High Commissioner for Refugees, *The State of the World's Refugees: The Challenge of Protection* (New York: Penguin Books, 1993).

7. These figures are from *World Refugee Survey* (Washington, D.C.: U.S. Committee for Refugees, 1994).

8. The United States Census Bureau has estimated that there are about 1.3 million illegal immigrants in California, most of them from Mexico. *New York Times*, February 6, 1994, p. 22.

9. Sharon Stanton Russell, *International Migration in Europe, Central Asia, the Middle East, and North Africa* (Washington, D.C.: The World Bank Population and Human Resources Division, 1993).

10. *New York Times*, August 23, 1993, p. B2.

11. *Far Eastern Economic Review*, April 8, 1993, p. 17.

12. These figures do not include return migration, which in some years can be quite substantial. According to the *1994 World Refugee Survey* an estimated 1,830,000 refugees returned home in 1993. During the Gulf War 5.5 million people were displaced within a single year, most of whom returned to their home countries and therefore are not classified as either refugees or immigrants. From most countries of migration there is also a significant return flow of former immigrants (about 200,000 yearly from the United States). Annual flows from one Third World country to another are not well reported and neither are worldwide statistics on illegal migration. The actual movement of individuals across international boundaries each year is thus highly variable.

13. Credit for this point goes to Michael Teitelbaum of the Sloan Foundation.

14. Michael Fix and Jeffrey S. Passel, *Immigration and Immigrants: Setting the Record Straight* (Washington, D.C.: The Urban Institute, 1994), p. 4. According to their estimates, the U.S. population is projected to rise from 249 million in 1990 to 355 million by 2040. Under current law about 70 million immigrants and their offspring will be added to the U.S. population in the next 50 years.

15. Governments with large and/or influential diaspora populations may be politically responsive to these populations' demands even when it results in conflicts with allies. In February 1994, the Clinton administration granted a visa to Gerry Adams, the political chief of the Irish Republican Army over the strong objections of the British government, notwithstanding the "special relationship" of the two countries. President Clinton evidently responded to pressures from two Irish-American senators, Patrick Moynihan (New York) and Edward Kennedy (Massachusetts), both of whom were critical for the president's health and welfare reform proposals.

5

Diasporas, the Nation-State, and Globalisation

Robin Cohen

The migration of peoples is a central theme in global history. As Wang Gungwu has convincingly argued, international migrants are the very embodiment of an extended sense of space, penetrating beyond, between, and underneath such conventional categories of international history as the nation-state, kingdoms, regions, and empires.[1] Of course, many long-distance migrants, whether through fate, circumstance, or choice, decide to conform to the demands of the nation-state system. They adopt new citizenships and fealties, new languages and social norms, and form new axes of community and association. But even in those countries (like, say, the United States) where adaptation, assimilation, or cultural conformity became requisite parts of the construction of a new nation, it has long been recognised that "the melting pot" has failed to erode prior group differences.[2]

Even if we accept that dissolving old loyalties into new national societies and polities works only imperfectly, a more challenging and complex argument turns on the precise nature of the migrants' continuing links between their places of origin and settlement (and, less significantly, their links with others of a similar origin in other settings). As Wang argues, cheaper and denser transport and communications have enabled people to move not just once, but again and again, to settle and remigrate, to move as small groups, families, or individuals, and to sell their skills to the highest global bidder.[3] He seeks to capture these qualitative and quantitative changes in migration patterns through elaborating on the phenomenon of "sojourning" a category that arose initially in his extensive studies of the overseas Chinese, but which he came to regard as having more universal implications.

My own discussion of "diaspora" is a complementary and parallel exercise, in that I too seek to find a theoretical and conceptual framework within which to locate issues of multilocality, displacement, complex social loyalties, and the overlapping identities so characteristic of what is sometimes characterised as the period of "late modernity", "postmodernity", or, more simply, "globalisation". How globalisation connects with "global history" I will address briefly later. As I see it, notions of diaspora have two advantages. They are particularly pertinent to history in that the expression is used of migrant groups in classical and modern times and in the current period of globalisation.[4] The second advantage is somewhat double-edged. On the one hand, concepts of diaspora have great variety and mutability (a plus if we regard the term as adequately meeting a shifting reality). More negatively, the proliferation of meanings of the word *diaspora* has the danger of multiplying confusion by suggesting meanings that are not pertinent to the particular group concerned. On the principle of "nothing ventured, nothing gained", I plan to probe a number of alternative concepts of diaspora, showing thereby, if only sometimes by inference, how migration, the nation-state, and globality are connected.

Diaspora as Dispersal

The term *diaspora* is found in the Greek translation of the Bible and originates in the words for *dispersion* and *to sow or scatter.*[5] The expression was used to describe the Greek colonisation of Asia Minor and the Mediterranean in the Archaic period (800–600 B.C.). Although there was some displacement of the ancient Greeks to Asia Minor as a result of poverty, overpopulation, and interstate war, *diaspora* essentially had a positive connotation. Expansion through trade, military conquest, and settlement were the predominant features of the Greek diaspora.

Subsequent definitions and explanations of the term are frequently casual or incomplete, but the use of the word *diaspora* often alluded to Jewish historical experiences. In particular, the idea that diaspora implied forcible dispersion was found in Deuteronomy (28:25), with the addition of a typically thunderous Old Testament warning that a diaspora constituted the punishment for a people who had forsaken the righteous paths and abandoned the old ways. The destruction of Jerusalem and razing of the walls of its Temple in 586 B.C. created the central folk memory of a diasporic experience (enslavement, exile, and displacement). The Jewish leader of the time, Zedekiah, had vacillated for a decade, then impulsively sanctioned a rebellion against the powerful Mesopotamian Empire. The Babylonian king Nebuchadnezzar showed no mercy for his impudence. His soldiers forced Zedekiah to witness the execution of his sons; the Jewish leader was then blinded and dragged in chains to Babylon. Peasants were left behind in Judah to till the soil, but the key military, civic, and religious personnel accompanied Zedekiah to captivity in Babylon.[6] Jews had been compelled to desert their "promised land" and thereafter forever became dispersed.

"Babylon" as the Site of Oppression

Babylon subsequently became a code word among Jews and, later, Africans, for the afflictions, isolation, and insecurity of living in a foreign place, being set adrift, cut off from their roots and their sense of identity, and oppressed by an alien ruling class. Ken Post,[7] for example, shows how Ethiopianism in Jamaica in the 1930s was

> by no means confined to the Rastafarians. Generally throughout Jamaican Ethiopianism, the sense of a Negro awakening combined with the feeling of being a scattered and oppressed, but nevertheless "chosen" people in a way which made it easy to identify "Babylon"—the white or near-white establishment. . . . It was thus a feature of Jamaican Ethiopianism as an ideology that it moved from a sense of being a chosen people to the identification of Babylon with the white enslaver, and thence to an interpretation of history which predicated the doom of the oppressor.

As a result of the perceived or actual trauma of their historical experiences *Babylon* assumed a pejorative connotation in the minds of many in the Jewish and African diasporas and evoked a sense of captivity, exile, loneliness, and isolation. However, if we examine the historical record, as opposed to the folk memory, of the Jews in Babylon, their experience can be understood in a far more positive or, at the least, more ambivalent way.

"Babylon" as the Site of Creativity

Perhaps the obvious starting point to a revisionist view of Babylon is that the benefits of integration into a rich and diverse culture were evident both to many of the first group of Judeans and their immediate descendants. A substantial number adopted Babylonian names and customs; the group as a whole used the Babylonian calendar and embraced the Aramaic language.

Even for those who wished to stay true to their roots, their enforced residence in Babylon provided an opportunity to construct and define their historical experience, to invent their tradition. Myth, folk tales, oral history, and legal records were combined into the embryonic Bible, and the earnest discussion groups at the homes of charismatic figures like Jeremiah and Ezekiel ("the prophets") turned into rudimentary synagogues.

It was, however, the stirring prophecies of a figure known as the second Isaiah (not his real name, but subsequent editors of the Bible perpetuated this error) that galvanised a return movement of the exiles. Isaiah hurled colourful imprecations at Babylon and the Babylonians:

. . . wild beasts of the desert shall lie there;
and their houses shall be full of doleful creatures;
and owls shall dwell there,
and satyrs shall dance there.
And the wild beasts of the islands shall cry in their desolate houses,
and dragons in their pleasant palaces;
and her time is near to come,
and her days shall not be prolonged.
(Isaiah 13:20–22)

While denouncing Babylon, Isaiah hammered home the message that "the remnant of Israel" had to return to Jerusalem to rebuild the Temple. If they did so redemption (another great diasporic theme) would surely follow. Return some did, but the purpose of the journey was neither quite so heroic, nor so spiritually pure, as Isaiah had suggested. Cyrus, the Persian king who had conquered Babylon, permitted and even encouraged the return of groups of Judeans as a form of enlightened colonialism. "It suited him to have an enclave of grateful Jews in Palestine, close to the Egyptian border".[8]

Moreover, the homecoming was far from a triumphant success. The restored Temple (completed in 515 B.C.) was a paltry affair, the priests were venal, and the returnees rubbed raw with the Judeans who had remained. It took a Persian-supported Babylonian priest, Ezra, to implement the law codified in Babylon (the Torah). His reforms led to a much greater ethnic particularism and religious fundamentalism. Although previously common, exogamous marriages were now frowned upon, and the highly prescribed purification rituals (circumcision, atonement, stringent dietary laws, etc.) also date from Ezra's period.

For the next five centuries, the evolution of Judaism in Palestine was marked by apocalyptic dreamers, messianic claimants, zealots, revolutionaries, and mystics. Crude attempts by the Greeks to Hellenize the country (a pig was sacrificed on an altar to Zeus set up in the Temple in 167 B.C.), then to Romanize it, only served to fan the flames of resistance and played into the hands of the fundamentalists.

By contrast, the Jewish communities in Alexandria, in Antioch and Damascus, in Asia Minor, and in Babylon became centres of civilisation, culture, and learning. The Exilarch (the head of the Babylonian Jews) held a position of honour among Jews and non-Jews alike, Jewish academies of learning flourished, and the centre-piece of theological exegesis, the Babylonian Talmud, comprising 2.5 million words, made the religious leaders, the Gaons, the cynosure of Jewish culture until the early eleventh century. Sassanian Persia had provided a cultural mélange of several brands of Christianity, astrology, a Persian literary revival, Zoroastrianism, and Indian and Hellenistic thought. Judaism thrived in this hothouse through engagement, encounter, competition, and the cut and thrust of religious and intellectual debate.

When the Romans destroyed the second Temple in A.D. 70, it was Babylon that remained as the nerve- and brain-centre for Jewish life and thought. Although the word *Babylon* often connotes captivity and oppression, a rereading of the Babylonian period of exile can thus be shown to demonstrate the development of a new creative energy in a challenging, pluralistic context outside the natal homeland. This ancient form of what we would nowadays call "multiculturalism" can be regarded as a precursor of the "hybridity" phenomenon that is celebrated by some contemporary writers in the period of globalisation.

Toynbee on Diasporas

Despite a more positive possible interpretation of the diasporic experience, the negative version of diaspora remained the predominant common and scholarly connotation, a use that was initially reinforced by Arnold Toynbee's powerful early work on the treatment of the Armenians by the Ottomans.[9] His conclusions were both explicit and graphic and he made no bones about accusing the Turks of the perpetration of mass genocide and large-scale atrocities. Nationalist Turkish politicians and historians still vigorously deny this charge and fight the ghost of Toynbee to this day.

What remains undeniable is that the Turkish government ordered the forcible deportation of two-thirds of the 1.75 million Armenians in northeast Turkey to Syria and Palestine and that something like 600,000 people died on the journey. This was a collective affliction that echoed the razing of Jerusalem and the African slave trade. But it was also an anticipatory "break event" in that it provided a rehearsal of the mass displacement of peoples in the face of the intolerant nationalisms and ethnic particularisms characteristic of the twentieth century. There is thus a clear moral, if not causal, connection between the Armenian deportations and events like the mass removals of the Palestinians by the Israelis in 1948, the population swaps between India and Pakistan in 1948–1949, the tit-for-tat expulsions between the Nigerians and the Ghanaians, and the "ethnic cleansing" of inconvenient groups in the microstates that emerged following the disintegration of Yugoslavia and other eastern European states after the collapse of state communism in the late 1980s. Nation-states often mark their birth and infancy with such events.

For the Armenians, the Turkish deportations marked the shocking start of their diasporic experience, with substantial groups settling in the Middle East, France, the United States, and Soviet Armenia. The collective anguish of the deportations meant that the Armenians had joined Jews and Africans to create a group of three traditionally conceived diasporas.

Toynbee's contribution to the interpretation of diasporas was, however, to take a new turn in his monumental *Study of History,* which he commenced in 1927, ultimately producing twelve volumes. The number of overlapping and popular editions, partial revisions, and abridged and compressed versions by his acolytes make it difficult to cite or derive his exact views. None the less, he seems to have been the first modern scholar to use the notion of diaspora in a comparative and analytical sense.

His starting point was a rejection of the nation-state as an effective unit of historical analysis. Instead he proposed to concentrate on "civilisations", twenty-one in the first edition of his work but, by the time the posthumous one-volume version of Toynbee's study was published, he was prepared to admit "up to at least 31, besides a few more that were abortive".[10] One important corrective to his earlier work is that "the formerly unknown history of the indigenous civilisations of Africa to the south of the Sahara has been given its due place side by side with the other regional civilisations".[11] Toynbee's revision was important for undermining those who had attacked his notion of civilisations for having a Eurocentric bias. Although there were undoubtedly Darwinian undertones in much that he wrote, it is doubtful that Toynbee can be meaningfully read as an apologist for European supremacy. Indeed, his celebration of Eastern civilisations was seen by some as an impious attack on the West,[12] and there are many places where he stresses his universal humanism.[13]

Toynbee's world comprised a progression of civilisations dominant until their deaths, a fate often brought about by self-inflicted wounds. But although the Greeks and Armenians qualified as having "civilisations", the Jews decidedly did not. They were either what he called an "abortive civilisation" or, elsewhere, a "fossil of Syriac society". In his posthumous volume, however, Jews are somewhat more flatteringly described as a "model diaspora"—a group he understood as filling the cracks and crannies between the great civilisations and acting as transmission agents, or a sort of service class, to the dominant civilisations of the time. This conception serves to reinforce the view of those who see some diasporas as essentially trading networks.[14]

Diasporas were also important to Toynbee insofar as they typified two possible reactions to the onslaught of a superior civilisation. The two alternatives he suggested were "Zealotism"—an excluding, defensive choice—or "Herodianism"—an accepting, openminded choice—by which he clearly meant, assimilation. In fact, as I hinted in my discussion of Babylon, a diaspora that remains a visible minority (through phenotypical difference or through the maintenance of heterodox rituals, dress codes, or religious practices) rarely has a full Herodian choice. Instead, I would argue that a positive acceptance of difference in an atmosphere of mutual engagement is a third and, in many ways, optimal, choice for a diaspora to survive and thrive. I will return to this argument in my conclusion.

Other Components of the Traditional Notion of Diaspora

The experience of dispersal and collective suffering constitute the key starting points in the definition of the classic diasporas. But if these factors are necessary, they are also insufficient. Three other dimensions were also characteristic of a traditionally conceived diaspora:

- The relationship between a diaspora and its host societies was generally a troubled one.
- A diaspora evidenced a sense of community that transcends national frontiers.
- A diaspora actively participated in the promotion of a return movement (although all certainly would or could not return) and the constitution or reconstitution of a national homeland.

A Troubled Relationship

Each of these features may be observed in the case of the diasporas (Jewish, Armenian, and African) so far identified. With respect to the uneasy social position in host societies, the tortured, self-deprecatory Jewish intellectual has already been magnified into stereotypical cinematic clipboard paste-ins. (Woody Allen has milked this cow virtually dry.) So let me instead cite some illustrative literary quotes of "the troubled relationship" in the cases of Armenians and Africans.

The California-born writer William Saroyan recounts[15] his school days in Fresno and a dialogue with his teacher, Miss Chamberlain. She had reprimanded him for speaking Armenian in class and making the other pupils laugh. Was he making fun of her?

> "No, we just like to talk Armenian once in a while, that's all."
> "But why? This is America, now."
> "The Americans don't like us, so we don't like them."

"So that's it. Which Americans don't like you?"
"All of them."
"Me?"
"Yes, you" . . . ["Americans always stick together"]
"Well maybe we do, but then this *is* America, after all."
"But we're here, too, now, and if you can't stand the only way we can be Americans, too, we'll go right on being Armenians."

This dialogue is instructive in that Armenians are widely thought to have been one of the most dissolvable of the peoples tossed into the so-called American melting pot. At the other end of the spectrum are the New World Africans whose unassimilability is acutely depicted by the African-American writer Richard Wright. Wright[16] uses what he calls a "frog perspective" to

> . . . describe someone looking from below upwards, a sense of someone who feels lower than others. The concept of distance involved here is not physical, it is psychological. . . . A certain degree of hate combined with love (ambivalence) is always involved in looking from below upward, and the object against which the subject is measuring himself undergoes constant change. He loves the object because he would like to resemble it, he hates the object because his chances of resembling it are remote, slight.

Coethnic Communities Abroad

The sense of unease or difference that diaspora peoples feel in their country of settlement is paralleled by a tendency to identify instead with coethnic communities in other countries. Bonds of language, religion, culture, and a sense of a common fate impregnate such a transnational relationship and give to it an affective, intimate quality that formal citizenship or even long settlement frequently lack.

Nonetheless, there is often a great deal of tension in the relationship between scattered coethnic communities. A bond of loyalty to the country of refuge/settlement competes with ethnic solidarity, although there frequently is a considerable reluctance by those who have stepped quite far down Herod's path of assimilation to the majority around them to accept too close a link with a despised or low-status ethnic group abroad, even if it happens to be one's own.

For example, that the image of Africans for many African-Americans was initially largely negative, is indicated by the very recency of the adoption of this hyphenated self-description. Previously, Africa signified enslavement, poverty, denigration, exploitation, white superiority, the loss of language, and the loss of self-respect. It is little wonder that the key basis of the appeal of populist leaders like Marcus Garvey was to the desperate need to escape abasement and to express self-esteem and dignity. Again, Richard Wright, although too sophisticated to sign up himself, was a perceptive observer of the early movements of black consciousness. To him[17] the Garveyites showed

> a passionate rejection of America, for they sensed with a directness of which only the simple are capable that they had no chance to live a full human life in America. . . . The Garveyites had embraced a totally racialist outlook which endowed them with a dignity I had never seen before in Negroes. On the walls of their dingy flats were maps of Africa and India and Japan . . . the faces of coloured men and women from all parts of the world. . . . I gave no credence to the ideology of Garveyism; it was, rather the emotional dynamics of its adherents that evoked my admiration.

The issue of "loyalty" to a country of settlement being challenged by loyalty to one's ethnicity, expressed here for African-Americans, was posed most acutely for European Jewry in the 1840s. At the beginning of that decade the Sharif Pasha of Syria arrested a Jewish barber on the charge of ritual murder, after the mysterious disappearance of an Italian friar and his servant. Confessions under duress, the arrest of Jewish children, and mob violence followed. Because of the then heated European rivalries in the Middle East, the "Damascus Affair" commanded much attention. The French government got drawn into supporting the charges, the Austrian and British governments denounced them.

For French Jewry, a critical moment of crisis had arrived. Although legally emancipated, with long-held views that their adherence to the Jewish religion was no barrier to full citizenship in France,[18] French Jews were suddenly confronted with an impossible dilemma. To advance French international ambitions, the state that had emancipated them was prepared to countenance an anti-Semitic libel. Finally, the initiative was seized by Adolphe Crémieux, a Jew and prominent French politician, who cooperated with eminent Jews in Great Britain and Austria (France's enemies!) to secure the release of the prisoners in Damascus.

The outcome was an apparent victory in humanitarian terms but, as Albert Lindemann shows,[19] it was a Pyrrhic one. Thereafter, French patriots argued that love of their brethren would always be greater than the love of French Jews for France. Jews would always be Jews. Moreover, their increasing prominence in commerce and banking meant that wealthy and powerful Jews could act against the nation's interest. It was but a small step to convince fellow patriots that Jews were part of an omnipotent global conspiracy. Such a widely held perception was later to fuel nineteenth- and twentieth-century anti-Semitism.

Support for a Homeland

The final additional aspect of the traditionally conceived diasporas, their promotion of a national homeland, lends some support to the charges of dual loyalty, even if not to the more fanciful notions of an international conspiracy.

In the case of French Jewry, for instance, the Damascus Affair was followed by an equally momentous event, the Dreyfus Affair, when, in 1894, a French Jewish army officer was falsely accused of spying for the Germans. "The affair" led to a profound change of heart in Teodor Herzl, hitherto a Herodian, bourgeois, Viennese journalist, who had been sent to cover the Dreyfus trial and later became the key advocate of Zionism. More in sadness than in anger, he concluded: "Everywhere we Jews have tried honestly to assimilate into the nations around us, preserving only the religion of our fathers. We have not been permitted to. . . . We are a nation—the enemy has made us one without our desiring it . . . We do have the strength to create a state and, moreover, a model state."[20] Similar feelings of frustration on the part of New World Africans led to the Ethiopian, Garveyite, and Pan-African movements. Just as "Zion" and "Israel" were imagined entities, the African homeland was an equally problematic and fictive community. African hopes sometimes centered on Ethiopia itself particularly after the crowning of Ras (Prince) Tafari as Emperor Haile Selassie of Ethiopia in November 1930. This led directly to the formation of the Rastafarian movement in Jamaica. But for many New World Africans, "Ethiopia" was more of a concept of "blackness" or "Africanity", only loosely connected with the country of Ethiopia itself.[21]

Other Africans in the Americas looked to Liberia—founded by repatriated postemancipation American slaves—for guidance and leadership. Regrettably, the often venal Americo-Liberian élite rarely showed themselves worthy of this regard. Another strand of support for an African homeland came from Caribbean intellectuals who were decisive actors in the Pan-African and nationalist movements of the post-1945 period. The influence of George Padmore and C.L.R. James in anglophone Africa, and Frantz Fanon and Aime Césaire in francophone Africa, has been attested to in many accounts.

In the case of the Armenians, the nationalist movement also developed in the nineteenth century, but the Turks held on fiercely and, as previously discussed, engaged in mass deportations rather than concede to demands for independence. A powerful friend of the Armenians emerged in Joseph Stalin, who, no doubt for his own interests, recognised the Soviet Socialist Republic of Armenia, created in 1920. This provided a homeland of sorts, although the Armenian diaspora in France and the United States felt torn in two ways—between the anticommunist policies of their countries of settlement and their homeland within the Soviet empire, imperfect and incomplete as that undoubtedly was. With the end of the Cold War the prospect dawned for a more open and public identification between the Republic of Armenia (proclaimed in 1990) and the Armenian diaspora, an alliance still complicated, however, by continuing Armenian claims to Turkish Armenia and part of Azerbaijan.

Although the Greek diaspora had been created more by colonisation than by forcible dispersal, the subsequent weakness of the natal country also led to a nationalist awakening. Before the nineteenth century it would have been stretching credulity to call the Greeks "a nation". Dorians, Ionians, and Aeolians were significant subethnicities in ancient Greece, however the major city-states had virtual autonomy one from another. Modern Greek nationalism was much nurtured by what Benedict Anderson called "the golden age of vernacularizing lexicographers, grammarians, philologists, and litterateurs" and by the growth of Philhellenism in the European universities.[22] Modern Greeks were "debarbarized" by this process of rediscovery and urged to be worthy of the likes of Plato, Socrates, and Pericles. The Greek War of Independence attracted the active support of the Philhellenists: The glamorous poet, Lord Byron, joined the Greek insurgents in 1823 and died in the cause. On the success of the insurgency, those bits of ancient Greece that were prised from the Turks were guaranteed independence by British, Russians, and later, the French. The expulsion of nearly 2 million Greeks from Turkey and Bulgaria to Greece and Crete over the period 1919–1920 also dramatically narrowed the ethnic diversity of the area, especially as considerable numbers of Turks and Bulgarians streamed the other way.

Trade and Entrepreneurial Diasporas

Whereas conventional notions of diasporas have often emphasised their catastrophic origins, their mass nature, and their disturbing effects, the expression *diasporas* has also been used to describe networks operating on a smaller scale and on a more benign level. In the classical and early modern periods, small groups of proactive merchants established extensive trading networks to buy and sell their goods, a phenomenon that has been documented for a number of the world's regions.[23] Often vast wealth was accumulated, although in some cases a lucrative trading monopoly combined with great diplomatic skill allowed middlemen to transform themselves into the notables of viable city-states. The most significant example of this outcome is found in sixteenth-century Venice, which commanded the trade between Europe and Asia and sponsored and supported an advanced artistic, cultural, and civic life. However, the power of the Turks in the eastern Mediterranean and the growth of competitive nation-states in western Europe ultimately put paid to Venice's powerful trading position.

With the rise of the imperialist nation-states, trading diasporas often ended up as camp followers of military conquests and colonial expansion by other nations. Take the example of the Lebanese who, from the seventeenth to the nineteenth centuries, went as independent merchants to Egypt and to the centres of trade between Europe and the Middle East (Livorno, Marseilles, and Manchester). The next phase constituted a largely unrestricted migration to North and South America. Finally, after World War I the Lebanese merchants established niches in West Africa and the Caribbean under the aegis of French and British colonial rule. Although many Lebanese started their travels as poor pedlars, by the late twentieth century their descendants boasted a president of Colombia, a prime minister of Jamaica, a majority leader in the U.S. Senate, a Nobel prize-winner for medicine, a president of the Royal Society, a world-famous heart surgeon, and a prize-winning Australian novelist.[24]

Of course, rags-to-riches stories of successful migrants are as common as immigration statistics to the scholar of migration. But the new twist to the argument is the insistence that entrepreneurial success hinged on membership of a trading or business diaspora. Probably the most assertive analysis along these lines is provided by Joel Kotkin in his comparative study of the Jews, the British, the Japanese, the Chinese, and the Indians.[25] Gone, for Kotkin, are the traumas of exile, the troubled relationships with the host culture, Toynbee's somewhat demeaning service-class status, and other negative aspects of the traditionally upheld diasporic condition. Instead, strong diasporas are now represented as the key "to determine success in the global economy". The Jews (once again!) appear as the archetypal "global tribe", possessing the three desiderata of success in the emerging transnational "ethnic economy":

- A strong identity ("a vocation of uniqueness"). This engenders a useful distance from the larger society, fosters self-help and self-employment (nearly half of the Jewish population in diaspora societies are self-employed).
- A global network of mutual trust. Capital and credit can flow freely between family, kin, and even more loosely associated coethnic members. Compared to other ethnic groups, Kotkin asserts, Jews have an extraordinary amount of mutual-aid societies exercising "entrepreneurial collectivism".
- A passion for knowledge. Usually this is reflected in a desire for education or an obsession with certification. But the passion is also adequately or even spectacularly served by intense curiosity, which in Yiddish is called *sechal* (being streetwise or quick-witted). Those with

> sechal often do not need capital because they can quickly intuit business niches (for example in textiles, communications, or the retail sector) left by other more established groups.

Although flawed by being in the breathless, business school "guide-to-success" genre, Kotkin's comparison of European and non-European groups and his unusual inclusion of the British as one of his "business diasporas" provides an effective blend of economic and cultural analysis. The crudities of neoliberal economic-speak are abolished in favour of a more sophisticated Weberian-style account; the implausible invisible hand of the market is replaced by the intimate handshake of ethnic collectivism. Far from being superseded in the age of globalisation, "business diasporas" are seen as a means for adapting to rapid capital flows, the international market for skills, and to the demands of the powerful multinational corporations.

Labour Diasporas

Although trading diasporas were formed by politically and commercially important groups, diasporas could also be constituted by those who left their homelands to find land or work in the New World. In particular, labour migrants flowed to the countries where industrialisation was strongest (particularly in the Americas). The turn away in labour recruitment from the depressed areas of northwest Europe to Southern Europe (particularly Italy, Spain, Portugal, and Greece) occasioned much disquiet in U.S. immigration debates at the end of the nineteenth century. Not only were such migrants regarded as racially inferior, they were seen as bearing dangerous cosmopolitan and international ideas. Indeed, international socialism, anarchism, and labour unionism were often spread by turn-of-the-twentieth-century labour migrants. There were brief moments when the economic and political activities of the imported labourers looked like they might constitute a serious potential threat to local capital accumulation in Canada, the United States, Argentina, Peru, Australia, and so on. But, in the end, militant political unionism in the United States[26] gave way to bread-and-butter unionism or to relatively benign forms of corporatism, like Peronism in Argentina. Most labour migrants adopted local citizenships and local loyalties that did not fundamentally threaten the construction of the nation-state.

In what sense then can labour migrants become a diaspora? Clearly a powerful and continuing link with the homeland is the sine qua non. In the modern period this is true perhaps, above all other contenders, of the Italian workers. However, it is easy to over-simplify a much more complex tug of loyalties. Donna Gabaccia's sensitive study[27] of Italian labour migration shows how internationalism (in anarchist and socialist varieties), exile politics, Italian worker solidarity, natal village and regional sentiments, and fealty to "the country that gave them their bread", all made claims on Italian workers. However, "the bottom line", as Gabaccia acknowledges, was that at the outbreak of war in 1914, the countries of residence were able to force a primacy of loyalty on nearly all of their residents.

The Newer Claimants to Diaspora Status

In 1991 the UN recognised 160 states; by the end of the century perhaps another 30 will be added to its membership. However, the number of "nation-peoples" (groups evincing a "peoplehood" through the retention or expression of separate languages, customs, folkways, and religions) is estimated at 2,000, over ten times the anticipated number of recognised nation-states. There is an increasing recognition that such peoples are only imperfectly, and sometimes only violently, held within the confines of the existing nation-states as the multiplicity of secessionist movements, ethnic demands, civil wars, and the fragmentation of the former USSR and several of the eastern European states testify.

Even within settled liberal democracies, the old assumption that immigrants would identify with their adopted country in terms of political loyalty, culture, and language can no longer be taken for granted. To the largely free immigrants of old, are added refugees and exiles (now numbering 17 million worldwide) whose movement was primarily dictated by circumstances in their home countries rather than by a desire to establish a new life. Often received with hostility and resentment by the indigenous populations, there is little bonding in the new setting.

In short, "homeland", that "other place", often buried deep in language, religion, custom, collective historical memory, or folklore, has a continuing claim on the loyalty of many contemporary minority communities. That claim may be strong or weak, boldly or meekly articulated in a given circumstance or historical period, but a member's adherence to natal community rather than a country of settlement is demonstrated by an acceptance that the link with the past is unavoidable and acknowledged to be inescapable. This crucial feature of a transnational identity has produced a rash of externally labeled and self-identified diasporas. I have already alluded to the Lebanese trading and Italian labour diasporas. Other claimants include the Chinese, Indian, Polish, Japanese, Ukrainian, Irish, Palestinian, Sikh, Caribbean, German, British, Portuguese, Turkish, and Kurdish diasporas. No doubt other serious candidates can be added to the list.

Do we, in our contemporary understanding of *diaspora,* wish to let "a thousand flowers bloom", thereby diluting the force of the original concepts, or should there be some clear criteria for membership of this hitherto rather exclusive club? My view is an intermediate one. It seems useful for comparative and analytical purposes to retain some of the defining characteristics of the traditionally conceived diasporas, while simultaneously striving to show openness to the newer aspects arising from the mass movements of population in the nineteenth and twentieth centuries and the crisis of the nation-state as we approach the twenty-first century.

At the risk of some repetition, it may be helpful to provide an initial indicative list of the criteria (implicitly) established earlier in the cases of the traditionally conceived, trading and labour diasporas, as a basis for comparing the superficially observed characteristics of some of the newer claimants to diaspora status:[28]

Dispersal and Scattering

Jews and Armenians were dispersed to such an extent that their diaspora populations massively outnumbered the homeland population: Indeed, although Zionists vehemently affirm the opposite, it is doubtful that a continuous history of settlement of the Jews in Palestine can be established. The number of diaspora Africans amounts to about 40 million people, about a tenth of the black African population.

On the list of newer claimants, the Palestinians have an unambiguous case of virtually complete population dispersal, whereas the Irish lost 25 percent of their homeland population between 1845 and 1851, the years of the potato famine. Lebanon also experienced very heavy population losses—again about 25 percent of the population before 1914 and a similar loss consequent on the civil war of the 1970s.[29] Although net migration losses were heavy in the case of some of the new claimants, they rarely constituted a serious drain on the capacity for internal reproduction. And, in the case of the larger population groups (for example, the Chinese and Indians), the proportion of the overseas to home population was very small. Although numbers are often significant in that a large loss of population can produce a sense of collective distress, who is lost to the homeland (for example, young people, or people of talent, education, and energy) can also create a source of deep anxiety in the homeland population.

A Collective Trauma

In general terms, it is remarkably difficult to separate out the compelling from the voluntary elements in the motivation to migrate.[30] But when we are talking of a trauma afflicting a group collectively, it is perhaps possible to isolate those events where the suddenness, scale, and intensity of exogenous factors unambiguously compel migration or flight. Being dragged off in manacles (as were the Jews and African captives) or being coerced to leave by force of arms (as were the Armenians) appear to be qualitatively different phenomena from the general pressures of overpopulation, land hunger, poverty, or an unsympathetic political regime.

Of the newly named diasporas, Irish writers emphasise the catastrophic origins of large-scale Irish migration, bitterly recalling both the brutality of English occupation and the ordeal of the famine. James Joyce in *Ulysses* (the title, significantly, is the Latin name for Odysseus) puts these words into the mouth of a Dublin citizen: "We have our greater Ireland beyond the sea. They were driven out of house and home in the black 1847 [the year of the potato famine].. . . Ay they drove out the peasants in hordes, twenty thousand of them died in the coffin-ships. But those that came to the land of the free remember the land of bondage." The language used here evokes the biblical Jews and the African slaves, a clear cross-identification with two of the classical diasporas. The Palestinians were also violently displaced by the Israeli Zionists who asserted the right—narrowly recognised in a United Nations vote—to a Jewish state. Some 780,000 Arabs were expelled from the territory controlled by the Israeli army, and a further 120,000 Palestinians were later classified as refugees, because they had lost their homes and livelihoods.[31]

The remaining diaspora claimants represent cases with a mixture of underlying causes (poverty, insecure land tenure, overpopulation, etc.) of migration combined with a variety of more immediate precipitating causes that served to accelerate the underlying movement or give to it a particular source or direction.

A Cultural Flowering in the Diaspora

I have alluded to the early case of the achievement of the Jews in Babylon as one example of this phenomenon. Despite their bitter privations, other groups have also made cultural contributions of global significance. Africans in the diaspora produced prominent musical forms like spirituals, jazz, blues, rock 'n' roll, calypso, and reggae; initiated major innovations in the performing arts; and generated a rich vein of literature and poetry. (The first two Nobel laureates for literature in the 1990s were New World writers of African descent.)

It is perhaps the case (although my view is very impressionistic here) that the Armenian and Greek contributions in the diaspora were somewhat less impressive, as both tended to concentrate on the preservation of their great traditions rather than on making a contribution to popular culture in their countries of settlement. Nonetheless, the interrogation of the old culture with the new provided noteworthy achievements among all groups. The Philhellenism movement allowed the diasporic Greeks to be living bearers of the received virtues of the ancient Greeks—in particular, to their philosophical insights, mathematical genius, and democratic spirit. Literature in the British diaspora (in Australia, South Africa, and the United States) soon rivaled, then outstripped native-grown English literature in its vigour and interest. V. S. Naipaul and Salman Rushdie are just two of the sparkling, creative writers of the Indian diaspora.

A Trading and Business Network

The suggestion that a diaspora could be considered a service class, which I drew from Toynbee's work, probably works best in those cases of modern diasporas where an intermediary trading role was assumed by a group whose numbers in any one country were insufficient to set up an ethnic enclave of any economic significance. I have already mentioned the case of the Lebanese. Chinese traders in Southeast Asia and Indian merchants in East Africa are analogous examples. The concept of "middleman minority" is a generally accepted sociological characterisation of such groups.[32]

Labour Migrants as Diasporas

Probably the most useful distinction to be drawn under this heading is that between diasporas that arose from the export of slave or unfree labour (for example Africans in the Americas or Indian indentured labour in the tropical plantations) on the one hand, and the diasporas of "free" labour on the other. The coerced labourers often clung tenaciously to old customs, languages, religions, and folkways, despite the brutal rupture arising from their mass transportation and exploitation. In the case of the "free" labourers, it would clearly be absurd to describe all who migrate for work as constituting a diaspora. Their reception in the place of work, their degree of autonomous organisation, the level of retention of the "old ways", and above all their links to their homeland or to other coethnic groups in other countries would determine whether the label "labour diaspora" is appropriate or meaningful.

A Troubled Relationship with the Majority

There is barely a migrant ethnic minority that did not at some stage experience discrimination in the countries of their migration. Whether it be Chinese in Malaya, Poles in Germany, Italians in Switzerland, Japanese in Peru, Irish in England, Palestinians in Kuwait, Caribbean peoples in Europe, Sikhs in Britain, Turks and Rom in Germany, or Kurds in Turkey—all these and many others experienced antagonism, legal or illegal discrimination, and have become the objects of violent hatred by majority populations. However, interethnic tension only becomes part of a diasporic phenomenon when disadvantaged groups look outside (for comfort, comparison, and identification) their immediate context to other coethnic communities elsewhere and to the possibility of return to the "homeland". In other words, the possibilities for the redress of their conditions through local representation, civic action, or political agitation must be limited.

I suggested that marginalisation of migrant ethnic groups is a fairly universal phenomenon. The major exceptions to this rule are those diasporas that were either aspiring or real settler colonies. The British in the Dominions and North America, the Portuguese in Brazil, and (for a time) the Spanish in the Americas, the French in Canada, and the Dutch in South Africa were able to establish their own hegemony in language, law, religious observance, property rights, and political institutions, thereby forcing the indigenees on to the defensive.

Transcending National Frontiers

So we arrive by a circuitous route to the point from which we started. Some diasporas were already scattered before the modern nation-state was invented or universalised. They are, if you like, survivals of a pre-nation-state form. The next wave—African, Chinese, Indian, Japanese, perhaps Irish—transcended the nation-state in another way—through being used by the advancing colonising powers as workers in their plantation colonies. The trading diasporas gained their comparative advantage precisely by moving between nations and modes of production (just as, for Toynbee, they acted as interlocuteurs between civilisations). But they had at least to become formally subordinate to the purposes of the imperial powers. Fully fledged "labour diasporas" were a rarer occurrence, but one can occasionally observe a transnational consciousness and pattern of organisation. Finally, it may be worth alluding to the case of the Rom ("Gypsies"), who have remained sublimely indifferent to the doctrines of national sovereignty that has pervaded much of the rest of humankind.[33]

Promoting a Return Movement

All the traditionally accepted diasporas ultimately were influenced by the lure of nationalism—the creation of an Armenian homeland, Philhellenism, Zionism, and Pan-Africanism—as the only certain means to protect their precarious and isolated existence outside their natal areas. Return movements, nationalist awakenings, and improvement schemes for homelands also were common in later diasporas. Although born in China, Sun Yixian (Sun Yat-sen) developed his political consciousness in Hong Kong and Hawaii. His Society for the Revival of China was a crucial instrument in the promotion of a modern Chinese nationalism. His career is interestingly paralleled by that of Mazzini; again born in Italy, but finding an echo for his republican and nationalist ideals largely in the Italian labour diaspora.

To conclude this section, my comparisons between the accepted diasporas and the newer claimants along eight criteria has yielded significant variations, but sufficient common ground to suggest that it is more than poetic license to describe a number of modern peoples as constituting a "diaspora". It is clear that their diasporic consciousness is often in direct contradiction to the exclusivist claims of the modern nation-state and that this has sometimes created major bifurcations of loyalty, identity, ideology, and consciousness.

Diasporas in "The Age of Globalisation"

What is meant here by *globalisation,* now such a powerful keyword in the social sciences? There is here a fortunate congruence of the common sociological preference for "process" with historian Raymond Grew's insistence that aspects of globality that are deemed unique may merely point to "a very long process of globalisation—one that could be extended much farther into the past".[34] I concur too with Grew in his view that global history starts with a sense that a transformation that recently became visible is destined to become universal. Thus, to designate a period "an age of globalisation" is neither to assume that all aspects of globality are in place, nor that they have not been prefigured. Instead, what is suggested is that a new tempo and intensity of existing features are now in evidence and likely to become dominant. Among the many features of globalisation that could be identified, I would like to emphasise four:

- A world economy with quicker and denser transactions between its subsectors and regions due to better communications, cheaper transport, and the effects of liberal trade and capital-flow policies.
- Forms of international migration that emphasise contractual relationships, intermittent postings abroad, and sojourning, as opposed to permanent settlement and the exclusive adoption of the citizenship of a destination country.
- Transnational social movements that have seriously undermined the nation-state as a focus of political organisation and action.
- A cosmopolitan and hybridised culture created and sustained by satellite transmissions, videos, tourism, advertisements, and the global media and entertainment industries.

Each of these aspects of globalisation, although in different ways, has opened up the spaces for diasporas to survive and thrive.

A World Economy

Let me start first with a world economy. By being attached to a strong, tightly integrated, and effective diaspora, economic transactions can adjust to the global scale and assume a rational, functional, productive, and progressive character.

International Migration

In the age of globalisation there are no countries that welcome mass migration. Even where selective migration is welcomed, states have sought to prevent the settlement of unskilled, old, or dependent migrants. This tendency has given new life to an old diasporic practice—that of "sojourning" (a cyclical pattern of migration and return common among Chinese, Mexicans, Italians, and others). As Wang Gungwu[35] has pointed out, many of today's "global" migrants are people of considerable wealth and portable skills, a group different from the unskilled labour migrants of the nineteenth century and the refugees and tightly controlled contract workers of more recent decades:

> new classes of people educated in a whole range of modern skills are now prepared to migrate or re-migrate and respond to the pull of centres of power and wealth and the new opportunities in trade and industry. Even more than the traditional sojourners of Southeast Asia, these people are articulate, politically sensitive and choose their new homes carefully. They study the migrant states, especially their laws on the rights of immigrants and the economic conditions for newcomers. . . . Furthermore many are masters not only in the handling of official and bureaucratic connection but also in the art of informal linkages.

As the same author notes, the Chinese sojourner *(huaqiao)* was regarded with considerable suspicion by nationalists in the emerging postwar states of Southeast Asia, especially after the governments in Beijing and Taipei sought to command the migrants' ultimate loyalty. Like the Indians in East Africa or the Lebanese in West Africa and the Caribbean, the colonial powers, notably the Dutch in Indonesia and the British in Malaya and Singapore, had "noted the usefulness of the Chinese as local experts and middlemen, more useful than other Asian traders who were not as widespread and who did not have their inter-port networks".[36]

Ultimately, the networks established in colonial times were superseded by the emergence of migration opportunities in Canada, the United States, and Australia. Sojourners to the new destinations were helped by the global communications and transport revolutions, the stronger legal protection accorded to minorities in the receiving countries, and by the adaptable tradition of sojourning itself.

Transnational Social Movements

In his discussion of nationalism, Eric Hobsbawm cites some telling figures charting the increasing shift away from the nation-state as a focus of political action and social engagement. The number of intergovernmental international organisations grew from 123 in 1951 to 280 in 1972 and 365 in 1984. The number of nongovernmental organisations showed an even more spectacular leap—from 832 in 1951, to 2,173 in 1972, and 4,615 in 1984.[37] The emergence of the three great regional economic blocs—the European Community, the North American Free Trade Area, and the Asia-Pacific region—will increasingly involve a network of political, cultural, and social organisations designed to build affiliations of a more social kind to the compelling economic logics of these blocs. Finally, global social movements linking women, the greens, the antinuclear and disarmament movement, human rights, and charitable organisations, have all been added in the post-war world to virtually the only transnational social movement in the pre-1945 period—the international labour movement.

When the followers of the labour Internationals proclaimed that workers had no country, they were decisively contradicted by the appeals to patriotism and jingoism in 1914: The workers meekly lining up behind the kings, kaisers, and czars to slaughter each other. Given the spread of supranational, inter- and nongovernmental organisations and global social movements, one can hardly imagine a nation-state being able today to command a similar obedience. (Governments in liberal-democratic states, Israel excepted, now have to rely on professional soldiers to fight their wars; the attempt by the United States to use drafted soldiers in Vietnam having ended in defeat.)

What has all this to do with diasporas? The point here is a simple one. Like the worker internationalists of 1914, those who wanted to retain open diasporic links were pitched against powerful, hegemonizing nation-states who sought to make an exclusive citizenship a defining focus of allegiance and fidelity. The world is simply not like that anymore; the space for multiple affiliations and associations that has been opened up outside and beyond the nation-state has also allowed a diasporic affiliation to become both more open and more acceptable.

Cosmopolitan and Hybridised Cultures

The final aspect of diasporas in the age of globalisation that I want to consider here is the cultural one. Diasporic communities have always been in a better position to interrogate the particular with the universal. They are better able to discern what their own group shares with other groups and where its cultural norms and social practices threaten majority groups. Such awareness, to echo an earlier remark, constitutes the major component of sechal, without which survival itself might be threatened. It is perhaps because of this need to be sensitive to the currents around one, that diaspora groups are typically overrepresented in arts, the cinema, and the entertainment industry. Awareness of their precarious situation may also propel members of diasporas to advance legal and civic causes and to be active in human rights and social justice issues.

Although knowledge and sensibilities might have enlarged to the point of cosmopolitanism (or universal humanism), at the same time traditional cultural values have often been reasserted. Thus, as the postmodernists have argued, a perverse feature of globalisation at the cultural level is that it has also brought about the fragmentation and multiplication of identities. This may require, paradoxically, a return to the local and the familiar. Stuart Hall is perhaps the most insightful observer of this condition:

> The face-to-face communities that are knowable, that are locatable, one can give then a place. One knows what the voices are. One knows what the faces are. The re-creation, the reconstruction of imaginary, knowable places in the face of the global post-modern which has, as it were, destroyed the identities of specific places, absorbed them into this post-modern flux of diversity. So one understands the moment when people reach for those groundings, as it were, and the reach for those groundings is what I call ethnicity.[38]

Although this is a rather idiosyncratic view of ethnicity in general, elsewhere Hall reminds us that an ethnicity, a cultural identity, is not a "fixed essence".[39] Instead, it is constructed though a blend of memory, fantasy, narrative, and myth. (Many anthropologists, of course, were aware of this already: So this insight was not quite so innovative as postmodernists appear to believe.) But Hall takes this idea much further trying, in particular, to battle with how a Caribbean identity might be defined.

This, he suggests, cannot be rendered simply as a transposition of a New World African identity because the rupture of slavery and the admixture of other peoples built into a Caribbean identity a sense of hybridity, diversity, and difference. He poses the question, "What makes African-Caribbean people already people of a diaspora?" and answers as follows:

> diaspora does not refer us to those scattered tribes whose identity can only be secured in relation to some sacred homeland to which they must at all costs return, even if it means pushing other people into the sea. This is the old, the imperializing, the hegemonizing form of "ethnicity". We have seen the fate of the people of Palestine at the hands of this backward conception of diaspora—and the complicity of the West with it. The diaspora experience as I intend it here is defined not by essence or purity, but by the recognition of a necessary heterogeneity and diversity; by a conception of identity which lives with and through, not despite, difference; by hybridity. Diaspora iden-

tities are those which are constantly producing and reproducing themselves anew, through transformation and difference.[40]

Hall's notion of diaspora I shall crudely designate as "postmodern", even though he distances himself from some aspects of this intellectual movement. It is postmodern in the sense that he wants to use the notion of diaspora to describe contemporary identities, while nonetheless lifting the notion from its history—in particular from its moorings in the catastrophic and territorializing tradition.

His work is paralleled and extended by that of Paul Gilroy who also wants to free *diaspora* from its associations with kinship and territory and can see in the notion a means of describing a creative, syncretic culture that draws on African, American, Caribbean, and European elements.[41] This emergent culture is briefly characterised as "the Black Atlantic", but his ambitious work (which needs much more exegesis than I have time to give it here) is also a comment on the nature of modernity, on the idea of a nationalism without a nation-state (or a territory), and on the idea of a "double consciousness" prefigured in Hegelian phenomenology. Two observations can be made of Gilroy's work. First it is suggestive to note that both he and Stuart Hall articulate the "double consciousness" of Caribbean peoples in Europe. Like many Chinese in the Pacific Basin, Australasia, and the United States, and like the East African Asians, the Caribbean peoples in Europe are remigrants, twice migrants, or (what I've called elsewhere) "a diaspora of a diaspora".[42] This feature may make such groups particularly open to creative hybridity in their cultural and intellectual responses. (This is certainly true of the individuals themselves, both Hall and Gilroy being widely regarded as two of Britain's leading intellectuals.) My second observation is that Gilroy and Hall have very different trajectories with respect to the relationship between the postmodern diasporas and the Jewish diaspora. Whereas Hall (in the quotation I used previously) explicitly distances himself from an old "imperializing", "backward", diaspora, Gilroy explicitly acknowledges his debt for the "inspiration and resources" provided by Jewish thinkers who helped him "to map the ambivalent experiences of blacks inside and outside modernity". He hopes that this appreciation "might contribute to a better political relationship between Jews and blacks at some distant future point".[43] A brave wish indeed, in view of the current climate of opinion in the United States between the two groups.

Conclusion

What I have suggested in this account is that notions of "diaspora" are remarkably diverse. The original Greek word, which signified expansion and settler colonisation can best be compared to the European (especially British, Portuguese, and Spanish) settlements of the mercantile and colonial period. But the expression was "hijacked" to describe a catastrophic dispersal of a people and their subsequent unhappiness (or assumed unhappiness) in their countries of exile. More specialist uses of the expression can also be found in the notions of trade and labour diasporas.

Straddling these meanings is Toynbee's apparently idiosyncratic notion of a diaspora forming the transaction points between two or more great civilisations. But, although this notion of a service class is specific to Toynbee, it is a kindred concept to the notion of a "middleman minority" in the colonial areas and among other modern diasporas. It may also work quite well to describe the skilled sojourners in the period of globalisation. The modern period introduced a whole host of new diasporas although the very attribution of the term, and therefore the characteristics associated with diaspora, are both still a matter of contestation and debate. Clearly some parallels persist, but there is still uncertainty as to which features of diaspora are necessary or merely contingent.

This sense of dropping off inconvenient bits of the descriptions of classical diasporas that do not apply, or that the authors do not wish to apply, is apparent particularly in the global phase. At one level globalisation has simply allowed diasporas to "come out"—rather like a more relaxed attitude toward gender issues allowed gays to declare themselves. At another level, globalisation has enhanced the practical, economic, and affective roles of diasporas, showing them to be particularly adaptive forms of social organisation. Some diasporas appear to have mutated across several phases and assumed different forms, refurbishing themselves as they go along. (It seems uncanny, for example, how Jews are singled out as the exemplary case by different authors, at different periods, whatever notions of diaspora are being advanced.)

Diasporas have also been at some level an alternative form of social organisation to the singular identity demanded by the hegemonising nation-state. Just as prior ethnic identities were not melted in the melting pot, so too did a diasporic consciousness survive in the interstices of the modern nation-state. Just as anti-Semites sigh with apparent resignation at the reappearance of "the eternal Jew" (despite forcible conversion, discrimination, and genocidal onslaughts), it may be that diasporas, seen as forms of social organisation, have predated the nation-state, lived within it, and now may, in significant respects, transcend and succeed it.

Finally, although this is as yet unfinished business, we should bear in mind the challenging notions of Hall and Gilroy that global diasporas have themselves become the sites for the creation and elaboration of new, original, hybridised cultures. The plasticity and complexity of postmodern identities are such, so these writers suggest, that there is no question of recovering the essence of the original identity. Instead, fragments of a mythologized past are combined with a fractured, multicultural, multi-sourced present to create a new "ethnicity". This form of local bonding, this "grounding", is necessary precisely because globalisation has threatened our structures of meaning and meaningfulness. Diasporas, traditionally conceived, modern, global, and newly affirmed, may provide a vital bridge between the individual and society, between the local and the global. The sense of uprootedness, of disconnection, loss, and estrangement, which hitherto was morally appropriated by the traditionally recognised diasporas may now signify something of the human condition. Emphasising the creative, enriching side of "Babylon", the radiance of difference, may provide a new form of universal humanism.

Notes

1. Wang Gungwu, "Migration and Its Enemies", in Bruce Mazlish and Ralph Buultjens, eds., *Conceptualizing Global History* (Boulder: Westview Press, 1993), pp. 131–132.

2. Nathan Glazer and Patrick Moynihan, *Beyond the Melting Pot: The Negroes, Puerto Rican, Jews, Italian, and Irish of New York City* (Cambridge, Mass.: Massachusetts Institute of Technology Press, 1963).

3. Glazer and Moynihan, *Beyond the Melting Pot.*

4. The use of *globalisation* here is not to say that all aspects of globality are only recent phenomena but merely to imply that only in more recent decades is there a sufficient density of flows of technology, peoples, ideas, and cultures for us to designate our age as "the age of globalisation" (see later).

5. See Stefan Helmreich, "Kinship, Nation, and Paul Gilroy's Concept of Diaspora", *Diaspora 2* (2)1992, who also notes that the patriarchal connection to the word is quite strong, the scattering or sowing of seeds being closely related, in Judeo-Christian and Islamic cosmology, to male sperm. A more gender-neutral inflection is given by Liisa Malkki, "National Geographic: The Rooting of Peoples and the Territorialization of National Identity Among Scholars and Refugees", *Cultural Anthropology,* vol. 7, 1992, pp. 24–44, who shows that arboreal metaphors ("roots", "soils", "family trees", etc.) are closely related to ideas of kinship and national identity.

6. David J. Goldberg and John D. Raynor, *The Jewish People: Their History and Their Religion* (Harmondsworth, Engl.: Penguin, 1989), pp. 46–48.

7. Ken Post, *Arise Ye Starvelings: The Jamaican Labour Rebellion of 1938 and Its Aftermath* (The Hague: Martinus Nijhoff, 1978), p. 172.

8. Goldberg and Raynor, *The Jewish People,* p. 53.

9. Arnold Toynbee, *Armenian Massacres: The Murder of a Nation* (London: Hodder and Stoughton, 1915); Arnold Toynbee, ed, *The Treatment of Armenians in the Ottoman Empire, 1915–1916* (London: Her Majesty's Stationary Office, 1916).

10. Arnold Toynbee, *A Study of History,* abridged ed. (with Jane Caplan) (London: Oxford University Press, 1988). First published 1972.

11. Toynbee, *A Study of History,* abridged ed., pp. 12–13.

12. Douglas Jerrold, *The Lie About the West: A Response to Professor Toynbee's Challenge* (New York: Sheed and Ward, 1953).

13. For example, Toynbee, *A Study of History*, vol. 1, 1934, pp. 207–249; Toynbee, *A Study of History*, abridged ed., p. 11; Arnold Toynbee, *A Study of History*, 12 vols. (London: Oxford University Press, 1934–1961).

14. This interpretation of Toynbee is strengthened by his reference (Toynbee, *A Study of History*, 12 vols.) to the Scots and the Lebanese as "diasporas". He even surmises that the professional classes from all cultural backgrounds may become a sort of diaspora in themselves, in that their skills had become in demand worldwide, rather than in particular countries.

15. William Saroyan, *Here Comes There Goes You Know Who: An Autobiography* (London: Peter Davies, 1961), pp. 87–88.

16. Cited in Bernard Makhosezwe Magubane, *The Ties That Bind: African-American Consciousness of Africa* (Trenton, N.J.: Africa World Press, 1987), p. 19.

17. Richard Wright, *American Hunger* (New York: Harper and Row, 1944), p. 28.

18. The compatibility between citizenship of a country of settlement and religious belief was a common, although not of course universally held view among emancipated European Jews. Notable dissenters included Daniel Halévy, an eminent Frenchman of letters, who thought it essential to escape the confines of a traditional religion: "How happy I am to have left that hell, to have escaped from Judaism". The German poet Heinrich Heine, who also had Jewish ancestry, was equally blunt. Judaism was not a religion but a misfortune: "Those who would say Judaism is a religion would say that being a hunchback is a religion". Quotes from Albert S. Lindemann, *The Jew Accused. Three Anti-Semitic Affairs: Dreyfus, Beilis, Frank, 1884–1915* (Cambridge: Cambridge University Press, 1991) pp. 15 and 62.

19. Lindemann, *The Jew Accused*, pp. 35–93.

20. Cited in Goldberg and Raynor, *The Jewish People*, p. 166.

21. This usage is closer to the Greek meaning, which translates as "burnt face", and to the seventeenth-century English understanding, which equated "Ethiopian" with "black".

22. Benedict Anderson, *Imagined Communities: Reflections on the Origin and Spread of Nationalism* (London: Verso, 1983), p. 69.

23. Philip Curtin, *Cross-Cultural Trade in World History* (New York: Cambridge University Press, 1984); Wang Gungwu, *China and the Chinese Overseas* (Singapore: Times Academic Press, 1992). Chapter 4, "Merchants Without Empires: The Hokkien Sojourning Communities" is especially significant.

24. Albert Hourani, "Introduction", in Albert Hourani and Nadim Shehadi, eds., *The Lebanese in the World: A Century of Emigration* (London: I.B. Tauris Centre for Lebanese Studies, 1993), pp. 5–9.

25. Joel Kotkin, *Tribes: How Race, Religion, and Identity Determine Success in the New Global Economy* (New York: Random House, 1993). His headline-grabbing principal title to describe the phenomenon he observes, "Tribes", does not merit serious dissection as it is not used analytically but is simply meant to evoke a powerful sense of ethnic solidarity among the five groups he depicts.

26. See Sidney Lens, *The Labor Wars* (New York: Anchor Books, 1974).

27. Donna Gabaccia, "Worker Internationalism and Italian Labour Migration, 1870–1914", *International Labor and Working-Class History* (forthcoming). See also

John A. Armstrong, "Mobilized and Proletarian Diasporas", *American Political Science Review* 70 (2)1976, pp. 393–403.

28. I emphasise again the tentative and rough-and-ready basis of this comparison. However, this chapter will later form part of an introductory volume to a more systematically conceived seventeen-volume, multiauthored series on diasporas to be produced by UCL Press, London, and edited by the current author.

29. Hourani and Shehadi, *Lebanese,* 1992.

30. Relevant discussion can be found in Robin Cohen, *The New Helots: Migrants in the International Division of Labour* (Aldershot, Engl.: Gower, 1987), pp. 33–42; Anthony H. Richmond, "Sociological Theories of International Migration: The Case of Refugees", *Current Sociology* 36 (2)1988, pp. 7–26; and Aristide Zolberg et al., *Escape from Violence: Conflict and the Refugee Crisis in the Developing World* (New York: Oxford University Press, 1989), pp. 258–282.

31. Janet Lippman Abu-Lughod, "The Palestinians in 1948", in Robin Cohen, ed., *The Cambridge Survey of World Migration* (Cambridge: Cambridge University Press, 1995).

32. This concept is richly developed in Edna Bonacich and John Modell, *The Economic Basis of Ethnic Solidarity* (Berkeley: University of California Press, 1980).

33. But, by the same token, their lack of interest in a national homeland (other than some putative affiliations to Indian roots) may mean that the Rom should not be counted as a diaspora at all.

34. Raymond Grew, "On the Prospect of Global History", in Mazlish and Bultjens, *Conceptualizing Global History,* p. 228.

35. Wang Gungwu, "Sojourning: The Chinese Experience in Southeast Asia", Jennifer Cushman Memorial Lecture, mimeo., 1992.

36. Wang Gungwu, "Sojourning".

37. Eric Hobsbawm, *Nations and Nationalism Since 1780* (Cambridge: Cambridge University Press, 1992), p. 181.

38. Stuart Hall, "The Local and the Global: Globalisation and Ethnicity", in Anthony D. King, ed., *Culture, Globalisation, and the World-System: Contemporary Conditions for the Representations of Identity* (Basingstoke, Engl.: Macmillan, 1991), pp. 35–36.

39. Stuart Hall, "Cultural Identity and Diaspora", in Jonathan Rutherford, ed., *Identity: Community, Culture, Difference* (London: Lawrence and Wishart, 1990), pp. 222–237.

40. Hall, "Cultural Identity and Diaspora", p. 235.

41. Paul Gilroy, *The Black Atlantic: Modernity and Double Consciousness* (London: Verso, 1993). See also Gilroy's *There Ain't No Black in the Union Jack* (London: Hutchinson, 1987) and his "Cultural Studies and Ethnic Absolutism", in Lawrence Grossberg et al., eds., *Cultural Studies* (New York: Routledge, 1991). A premature and not very fleshed-out critique of Gilroy's ideas was provided in Stefan Helmreich, "Kinship, Nation, and Paul Gilroy's Concept of Diaspora", written before the crucial work was published.

42. Robin Cohen, "La diaspora d'une diaspora: le cas des Antilles", in R. Gallissot, ed., *Pluralisme Cultural en Europe* (Paris: L'Harmattan, 1993), pp. 61–77.

43. Paul Gilroy, *Black Atlantic,* pp. 205–206.

6

Migrant Workers, Markets, and the Law

Yash Ghai[1]

Migration, markets, and the law are among the major factors that have facilitated globalisation across regions and continents. Starting from the 1500s, migration has brought the world closer and resulted in the diffusion (and sometimes the destruction) of cultures, linking people across continents and sovereignties. The causes of migration were several, ranging from the escape from religious persecution and the search for a better life to slavery and servitude, but the market has been the major incentive for, and organiser of, migrations.[2] The spread of the market is responsible more than any other factor for the integration of the world (not just its economies), the hegemony or demise of cultures, the universalisation of production processes, and the emergence of a common worldview. It has, in Marx's evocative expression, destroyed the Great Wall of China. For the market requires more than economic processes for its operation; it needs the politicisation of space—an organised community, legalisation of the use of force, rules, adjudication, and ideology (and more, especially in the days of mercantilism, which appeared in the early days of our story).

The law has played an important (even though secondary) role in the globalisation of the market, at least after the initial processes of "primitive accumulation" when lands were appropriated and labour generated through the compulsion of armed force. The market was built on and reinforced "asymmetries" in the world, and law played its due role in that process. But the law also bore elements of liberalism within it and the contradictions within the law generated dialetics between crude market forces and the humanising and civilising influences that have been so visible in the gradual development of the legal and social position of migrants. The needs of the market may be affected by other factors such as racism, a theme which is explored later through an examination of the post-1971 reaction in the West to immigration. There is, however, another sense in which the law has been part of the globalisation process: in the spread across the world of major families of legal regimes and in the interaction between (and subjugation of) legal systems. Migrants carried their law with them (except for the most oppressed, the slaves): the workers merely their personal law, the privileged European settlers, colonising vast spaces of the world, also their public law. European merchants, in alien places, carved their own legal enclaves (as in Macao) and elsewhere secured their native law through regimes of extraterritoriality (as in China, Egypt, etc.). The law, as ever, reflects and reproduces hierarchies, while professing equality of all before it.

Thus migration, markets, and the law intersect at so many points and in so many varied ways that the scope of a paper on this subject would be vast. And it would be also an untidy paper, since the legal regime governing migration and the rights and liabilities of migrants is diverse and fragmented, its underlying principles confused and inchoate. The right to enter and leave a country, protection against expulsion from a country, the rights to seek and keep employment, to a pension, to equality, to the family, social security, language, education and culture, and to participate in trade union affairs, for example, which are inextricably connected to the legal situation of migrants, are covered by different systems, principles of the law and disparate sovereignties. These are dealt with in different ways in different jurisdictions, determined in part by historical traditions, making it extremely hard to generalise in this area. Doctrines of state sovereignty still govern many of these matters, although there has been a progressive development of regional and global regimes and principles. It is in the interaction between the domestic and international systems and principles that lies the solution to many of the legal issues relating to migration and migrants. Not surprisingly more progress toward universalisation and harmonisation of the position of migrants has been made at the regional levels than the international, with nationality still a central, although diminishing, criterion for the enjoyment of rights of mobility, employment, and equality. Some migrants are clearly more privileged than others. Recent legal developments reflect the numerous categories of migrants and deal specifically with several of them. We thus have an intricate network of rules, jurisdictions, and tribunals vested with the law on this matter.

The legal framework for migrants has thus been diverse, complex, and changing, and it is impossible to give an adequate account of it in this short space. The general point is that whereas the process of migration (and the economic processes underlying it) has been "global", the legal frameworks have been diverse, nationally oriented, and fragmented. There was an element of "globalism" in the legal framework when migrations took place within empires, because of the availability of a central authority. The rise of nation-states makes for diversity. However, in the twentieth century there are attempts to overcome this fragmentation, and there has been some concern with the rights of migrants. This concern has been part of the wider movement for human rights in the second half of the twentieth century; it has also been a response to the emergence of communist states. So there are elements of globalisation in this, although state sovereignty still remains a fundamental assumption of these attempts.

State sovereignty is a barrier to the globalisation of laws that would parallel the globalisation of the economic processes that underlie the globalisation of migrations. This has produced a certain degree of asymmetry in the global marketplace, because we have a greater freedom for the movement of capital than of workers. Other factors (like exports) are also being freed from national control. State regulation of migration in recent decades has produced a strange patch quilt of laws, concerned more with politics than economy.

In a study of the law, one must be attentive to its evasions; their consequences are contradictory, sometimes assisting migrants to overcome formal barriers to movement and frequently disadvantaging them through their inability to invoke rights they might otherwise enjoy. For governments too, the evasion of the law can be functional. It can be argued that illegal immigration is tolerated by the state because it deflects racist criticism of official migration policies, yet allowing the state to win popularity by claiming to have an energetic policy of catching illegal immigrants. Thus it creates a new species of unfree labour suffering worse conditions than indentured labourers. The result is various groups of workers with varying stakes in the economy and society. In this way "real" immigration policies reflect the different needs of the market.[3]

In order to get some purchase on this vast and complex subject, this chapter focuses on the legal position of migrant workers, defined as those workers whose movement is determined by economic factors, not necessarily of their own choosing. It thus excludes other forms of migrations, for example, refugees, or as a result of partition, war, natural calamities, or special settlements of convict colonies, and so on, on which there are specialised bodies of laws. Three "waves" of migration are discussed—slaves, indentured labourers, and free migrants—free migrants of course in a formal sense, because most of them have been driven by economic or political pressures. The development of the rights of migrants represent the interaction of market forces, changing notions of what is acceptable and moral—and expedient, and the balance between state sovereignty and the claims of international community.

Migrations, their ebb and flow, have been largely determined by the market. But it was not the market of the classical economists; most early migrations were connected with plantations, with their own social and economic logic, which the law reflected well. In later times, with better-established markets, there was again a conflict between the aspirations of individual employers (leading to the growth of illicit migration) and of the market in general, which required stability, mobility of labour, and competition. The market has been a key determinant also of the scope of the rights and duties of the workers, although political and cultural considerations have not been unimportant, and in recent years perhaps decisive. For the most part the migrants were in a weak position, and the employers and various forms of "protectors" have bargained on these rights and duties. For the greater period, governments were not democratic and so were less sensible of the interests of the migrants than of their employers.

Migration not only gives rise to a set of laws but also to its ideological justifications. It also gave rise to particular tensions within the legal system as two different sets of principles had to be accommodated. White migrants carried their laws, particularly public law with its civil liberties, with them, and so benefitted from a generous regime, but its benefits were not extended to coloured migrants. It is wrong to overdo the colour distinctions (the class nature of Western states ensured that coloured were not their only victims), but they were salient.

The broad periods of migrants' rights may be said to move from status (slavery) through semicontract (indenture) to free labour (contract). The law on the whole has reproduced rather than redressed the inequalities between the parties. The lawmaking process has been heavily influenced by the dominance of the employer class. The pressures of the economic imperative have nullified much of the protection the law may have provided. Enforcement has always been a problem. Law is not an instrument that lends itself easily to use by the oppressed.

Slavery

One of the earliest forms of migrant labour was slavery, and one of the major manifestations of it was the capture and transportation of Africans as slaves to the Caribbean and North America from the sixteenth century onward. It is hardly possible to talk of the rights of this category of migrants. There were no rules for the capture and sale of slaves. Abductions and purchase from local headmen were the usual means of acquiring them for transportation. A sort of market existed for these transactions, but no official regulation. Some royal charters of European monarchs did provide for monopolies or privileges in the sale of slaves (Verzil 1972, chap. 5).

The legal basis for slavery seems unclear; the American and Caribbean courts assumed rather than proved its lawfulness. As a U.S. court said in

1817, "It is an admitted principle, that slavery has been permitted and tolerated in all the colonies established in America by the mother colony. Not only of Africans, but also of Indians. No legislative act of the colonies can be found in relation to it" (Wheeler 1837, p. 9). The last sentence is inaccurate because various states did promulgate laws prescribing slavery for Africans. It did not matter greatly to the judges of this period what, and indeed if any, legal basis existed for slavery. They took it as a "legal axiom", that in all governments in which municipal regulations were not absolutely opposed to slavery, persons already reduced to that state could continue to be held in it. Equally fundamental to them was the initial legality of slavery; hence the absence of any legislative act of European powers for the introduction of slavery into their American dominions (Wheeler, p. 15). The basis of this legality appears to be merely the official toleration of slavery; on such slender foundations was a huge edifice of the jurisprudence of slavery built.

An attempt was, however, made to establish a jurisprudential basis for slavery. At first it was considered to be a part of social order, sanctioned by long custom. It was deemed to be allowed by the law of nations, and venerable authorities like Grotius could be invoked as evidence and justification. Slaves had long been treated in international law as articles of commerce, and in war, as contraband. Different legal systems recognised rights of property in slaves based on the laws of other countries, partly because of the rule of comity and partly because of the uncontroversial nature of slavery. Under this system, the detailed rules governing slavery were laid down by courts. Whereas at one level this meant that although the justifications or the legality of slavery was "universal" (i.e., Western), the detailed rules were nationally determined. But even here there was a wide degree of convergence, for three reasons: (1) since slaves were regarded as chattels, the concept of ownership provided a common framework; (2) there was reference to a common body of learning, the rules of Roman law on slavery (although common law courts made rather selective use of Roman law); and (3) among British or former British possessions, the unity was promoted by the common law as the rules were developed principally by the judges.

However, this well-ordered jurisprudence came under stress as doubts about the morality of slavery or its compatibility with evolving ideas of individual freedom in the common law arose. The sentiment developed that although slavery was not contrary to the law of nations, it was contrary to the law of nature. But this was now also the age of the positive law, and it was conceded by courts that despite the doubts about the compatibility of slavery with justice, they would enforce it if it was sanctioned by positive law (and indeed some went so far as to regard long practice as instance of positive law). Moreover the concept of the comity of nations helped to perpetuate slavery; for at this point comity was deemed to override public policy.

This area of the law was left largely to courts, reflecting, paradoxically, at first the general global consensus on the validity of slavery and then the lack of consensus that made legislative policy difficult. As I will show later, the judges were mindful of the dominant commercial interests, and the rules of slavery were bent to their hegemony. Two preliminary points are worth making. One is that the master-slave relationship permeated social life; the hegemony of the slave holders, presupposing the social and economic preponderance of great slave plantations, determined the character of the place (Genovese 1961). Judges operated within the dominant values of such a society, socialised with the slave-owning elites, and promoted their interests (as indeed judges promoted the interests of planters under the later system of indenture) (Tinker 1974). The other point is that court decisions reflected changing views of society on slavery and brought about the gradual amelioration of the conditions of slaves. For the most part, there is a strong sense of the binding force of precedents and legislation, a kind of perverse rule of law.

The courts conceded few rights to slaves. The slaves themselves were not objects of rights. They had no choice in decisions over transportation or the means for it. As slaves, they were nonpersons. An American court said in 1828 that

> A slave is in absolute bondage; he has no civil right, and can hold no property, except at the will and pleasure of his master . . . and all his rights and acquisitions and services are in the hands of his master. . . . A slave cannot take property by descent or purchase. . . . No legal contract whatever could be made with a slave without the consent of his master . . . a slave at common law could not contract matrimony, nor could the child of a slave take by descent or purchase (Wheeler, p. 7).

A great deal of the law relating to slavery was concerned with property—property in slaves. In one case, where there was a doubt about the status of an Indian, the judge gave the benefit of the doubt to the alleged owner of the Indian, contrary to the general rules of interpretation that favour the liberty of an individual, because he valued more highly "the rights of property" (Wheeler, p. 20). There was much learning about the issue of ownership of slaves (including the vexed question of whether they were to be regarded as personal or real property, the latter tying them more closely to the land) and the scope of and the forms for the transmission of such ownership (including the doctrine of uncontested adverse possession). In most of these matters, the position of slaves was assimilated to ordinary chattels; and much of this was done under the auspices of the judiciary through reasoning by analogy.

The welfare of the slaves and their progeny never featured in judicial decisions. The owners—and the courts—were quite happy to split families for what they regarded as equitable distribution of assets among their own descendants or the maximisation of products (Wheeler, p. 28). There were, however occasions when courts would not sanction splitting infant children from the mother, "which humanity forbids" (Wheeler, p. 183). Indeed a particular proprietary interest of slave owners was in their reproduction for sale, especially as the difficulties of getting replacements from Africa mounted. Because the slaves were regarded as chattels, there was much case law on guarantees and warranties as to their health and fitness, and the rules governing their mortgage (but that jurisprudence need not detain us here since it affected rights of parties in transactions of sale or hire of slaves, rather than the rights of slaves themselves).

An interesting illustration is the debate on whether a slave should be tried by a jury of slave owners. The court recognised the need to

> surround the life of the slave with additional safeguards, and more effectually to protect the property of the owner, by infusing into the trial, that temperate and impartial feeling, which would probably exist in persons owning the same sort of property. That the master would have assurance of an equitable trial by persons who had property constantly exposed to similar accusations, and would not wantonly sacrifice the life of a slave, but yield it only to a sense of justice, daily experience is sufficient to convince us. The property of a man is more secure when he cannot be deprived of it, except by a jury, part of whom at least, have the like kind of property to lose (Wheeler, p. 213).

In another context, courts justified the absolute dominion of the master over his slave as the means to secure the "value of slaves as property" (Wheeler, p. 248).

That the law treated slaves as chattels (things) and not persons defined their civil status and their civil rights (or the lack of rights). They had no power to make contracts and they could not own or transfer property. They had no entitlement enforceable in law to any gifts that might have been devised to them or for their benefit.

> It is indispensable to the validity of every devise, that there be a devisee appointed who is competent to take. Slaves have not that competence; for a civil incapacity results from the nature and conditions of slavery. And it would be a solecism, that the law should sanction or permit the acquisition of property by those from whom it afterwards withholds that protection without which property is useless (Wheeler, pp. 193–194).

Slaves could not initiate legal proceedings, except in one instance—to establish their freedom under the law. And they were not competent to appear as witnesses in courts, except again in proceedings to establish their freedom. Indeed incompetence as witnesses appears to have been not only a consequence of slavery but also of colour. In 1821 a U.S. judge said

> there is not instance in which a negro has been permitted to give evidence, except in cases of absolute necessity; nor has the court ever recognised the propriety of admitting them in any case where the rights of white persons are concerned. When we consider the degraded state in which they are placed by the laws of the state, and the ignorance in which most of them are reared, it would be unreasonable, as well as impolitic, to lay down as a general rule that they were competent witnesses (Wheeler, p. 195).

This was a rule of common law rather than of statute, and indeed some statutes allowed the evidence of free Indians and slaves, without oath, for or against any other slave accused of a crime. Free coloured persons were competent in civil proceedings where the parties were themselves coloured.

Since slaves had no capacity to make contracts, they were unable on their own to enter into matrimony. They could marry with the consent of their master, but such "marriage" was devoid of any civil effect. Marriage between a slave and a free person seems to have been possible, although such a marriage too did not produce its normal legal consequences. In the case of a marriage between a slave and a free woman, the court treated the children as belonging to the mother, as to their civil rights and duties, and she was given the sole custody and control of them "as though the father was dead" (Wheeler, p. 200).

It was not possible to treat slaves exclusively as chattels. Chattels do not have a consciousness and cannot be liable in law. Considerations of both residual humanity and law and order dictated that for some purposes slaves be treated as persons. I take first the case of the liability of the master or others for the mistreatment of slaves. In principle the master could, on analogy with chattels, treat his slave as he wished. The slave had no redress against the master (and in logic of course he could not, for any damages he obtained would belong to the master). And the master did not commit any criminal offence by physically punishing his slave. However, if he inflicted "cruel punishment", causing serious physical injury or death, he could be liable (on the analogy that in some circumstances the law punished even cruelty to animals). The argument was indeed made that the injury to, or the death of, the slave was a matter solely for the master.

The courts took the line that the law vested in the master the absolute and uncontrolled right to the services of the slave; "the means of enforcing these services, follow as necessary consequences; nor will the law weigh with the most scrupulous nicety, his acts in relation thereto" (Wheeler, p. 211). The courts would not allow

> the rights of the master to be brought in the courts of justice. The slave, to remain a slave, must be made sensible that there is no appeal from his master; that his person is, in no instance usurped; but is conferred by the laws of man, at least, if not by the law of God. The danger would be great indeed, if the tribunals of justice should be called upon to graduate the punishment appropriate to every temper, and every dereliction of menial duty. No man can anticipate the many and grave provocations of the master which the slave would be constantly stimulated, by his own passions, or the instigation of others, to give; or the consequent wrath of the master, prompting him to bloody vengeance, upon the turbulent traitor; a vengeance generally practised with impunity, by reason of its privacy. The court therefore disclaims the power of changing the relations in which these parts of our people stand to each other (Wheeler, p. 247).

But it was not necessary for the life of the slave to be placed in the hands of the master for him to enjoy the former's services. Any other view would be "abhorrent to the hearts of all those who have felt the influence of the mild precepts of christianity" (Wheeler, p. 211).

Mistreatment by others was generally dealt with as trespass or harm to the property of the master (and damages awarded to him for injury to the slave). This meant that mere battery that did not incapacitate the slave temporarily or permanently would not be actionable (Wheeler, p. 243). But outsiders were also liable to criminal sanctions if unjustified force was used and caused serious injury to the slave, and indeed capital punishment was prescribed for the murder of a slave.

The more important reason, however, for relaxing the rule that the slave is a chattel and treating him as a person was to maintain law and order. Courts realised that a slave society is always vulnerable to rebellion or serious acts of disobedience and that there are limits to control through hegemony in such society. Appropriate punishments had to be provided to deter rebellion, and it was necessary in order to create responsibility and liability that slaves be ascribed the capacity to form intention and execute it. A special court, with a mixture of justices and freeholders, which could be quickly convened, was established in many states for the trial of slaves. The rules of procedure as well as of substantive law were less favourable to slaves than freemen (Wheeler, p. 221). For the same reason the courts were willing to disregard acts of petty and sometimes more serious violence upon the person of the slave by others than the master (often on spurious grounds of maintaining order) as reinforcing the dominance of the white man.

The last paragraphs give an indication of the relationship of the slave to the state. If the slave is a nonperson, merely a chattel, then he or she can be of little concern to the state. Indeed, this was the attitude occasionally taken by the courts. In one case the court refused to punish a freeholder for assault upon a slave since it regarded the slave as a chattel, whose protection may be a matter for the master but not the state. "There can be therefore no offence against the state for a mere beating of a slave unaccompanied by any circumstances of cruelty, or an attempt to kill and murder. The peace of the state is not thereby broken; for a slave is not generally regarded as legally capable of being within the peace of the state. He is not a citizen, and is not in that character entitled to her protection" (Wheeler, p. 243). But, as indicated previously, questions of slavery were implicated in law and order, and a great deal of jurisprudence was built on the need of society to subordinate slaves. Some protection to the slave against excessive cruelty by nonmasters was justified on the need to preserve peace, because although a slave was accustomed (and expected) to accept all manner of chastisement from the master, he might well be provoked into retaliation if beaten by others. The state had of course a general interest in maintaining the institution and incidence of slavery, as central to the well-being of powerful social classes.

It was in cases dealing with the manumission of a slave by the master that the courts developed at some length the interest of the state in the slave. Although in other contexts the courts had asserted the absolute dominion of the master over his slave, they balked at his unrestricted powers to emancipate him/her. The additional consent of the state was central. Manumission

> is adopting into the body politic a new member, a vastly important measure in every community, and especially in ours, where the majority of freemen over twenty-one years of age, govern the balance of the people, together with themselves; where the free negro's vote at the poll, is of as high value as that of any man. Degraded by their colour and condition in life, the free negroes are a very dangerous and most objectionable population where slaves are numerous. Therefore, no slave can be safely freed but with the consent of the government where manumission takes place (Wheeler, p. 291).

The court argued further that it would be unfair (indeed "a violation of moral duty") to impose freed negroes on other states of the United States, since on manumission they would acquire the right of free movement within the federation. Freed slaves would also provide a constant temptation for existing slaves to run away to their settlements. The court anticipated racial problems on the emancipation of slaves. They were anxious to avoid the burden on society of looking after freed slaves. They consequently reached, for them, the logical conclusion that manumission would be allowed so long as the freed man was removed beyond the jurisdiction of the United States (hence the origin of the settlement in Liberia).

Manumission affected, apart from the general interests, interests of particular groups or individuals, like the creditors or descendants of the slave owner and the descendants of the slave. Manumission could not be conferred in fraud of the creditors (on principles that are familiar to the modern laws on security). Courts developed complex case law on these matters. They placed no particular value on emancipation (although some paid lip service to freedom); within the constraints of satisfying previous obligations, the dominant factor was the intention of the slave owner—in keeping with the equation of the slave to the property of the master. In one case the court said, "Though this is a claim of freedom, we are not so much in favour of liberty so as to lose sight, that this class of people are acknowledged as slaves. The master has a property in them, and contracts respecting this species of property are to be construed by the same rules of interpretation that contracts respecting any other species of property are" (Wheeler, p. 331).

A number of difficult and complex problems were raised for the courts once slavery was abolished in some of the U.S. states. What was to happen to the slaves if they went with their masters or on their own to such states? There was of course the precedent of the *Somerset* case (1772), which was generally interpreted to mean that when a slave entered a country that did not recognise slavery, he or she became free. This doctrine may be suitable for England, far away from the major sites of slavery, but its potential for conflict between contiguous states that diverged on the question of the legality of slavery was recognised by the courts in the United States. The resolution of the claims of slave-owning and slave-free states posed a major dilemma for the courts, because these conflicts not only posed the question of the role of the rule of comity but were also reflective of divergent moral orders. It is fair to say that the courts developed no consistent line of authority (any more than the English courts did despite the ringing rhetoric of *Somerset*).

In a sense the task of the courts was facilitated by the variety of circumstances in which the issue of freedom arose, which allowed them a measure of pragmatism or casuistry, avoiding hard doctrine or principle: the absconding slave, the slave on a sojourn with his/her master, the slave with his/her master on a permanent change of residence or domicile, the slave reluctant (or willing) to return with the master to place of original residence, and so on. In these ways the courts were enabled, on the whole, to maintain the interests of slave owners and slave-owning societies. In general they held the rule of the comity of nations (whereby they gave effect to the laws of another state) more important than the rule of public policy (which subjects foreign laws to the test of what is morally or otherwise acceptable in the jurisdiction of courts). Here again the courts were much influenced by notions of the sanctity of property and the desirability of facilitating international transactions.

In an important case from Massachusetts (one of the first states to abolish slavery), in a learned judgment, Chief Justice Shaw defined the rule of comity as follows:

> Each independent community, in its intercourse with every other, is bound to act on the principle, that such other country has a full and perfect authority to make such laws for the government of its own objects, as its own judgement shall dictate, and its own conscience approve, provided the same are consistent with the law of nations; and no independent community has any right to interfere with the acts or conduct of another state, within the territories of such states, or on the high seas, which each has an equal right to use and occupy; and that each sovereign state, governed by its own laws, although competent and well authorised to make such laws as it may think most expedient to the extent of its own territorial limits, and for the government of its subjects, yet beyond these limits, and over those who are not her own subjects, has no authority to enforce her own laws, or to treat the laws of other states as void, although contrary to its own morality (Wheeler, p. 363).

The crucial point therefore was whether slavery was contrary to the law of nations, and here Chief Justice Shaw had to concede that it was not. The practice of European states, particularly in their colonies, had produced custom that legalised slavery. Until slavery was abolished with the consent of major world powers, courts operated in this ambiguous way. Yet the judiciary itself had foreshadowed its demise, because Chief Justice Marshall had said in an earlier case of slave trade, "That it is contrary to the law of nature will scarcely be denied. That every man has a natural right to the fruits of his own labour is generally admitted, and that no other person can rightfully deprive him of those fruits, and appropriate them against his will, seems to be the necessary result of this admission" (Wheeler, p. 363).

I conclude with some general observations on slavery. It is an early instance of globalisation of the world economy and politics. This globalisation could, however, be achieved only by denying the universalism of men and women. This early pattern set the example for subsequent acts of globalisation. Its outstanding feature was the subjugation of the east by the west, of black people by the white people. The notion of black man as a nonperson symbolised the asymmetry of globalisation (with resonances in the contemporary period). Juridically, the forerunners of legal systems, which pride themselves on the rule of law and human rights, had little difficulty in accommodating inequalities and racism. This was bolstered by a so-called law of nations, an early attempt at the universalisation of legal norms, but which was in fact another form of white man's law and rule. Since then it is the white man's law that has determined the rights and duties of black men. With its presumptions of the inferiority of blacks built into the substance and procedure of the law, the seeds of racism were effectively sown and a rich harvest was garnered. The basic principle of slavery law (one, privileged, law for the free, i.e., white, and another, for the slave, i.e., black) has many resonances in contemporary law or practice. The ending of slavery did not therefore mark any great watershed for its dominant assumptions and many of its practices were continued in new legal forms and ideologies (as immediately with indenture).

Indenture

The abolition of slavery and the reluctance of former slaves to work on plantations led to the search for new types of labour. The most effective of these was the system of indentured labour under which millions of Indians, Chinese, and Pacific Islanders were transported to faraway lands. India was the major source of cheap labour that could be exploited within the framework of the empire. The market impulses behind this form of labour were the same as had motivated slavery. In juridical terms, however, it could be argued that there was a qualitative difference. The underlying basis of indenture was consensual and not coercion. It recognised the person of the labourer and represented a transformation from status to contract. It was delimited in time. In practice the change was less striking or decisive. Economic compulsion, the demands of the organisation of production, and lax enforcement of the law meant that the labourer was not necessarily better off.

Indenture was what in modern parlance we would call standard form contract, and the rights and duties implied in it were not negotiated or negotiable by the migrant. The sanctions for the breach of the terms of indenture by the labourer were penal and not civil, denying the form of his contractual engagement. An extensive set of regulations defined these terms and tied him to a particular employer and a particular residence. This extensive regulation and the lack of the legal capacity of the indentured labourer to change employment meant that this form of regulation, like slavery, did not meet standards of economic or market rationality, and therefore political considerations were paramount.

Rights and duties (and other incidents of indenture) were negotiated by parties other than the migrant (reflecting the weak position of the labourer). In time a complex legal regime developed to govern the system of indenture. Here is another contrast with slavery. Slavery, including the massive transfers of population across vast spaces, was privately organised. So were many of its incidents, for in the absence of legislation, courts tended to follow the customs of the slave owners. The coercive powers of the state were no doubt necessary to sustain the system of slavery, but the initiative was left to slave traders and owners. Indenture, in contrast, involved a large number of official agencies acting under the authority of domestic and international law negotiated by governments (even if at the instigation of and to the benefit of private parties). Indenture therefore represents the beginnings of the formalisation of global migrations. Transfers within the British Empire were concluded within a set of administrative agreements and regulations, the common sovereignty of the Crown dispensing with the form (if not the reality) of international transactions in migrant labour. The usual procedure was to enact legislation setting out the terms of emigration from India and immigration legislation in the receiving country that satisfied the conditions on which indentured labour was permitted. When other European powers wanted Indian labour (or when British colonies wanted Chinese or African labour outside the British dominions), the machinery of international relations and transactions needed to be mobilised. Bilateral treaties, which even today play a key role in international migration, had its roots in indentured labour. Reflecting the more active engagement of states in the migration process, the framework of migration labour was largely statutory, compared to the largely judicial framework of slavery. Courts still had a role to play in the enforcement of statutes, but the great discussions of policy, which marked the judicial process during slavery, gave way to narrower rules of statutory construction.

The form and legal incidents of indenture were influenced by the horrors and abuses of slavery. "In the moral and intellectual climate of the 1830s and 1840s, it was necessary that any systematic movement of emigrants should satisfy the ethical and economical beliefs of the industrial and professional middle class of Britain; beliefs mainly formed by the teaching and preaching of the Utilitarians and Evangelicals" (Tinker, p. 61). These concerns manifested themselves in the debate on the balance between laissez-faire methods and governmental control. Another factor that entered into decisions on the form of migration was more overtly political; the satisfaction of the Indian government that there were sufficient safeguards for the protection of migrants. The Indian government was at that time of course the British Indian government, and the influence of Indians on it remained tenuous until the end of indenture in the early part of the twentieth century. For a long time the Indian government was more susceptible to the demands of British planters in the Caribbean, Mauritius, and Fiji, particularly because it was mediated through the Colonial

Office and other departments in London (Richardson 1982, pp. 28–29; Tinker, pp. 92–94). As it became increasingly necessary to rule India with a measure of the consent of its people, Indian opinion had to be placated, and Indian opinion, humiliated by the third-rate status accorded to Indians in the empire, became vocal on this point (Tinker, chaps. 7 and 8). The Indian government consequently began to assert an independent position in the politics of the empire.

The year 1837 may be regarded as the start of official indenture, when the Indian government passed an act governing emigration from India. It contained the rudiments of principles that were elaborated in subsequent laws and conventions. The contractual basis of indenture was emphasised by the requirement that the terms of employment must be in written form, and that the intending migrant must demonstrate his knowledge of them, to the satisfaction of an agent of the government. Emigration agents, representing potential employers, were established to ensure that the provisions of the law on recruitment and passage were honoured. The length of indenture was five years, renewable for a further five years. At the end of his service, the labourer was to be returned to the port of his departure. Conditions for the passage to the place of employment were also laid down: dietary, spatial, and medical.

The Indian indentured labour provided the model elsewhere. For example, when, under pressure from mining interests in the Transvaal, Britain opened negotiations with China for Chinese indentured labour, considerable reliance was placed upon the system and terms of the Indian indenture (Richardson). Under a convention of 1860, the Chinese Emperor had agreed to allow his subjects to take service in British colonies. A convention in 1904 spelled out the terms on which Chinese labour would be exported. These included the appointment of a Chinese inspector, who, together with the British consular at the port of departure, would publicise by proclamation and "by native presses" the text of the indenture and "any particulars of which the Chinese officer considers it essential that the emigrant shall be informed, respecting the country to which the emigrant is to proceed, and respecting its laws", including where applicable, any immigration ordinance. The recruitment was to be supervised by the inspector; the terms of indenture had to be drawn up in both Chinese and English. These had to provide clearly

> the name of the country for which the labourer is required, the duration of the engagement, and, if renewable, on what terms, the number of hours of labour per working day, the nature of the work, the rate of wages and mode of payment, the rations, clothing, the grant of a free passage out, and where such is provided for therein, a free passage back to the port of embarkation in China for himself and family, right to free medical attendance and medicines (ART. 7).

An indentured labourer could not be transferred to another by his employer without the labourer's consent (a provision designed to prevent speculation in labour) (ART. 12). Provision was made for a medical examination before the ship's departure.

The convention also attempted to secure the protection of labourers once they reached their destinations. In order to ensure that the terms of the engagement were observed, China was to establish a consul, whose expenses were to be met out of a levy on the employers (ART. 13). The host country was also to appoint one or more officers to ensure that "the emigrant shall have free access to the Courts of Justice to obtain redress for injuries to his person and property which is secured to all persons, irrespective of race, by the local law" (ART. 9). The emigrant was to have access also to postal services in order to keep in touch with the home country and to have facilities for making remittances to his family (ART. 10).

These provisions were frequently hard to enforce. Most emigrants were illiterate and understood little of the terms to which they signed themselves or of the conditions in the place for which they were destined (Richardson, p. 74). The demand for labour seemed insatiable, and recruitment practices were generally little short of forced conscription (Tinker, pp. 122–131). The Indian government, which was supposed to prescribe and then supervise policy for emigration, was "largely in the dark about conditions in the colonies where their people had settled" (Tinker, pp. 103–104). The machinery for the enforcement of the conditions of emigration and indenture was for the most part ineffective (Tinker, pp. 103–104), and the regulators were routinely co-opted by the regulated—the planters and mining interests (Tinker, p. 101). Various devices were employed to prolong the period of indenture, and a variety of fines reduced the real income of the labourers (Tinker, pp. 107, 188, and 195). Salaries were frequently in arrears for several months and were seldom paid in full; a contemporary commentator reported that the planters had not gotten over the habits of the slavery system and did not really accept the obligation of giving their people salary (Sewell quoted in Tinker, p. 186). The working conditions were determined by the custom of slavery, and labourers sometimes had to work for twenty-four-hour stretches.

> The coolies, like the slaves before them, formed a compulsory labour force which the planter had in his employ, whether he wanted them or not.
>
> The absence of flexibility in the deployment of labour shaped the approach to job allocation. The planter could bring in extra labour at crop time by paying the Creole Blacks higher rates for the more demanding tasks, and he could sometimes hire coolie labour from job contractors. But he was saddled with his regular work-force of indentured coolies who had to earn their keep throughout the year. As in the slave-time, the planter used men and women for work hauling loads and ploughing which could better have been per-

formed by draught animals. The coolie remained the all-purpose animal, though even in the early 1870s it was being argued in Trinidad: "the reform . . . most urgently needed is to spare the life-blood of the coolie by the more extended use of implements worked by steam machinery, mules or oxen . . . instead of the primitive system of manual labour" (Tinker, p. 191).

It proved singularly hard to enforce the limit on the number of hours a labourer had to work. The need to maximise the returns from the labourer during the period of indenture led to his super-exploitation (Tinker, p. 183). This was merely a special instance of the more general problem of law enforcement. Numerous commissions highlighted the shortcomings of the system and its inefficient policing, although protection agents were employed in the country of destination to ensure that the terms of the law and the indenture were observed and the Indian government reserved the power to scrutinise the immigration legislation of countries wanting to import Indian labour and to suspend emigration as sanction. The reasons for the lax enforcement were connected in part to the nature of the organisation of plantation—just as the courts had recognised during slavery. Every planter behaved as if he was a magistrate on his own estate, and only the most severe mistreatment of a labourer was dealt with officially. Planters continued to administer punishments as in the times of slavery.

If the rights of the labourer were disregarded in practice, the same cannot be said of his duties and obligations. For the most part these were enforced through criminal sanctions, although they arose out of contract. Conviction rates were high, covering a high proportion of workers. Penalties were severe (Naidu 1980). Laws on "vagrancy" were employed to keep control on those whose indenture had run out and to force them back into employment, so that "status" in itself had no particular significance.

This uneven and partial administration of the law was possible in part because the planters' domination in these societies was supreme and not liable to be challenged by magistrates and other officials. "Most of the planters in the Caribbean were Justices of the Peace, exercising by legal right the authority which they asserted by means of their dominant place in the economy. The Mauritius Royal Commission emphasised the 'extreme deference' shown by magistrates to 'the wishes of the masters'" (Tinker, p. 220). This description is similar to Eugene Genovese's account of justice in the slave societies of the United States. It was justified on the basis of the culture and productive capacities of the ruling class and the laziness and ignorance of the working people.

To conclude the discussion of indentured labour: Indentured labour shared many of the characteristics of slavery. This was so particularly in the case of the organisation of work, which for the most part was based on plantations. The indentured labourer was also like the slave in having few enforceable rights. Likewise he had little influence in shaping or mobilising the law that determined his situation. He suffered similarly from the imbalance between the number of men and women, making family life and family rights illusory.

The factors that distinguished him/her from the slave were for the better part negated in practice: contract (not status), legal personality, and access to the legal system. The rights that the law gave him (and the administrative machinery to effectuate them) were largely symbolic; and in this, of course, the law served ideological functions that it had served before and serves today. The legal situations of both the slave and the indentured labourer, with their numerous restrictions and the lack of mobility, prevented the complete commoditisation of labour.

Such labour was essential to the project of capitalist development, but in itself it failed to observe the rules of the market: competition, mobility, universal norms, and equality. The peculiar needs of the planters and the mining companies, rather than the impersonal market, defined its roles, regulation, and duties. Slavery and indenture arose in conditions of scarcity of labour, with entrepreneurs anxious for workers. Yet the political economy of slavery and indenture disempowered the workers; and other groups reaped the monetary benefits of the demand for labour.

Although the legal foundations of slavery were said to lie in the law of nations (and therefore partake of a process of globalisation), it was indentured labour that brought about the greater interaction of states, in the attempts to regulate and cooperate in transstate migration, leading to the development of some increasingly general norms (just as the abolition of slavery required concerted interstate cooperation and norm setting). The emergence of slavery covered the period when states (at least in the West) were being formed, and its demise came when the Western state system was well established. The beginning of the indentured period saw the rise of European empires, and its end coincided with the start of their disintegration. The system of indenture therefore had a peculiarly imperial character. It was either a "domestic affair", within the domain of a common sovereignty, or mediated through the grace of the imperial power. Insofar as it was the former, it pointed to the contradictions of the legal ideology of the empire: that of the equality of His/Her Majesty's subjects wherever they might be. The ideology of common and equal citizenship was inconsistent with the colonial enterprise and ambitions in the Caribbean, Africa, and Australasia; and on this contradiction foundered in one sense, the system of indenture, as Indians became preoccupied with their status in the emperor's dominions.

In a more realistic sense, the system of indenture foundered on economic realities. The agitation for its repeal was overtaken by World War I and the consequent disorientation of Western economies, when labour lost its scarcity value. So, as in its inception, so in its end, the scope and parameters of indenture were determined by the market. The collapse of indenture brought to the fore the other aspect of its organisation—interstate cooperation and the system of treaties. But the context was now changed. The bilateralism of the indenture system was supplemented by multilateralism or globalisation. The postwar settlement saw the rise of truly global institutions, with a mandate for international public policy. It was recognised that the globalisation of markets and economies required a corresponding supranational superstructure. The League of Nations and the International Labour Organisation, the first of such global organisations, had vast agendas, and migration, with the national preoccupation with economies, was by no means dominant. But the rise of the socialist world had given urgency to the question of the position of workers within capitalist economies, and the lot of migrant workers could not be ignored. The postwar settlements also engaged these institutions in policymaking and establishing new norms for interstate relations and, to some extent, the relationships of the state to its own people. The international movement for human rights was to flourish after World War II, but it was foreshadowed in the interwar period. It is within this constellation of factors that the next stage in the development of the rights of migrant workers was set.

Free Migration

My principal concern is with immigration from developing countries to the West, particularly Europe, after World War II. The major legal developments of this period had been prefigured earlier in the twentieth century and were marked by two parallel (and occasionally intersecting) movements: the establishment of national regimes for the control of migration and the development of international or regional standards governing the status and rights of migrants. Both regimes have undergone significant modifications since the beginning of the twentieth century and the process is by no means over. Ironically, the era of free migration was marked by the rise of national restrictions on immigration and employment. Until the beginning of the twentieth century, there were few restrictions on entry into a country; indeed the liberal economic theories of the time supported the free movement of persons. Various countries, especially Britain, France, and the United States, had promoted legislation in the eighteenth and nineteen centuries, imposing specific rather than general restrictions on entry (the power to deport being more important) (Plender 1988, chap. 2).[4]

It is interesting that the more serious restrictions on entry came with the fear of Asian migration (even before the end of indenture, which had largely involved Asians)—it was considered that there was now no need for Asian labour after its contribution to the initial opening up of the West. The United States passed the Chinese Exclusion Act in 1882, requiring the registration of Chinese (and authorising their deportation for failure to register). Australia followed suit in 1901, laying the foundations of its white Australia policy. In 1885 Canada also introduced restrictions on Chinese immigrants (Chinese Immigration Act). White self-governing dominions within the British Empire introduced restrictions on the entry of Indians, which, as subjects of the Crown, they would otherwise have been entitled to. Restrictions were introduced also to regulate the entry of Jews and other emigres from Eastern Europe, in the United States, the United Kingdom, and Canada. In the United Kingdom the Aliens Act of 1905 was the first of the modern laws controlling immigration; "immigrants" henceforth had to secure the permission of an immigration officer. The imminence of World War I reinforced similar restrictions in the United Kingdom and elsewhere and universalised the system of passports for foreign travel. Meanwhile the United States and Canada introduced national quota restrictions, which had the effect of excluding communities whose members were not already settled there—its purpose was widely assumed to be the exclusion of coloured people, who were also denied the right to naturalisation. Racially discriminatory immigration laws therefore became, at the early stage of regulation, the characteristic of Western states. An attempt by Japan to outlaw them by inserting the principles of the equality of nations and just treatment for nationals of all states in the Covenant of the League of Nations was defeated by Western powers.

In the interwar years there was relatively little migration from the developing countries to the West because of the recession and few changes in the legal regime of migration. There were some attempts to develop international standards under the auspices of the International Labour Organization (ILO) (discussed later), but these did not have much influence on national laws or practices. However, rapid economic development in the West after World War II led to acute labour shortages. Western countries dealt with the shortage by promoting immigration from the developing countries (as well as southern Europe), through a combination of national regulations and bilateral treaties. Racial discriminations in immigration laws or policies were removed or attenuated (the United States abolished the Chinese Exclusion Act in 1943, and Canada, in 1947, and in 1946 the United States removed restrictions on Filipinos and Indians from entering the United States and acquiring naturalisation). As the need for labour was selective, governments in Europe and North America armed themselves with wide discretionary powers as to the admission of foreigners for work, so as to admit those with skills lacking domestically and to keep others out. The legislation provided only the broad principles, so that the detailed regulations were established in executive decrees, ensuring considerable flexibility as well as the dominance of the bureaucracy. A vast network of bilateral and regional treaties and national legislation developed.

Labour shortages, and immigration, continued until the early 1970s, when the rise in the cost of energy and economic recession in the West once again led to restrictive practices, in many instances leading to the total stoppage of fresh primary immigration. In most countries, the underlying rationale was the same—the needs of the labour market. For France, Gilles Verbunt has said that the immigration policy has been determined by the needs of the moment, and that even illegal immigration has been tolerated so long as it served economic needs (Verbunt 1985, pp. 134 and 137). Similar claims have been made for Germany by Hartmut Esser and Hermann Korte, who say that immigration policy has been restricted to controlling the entry and residence of foreigners in accordance with German economic interests, and that "the 1973 recruitment stop was the clearest manifestation of the central role that economic interests have in the employment of immigrant labour" (Esser and Korte 1985, pp. 178 and 180). Hoffman-Nowotny says about Switzerland that "there is no doubt that immigration since the second world war has been seen primarily as an economic phenomenon: in other words, immigrants have been desirable only as manpower" (1985, p. 216).

The legal framework and the ability to regulate immigration and deal with migrants were however determined in part by different historical and legal traditions, political systems, and colonial connections of Western countries. In general, whereas the ebb and flow of migration was governed by the market (even when the laws were laissez-faire), the treatment of immigrants was governed by domestic political traditions (to deal in large part with the unforeseen social and cultural consequences of the market-driven migration). Even here, there was similarity among the different states since Western political systems have moved toward some kind of convergence (Hammar 1985b and Collinson 1994). It is difficult to describe briefly the national systems, but some salient features—and differences—are referred to.

In Europe a distinction may be drawn between states with colonial connections and those without. The laws in the former (e.g., the United Kingdom, France, and the Netherlands) allowed the free entry of the inhabitants of their colonies and in many cases, ex-colonies. Colonies and ex-colonies were the principal source of immigrants. Their citizens enjoyed many of the social and political rights of local citizens, including that of residence. These countries did not rely much on bilateral agreements, except when they wished to exercise control over numbers (as

France with Algeria). The result was the lack of control over numbers, skills, and location of immigrants. In all cases legislation was introduced to impose restrictions (most severely in the United Kingdom), at first for social and political reasons, and later also for economic reasons with the onset of recession, so that the position of ex-imperial migrants was assimilated to other migrants (including the obtaining of the necessary permissions and documentation in the country of origin of the migrant) (Layton-Henry 1988). Countries that did not have a colonial connection (e.g., Switzerland, Germany, and the Scandinavian countries) relied more upon bilateral treaties with labour-exporting countries and tended to restrict recruitment to European states, at least initially. Bilateral treaties were implemented through national legislation, which in most cases provided for strict controls through visas, residence permits, and work permits. Bilateral treaties facilitated greater control over numbers because there were generally provisions for the repatriation of workers.

Another distinction may be drawn between states that allowed migrants on a temporary and rotational basis (pursuing policies of "guest workers" as in Germany, Switzerland, and the Netherlands) and those that accepted policies of settlement (e.g., the United Kingdom, France, and the Scandinavian countries). The former were more liberal in allowing entry but imposed tough conditions once workers were admitted. They were given permission for a specified (generally short) duration, for a specific job, and a specified locality. They had to return to their country of origin on the expiry of the permit, although they could come back after a period. Thus they had no, or limited, rights of mobility and no security of residence.

Countries of immigration or settlement had, except initially in the case of ex-colonials, stricter provisions for entry but granted greater rights of residence and employment. These differences can be illustrated by an examination of the principal devices of control: the residence permit, the work permit, the right of permanent residence, naturalisation, and the right of family reunion (although it is important to keep in mind that the regulations have changed from time to time). In the former metropolitan countries none of these controls were necessary at first for ex-colonies. And for residents of ex-colonies and other countries of immigration, the waiting period required before the right of permanent residence could be secured was quite short. Sweden was particularly generous in requiring only one year, after which most restrictions were removed (so long as the person maintained residence in Sweden). In the Netherlands a permanent work permit may be granted only after three years of ordinary residence, based on a permit that is given only for a specific job (that restriction being removed at the time the permanent work permit is granted). However, a right of permanent residence is obtained only after five years (subject to a guaranteed income). In Britain, work permits, tied to a particular job, are issued initially for twelve months, subject to annual renewals; after four years a permit holder becomes eligible for (rather than entitled to) the removal of time and employment restrictions. In France there are three categories of work permits, depending on duration; the normal rule is one or three years' duration, during which a person is tied to a specified job. It would seem that there is no entitlement to a permanent residence.

In Germany the permit is restricted as regards duration and job; one year is standard, and after three years, permits of two or three years may be granted. After five years a person is eligible for, but not entitled to, permanent residence. In Switzerland the initial permit is valid for a limited time (one year or less) and tied to a specific job. Other conditions may be attached, breach of which is a ground for expulsion. The permit may be renewed on a yearly basis, for the first five years, and thereafter for two-year periods. It is only after ten years that a person becomes entitled to a permit authorising permanent residence, and until that is granted, he or she has little security of employment or residence.

Similar differences prevail as regards naturalisation. In no country is naturalisation now a matter of right. In Sweden, the United Kingdom, the Netherlands, and France it becomes available after five years of residence, subject to language tests, or evidence of "assimilation", or, as in France, "loyalty" (which has tended to bring in questions of support for the ruling party). In Switzerland the period is twelve years, which may be increased if there has been a change of residence from one commune to another. Naturalisation removes all the restrictions on the migrant, who is then placed in a position of equality with the citizen. Given this principle, it is surprising that more applications have not been made for naturalisation than is the case.

One reason is that the legal regimes of these countries no longer recognise sharp distinctions between citizens and other residents. Migrants became entitled at an early stage to several economic rights of citizens—the right to join trade unions, equal pay, and other terms of employment, like social security, and so on. Once migrants acquire permanent residence, remaining restrictions on employment and mobility (if any) are removed. Most countries are still reluctant to grant equal political rights (Layton-Henry 1990), although migrants can join and support political parties. In the UK Commonwealth, citizens are entitled to full political rights, whereas the Scandinavian countries and the Netherlands allow participation in local government. Most migrants did not appear to regard political rights as important to them, although there is little doubt that the exercise of economic rights is more effective if they are backed by political participation (as is demonstrated by the relatively better position of migrants in the United Kingdom than in Germany, where naturalisation is very difficult).

In Europe the distinction between countries favouring immigration and those favouring temporary workers has tended to disappear since the 1970s, which period was a turning point in many respects. States whose policies were based on the assumption of temporary and rotating workers realised that some foreign workers were bound to stay on (financial and economic incentives for them to return to their countries of origin having been ineffective) and that the children of these workers had to be integrated into society. However, countries like the United Kingdom tightened immigration controls on migrants from the Commonwealth and changed the basis for citizenship to exclude children born in the United Kingdom of non–United Kingdom citizen parents, a change from jus soli to jus sanguinis, although children of settled parents could obtain nationality by birth in the United Kingdom (Layton-Henry 1985 and Plender 1988). Moreover it was necessary to stabilise the market, particularly in sectors to which local workers could not be attracted.

States with immigration orientation realised that they had no sensible and coherent policies for the integration of immigrants and, more importantly, their children. Commissions were established in most of these countries to examine the social and cultural consequences of immigration and resulted in largely common conclusions that in order to avoid industrial and social unrest and racial conflicts, important changes were necessary. Legislative and administrative steps were taken to remove restrictions on long-term migrants and ensure them complete equality in employment-related rights and to integrate their children into the mainstream educational system while recognising their cultural distinctiveness. This was coupled with the halt to further primary immigration—a kind of social compact that was politically necessary, particularly in Germany and Switzerland. The result of these and some earlier policies was that in the economic field the migrant workers secured formal, legal equality with the locals. There was considerable integration in the labour market, and migrants were more significantly unionised than local workers.

These benign developments were also helped by domestic constitutional values—thus the German Constitutional Court held the wide discretion given to officials as inconsistent with various constitutional as well as treaty provisions (Ansay 1991). It also held that the rights of the family guaranteed by the constitution applied also to non-German nationals (facilitating reunion). The protection of the rule of law and the right to develop freely one's personality was inconsistent with the uncertainty regarding residence permits, developing a presumption of renewal. Restrictions on residence or employment with a specified employer have been interpreted to be violative of the dignity of the person as well as the prohibition against forced labour. The concept of proportionality has been used to prohibit deportation for minor offences. These judicial advances have been consolidated in new legislation (Aliens Act 1991). In Canada the Supreme Court has extended the benefits of the 1982 Charter of Rights and Freedoms to noncitizens, ensuring rights of fair hearing and rejecting the notion that immigration involves privilege (and executive discretion) rather than rights (*Singh* v. *Minister of Employment and Immigration* [1985] 1 SCR 177; Goodwin-Gill 1989, p. 544). The U.S. courts have given the protection of the Civil Rights Act to illegal migrants (Helton 1991, pp. 851–852). The European Convention of Human Rights has also been used, although infrequently, as a basis for some rights for migrants. However, not all judicial contests have gone in favour of migrants (reflecting society's ambiguities toward the acceptance of migrants). It is also important, as always, to make a distinction between formal legal provisions and the reality on the ground, for migrants continued to suffer discrimination in job opportunities and promotions, existed on the margins of society and economy, and lived in poor accommodation in the less-salubrious parts of industrial towns. And even as national laws were equalised, further discriminations were appearing, particularly in the form of EEC (European Economic Community) regulations, which created new distinctions in economic rights between migrants who were citizens of a member state and those who were not. This privileged regime for a class of workers and the halting of further non-EEC migration established the mentality and reality of "fortress Europe", which paradoxically was as much a response to globalisation as was the migration itself.[5]

The convergence among Western states and the special regimes were products not only of domestic politics and economies but also of international legal developments, which are a distinguishing characteristic of this period. There are three strands to these developments: bilateral treaties between labour-importing and labour-exporting states, regional arrangements for labour mobility, and international conventions and declarations. At present they do not add up to a tidy picture; and there is no consensus on essential principles and procedures.[6] Nevertheless some core principles are getting increasing acceptance, and the recent adoption of the International Convention on the Protection of the Rights of All Migrant Workers and Members of Their Families (1990) is a symbolic recognition—but no more—of the extension of the general regime of human rights to migrants.

In both the bilateral and international treaties there is a clear pattern of development: First there is the regulation of the recruitment process and the travel, and some minimum conditions of work and residence in the country of employment (reflecting the nature of indenture treaties); then the principle of the equality of the migrant with nationals in employment and work conditions; the extension of the principle of equality to housing and social security; and finally there is a more global approach, equality across a wider spectrum, and increasing security of work and residence permits.

Bilateral treaties are descendants of treaties of friendship whereby nationals of one state were granted rights in the other signatory state, on the basis of reciprocity. However these treaties were concerned not with workers but business and merchant classes. The true ancestors are therefore the treaties underpinning the system of indenture, dealing with cooperation between the labour-importing and exporting states on the flows of workers and their regulation (a useful summary is provided in Lillich, pp. 105–120). Bilateral treaties have been more important for intra-European migration than migration from developing countries (although the United States had a treaty with Mexico and France, with Algeria, the latter concerned principally with repatriation of workers). States favouring policies of transient workers have made use of these treaties since they oblige the exporting countries to cooperate in their repatriation.

The treaties provide for migration under the auspices or supervision of states, which also undertake the responsibility to solve difficulties that may arise. Contracts of employment have to be signed before migration takes place. In general they provide for equality between migrant workers and nationals in respect to employment, working conditions, and social security. Some include aspects of cultural rights, others provide for family reunion, and many provide for continued, although conditional, residence beyond the expiration of the original contract. As Lillich points out, these treaties can hardly be considered broad charters of the rights of migrants and their families. Their purpose is to secure an orderly flow of labour to the industrial states, and they contain little more in the way of human rights guarantees than is necessary for this goal in a humane way (Lillich, p. 110). The ILO recommendations on the terms of such treaties represents little advance on existing practice (the 1949 Convention will be discussed later).

Little needs to be said about regional arrangements, because they have no direct effect on migration from developing countries. For our purpose the importance of regional arrangements is that they establish a dual regime, the more favourable of which is denied to developing-country migrants. But they also establish higher standards for migrant workers, and thus point the direction for the development of general norms (just as at an earlier stage bilateral treaties set the standards to which national legislation should aspire).

An innovation of this period is the development of an international regime for migrants. Previously there was little protection under international law for the migrant workers. The traditional and general rules of international law, which evolved over the years, reflected the needs of international commerce or imperialism. There was no right of immigration into another country under general international law (Goodwin-Gill 1977). If a country is the one to which the migrant belongs through the bonds of nationality, the weight of opinion is that there is a right to enter. There is a similar ambiguity about the right to leave a country. Although the power of a state to prevent a migrant from leaving that state, except in circumstances limited to ensure the enforcement of his legal obligations and liabilities, is denied, the matter is different if the person is a national of the state. A number of countries have imposed restrictions on the right of their nationals to leave, and it would be correct to say that the preponderance of opinion is that the matter was one of domestic jurisdiction. As for the protection of the migrant, there is surprisingly little law. Much of the subject has been concerned with the protection of the property of aliens and their access to the legal system of the country of residence. Thus, there is very considerable literature on the law of nationalisation and on the concept of denial of justice and the exhaustion of local remedies, but not much on the migrant who is an employee. Some rudimentary rules of limitation on expulsion would cover such a person, but their purport and extent are far from clear.

International concern with the rights of migrants began with the establishment of the International Labour Office, whose mandate under the Peace Treaty of Versailles included responsibility for the improvement of the conditions of workers, "involving such injustice, hardship and privation to large numbers of persons as to produce unrest so great that the peace and harmony of the world are imperilled" and highlighted the need for "the protection of the interests of workers when employed in countries other than their own". Since then the ILO has promoted a number of conventions and recommendations for this purpose. In addition to the work of the ILO, some progress has been made through machineries for regional economic cooperation (most prominently the European Union and its predecessor, the EEC, and the Nordic labour market). The international community itself has supplemented the initiatives of the ILO through a series of general declarations and conventions on human rights, which has become a truly global enterprise, not without controversy.

Early UN initiatives in the area of human rights did not directly concern themselves with the situation of migrants or aliens, although several provisions in the Universal Declaration of Human Rights, the International Covenant on Civil and Political Rights, the International Covenant on Economic, Social, and Cultural Rights, and the Convention for the Elimination of all Forms of Racial Discrimination would assist aliens. The UN has also banned slavery and similar institutions, forced labour, traffic in persons, and illicit and clandestine trafficking in migrant labour have either been expressly outlawed or strongly condemned. I do not propose to discuss the scope and limitations of these provisions for this purpose (useful analyses may be found in Lillich 1984, Goodwin-Gill 1977 and 1990, and Plender 1988). At first, the ILO tended to treat the problems of migrant workers in Europe differently from those in the developing countries. Although it now adopts a global approach, there still exist its conventions and recommendations, which apply exclusively to some developing regions. Of the numerous ILO conventions and recommendations, I examine two that have the most extensive and global elaboration of migrants' rights.[7]

The Migration for Employment Convention (Revised), 1949, adopted at a time of labour shortages, contains a number of core compulsory principles and provisions and three optional annexes. The former seek to ensure that migrants have accurate information about their prospects and are given assistance for their journeys, including the provision of medical services. More importantly, it ensures to migrants the same rights as citizens in relation to remuneration, overtime, holidays, apprenticeship and training, membership in trade unions and collective bargaining, accommodation, and social security. Migrants and their families who have been admitted for permanent settlement cannot be forced to return to their country of origin if the migrant is "unable to follow his occupation by reason of illness contracted or injury sustained subsequent to entry", although a country may provide that this right accrues only after a residence not exceeding five years (ART. 6). Migrants may remit savings to their country of origin "taking into account the limits allowed by national laws and regulations" (ART. 7).

The convention thus deals with only a limited number of matters of immediate concern to the migrant, and even then in somewhat tentative terms. To some extent, the annexes, especially the first two, make up for the weaknesses of the convention. The first two annexes deal with the recruitment, placement, and conditions of employment—the first when recruitment is other than under Government-sponsored arrangements for group transfer, the second when it is so. The latter annex provides more extensive protection than the former. Both provide that recruitment may be undertaken only by public authorities or by private agencies licensed for this purpose, which must be supervised by public authorities. Illegal and clandestine recruitment or migration is prohibited and punishable. Both state the principle that the migrant should not have to pay for any services in connection with his recruitment or placement. In countries where there exists a system for supervision of employment contracts of migrants, the migrant has to be given a copy of the contract before his departure, if possible, otherwise, he must be given a memorandum of some kind that states the main provisions of the contract as well as the general conditions of work. States undertake to supervise such contracts and to punish violations thereof. Additionally, the second annex provides that if the migrant, through no fault of his own, is unable to secure the employment for which he was recruited, or any other suitable employment, he shall not be responsible for the costs of transportation home for himself and his family. The recipient state is obliged to try to find him suitable employment, which, however, does not prejudice the welfare of the national workers, and, in some instances, the state is obliged to provide maintenance and arrange for his resettlement.

The ILO has also adopted a Recommendation Concerning Migration (1949), which elaborates the provisions of the Convention and states, in particular, how the state should discharge its responsibilities with regard to the rules of recruitment, information services, facilities for reception of migrants, and help with initial problems of settling in the new country. It goes beyond the convention in suggesting greater protection against expulsion, easing of restrictions on employment opportunities, and provision of social services, especially schooling.

The other principal instrument is the 1975 Convention Concerning Migrant Workers. One part of each deals with migrations in abusive conditions (the response to illicit smuggling of foreign workers in terrible and dangerous conditions) and aims at the elimination of illegal migration. The other part seeks to ensure the equality of opportunity and treatment of migrant workers with respect to employment and other economic rights and to safeguard their cultural rights. The latter is to be done by measures to "preserve their national and ethnic identity and their cultural ties with their country of origin, including the possibility for children to be given some knowledge of their mother tongue" (ART. 12 [f]). There is a vague mention of the reunification of the families of migrant workers. There are similarly vague provisions for the right of free employment after a maximum period of two years or the completion of the first contract if of shorter duration and the recognition of qualifications obtained by a migrant in his or her own country. More far-reaching is the Recommendation 151 Concerning Migrant Workers (1975), in which members states are urged to take "account not only of short-term manpower needs and resources but also of the long-term social and economic consequences of migration for migrants as well as the communities concerned" (ART. 1). Apart from the principle of equality, there is an emphasis on vocational training, security of employment, and security of residence (so, for example, a person who has lost his or her job has to be given a reasonable opportunity to seek alternative employment and social benefits). The reunification of families is stressed, subject to the availability of appropriate accommodation.

The most significant development in the international regime for migrant workers is the Convention on the Protection of All Migrant Workers and Members of Their Families, which was adopted by the United Nations in 1990 (rather than the ILO—allegedly due to preference of developing countries who carry more clout in New York than in Geneva—Roger Bohning 1991, p. 700). Unlike the ILO conventions, this convention covers a wide spectrum of migrant workers (including those in "irregular situation", largely illegal migrants) but excludes "investors", seafarers, and workers on offshore installations. More fundamentally, it preserves to states the right to establish the criteria for admission of migrant workers and their families (ART. 79). The convention therefore deals not with migration as such but the situation of workers once they have been admitted into another country.

Most rights under the convention are granted to all migrant workers, but the rights of seasonal and frontier workers are necessarily limited because of their situation, and illegal migrants do not enjoy all the rights that accrue to legal migrants. The question of illegal migration has been vexed; its formal recognition may, it is feared, lead to excessive and uncontrolled migration, whereas its nonrecognition allows the severe exploitation of illegal migrants. The compromise in the convention, whereby some minimal rights are granted to migrants but the threat of expulsion remains, means that the rights are unlikely to become effective (Bosniak 1991). To a large extent the convention consolidates rights provided under different ILO conventions (e.g., rights to equality in employment relations and trade union rights). It also repeats rights granted under general UN international instruments on human rights, which are not specifically related to migrants, for example, protection against torture or degrading punishment, right to a fair trial, freedom of conscience, and so on, reproducing in fact most of the provisions of the International Covenant on Civil and Political Rights (for a comparison of the convention with other human rights and migrant worker conventions, see James Nafziger and Barry Bartel 1991). Rights that are specifically concerned with migration include the right to leave any state and to return to the state of origin (ART. 8), the right to consular protection (ARTS. 16 and 23), specific protections of the law (e.g., that verifications of the identity of a migrant or his/her family by officials must be carried out in accordance with procedures established by law [ART. 16], protection against arbitrary destruction of identity or travel documents [ART. 21], protection against collective or arbitrary expulsion [ART. 22]), protection against expulsion or revocation of work permit merely for failure to fulfil an obligation of the work contract, unless the fulfillment of that obligation constitutes a condition for residence or work permit (ART. 20), equality with nationals with respect to remuneration and other conditions of employment (irregular situation being no disqualification) (ART. 25), equality of migrants with respect to social security "in as far as they fulfil the requirements provided for by the applicable legislation of that State and the applicable bilateral and multi-lateral treaties" (ART. 27), equality with nationals with respect to emergency medical treatment (ART. 28) and education of children (ART. 30), respect for and official help toward maintaining the cultural identity of migrants, including maintaining their cultural links with countries of origin (ART. 31), the right to transmit earnings and savings on termination of stay in the employing country as well as, "in accordance with the applicable legislation", personal belongings and effects (ART. 32), and the provision of relevant information about migration procedures and rights under the conventions (ART. 33).

A further set of rights is available only to migrants and their families who are "documented or in a regular situation". These are: information on conditions of work and residence before departure from country of origin (ART. 37), the right to liberty of movement in the territory of employment and to choose place of residence (ART. 39), the right to form trade unions and other associations for promotion and protection of economic, social, cultural, and other interests (ART. 40), the right to participate in public affairs in their state of origin, including the right to vote in and stand for elections there (ART. 41), equality of treatment with nationals in relation to access to educational institutions and services, vocational guidance and placement services, vocational training, housing, including social housing schemes, and protection against exploitation with respect to rents, social and health services, cooperatives, and self-managed enterprises, and cultural life (ARTS. 43 and 45), subject to the terms of their permit for residence and employment, equality of treatment with nationals with respect to protection against dismissal, unemployment benefits, access to public work schemes intended to combat unemployment, and access to alternative employment in the event of loss of work or termination of other remunerated activity (ART. 54), prohibition of expulsion for the purpose of depriving a migrant worker or a member of his or her family of rights arising from residence and work permits and in any case the need to take humanitarian considerations into account when deciding on expulsion (including the length of stay) (ART. 56), and equal tax treatment (ART. 48).

Migrants are also to enjoy exemption from export and import duties with respect to their personal and household goods and work equipment upon departure for employment or return to country of origin (ART. 46). Migrants are to have the right to transfer earnings and savings to the country of origin, "in conformity with procedures established by applicable legislation of the State concerned and in conformity with applicable international agreements" (ART. 47).

In addition the states of employment are urged to establish institutions, on which migrants themselves should be represented, for dealing with the special needs, aspirations, and obligations of migrants (ART. 42) as well as to grant permission to them of temporary absences without jeopardy to their work or residence permits (ART. 38). There are a number of provisions about rights of employment and residence. The general principle as to the former is that migrants should be free to choose their employment, subject to restrictions that are in the interests of the state or that depend on particular qualifications. For migrants whose stay is limited, the right of free employment may be subject to a prior maximum stay of two years or to other conditions that may be authorised under bilateral or multilateral agreements, except that such restrictions must cease after a maximum of five years' residence (ART. 52).

States that separate residence from work permit are urged to ensure that the authorisation for residence is coextensive with the period for which the right to work is granted, and migrants who are allowed to freely choose their employment shall not be deemed to be in irregular situation merely by terminating their employment prior to the contractual period; instead they would be granted sufficient time to find alternative employment (ART. 49). Even where a migrant has not been granted the right of free employment, he or she would be allowed time to find alternative employment (including in state-sponsored schemes) for the remaining period of their permit (ART. 51). There are a number of special rights to protect the family and family life of the migrant: States are under a general obligation to take appropriate measures to ensure the protection of the unity of the family (including reunification facilities) and are urged to extend equality of treatment with nationals to members of migrants' families in relation to employment and training (ARTS. 44 and 45). States that admit members of families on the basis of unification should consider sympathetically their right of continued residence in the case of the death of the migrant or in the event of divorce (ART. 50). Children of migrants are to be integrated into the host community via the educational system as well as to have the facilities to learn their mother tongue and culture (ART. 45).

In line with international human rights instruments, the convention makes provision for the supervision and (to a more limited extent) the enforcement of its rights. The ability of a member state to enter reservations reflects the general "compromise" nature of the convention: A state may make reservations, but cannot exclude any part of it (meaning that reservations may be made to specific rights) or disapply it to particular categories of workers (except as provided in the convention itself) (ART. 88). It should also be remembered that many provisions are made subject to national legislation or are merely hortatory. Three methods of supervision or enforcement, only one of which is compulsory, are provided. A committee of experts is to be established to whom member states have to submit periodic reports on the implementation of the convention (ARTS. 72 and 73). The application of one or both of the other methods depends on the choice of the state concerned. A state may agree that another state may complain to the committee against its violation of the convention (ART. 76), and it may also agree that a resident of the state may have direct access to the committee (ART. 77). The committee has in no instance the power to order enforcement, but the assumption—not always justified by the experience under other instruments—is that its rulings or conciliation efforts will solve the problem.

There is no doubt that the convention marks a significant advance in migrants' rights. For the first time it places these rights within the international regime of human rights (even if this is achieved through redundancy—the first set of rights under the convention is for the most part merely a repetition of existing UN instruments, particularly the Covenant of Civil and Political Rights). However, it is inevitably a compromise between the views of labour-exporting and labour-importing countries. The latter, anxious to maintain as much freedom of action as possible, are unlikely to rush to ratify the convention and the prospects of it coming into force in the near future are remote (a fate it will share with previous ILO conventions—only thirty-eight countries have signed the 1949 convention, excluding major immigration countries like Germany, Sweden, Denmark, the United States, Canada, and Switzerland, and only fourteen states have adhered to the key ILO convention of 1975). The internationally defined rights of migrants will, for the foreseeable future, subsist merely on paper, aspirations rather than reality.

Conclusion

The legal regime of migrant workers has varied over the long period of migrations sketched in this chapter. The regime of slavery reflected the laissez-faire economy of the time, with the major responsibility for developing juridical norms vested in the judiciary. The slave was reduced to a commodity, and his or her owner disposed of him or her like any other chattel. The system of indentured labour was founded on a statutory scheme, with the rudiments of regulation (in other areas too, the nineteenth century was indeed the age of statute). It represented an increased involvement of the state and the bureaucracy in economic matters. It was a consensual regime, however unreal effective consent may be under economic or political stress. The twentieth century regime, based on consent and voluntariness, is complex and variegated. The complexity owes itself to a new balance of claims and interests as well as to the internationalisation of the issue of migrant labour. It is compounded of national and international norms, administered by state functionaries, and supervised by the judiciary.

The early years of the twentieth century marked the decline of imperial hegemony, and with it the rise of a more multilateral world. The legal regimes of slavery and indenture had reflected imperial hegemony, providing a kind of both uniformity and unity. This was replaced in the twentieth century by a plethora of legal regimes, a manifestation of diverse national traditions, and the break up of sovereignty tying labour importing and exporting territories. If everywhere the market determined the incidence of migration, national juridical traditions supplied the technique to regulate it. However a convergence of sorts has begun, imposed by both the imperatives of the market and social order and the emerging international regime of rights and justice. The democratisation of the political orders in the West produce a contradiction: populist pressures that seek to deny rights to migrants and the rights-oriented values of democracy that impel the law toward the equality of all. The political emergence of the Third World (the exporter of labour) has redressed, even if partially, old imbalances. The development of an international regime of rights has greatly affected the norms governing migrant labour. They are imperfectly applied to this area—denying a major premise of the Western theory of rights as universal and inalienable (and calling into question the quality of the West's commitment to rights). In its early days migrant labour was of course based on the forced or voluntary alienation of rights, and despite the progress since then, a migrant worker even today alienates some of his or her rights in order to earn a living.

In recent decades it was sovereignty that came between a migrant worker and his or her rights (and increasingly it is her—reflecting the present state of the international division of labour). But the stranglehold of sovereignty has slowly been prised loose—equality of economic rights is acknowledged (if not always practised), and a state's right to expel foreigners is no longer unqualified. Regional labour markets have further attenuated the links between a state and its subjects, and citizenship in its emotional and legal terms is no longer what it was. Indeed international, regional, and national norms increasingly secure to a migrant in his or her country of employment and residence the enjoyment of the culture of his or her country of origin. Multiculturalism has become a shibboleth of our age, and migration is at the centre of it.

Consequently the market determines rights and obligations less directly than in the days of slavery and indenture. It is somewhat ironical that whereas during slavery and indenture, the movements of people were driven by the global market (even if "national" markets implemented the market principle of labour imperfectly), in our own more global age, movements are less determined purely by market considerations, although national markets themselves have, domestically, applied more rigorously the market principles of mobility, equality, and competition. I have suggested that there are two factors that have contributed to this result: political pressures and imperatives in Western states (tending toward the halt to migration but the improvement of the position of existing migrants) and the international movement toward human rights.

It is appropriate to end this chapter with a few brief reflections on the human rights movements since it is seen as such a distinctive feature of the present global processes. Except for a short period of anticolonial struggles, the pressures for international human rights have come from the West. It has sought to emphasise the common humanity of the peoples of the world by declarations about the inherent dignity of the person and the universalism and inalienability of his or her rights. The ideas themselves are not new; what is new is that the international community claims a responsibility for the protection of rights, and thus empowers a citizen vis-à-vis his or her state, and other states. Rights are no more a matter of only domestic jurisdiction. This globalisation is undermined by the persistence of the state as the framework for the definition, enjoyment, and qualifications of rights and by the special status accorded to citizenship. Nowhere is this dilemma more clearly highlighted than in the case of migrants' rights. The West, the champion of universalism and inalienability, has been reluctant to recognise the equality of migrants with nationals, and migrants rights have been something of a Cinderella in the family of human rights (as is clear from the slow progress over, and the limited scope of, the 1990 Migration Convention and its studied disregard since its formal adoption). It is necessary to guard against the optimism that the world has achieved other kinds of rights, for the fact is that the international human rights movement has made remarkably little impact on international practice, as we are reminded daily. It exists primarily in the sphere of rhetoric and ideology, and even there it has become a matter of great controversy (Ghai 1994). Yet migration, by itself and as part of globalisation processes, has made the most fundamental challenges to the state, making borders porous, attenuating the bonds of citizenship (extending more and more rights to nonnationals), and detracting from the distinctiveness of "national" cultures, making multiculturalists of us all. By a further irony it is in the West that these developments have advanced the most, for with the lapse of the economic hegemony of the West, migration has become increasingly a south-south phenomenon. It is in the new labour-importing countries like Japan, Hong Kong, Singapore, Malaysia (Battistella 1993) and the Gulf states (Amjad 1989) that there occur the most serious violations of the (internationally defined) rights of migrants. It is necessary to caution overselves against optimism regarding the positive impact on human rights of globalisation processes.

Notes

1. This paper is a revised version of a paper presented at the International Conference on Global History and Migrations held at the University of Hong Kong in January 1994. I am grateful to Professors Wang Gungwu and Robin Cohen (and other participants at the conference) for their helpful comments.

2. A vivid illustration of the market organisation of slave trade, with the slave trading companies being granted the attributes of government, with procurers and middlemen, discounts for favoured or powerful clients, the risk of the ill health of the slave passing with property in him or her, with insurance policies that made it more expedient to throw slaves overboard to sharks in the mid-Atlantic than have them transported in safety in an emaciated condition, all the while weaving a triangular web of commercial intercourse between three continents, is the powerful novel of Barry Unsworth, *The Sacred Hunger* (1993).

3. I am grateful to Abdul Paliwala for this point.

4. Britain imposed restrictions on refugees fleeing from the French Revolution, and the United States and Switzerland imposed restrictions on what they regarded as Jacobin emissaries trying to infiltrate immigrant groups. Just before the outbreak of the Napoleonic Wars, France introduced legislation requiring passports.

5. There is no space to discuss in detail regional arrangements for labour mobility, since workers from developing countries did not benefit from them. The most advanced regime of rights for migrant workers is the European Convention on the Legal Status of Migrant Workers (1977), which is restricted to the nationals of member-states of the Council of Europe (Lillich 1984, pp. 89–94).

6. A distinguished scholar, Richard Lillich has written of contemporary developments, "the law governing the treatment of aliens—in its broadest sense—resembles a giant unassembled juridical jigsaw puzzle. . . . Actually, this figure of speech is not entirely apt, since it conveys the impression that there exists a certain number of pieces which, when assembled, will complete a predetermined design. With respect to the treatment of aliens, however, the number of pieces is uncertain and the grand design is still emerging, as is obvious from a perusal of the preceding chapters. . . . Thus another figure of speech, taken from the fashion world, might be more appropriate: 'the layered look'. For over the basic garment (the customary international law of state responsibility for injuries to aliens), nation-states have placed shirts, sweaters, and jackets (bilateral treaties, regional arrangements, and multinational conventions), leaving the alien's body protected by a varying number of layers (legal regimes) depending upon the sartorial tastes of the State involved. While the trend has been towards greater protection of the alien from the chilling effect of the State's far-reaching sovereign powers over his or her admission, stay and expulsion, the extent of such protection varies greatly, leaving aliens in many States inadequately protected, both substantively and procedurally, as the present time" (Lillich, p. 122).

7. Of these the important ones are: Convention on the Recruiting of Indigenous Workers (1936); Convention on the Contracts of Employment (Indigenous Workers) (1929); Convention concerning Social Policy (Non-Metropolitan Territories) (1947); Convention concerning Equality of Treatment in Social Security (1962); and Convention concerning Rights in Social Security (1982).

References

Amjad, R., ed. (1989) *To the Gulf and Back* (Geneva: ILO).

Ansay, T. (1991) "The New UN Convention in the Light of German and Turkish Experience", *Twenty-fifth International Migration Review*, 831–847.

Battistella, G. (1993) *Human Rights of Migrant Workers: Agenda for NGOs* (Quezon City, Philippines: Scalabrini Migration Center).

Bosniak, L. S. (1991) "Human Rights, State Sovereignty, and the Protection of Undocumented Migrants Under the International Migrant Workers Convention", *Twenty-fifth International Migration Review*, 737–770.

Cohen, Robin. (1987) *The New Helots: Migrants in the International Division of Labour* (Aldershot, Engl.: Gower Press).

Collinson, S. (1994) "Public Policies Towards Immigrant Minorities in Western Europe" (Geneva: United Nations Research Institute for Social Development).

Corris, Peter. (1973) *Passage, Port, and Plantation* (Melbourne: Melbourne University Press).

Davis, D. B. (1975) *The Problem of Slavery in the Age of Revolution* (Ithaca: Cornell University Press).

Entzinger, H. B. (1985) "The Netherlands", in Tomas Hammar, *European Immigration Policy* (Cambridge: Cambridge University Press).

Esser, H., and H. Korte (1985) "Federal Republic of Germany", in Tomas Hammar, *European Immigration Policy*.

Genovese, Eugene. (1961) *The Political Economy of Slavery*.

Ghai, Yash. (1994) *Human Rights and Governance: The Asia Debate* (San Francisco: The Asia Foundation).

Goodwin-Gill, G. (1978) *International Law and the Movement of Persons Between States* (Oxford: Clarendon Press).

Goodwin-Gill, G. (1989) "International Law and Human Rights: Trends Concerning International Migrants and Refugees", *International Migration Review* 23:526–546.

Hammar, T. (1985) "Sweden", in Tomas Hammar, *European Immigration Policy*.

Hammar, T. (1985b) "Comparative Analysis", in Tomas Hammar, *European Immigration Policy*.

Helton, A. C. (1991) "The New Convention from the Perspective of a Country of Employment: The U.S. Case", *International Migration Review* 25:848–858.

Hoffman-Nowotony, H.-J. (1985) "Switzerland", in Tomas Hammar, *European Immigration Policy*.

Layton-Henry, Z. (1988) "The UK", in Tomas Hammar, *European Immigration Policy*.

Layton-Henry, Z. (1990) "The challenge of political rights", in Z. Layton-Henry, ed., *The Political Rights of Migrant Workers in Western Europe* (London: Sage Publications).

Lillich, R. B. (1984) *The Human Rights of Aliens in Contemporary International Law* (Manchester: Manchester University Press).

Lonnroth, J. (1991) "The International Convention of the Rights of All Migrant Workers and Members of Their Families in the Context of International Migration Policies: An Analysis of Ten Years of Negotiation", *International Migration Review* 25:710–736.

Martin, D. A. (1989) "Effects of International Law on Migration Policy and Practice: The Uses of Hypocrisy", *International Migration Review* 23:547–578.

Nafziger, J. A., and B. C. Bartel (1991) "The Migrant Workers Convention: Its Place in Human Rights Law", *International Migration Review* 25:4, pp. 771–799.

Naidu, Vijay. (1980) *The Violence of Indenture in Fiji* (Suva, Fiji: University of the South Pacific).

Nanda, Ved. (1993) "The Protection of the Rights of Migrant Workers: Unfinished Business", in G. Battistella, ed., *Human Rights of Migrant Workers: Agenda for NGOs* (Manila: Scalabrini Migration Centre).

Plender, Richard. (1988) *International Migration Law,* rev. 2d ed. (Dordrecht, the Netherlands: Martinus Nijhoff).

Plender, Richard, ed. (1988) *Basic Documents on International Migration Law* (Dordrecht, the Netherlands: Martinus Nijhoff).

Potts, Lydia. (1990) *The World Labour Market: A History of Migration* (London: Zed Press).

Richardson, Peter. (1982) *Chinese Mine Labour in the Transvaal* (London: Macmillan Press).

Tinker, Hugh. (1974) *A New System of Slavery* (London: Oxford University Press).

Tushnet, Mark. (1975) "The American Law of Slavery, 1810–1860: A Study in the Persistence of Legal Autonomy", *Law and Society Review* 10:1, 2, and 119.

Unsworth, B. (1992) *The Sacred Hunger* (New York: Doubleday).

Verbunt, G. (1985) "France", in Tomas Hammar, *European Immigration Policy.*

Verzijl, J. H. N. (1972) *International Law in Historical Perspective,* vol. 5 (Leiden, the Netherlands: A. W. Sijthoff).

Wheeler, Jacob D. (1837) *A Practical Treatise on the Law of Slavery Being a Compilation of all the Decisions Made on That Subject by the Several Courts of the United States and State Courts* (New York: Negro Universities Press, reprint 1968).

Wolfrum, R. (1993) "The Emergence of 'New Minorities' as a Result of Migration", in Catherine Brolmann, et al., eds., *Peoples and Minorities in International Law* (Dordrecht, the Netherlands: Martinus Nijhoff).

7

Of Migration, Great Cities, and Markets: Global Systems of Development

Ronald Skeldon

In April 1976, before global issues and global history became as fashionable as they are today, there took place in New Harmony, Indiana, a conference on Human Migration: Patterns, Implications, and Policies. The perspective of that meeting was very clearly on global migration. Several of the papers at that 1976 meeting (see McNeill and Adams 1978) were seminal in their field, and it is interesting to look back to see how migration was viewed then and to venture an assessment of what we might have learned since. The compulsive element behind so much of human migration, rather than free choice, and the significance of state action appear to have been important themes of the discussions of that 1976 meeting (McNeill 1978). The geographer at the meeting, Terry McGee, questioned the relevance of the conventional approaches to the study of migration for the analysis of the situation in Asia (McGee 1978). He argued that the high population densities in the rural sector of Asian countries made the development of European-type urbanization patterns unlikely and that we needed to design new paradigms and models more appropriate to the Asian context. He saw the experience of socialist Asian countries, notably China, as offering a possible alternative (McGee 1978, p. 219).

This chapter will attempt to build upon this earlier work by examining recent trends in the relationship between migration and development and in the interpretation of urbanization and the growth of large cities. The focus will mainly be upon Asia, although the spatial perspective will be broadened in places as a preliminary attempt to search for more general patterns. The approach is one of work-in-progress and the sections are very much at a hypothetical stage, reflecting speculative thought rather than statements well grounded in empirical fact.

Separate or Parallel Evolutionary Patterns?

The core of Terry McGee's critique of the then "theoretical underpinnings" of the conventional approaches to the study of rural-to-urban mobility was that they ignored or misinterpreted the factors "which can be subsumed within the process of the penetration of capitalism" (McGee 1978, p. 206). McGee's search for a different model or different paradigm of migration has led him in subsequent work to continue to challenge the Western view of the urban transition (McGee 1991, McGee and Yeung 1993, see also Ginsburg 1991). He argues for the emergence of distinctive zones of agricultural and nonagricultural activities in the interface between rural and urban that, he maintains, were never found in the historical experience of urbanization in the West. These zones he calls *desakota,* meaning extensive, densely populated areas of intense interaction with both rural and urban areas.

The rejection of Western-type models of the urban transition was a fairly influential current of thinking from the mid-1970s. For example, Pryor (1981, p. 114) argued strongly that "western-derived theories and models may be fundamentally unsuited to Third World applications" and maintained that any quest for a single theory of migration was a "quest for utopia". The important role of natural increase in urban growth in developing countries, the significance of circulation rather than of permanent migration, and the growth of informal activities, unemployment, and self-built housing in the cities all appeared to suggest a process quite different from that of the historical experience of Europe.

That there are clear distinctions between the present developing world experience and the European experience seems incontrovertible. The former is occurring in a very different technological era, and one could not expect the patterns of mobility to be the same in an age dominated by the aeroplane and the automobile as they were in one that was characterized by the steamship or horse-drawn carriage. Nevertheless, there are similarities: circulation, informal sector activities, and unemployment were also clearly part of the Western experience of urbanization and cannot be seen as characteristic of just present developing countries (Skeldon 1990). Agricultural activities close to European core urban areas were also an integral part of that process.

It is also deceptive to talk of "present developing world experience" as if there are commonalities across the whole area that might be designated as "developing". To go back to the mid-1970s, the example of China was seen as providing an alternative to Western approaches to development (Aziz 1978). Its apparent success in "eliminating destitution and unemployment through a system of communes" provided an impetus for the search for new approaches in rural development (Lea and Chaudhri

1983a). The Indiana meeting on migration was held some five months before the death of Mao Tse-tung and almost three years before China embarked upon its reforms and opened its economy to outside forces. Today, we know much more of what occurred in China during the Maoist period, although the jury is still out on whether China over the medium term really pursued a radically different development path compared with other countries. In terms of population mobility, China certainly appears to have successfully controlled cityward migration from the late 1950s to the late 1970s. Without these controls, it has been estimated that China's urban population would have been about twice its size in the mid-1980s (Banister 1987). McGee is correct in identifying China as a critical test case of general models of migration. Simply because of China's sheer size in terms of population, what occurs there is going to affect global patterns one way or another. The issue of whether migration in China has indeed been different from that in other countries will be raised in a little more detail toward the end of this chapter.

Although the trend toward "interdependent development" (Brookfield 1975) has been clear from long before the 1976 conference, there has been a veritable explosion of writing on global issues, globalization, and global systems since that time. This chapter will, following its mandate, focus more on the economic aspects, but here too the literature is extensive. The range of writing on these global issues can be gathered from the works of Bennet and Estall (1991), Chase-Dunn (1989), Dicken (1992), Henderson (1989), King (1990), Peet (1991), Sklair (1991), and Wallace (1990), with global approaches to migration in Kritz, Lim, and Zlotnik (1992), Kritz, Keely, and Tomasi (1981), and Potts (1990). Much of this writing explicitly or implicitly has been influenced by Marxist thought. The ideas centre essentially around the spatial expansion of economic activities around the world so that no national, let alone regional, economy can be self-sufficient. An international division of labour has arisen that capitalizes on the relative costs of factors of production in different parts of the world. The transnational corporation has been at the heart of this development and introduces tensions between the sovereignty of individual states and these dynamic and powerful capitalist enterprises. As the various sites of production have extended over space, so the need to control these from a central point has increased, paradoxical though this may at first appear. These centripetal forces have given rise to the emergence of the "global city". Sassen (1991) has attempted to show from an analysis of the structural change in these cities that there are parallels that appear to transcend the very different cultural, geographical, and historical contexts of three global cities, New York, London, and Tokyo.

There thus appear to be two opposing interpretations. On the one hand, there is the call to reject Western models as appropriate to describe the situation in developing countries, and on the other hand, the impact of global processes appears to draw attention to parallels between the situations in very different parts of the world. Rather than seeking out absolutely new paradigms, it might be more appropriate to modify existing approaches while still maintaining a unitary framework. This chapter will attempt to see whether the patterns of migration associated with development can in some way be fitted into a unified framework or whether separate paradigms for Western and nonwestern areas are required.

The Penetration of Capitalist Industrial Systems

The starting point of Terry McGee's argument, the core of the global city idea of Sassen, and the basis for previous work I have carried out on the evolution of migration in developing countries (Skeldon 1990) all appear to have one fundamental point in common: The key force setting change in motion is the extension of capitalism—or the "penetration of capitalism" if we take the point of view of the developing areas. (See also the work of Potts [1990] and Cohen [1987].) The examination of migration in relation to this penetration is commonly restricted to the recruitment of migrant labour: of indentured Indians or Chinese coolies in the nineteenth century, of African labour to the mines of southern Africa, or of Asians to the oil-rich countries of the Middle East in the second half of the twentieth century, for example. Important though these flows have been, they represent but part of the total mobility associated with "development" or the spread of capitalism. These labour flows are often separated from the matrices of population movements in the areas of origin and the areas of destination, and this focus on only one part of total population mobility diverts attention from the whole system of change. This chapter will take one area where, by any measure, the penetration of capitalism has been intense, to chart briefly the changing migration patterns. The discussion will then be changed to a global level in an attempt to "fit" the model developed into a broader framework. The region is that of the newly industrializing economies of East Asia.

The four little tigers of East Asia—South Korea, Taiwan, Hong Kong, and Singapore—have experienced one of the longest periods of sustained economic growth in recent history. Combined, they registered annual average per capita growth rates of GNP from 1960 to 1985 of just under 10 percent—a remarkable performance indeed. They increased their share of world exports from 1.5 percent in 1965 to 6.7 percent in 1990, and their share of world export of manufactured goods, from 1.5 percent to 7.9 percent over the same period (World Bank 1993b). These bald figures, however, hide a major structural transformation in the nature of their economic base. There has been a shift from a limited number of light, labour-intensive industries through to a complex range of capital-intensive, knowledge-based industries. The progression of South Korea's industrial development is given in Table 7.1. Not all the newly industrialized economies have followed the same combination of industries, but they have all specialized in particular groups of industries, and all have moved from labour-intensive, to capital-intensive, to knowledge-intensive industrialization. Within this transition is the shift from import-substitution industries to export-oriented industries, a story that has been well told elsewhere—see, for example, World Bank (1993b) and Haggard (1990).

The implication that this shift has for migration lies partly in the changing nature of the labour demand of the various industries. At the most obvious level, the initial demand is for large volumes of relatively unskilled labour, whereas later the demand is for greater skill levels. Unskilled labour can be turned around fairly rapidly, and there are advantages to employers in doing so. Employers' commitments to employees in terms of protection and benefits can be minimal, and any attempts to improve conditions on the part of the employees can be dealt with by dismissal at little cost to the company. Organizations among labour are weakly developed, if they exist at all—rapid turnover of personnel does not allow the generation of the kinds of experience necessary for the emergence of such organizations—and much of the labour is female. The nature of this industrial complex favours close linkages with the rural hinterland, with a high incidence of circulation between town and country. Some of this will be seasonal in East Asia, depending upon demands in the rice economy, but essentially we are dealing with intense systems of rural-to-urban circulation such as have been described in Indonesia, Thailand, and elsewhere in the developing world (see Hugo 1982, Goldstein 1978, Skeldon 1990, and Prothero and Chapman 1985). The costs of reproduction of this labour force are borne by the origin rather than the destination societies (Burawoy 1976, also Smith 1982, pp. 29–30).

As the skill levels demanded by the industrial enterprises rise, then the training costs increase and turnover is discouraged. This transition in skill demand will contribute to discouraging labour circulation and encouraging a more permanent labour force. Clearly, this shift does not occur over the short term or simultaneously across all industries—there are low-skill industries that persist throughout the industrial structural transformation, for example, construction—but, over the long term, there will be a reduction in circulation from rural origin of migration to the main urban centres. One of the clearest cases to illustrate this progression comes not from Asia but from South Africa, where technological shifts in the gold-mining industry encouraged a stabilization in the labour force (Lemon 1982). This was certainly reinforced by the increasing importance of sec-

TABLE 7.1 Stages in South Korea's Export-Oriented Industrial Development

	1961–1966	*1966–1971*	*1971–1976*	*1976–1981*	*1981–1986*
Infant industries	Textiles Clothing Footwear	Electronic assemblies Shipbuilding Fertilizers Steel	Motor vehicle assembly Consumer electronics Special steels Precision goods (watches, cameras) Turnkey plant building Metal products	Automotive components Machine tools Machinery assembly Simple instruments Assembly of heavy electrical machinery Semiconductors	
Industries becoming competitive		Textiles Clothing Footwear	Electronic assemblies Shipbuilding Fertilizers Steels	Motor vehicle assembly Consumer electronics Special steels Precision goods Turnkey plant building Metal products	Automotive components Machine tools Machinery assembly Simple instruments Assembly of heavy electrical machinery Semiconductors

Self-sustaining industries	Textiles Clothing Footwear	Electronic assemblies Shipbuilding Fertilizers Steel	Motor vehicle assembly Consumer electronics Special steels Precision goods Turnkey plant building Metal products

Source: Adapted from Boston Consulting Group, 1978, Appendix 5, p. 30. Cited in G. J. R. Linge and F. E. Hamilton, "International Industrial Systems", in F. E. I. Hamilton and G. J. R. Linge, eds., *Industry and the Industrial Environment. Volume II International Industrial Systems* (London: Wiley), 1981, p. 33.

ondary industries, but the new technologies of mining meant that it was no longer economic to turn labour around after every contract, and the skilled workers required by the industry were encouraged to remain. The stabilization of the black labour force and the emergence of middle-income groups have surely been important factors in the recent demise of apartheid. The transition toward a reduction in circulation over time has also been clearly documented for other parts of the developing world (Skeldon 1990).

It would be naive to associate the concentration of populations and forms of mobility directly to the establishment of jobs in labour-intensive firms. All the experience of urban growth in the developing world over the last four decades has shown that job creation does not keep pace with additions to the urban population. Large proportions of these populations, in some cases the majority, enter into self-created jobs in the so-called "informal sector". This sector has been seen as distinct from the formal sector, yet the differences are more apparent than real when comparing the labour-intensive "formal" industries with informal industries and service activities. In neither sector is there job security. Earnings in the informal sector may be as high as or higher than those in the formal sector. For example, in a study in New Delhi, no great difference in income-earning opportunities between the two sectors was found (Bannerjee 1986), and in Lima, Peru, where much detailed analysis of the informal sector has been carried out, per capita earnings in the informal sector were 38 percent higher than the minimum legal wage (De Soto 1989, p. 62). Both sectors consist of segmented labour markets that are controlled by specific groups. These groups are often migrants from particular areas of origin, and villagers have been shown to control access to specific occupations in localities as widely different as Peru, Indonesia, and Papua New Guinea (see Prothero and Chapman 1985, also Skeldon 1990).

The essence of the previous argument is that the simple dualistic interpretations so common in development studies are insufficient. The transformation is not simply from agriculture to industry but to an ever-changing mix of industries and services, each with their own skill demands and ultimately their own forms of spatial mobility. With the initial shift toward more capital-intensive industrialization and less-segmented labour markets, there is a tendency for the incidence of internal circulation to slow as people stay longer at destinations and at particular jobs.

However, while these changes occur, other forms of movement emerge, many of these associated with circulation. The increasing demand for ever-higher skills generates two forms of international migration: the movement of students overseas and the importation of skills from core developed areas. Although significant numbers of students may remain at the destination after completing their studies, many do return to transfer skills and assume entrepreneurial roles in their home economy. It is estimated that between 20 and 30 percent of professionals in South Korea, for example, were trained overseas (Kuznets 1987), and return movements are a major factor in the other East Asian economies. The numbers of students from the Asian (and other) economies studying in the United States are given in Table 7.2.

Labour-intensive development in the East Asia economies developed at such a rate that labour demand was exceeding supply from the early 1960s in the case of Hong Kong, from the mid- to late 1960s in the case of Taiwan, and from the mid-1970s in the case of South Korea. Malaysia, too, in the 1980s became a labour-deficit economy. The initial rapid growth of the labour forces and the incorporation of female labour partially relieved acute labour shortages, but pressure has built up over the last decade to reduce labour-intensive activities both in industries and in some services; the informal sector, or the hawker or bazaar economy, has virtually disappeared as a significant employer of labour in Hong Kong, for example. There has been a shift in the location of the initial labour-intensive industries as the local costs of labour have increased with rising skill levels. These are moving offshore in the cases of South Korea and Taiwan, although the clearest cases are the movements to the immediate hinterlands of Hong Kong and Singapore. Employment in the manufacturing sector of Hong Kong has dropped markedly since the first half of the 1980s (Figure 7.1) and a regional division by functional activity is emerging around the eastern side of the Pearl River Delta (Figure 7.2). Similarly, Singapore is exporting its labour-intensive industries into the so-called "growth triangle", incorporating the Riau Islands in Indonesia and Johor in Malaysia (Figure 7.3).

The expansion of the transnational capitalist system, initially from the core growth areas of Eastern Europe and North America and later from Western North America and Japan implies an evolution of industrial systems and their diffusion outward. Two of the leading exponents of this capitalist system have invoked the spirit of Frederick Jackson Turner in their recent work, even if they disagree on the primary driving forces (Storper and Walker 1989, p. 208). The diffusion, however, need not be in regular waves across contiguous space but can vault to favoured regions; and the main innovations do not necessarily always originate in the centre. The shifts in products that are consequent upon technological innovation are reflected in international business long cycles. Each cycle is centred around particular locations that undergo restructuring as the new industrial zones of the next cycle emerge. Although, in some cases, these zones may be contiguous—the transformation of central Hong Kong and Singapore are clear as the labour-intensive industries of the previous cycle are pushed toward the peripheries in China and Malaysia, for example—

TABLE 7.2 Leading Ten Places of Origin of Foreign Students and Percentage Share, 1954/1955–1991/1992

Locality	*Foreign Students*	*% of Total*
1954/1955		
1. Canada	4,655	13.6
2. China	2,553	7.5
3. India	1,673	4.9
4. Japan	1,572	4.6
5. Philippines	1,476	4.3
6. Colombia	1,301	3.8
7. Mexico	1,247	3.6
8. South Korea	1,197	3.5
9. Iran	997	2.9
10. Venezuela	882	2.6
1964/1965		
1. Canada	9,253	11.3
2. India	6,813	8.3
3. Taiwan	6,780	8.3
4. Iran	3,719	4.5
5. Japan	3,386	4.1
6. Hong Kong	3,279	4.0
7. South Korea	2,604	3.2
8. Philippines	2,473	3.0
9. United Kingdom	1,959	2.4
10. Thailand	1,630	2.0
1974/1975		
1. Iran	13,780	8.9
2. Hong Kong	11,060	7.2
3. Taiwan	10,250	6.6
4. India	9,660	6.2
5. Canada	8,430	5.5
6. Nigeria	7,210	4.7
7. Thailand	6,250	4.0
8. Japan	5,930	3.8
9. Mexico	4,000	2.6
10. South Korea	3,390	2.2

(continues)

but, in other cases, these zones may be separated by considerable distances. Modern systems of communication in an era of "post-Fordism" industrial production, which depends upon flexible high-technology production, allow the assembly of components that may have been made on different continents.

TABLE 7.2 *(continued)*

Locality	*Foreign Students*	*% of Total*
1984/1985		
1. Taiwan	22,590	6.6
2. Malaysia	21,720	6.3
3. Nigeria	18,370	5.4
4. Iran	16,640	4.9
5. Canada	16,430	4.8
6. South Korea	15,370	4.5
7. India	14,610	4.3
8. Venezuela	13,160	3.8
9. Japan	10,290	3.0
10. Hong Kong	10,130	3.0
1991/1992		
1. China	42,940	10.2
2. Japan	40,700	9.7
3. Taiwan	35,550	8.6
4. India	32,530	7.8
5. South Korea	25,720	6.1
6. Canada	19,190	4.6
7. Hong Kong	13,190	3.1
8. Malaysia	12,650	3.0
9. Indonesia	10,250	2.4
10. Pakistan	8,120	1.9

Source: Open Doors 1991–1992: Report on International Educational Exchange (New York: Institute of International Education), 1992.

The coordination and the financing of these activities are controlled through a hierarchy of cities, with the global cities of New York, London, and Tokyo at the apex. In essence, these cities create global space based upon functional divisions of labour. From being local-level and then national-level centres, these cities have grown to have a global influence primarily through their role as headquarters for multinational corporations and international banks (Cohen 1981). These cities are linked down to regional and national cities in a system of nested hierarchies that articulate the global system. The evolution of these global cities from the sixteenth century has been traced by King (1990) and by Chase-Dunn (1985). What seems important is that each new cycle over the last 150 years has given further impetus for expansion into the periphery, with an increasing number of global cities to be found there. In Asia, the Hong Kong–Guangzhou axis has clearly emerged as a global city, with predictions made by the generally conservative Hong Kong Bank that it will be the largest finance

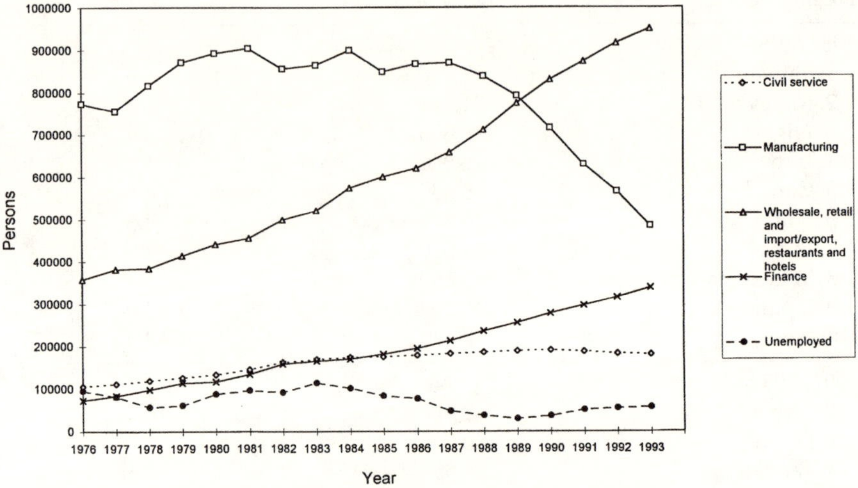

FIGURE 7.1 Employment and Unemployment in Hong Kong, 1976–1993

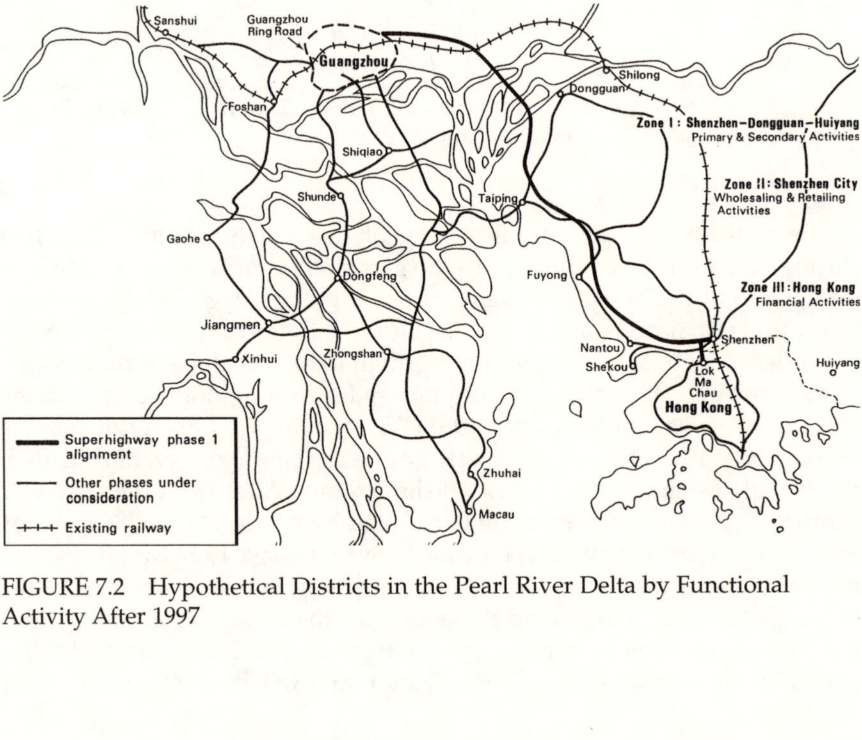

FIGURE 7.2 Hypothetical Districts in the Pearl River Delta by Functional Activity After 1997

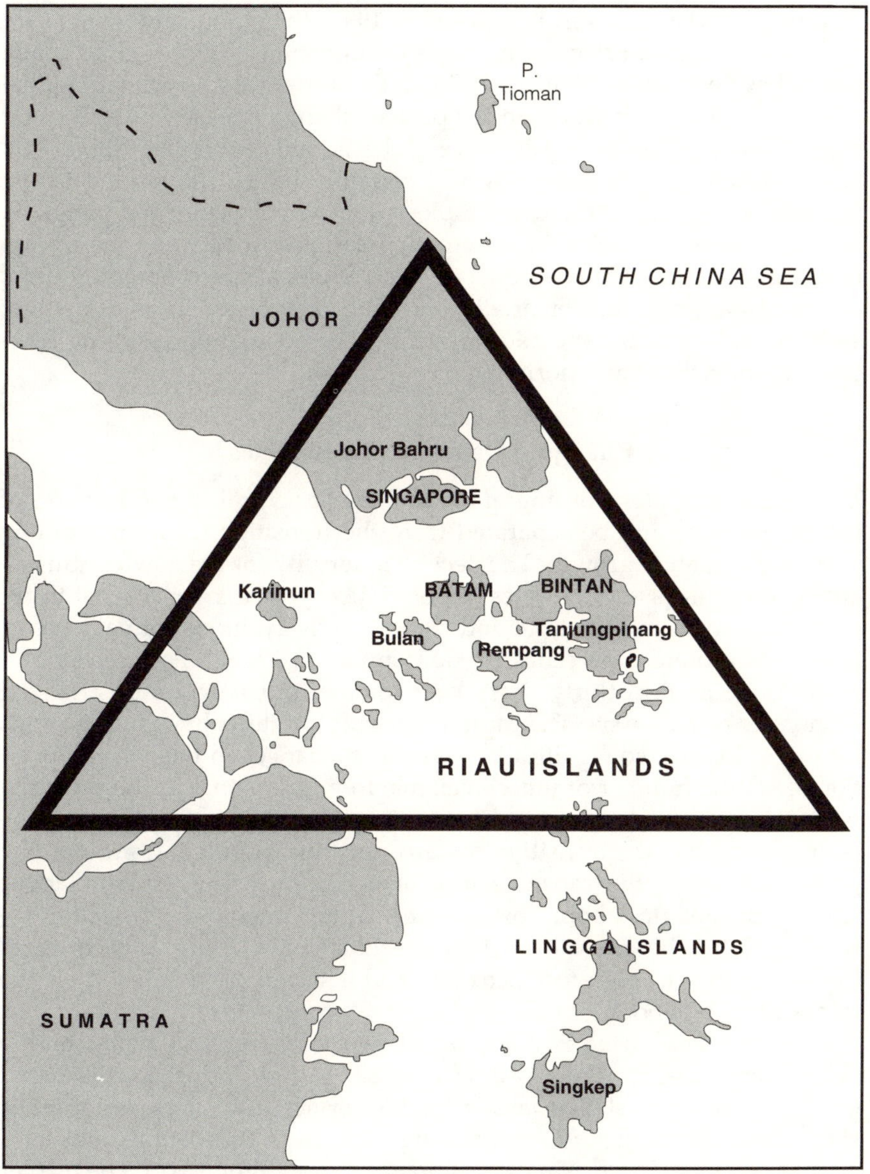

FIGURE 7.3 The Growth Triangle of Singapore

Source: Lee Tsao Yuan, ed. *Growth Triangle: The Johor-Singapore-Riau Experience* (Singapore: Institute of Southeast Asian Studies), 1991

centre in the world within the first two decades of the twenty-first century (*South China Morning Post*, 11 November 1993). Singapore and Sydney are also in this league. Friedmann, in his examination of global cities made only a few years ago (1986), identified only Singapore as a primary global city in Asia, but such has been the pace of change in east Asia that other cities almost certainly would have to be added to his list (Table 7.3). Shanghai and Beijing-Tianjin would certainly have to be added to the "secondary" global cities, for example, to join Taipei, Seoul, and Bangkok. Before attempting to draw a schematic relationship between the formation of global cities, the functional division of global space, and migration, it is necessary to consider briefly one other key factor in the equation: shifts in the structure and rates of growth of population resulting from changes in fertility and mortality.

Changing Demographic Regimes

The changing pattern of migration and the structural transformation of the economy cannot be separated from the transition from high to low rates of population growth. The decline in fertility for the newly industrializing economies and the rates of population growth over the last thirty years are shown in Tables 7.4 and 7.5, respectively. From annual rates of growth of around 3 percent in 1960 population growth had declined to around one percent thirty years later for the four newly industrialized economies of East Asia. The rapid demographic shifts have implications for migration in two significant ways. First, changes in the age composition affect the number of those available to migrate, that is, the potential pool of migrants. And, second, reductions in the rate of growth of the labour force and the transition toward negative population growth is a powerful force for the transformation of an economy. The resultant labour scarcity pushes up labour costs forcing labour-intensive production toward peripheral zones where there is still surplus labour, it encourages the switch toward high-tech activities and it stimulates a demand for the importation of labour.

The labour imported is made up of two very different types: highly skilled personnel for the fast-developing high-tech industries discussed previously and nonskilled labour for the service industries, restaurants, shops, and the dangerous, demanding, and dirty occupations that local people, with their increasing aspirations, are unwilling to do. The former tend to come from other global cities, whereas the latter will come from cities further down the regional hierarchy—not necessarily just from these cities themselves but also from their hinterlands. Although activities in the global city may have low-skill demands, those who fill the positions may have considerable skills, because the difference between earnings in

TABLE 7.3 The World-City Hierarchy

Core Countries				*Semi-Periphery Countries*			
Primary		*Secondary*		*Primary*		*Secondary*	
London +	***	Brussels+	*				
Paris+	**	Milan	*				
Rotterdam	*	Vienna+	*				
Frankfurt	*	Madrid+					
Zürich	*					Johannesburg	*
New York	***	Toronto	*	São Paulo	*	Buenos Aires+	***
Chicago	**	Miami	*			Rio de Janeiro	***
Los Angeles	***					Caracas+	*
		San Francisco	*			Mexico City+	***
Tokyo+	***	Sydney	*	Singapore+	*	Hong Kong	**
						Taipei+	*
						Manila+	**
						Bangkok+	**
						Seoul+	**

Source: J. Friedmann, "The World City Hypothesis," *Development and Change*, vol. 17 (1), 1986, p. 72.

Notes: Population size categories (recent estimates referring to metro-region)

- * 1–5 million
- ** 5–10 million
- *** 10–20 million
- + National capital

TABLE 7.4 The Decline in Fertility in the Asian Newly Industrializing Countries: Total Fertility Rates, 1961–1991

	Hong Kong	*Singapore*	*Taiwan*	*South Korea*
1961	5.0	5.5	5.6	5.9
1966	4.5	4.4	4.8	4.8
1971	3.4	3.1	3.7	4.1
1976	2.5	2.1	3.1	3.0
1981	1.9	1.7	2.5	2.6
1986	1.3	1.4	1.7	1.7
1991	1.2	1.7	1.6	1.6

Sources: Hong Kong: Demographic Trends in Hong Kong: 1979–1989, mimeo, Department of Census and Statistics, 1990, and updates; *Population of Hong Kong,* Country Monograph Series No. 1, ESCAP, Bangkok, 1974. Singapore: Saw Swee-Hock, *Changes in the Fertility Policy of Singapore,* The Institute of Policy Studies, Singapore, 1990. Taiwan: *Statistical Yearbook* of the Republic of China, Directorate-General of Budget, Accounting and Statistics, Taipei, various years. South Korea: *Korea Statistical Yearbook,* National Statistical Office, Seoul, various years.

the service activities in the destination areas and those in more highly skilled activities in origin areas may be substantial. For example, earnings for domestic servants in Hong Kong and Singapore are much higher than for teachers, nurses, or technical office staff in the Philippines. There is thus a deskilling of the mainly female labour force in this example.

Both the highly skilled and more lowly skilled international migration systems just sketched have one aspect in common, at least in Asia: They are essentially circular in nature, being based on limited-term contracts. Migration into the lower circuit of other global cities, for example, New York, from the Caribbean and Central America, may be of a more long-term nature, although there is also annual circulation of, for example, street sellers (hawkers) from West Africa.

Population migration cannot, however, be related simply to labour-market demand or relative degrees of unemployment as the following example demonstrates. The transition from a labour-surplus to a labour-deficit economy has been associated with a shift from emigration to immigration or a "turnaround" in international labour migration (Fields 1994). In the East Asian case, and particularly in the case of Hong Kong, I have argued that this interpretation does not hold. There was little evidence of pronounced emigration from East Asian economies when growth rates were highest and unemployment was a feature (Skeldon 1994c). The periods of maximum outflow from all the economies were associated with a time of gradual but growing labour shortages, although, to be sure, as these have intensified, so too has immigration. There has

TABLE 7.5 Rates of Population Growth of the Asian Newly Industrializing Countries, 1955–1990

	Hong Kong	*Singapore*	*Taiwan*	*South Korea*
1955–1960	4.2	4.5	3.5	2.9
1960–1965	3.7	2.8	3.2	2.7
1965–1970	1.3	2.0	3.1	1.9
1970–1975	2.2	1.7	1.9	2.0
1975–1980	2.7	1.3	2.0	1.5
1980–1985	1.6	1.2	1.6	1.6
1985–1990	0.9	1.2	1.1	1.5

Source: See Table 7.3 and E. K. Y. Chen, *Hypergrowth in Asian Economies: A Comparative Study of Hong Kong, Japan, Korea, Singapore, and Taiwan* (London: Macmillan), 1979, p. 14.

been no simple switch from emigration to immigration, with both coexisting simultaneously, even if there has been a general trend toward diminution of the former from some economies, notably South Korea, and pressure for increased immigration has increased. Any explanation of the flows cannot be divorced from the international political environment, a theme that will be developed later in the paper.

A Schematic Representation of Migration and Global City Development

Hypothetically, we can envisage a relationship between a functional division of space and patterns of population mobility. Let us take a general division of space of three zones: (1) labour-intensive industrialization; (2) more capital-intensive industrialization and wholesale and retailing activities; and (3) knowledge-based industrial and financial services. This schema finds its basis in reality in the zonation evolving around Hong Kong, as was seen previously in Figure 7.2. The boundaries of these zones are clearly not fixed or immutable, or even observable on the ground. And it is not necessary to conceptualize the zones as contiguous, because the labour-intensive periphery of such global cities as Tokyo or New York can be thousands of kilometres away in Southeast Asia, China, or Mexico, but with company headquarters in the cities themselves. The zones do appear, nevertheless, to be constantly shifting outward from the global cities in an irregular frontier pattern, but with the driving force being the search for labour rather than land.

In Zone 1, mobility is characterized by intense rural-to-urban circulation, with high rates of turnover. The local economy is labour-surplus, both from rapid natural rates of labour-force growth and from internal in-migration. Zone 2 is the transition toward more highly skilled, more capital-intensive industrialization, but with strong development of wholesale and retail service activities. In this zone, labour turnover is reduced and the in-migration is much more of a long-term nature. The informal bazaar economy is reduced and unemployment rates are low. The third zone is the core of the global city region itself, with high-cost, high-skilled, knowledge-based industries. The growth of the indigenous labour force is very slow and there are acute sectoral labour shortages. These are met through the importation of high-skilled labour, primarily from or through other global cities, often within the networks of transnational corporations. There is also the importation of labour to carry out the kinds of activities that the highly educated indigenous labour force is unwilling to do. This labour is kept in a vulnerable position, it is foreign labour recruited from or through regional city networks. There is little long-term internal migration from the immediate hinterland into the core of the global city. Rather, there is a dispersal of residents from that core. This has been observed as a turnaround of urbanization in the developed countries of the West. This has led to urban-to-urban migration down the regional hierarchy as urban growth has become more dispersed from traditional core areas.

In East Asia, there has also been a dispersal, but one that has been associated with the movement of the highly skilled for destinations in North America and Australasia. Although this emigration has characterized all the newly industrialized economies of Asia, it has been seen to be more a characteristic of Hong Kong where political uncertainty over the return to Chinese sovereignty in 1997 has been seen as the primary driving force. I have shown elsewhere that political uncertainty is but one factor, and this population movement is part of the evolution of trans-Pacific family and business networks that allow access to economies at different stages of business cycles (see Skeldon 1994b). These "emigrants" are retaining homes and businesses in the origin areas as well as establishing offshoots or new opportunities in areas of destination. The result is a "managed mobility", which allows people to flow around the Pacific within the networks depending upon perceived economic and political risk. This migration is, in essence, a global variant of the deconcentration observed from the largest cities of core developed countries in the 1980s, although residents of these areas also are participating in global economic networks. The core regions of Asia are thus already participating in deconcentration, albeit, as yet, of an incipient and different kind.

Although the previous scheme is presented in spatial terms, it could equally be presented in temporal terms for any of the global city regions of East Asia. The central parts of Hong Kong, Seoul, or Taipei have seen a transformation from labour-intensive manufacturing of labour-surplus economies through to knowledge-based, labour-deficit economies as outlined earlier in the chapter.

What we have just seen is clearly a highly generalized model of what has occurred in East Asia, and the fundamental issue remains whether this system will diffuse throughout the world to create a truly global system of development or whether this is a unique form of development, different from what has occurred in the past and what will affect the rest of the world in the future.

Global Patterns of Migration and Development

There is considerable debate about which indicator is the "best" measure of development—whether it is GNP per capita, the human development index (HDI), the physical quality of life indicator (PQLI), or some other measure. Despite its drawbacks, GNP per capita is still the most commonly accepted indicator of development as enshrined in the ranking of countries by the World Bank. A map of the countries of the world by their general level of development—high-income, upper-middle-income, lower-middle-income, and low-income economies—is provided in Figure 7.4. At the simplest level of spatial analysis, there are clear development blocs; areas of high development as well as of low development are spatially concentrated. The countries of high income and upper-middle income are, with a few exceptions, found in areas of higher latitude and primarily in the maritime parts of those areas. The low-income countries are found in central and eastern Africa and in south and east Asia.

This very simple division immediately raises the tension between the state, or the area over which governments have control and on which universal basis population and development statistics are released, and the underlying spatial pattern of development as outlined in the previous section. There are major differences within countries that are obscured by the even shading of the map but are often ignored when the statistics appear as listings in tables. Equally clearly, these differences are more significant the larger the country and the greater its population. This is particularly the case for the giants of Asia, China, and India, and also for Indonesia, and for Mexico and Brazil in Latin America.

There is considerable debate as to the real value of China's GNP, which is published as $US370 per capita in the latest World Bank *World Development Report* (1993a). This is assumed to underestimate considerably the significance of China's economy. Nevertheless, it will be accepted here as the only figure that is generated by a common methodology to allow comparison among countries. Mapping intrastate spatial differences in income per capita for China and India shows that the city areas

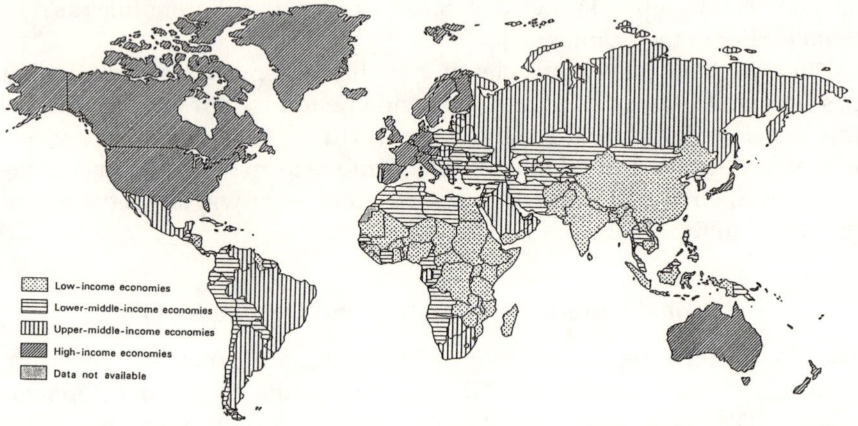

FIGURE 7.4 Groups of Economies

of Beijing-Tianjin and Shanghai and the provinces of Liaoning and Guangdong in China would join the ranks of the lower-middle-income countries. Although there are clear interstate differences in per capita income in India, not one of those spatial units would rise above the low-income country level. However, if data were available for local areas of the largest cities, Delhi and Bombay, like Shanghai and Beijing-Tianjin, these would almost certainly appear in the higher-income group. Attempts to map spatial differences in wealth in these two countries have been made widely available by *The Economist* for China (29 November 1992) and for India (4 May 1991).

It is in the superimposition of urban functional zones (such as those discussed earlier in the chapter) on the national patterns that difficulties arise, simply because of a lack of available data. Ginsburg, Koppel, and McGee have attempted to provide a general idea with the distribution of three *desakota* types, which are given in Figure 7.5. The three types are: (1) the population of core cities where there has been a rapid transformation of the economy; (2) core cities of rapid growth, but where agriculture still plays a major role; and (3) core cities of high population growth but slower economic growth. An alternative would be to map the three hypothetical functional regions discussed earlier. However, the available data do not allow this to be done with any accuracy. A variant is to provide a generalized diagram of a series of "tiers" of development within which the functional zones described earlier appear to be expanding. These tiers, as given in Figure 7.6, are the core represented by Japan; the extension of that core, the four newly industrializing economies (NIEs); the actively extending core in the hinterlands of the NIEs in China, in parts of Southeast Asia, and in parts of India; a future labour frontier; and

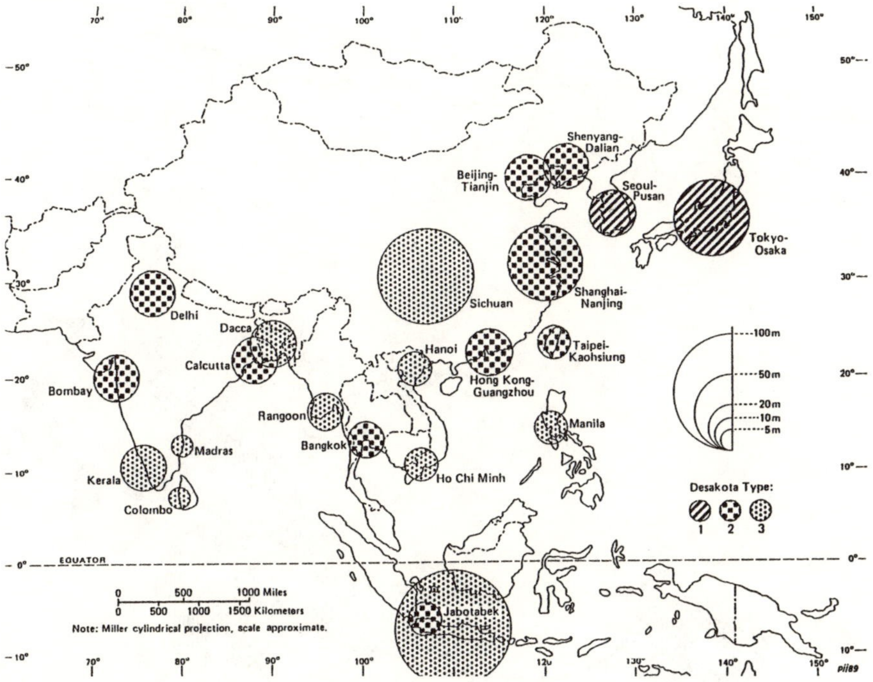

FIGURE 7.5 Growth of Core Areas in Asia

a resource niche. To fit the functional zones outlined earlier into this spatial system would put Zone 3, the knowledge-based industries, squarely into the core and, increasingly, into the core extensions; Zone 2, the capital-intensive, wholesale and retailing zone would be limited to the peripheries of the core and core extensions and, increasingly, to the actively extending core; and Zone 1, the labour-intensive activities, would be found in the actively extending core and pushing into the labour frontier along the edge of that extending core. Elsewhere, I have attempted to associate particular changing sequences of population mobility with these development tiers (Skeldon 1992). For example, declining spatial mobility, mainly for reasons of changing age structure, and spatial deconcentration appear to characterize the core. The concentration of more long-term migrant populations typifies the actively extending core, and intense circulation, which increasingly becomes urban-oriented, characterizes the future labour frontier tier. Rural-rural circulation dominates the resource niche. Although intraregional movement dominates the pattern of mobility of each development region, these areas are obviously not self-contained units. The movement among them does tend to be between regions immediately above or below in the development sequence in a definite hi-

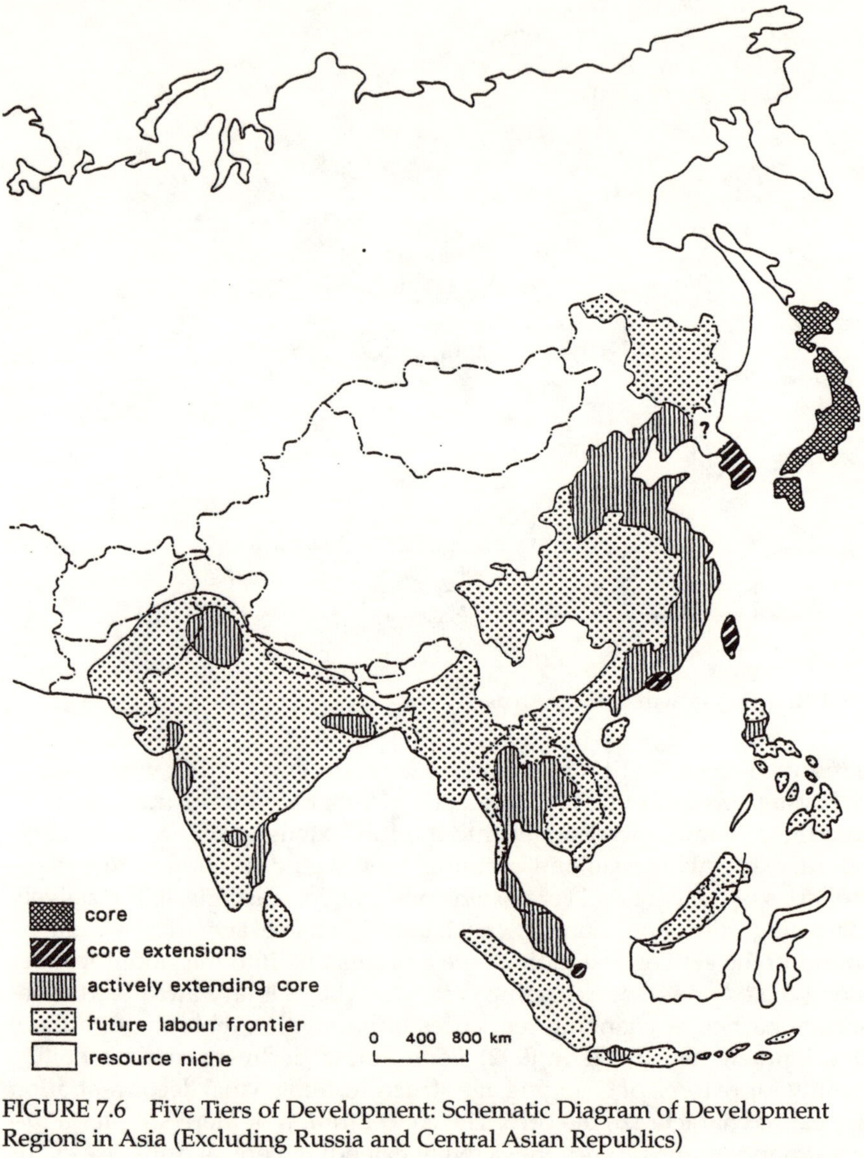

FIGURE 7.6 Five Tiers of Development: Schematic Diagram of Development Regions in Asia (Excluding Russia and Central Asian Republics)

erarchical pattern. For example, there is relatively little movement between the future labour frontier and the core relative to movements between that frontier and the actively extending core.

Similar development areas could be identified for other parts of the developing world. Areas of actively extending core development can be identified for southern Africa, where one could hypothesize an expansion from the Republic of South Africa north through Botswana, Namibia, and Zimbabwe. Other zones of actively extending core development could be identified in South America around the Plate River, and out from the São Paulo, Rio de Janeiro, and Caracas-Maracaibo axes in the southern and northern parts of that continent, respectively. Core extension, where urban deconcentration is already taking place, may have emerged around Buenos Aires and in central Mexico. The evidence available from the developing world suggests that, as in the case of the Western experience, there are clear periods of spatial concentration that are associated with development (Vining 1986). The *desakota* pattern of agricultural/nonagricultural land use is likely to be but a temporary phase in the process of concentration, although a clear difference with the Western pattern will lie in the sheer size of the resulting urban concentrations. For example, the Hong Kong-Shenzhen-Guangzhou urban area, which does not even figure among the large agglomerations identified by the United Nations, already has a population well in excess of 12 million (United Nations, 1993). The "official" 1991 figures for Guangzhou and Shenzhen in 1991 (*China Statistical Yearbook 1992*) were 3.6 million and 0.4 million, respectively. These would not include the "floating" population, which could, depending upon the estimate, add another 3–4 million. Hong Kong's population in 1991 was 5.7 million.

The extent to which the advancing zones identified previously will expand can only be the result of extreme speculation. Not all areas can rely only upon knowledge-based industries, at least in the medium term. Educated guesses of where the expansion of the actively extending core might occur in Asia over the short term can be ventured—Vietnam seems an obvious case, for example. However, more profitable than making a series of predictions from a cloudy crystal ball is to examine briefly the other major factor impinging on the penetration of capitalism—the role of the state.

The Political Dimension

In the debate over the emergence of the rapidly growing economies of East Asia, many have argued that free market forces were among the fundamental factors. However, the role of the state has also played an equally important part, even if there has been considerable variation in the type and degree of government intervention among countries in the region (World Bank 1993b). Common to all, however, have been strong, outwardly oriented prodevelopmentalist governments, a type that has been termed the *hard* state. These essentially autocratic regimes have had the stability to pursue and implement consistent economic policies over a considerable period of time without changes of direction that might have been introduced by governments more responsive to public opinion. Autocracy of course is not the necessary condition for this kind of development: There are many cases of autocratic governments that have sought self-sufficiency and cut themselves off from the international economy. There, the penetration of a system as described earlier in this chapter has not been possible. Extreme autocratic governments reflecting nationalist sentiment may attempt to homogenize their populations and rid themselves of potential entrepreneurial groups, among others. The population movements consequent upon these policies are discussed elsewhere in this volume. Other political systems will not favour the penetration of transnational enterprise either. Where the state has essentially ceased to exist as an effective political unit, as in parts of sub-Saharan Africa for example, multinational enterprises will not establish any kind of industrial system, and these areas will remain on the periphery.

The establishment and rapidity of development of the penetration of capitalist enterprise thus depends upon a very particular type of political system. It is oriented toward the international community, and many of the members of the government will be, in all probability, returned migrants from core countries. Although in principle favouring market forces, the government plays an important role in creating the necessary infrastructure to attract international capital and in devising policies to regulate effectively the allocation and distribution of resources through land or trade policies, for example. Although Adam Smith's "hidden hand" of the market may have described the process of economic development in the eighteenth century, state intervention was becoming increasingly important in the core developing industrial societies of Europe from the second half of the nineteenth century. There, too, the extension of effective state control over increasingly wider areas—jurisdictional integration (Olson 1982)—created nationwide markets that directly stimulated production. The degree of state interventionism has varied in the historical experience of Europe and varies in East Asia today but, before attempting to see whether we are dealing with a new type of development system or a variant of "old" European patterns, it is worth considering briefly the example of China, because it has for so long been seen as providing an alternative model.

The Case of Migration and Development in China

As mentioned earlier in the chapter, China indeed appeared to provide a different model of urbanization and development from the perspective of the mid-1970s. The growth of the cities from 1958 through the late 1970s was tightly controlled and, at particular times, millions, and in some cases tens of millions, of people were directed away from the cities to the countryside (Banister 1987). There have been few other cases where the movement of so many people has been directly controlled by the state for so long. Since the reforms initiated from 1979 the situation has, however, changed significantly in a number of ways. First, from a time of tightly controlled migration, China has moved into an era of massive population mobility. Second, from a period of managed migration to inland provinces, the direction of movement has changed toward the coastal provinces. And, third, from limited migration to towns and cities and policies of urban decentralization, the dominant pattern of movement is now toward the urban areas and principally toward the largest cities of China; among these, Shanghai, Beijing-Tianjin, and Guangzhou figure prominently.

Although we now know much more about migration in China than we did a decade ago, thanks primarily to several recent surveys and the 1990 census, which for the first time included questions on migration, it is still extremely difficult to gauge the real volume of migration. The definitions of migration do not capture much of the new mobility, which is short-term. For a discussion of definitions and the background to migration in China, see Goldstein and Goldstein (1992 and 1987–1988). This "floating population" has been estimated at between 50 and 70 million, and there may have been almost twice as many temporary migrants as there have been permanent migrants, the latter defined by a change in household registration (Taubman 1993). However, these numbers capture but part of the total recent migrant flows. In Shanghai alone, in 1993, a recent estimate has put the floating population at 2.5 million (cited in Pannell 1993). Much of this floating population appears to remain for fairly extensive periods in the cities with, in 1991, 22 percent in Shanghai and 29 percent in Guangzhou having been resident for more than one year (cited in Taubman 1993). Hence, much of the initially temporary movement appears to be evolving into semi-permanent movement, a trend that has been observed in other developing countries (Skeldon 1990). Over the last decade, China appears to have taken on features of mobility that are familiar to those who have studied migration elsewhere and, rather than providing a separate model of migration and development, may very much be following more general patterns as capitalism has penetrated along the eastern seaboard.

Discussion

This chapter began by referring to the issue raised by Terry McGee at a previous conference on global migration that we need paradigms different from those developed from the Western experience in order to make sense of the process of migration and development in the developing world today. I adopted McGee's key point that it is through an analysis of the penetration of capitalism that the most fruitful way forward is to be found, and I examined the recent development experience of East Asia in this light. This experience has indeed been different from that of Europe and one could not have expected it to have been otherwise. The mix of industries, each with their own skill demands, the technologies available, the types of communications, and the degree of government involvement have been different. Yet, despite these differences, there have been similarities. The general trend from labour-intensive to capital-intensive to knowledge-intensive industries is a common theme. Demographically these societies have moved from higher to lower fertility even if the pace and the reasons for the decline have differed markedly. The economic development of East Asia has also brought about a population concentration that is entirely consistent with the Western experience, even if the scale and time period over which the process has operated have been different. In the context of McGee's "extended metropolis" argument, it appears likely that, as land values and labour costs increase under a market economy, the *desakota* pattern will wither as agricultural and labour-intensive activities are progressively pushed out in an ever-moving periphery. The *desakota* pattern is a transient phase of Asian urbanization rather than a totally separate type of urban settlement. The only way it might persist is if a nonmarket economy were either to remain or to be introduced that would then render unlikely the "penetration of capitalism" thesis.

Both Western and nonwestern patterns of migration and development can be understood within a framework of capitalist expansion even if the particular form of that expansion has varied. The capitalist system has not expanded in a regular or uninterrupted fashion but rather in an inconstant manner (Storper and Walker 1989). The alternating periods of growth and recession are reflected in business cycles. Each of these cycles has its own "mix" of technologies and industries, and each has its own location in geographic space. As new technologies and industries emerge, those of the previous cycles are marginalized from core areas. Yet, the very process of marginalization will set off processes of development in specific areas that may eventually come to rival or even surpass those of core areas. This is illustrated by the case of East Asia where an accelerated development on the periphery of the traditional European and North American core has occurred since World War II. Within this area I traced the progression, both temporal and spatial, of labour-intensive to knowledge-intensive industrialization.

The principal argument against the "separate paradigm" approach to the migration and settlement in developing areas is that it gives the impression that the developments are occurring entirely separate from those in the core areas. The key issue is not whether the development of today's developing countries is the same or different from that of the historical experience of the core countries but how it has been brought about through linkages with those core countries. Previous patterns of colonial activity, present patterns of direct foreign investment, and the activities of transnational corporations are critical to an understanding of these linkages. Yet, perhaps the most fundamental of these linkages is the human contact through migration. Between the early 1960s and the early 1990s, the proportion of Asians entering the core settler societies of Australia, Canada, and the United States increased from around 5 percent to more than 40 percent of the total.

Prominent among the Asian group have been those of Chinese origin from Hong Kong, Taiwan, and Southeast Asian countries as well as China itself. This legal settler migration is but part of a much broader spectrum of movement that includes students, business travelers, tourists, and illegal migrants. However, much of this movement, including the settler migrations, is not a simple origin-destination movement but a complex system of return movements and circulation. The importance to the East Asian economies of the return of students after receiving higher-level education overseas has already been mentioned, but there are other forms of mobility about which we still know relatively little. Some of these involve long-distance commuting among two or more centres around the Pacific rim. This modern "new extended" or "diasporic" family often means that children are left in a residence in California or Auckland while both parents are working in Taiwan or Hong Kong—the "parachute kids" syndrome—or the wife and children are left in Vancouver, Toronto, or Sydney while the husband attends the family business in Hong Kong and commutes across the Pacific every few weeks—the "astronaut" syndrome. High youth dependency ratios and female dominance in the age cohorts of 30–39 years have been observed in some of the major destinations of Hong Kong migrants (see Skeldon 1994b and a summary in Skeldon 1994a).

This vast circulation of people and ideas pushes and regenerates the capitalist frontier out from the traditional core areas of Europe and North America. The intensity and great distances covered by this system of circulation are unique features allowed by modern communications, which had no direct counterpart in early European migrations. Yet these movements, and their consequences in the origin countries, are as integral a part of the experience of the traditional core areas as they are of the newly industrializing regions and must not be seen as independent developments. The key nodal points in this system are the global cities, which are both the principal targets of the circulation and the business centres coordinating global economic activity.

The factors controlling the diffusion of this system of mobility are clearly not simply economic: Political factors too are important. The idea of nationalism spread from Western Europe from the nineteenth century until, by late in the twentieth century, it had become virtually a global norm sanctified in and by the United Nations. An ideology of nationalism is created and reinforced by institutions such as the military and the education systems, which engender common values and a feeling of belonging to a community. These institutions can have a profound impact on population movement that is often not appreciated in discussions of migration (Skeldon 1990, pp. 196–201). It is not only agencies such as military recruitment or education policy that generate certain types of mobility but also political decisions that directly affect the economic system. These can vary from policies on labour recruitment to policies that promote the disbanding of local or regional tariffs to create wider trade areas. The latter will open up new areas to investment from dynamic growth centres and allow the free movement of the factors of production, including labour. The increased circulation of goods and, more importantly, of people—the result of these political decisions—in effect "creates" the nation. The nation is not immutable and, as global systems of circulation evolve, new identities, new political units based upon global cities, and new "imagined communities" (Anderson 1983) will emerge. The migration of individuals needs to be placed squarely within this political and institutional framework before an adequate understanding of the process can be achieved.

How far this system will diffuse out from the major cities in Asia cannot yet be known. It is predicated to a large extent on the willingness of state institutions to adopt the kinds of policies and activities being emitted from these global cities. The "modernization" of China is a case in point. Whether a communist state can absorb capitalist principles to produce a "socialist market economy" remains one of the intriguing issues for the end of the twentieth century. There could indeed be significant setbacks if increasing wealth differences within China exacerbate regional disaffection to create unrest. Interstate rivalries for resources and markets within the region could also provoke a significant breakdown of the progression of economic development. Hence, political development and the strength of political institutions are critical in determining how extensive and how fast the economic system will be allowed to develop.

There will be other areas that will never be fully incorporated into the system either because they are undesirable or because they are extremely harsh in terms of their physical environment or because, politically, they are intransigent and strenuously resist encroachment for one reason or another; or, most likely, because of a combination of these environmental and political reasons. These areas will remain permanently on the fringe and may indeed have forms of mobility that are unrelated to those discussed in this chapter.

There may, of course, be broader constraints to the diffusion of such a system. These constraints bring environmental concerns to the fore. The penetration of a capitalist system has ravaged certain environments; and the destruction of forests and the expansion of deserts through salination are often cited examples that will not only run counter to development but also can generate their own population movements, as people flee these areas. The penetration of capitalism may also push people toward more marginal areas by expropriating their own lands, further exacerbating environmental problems in these delicate marginal areas (Harrison 1992, pp. 130–132).

All migrants can be seen to move for environmental reasons of one type or another, but, in a narrower sense, the migration of increasing numbers can be attributed to the despoilation and/or degradation of the physical environment. This issue is reviewed by Suhrke (1993). Whereas indeed these migrations are of concern, it appears that the environment is generally but one factor in a complex system of causation rather than the primary cause. There is, however, the other side of the equation of the relationship between population movement and the environment: the impact of the transfer of people from areas of lower density and lower consumption to areas of higher density and higher consumption and its effect on the environment. The transfer has both local and more widespread, even global, effects. The local effects include increased levels of pollution caused by the natural wastes of expanding urban populations, the deteriorating air quality from clogged intracity transportation and from factory emissions, and all the land-use abuses brought about by the poorly zoned growth of megacities.

The more widespread effects are more difficult to gauge. These relate to changing consumer values and changing patterns of consumption. Although many of the migrants to cities may be at levels close to the poverty line, the vast majority appear to be positively selected with respect to education and skills relative to their populations of origin. They are therefore among the more innovative and dynamic elements of any population and among those likely to adopt new consumer norms. This may particularly apply to those international migrants who, as seen earlier, are becoming such an important part of global systems of human circulation. Just what the implications are of this movement for the global consumption of resources is not yet understood. It would seem, however, that this movement could transform lower consumers into higher consumers and they could then transfer these values and aspirations back to their places of origin during their periodic returns to home areas. Hence, there may be limits to the spatial development of the migration system imposed by global resource constraints, although these are likely to change with technology and any Malthusian scenario is almost certainly likely to be too simplistic. The issue of the interrelationship between population and resources is too complex to be dealt with here, but, clearly, it is not simply a matter of population numbers: Migration, too, needs to be incorporated into the equation if we are to come to a proper understanding of population and environment.

The relevance of global history is that it brings a historical perspective to contemporary global issues (Mazlish 1993). It attempts to transcend the nation-state as a unit of analysis by focusing on those processes and those institutions that are creating the global community. This chapter has focused upon population movements in East Asia over the last fifty years to suggest that the most effective way to understand global patterns of migration is to envisage them within a unitary framework of the expansion of a capitalist system. I have argued that, despite differences between the experiences of Europe and those of East Asia in their urban and industrial transformations, there are similarities of process that have been reflected in the general structures of demographic and mobility change. The functional economic differentiation of regions observed in this chapter and the associated patterns of population mobility are examples of the types of processes that are helping to create a global economy and global community. The approach adopted is offered as a framework for a comparative and interdisciplinary perspective on changing patterns of mobility within a global economy. It is clearly diffusionist, even if that diffusion is not necessarily regular in space or time and, as such, is a key element in the "web of connection" in the construction of global history (Grew 1993, p. 239).

References

Anderson, B. (1983) *Imaginal Communities: Reflections on the Origin and Spread of Nationalism* (London: Verso).

Aziz, S. (1978) *Rural Development: Learning from China* (London: Macmillan).

Banister, J. (1987) *China's Changing Population* (Stanford: Standford University Press).

Bannerjee, B. (1986) *Rural to Urban Migration and the Urban Labour Market* (New Delhi: Himalaya Publishing House).

Bennett, R., and R. Estall, eds. (1991) *Global Change and Challenge: Geography for the 1990s* (London: Routledge).

Brookfield, H. (1975) *Interdependent Development* (London: Methuen).

Burawoy, M. (1976) "The Functions and Reproduction of Migrant Labor: Comparative Material from South Africa and the United States", *American Journal of Sociology* 81:1050–1087.

Chase-Dunn, C. (1985) "The System of World Cities, A.D. 800–1975", in Timberlake, *Urbanization in the World Economy*, pp. 269–292.

———. (1989) *Global Formation: Structures of the World Economy* (Oxford: Blackwell).

Cohen, R. (1981) "The New International Division of Labor, Multinational Corporations and Urban Hierarchy", in Dear and Scott, *Urbanization and Urban Planning*, pp. 287–315.

———. (1987) *The New Helots: Migrants in the International Division of Labour* (Aldershot, Engl.: Avebury).

Dear, M., and A. J. Scott, eds. (1981) *Urbanization and Urban Planning in Capitalist Society* (New York: Methuen).

De Soto, H. (1989) *The Other Path: The Invisible Revolution in the Third World* (New York: Harper and Row).

Dicken, P. (1992) *Global Shift: The Internationalization of Economic Activity* (London: Paul Chapman).

Fields, G. (1994) "The Migration Transition in Asia." *Asian and Pacific Migration Journal* 3:7–30.

Friedmann, J. (1986) "The World City Hypothesis", *Development and Change* 17:69–83.

Ginsburg, N. (1991) "Extended Metropolitan Regions in Asia: A New Spatial Paradigm", in Ginsburg, Koppel, and McGee, *The Extended Metropolis*, pp. 27–46.

Ginsburg, N., B. Koppel, and T. G. McGee, eds. (1991) *The Extended Metropolis: Settlement Transition in Asia* (Honolulu: University of Hawaii Press).

Goldstein, S. (1978) Circulation in the Context of Total Mobility in South-East Asia. Paper no. 53, East-West Population Institute (Honolulu: East-West Center).

Goldstein, S., and A. Goldstein. (1987–1988) "Varieties of Population Mobility in Relation to Development in China", *Studies in Comparative International Developments* 22:101–124.

———. (1992) Censuses and Surveys as Sources of Information on Permanent and Temporary Migration in China. Paper presented at the International Seminar on China's 1990 Population Census, Beijing, October.

Grew, R. (1993) "On the Prospect of Global History", in Mazlich and Buultjens, *Conceptualizing Global History*, pp. 227–249.

Haggard, S. (1990) *Pathways from the Periphery: The Politics of Growth in the Newly Industrializing Countries* (Ithaca: Cornell University Press).

Harrison, P. (1992) *The Third Revolution: Population, Environment, and a Sustainable World* (Penguin Books).

Henderson, G. (1989) *The Globalization of High Technology Production: Society, Space, and Semi-Conductors in the Restructuring of the Modern Economy* (London: Routledge).

Hugo, G. (1982) "Circular Migration in Indonesia", *Population and Development Review* 8:59–83.

King, A. D. (1990) *Global Cities: Post-Imperialism and the Internationalization of London* (London: Routledge).

Klein, S., ed. (1987) *The Economics of Mass Migration in the Twentieth Century* (New York: Paragon).

Kritz, M. M., C. B. Keely, and S. M. Tomasi, eds. (1981) *Global Trends in Migration: Theory and Research on International Population Movements* (New York: Center for Migration Studies).

Kritz, M., L. L. Lim, and H. Zlotnik, eds. (1992) *International Migration Systems: A Global Approach* (Oxford: Clarendon Press).

Kuznets, P. W. (1987) "Koreans in America: Recent Migration from South Korea to the United States", in Klein, *Economics of Mass Migration*, pp. 41–69.

Lea, D. A. M., and D. P. Chaudhri. (1983a) "The Nature, Problems and Approaches to Rural Development", in Lea and Chaudhri, *Rural Development*, pp. 1–37.

Lea, D. A. M., and D. P. Chaudhri, eds. (1983b) *Rural Development and the State: Contradictions and Dilemmas in Developing Countries* (London: Methuen).

Lemon, A. (1982) "Migrant Labour and Frontier Commuters: Reorganizing South Africa's Black Labour Supply", in Smith, *Living Under Apartheid*, pp. 64–89.

Mazlich, B. (1993) "An Introduction to Global History", in Mazlich and Buultjens, *Conceptualizing Global History*, pp. 1–24.

Mazlich, B., and R. Buultjens, eds. (1993) *Conceptualizing Global History* (Boulder: Westview Press).

McGee, T. G. (1978) "Rural Urban Mobility in South and Southeast Asia: Different Formulations, Different Answers", in McNeill and Adams, *Human Migration*, pp. 199–224.

———. (1991) "The Emergence of *Desakota* Regions in Asia: Expanding a Hypothesis", in Ginsburg, Koppel, and McGee, *The Extended Metropolis*, pp. 3–25.

McGee, T. G., and Y. M. Yeung. (1993) "Urban Futures for Pacific Asia: Towards the 21st Century", in Yeung, *Pacific Asia in the 21st Century*, pp. 47–67.

McNeill, W. H. (1978) "Introduction", in McNeill and Adams, *Human Migration: Patterns and Policies* (Bloomington: Indiana University Press), pp. xi–xviii.

McNeill, W. H., and R. S. Adams, eds. (1978) *Human Migration: Patterns and Policies* (Bloomington: Indiana University Press).

Olson, M. (1982) *The Rise and Decline of Nations: Economic Growth, Stagflation, and Social Rigidities* (New Haven: Yale University Press).

Pannell, C. W. (1993) A Preface to China's Urbanization: The Role of Large Cities. Discussion Paper, Centre for Urban Planning and Environmental Management, University of Hong Kong.

Peet, R. (1991) *Global Capitalism: Theories of Societal Development* (London: Routledge).

Potts, L. (1990) *The World Labour Market: A History of Migration* (London: Zed Books).

Prothero, R. M., and M. Chapman, eds. (1985) *Circulation in Third World Countries* (London: Routledge and Kegan Paul).

Pryor, R. J. (1981) "Integrating International and Internal Migration Theories", in Kritz, Keely, and Tomasi, *Global Trends*, pp. 110–129.

Ramos, R., et al. (1994) *Population and Development in Macau* (University of Macau and Macau Foundation).

Sassen, S. (1991) *The Global City: New York, London, Tokyo* (Princeton: Princeton University Press).

Skeldon, R. (1990) *Population Mobility in Developing Countries: A Reinterpretation* (London: Belhaven).

———. (1992) "The Relationship Between Migration and Development in the ESCAP Region", in United Nations, ESCAP, *Migration and Urbanization*, pp. 45–62.

———. (1994a) "Migration and Development in Asia: From Sojourners to New Extended Families", in Ramos et al., *Population and Development*.

Skeldon, R., ed. (1994b) *Reluctant Exiles? Migration from Hong Kong and the New Overseas Chinese* (New York: M. E. Sharpe and Hong Kong University Press).

———. (1994c) "Turning Points in Labour Migration: The Case of Hong Kong", *Asian and Pacific Migration Journal* 3:93–118.

Sklair, L. (1991) *Sociology of the Global System* (New York: Harvester Wheatsheaf).

Smith, D. M., ed. (1982) *Living Under Apartheid: Aspects of Urbanization and Social Change in South Africa* (London: Allen and Unwin).

Storper, M., and R. Walker. (1989) *The Capitalist Imperative: Territory, Technology, and Industrial Growth* (Oxford: Blackwell).

Suhrke, A. (1993) Pressure Points: Environmental Degradation, Migration, and Conflict. Occasional Paper no. 3, of the project Environmental Change and Acute Conflict, A Joint Project of the University of Toronto and the American Academy of Arts and Sciences, Cambridge, Massachusetts.

Taubman, W. (1993) Socio-Economic Development and Rural-Urban Migration in China Since the Beginning of the 1980s. Discussion Paper Series, China Economic Research Centre, University of Macau.

Timberlake, M., ed. (1985) *Urbanization in the World-Economy* (New York: Academic Press).

United Nations. (1991) *World Urbanization Prospects: The 1992 Revision* (New York: Department of Economic and Social Information and Policy Analysis).

United Nations ESCAP. (1992) *Migration and Urbanization in Asia and the Pacific.* Asian Population Studies, Series no. 111. Bangkok.

Vining, D. R. (1986) "Population Redistribution Towards Core Areas of Less Developed Countries 1950–1980", *International Regional Science Review* 10:1–45.

Wallace, I. (1990) *The Global Economic System* (London: Unwin Hyman).

World Bank. (1993a) *World Development Report 1993* (New York: Oxford University Press).

———. (1993b) *The East Asian Miracle: Economic Growth and Public Policy* (New York: Oxford University Press).

Yeung, Y. M., ed. (1993) *Pacific Asia in the 21st Century: Geographical and Developmental Perspectives* (Hong Kong: The Chinese University Press).

8

Uncertain Globalization: Refugee Movements in the Second Half of the Twentieth Century

Astri Suhrke

The nature and extent of the globalization of the refugee phenomenon can be analyzed on several levels. One concerns the development of the international refugee *regime:* how did the progressive expansion of a common system to protect and assist refugees come to acquire a global scope? Another level deals with *causes.* Refugee problems exist in most parts of the world and are often attributable to similar events. Arguably, the concept of globalization is more appropriate when refugee flows appear across nations and regions as a result of causes that are structurally linked, rather than coincidental occurrences. Raymond Grew has made a similar point with respect to ecology: a global ecology can be said to exist in recognition of the interdependence of its constituent parts.[1]

This chapter will focus on these two levels of analysis. A third important perspective should be noted, however. By their *impact,* refugee flows can also contribute to the process of globalization, although the effects would seem to be less than those produced by other types of migrations. Analyzing the relationship between migration and globalization of history, Wang Gungwu points out that migrants (and sojourners) established traditions of "linked spatial relationships" over great distances by retaining ties with the homeland. Political and technological developments made it possible to do so with increasing ease in the second half of the twentieth century.[2] Like migrants, refugees have also been dispersed geographically, but some important differences between the two limit the globalizing impact.

Contemporary refugee flows have with a few exceptions remained within the region of origin.[3] Dispersion, moreover, has been counterbalanced by the principle of concentration, which occurs when diaspora seek protection in their actual or putative homeland (e.g., Hungarian minorities in Europe after World War I and, in another context, the forced movement of Muslims from the Caucasus to the central regions of the Ottoman Empire in the late nineteenth century). Most important, perhaps, the nature of the refugee condition makes it difficult to maintain links with the country of origin and hence keep alive these ties.

On the contrary, networks of support for, and control of, refugee movements have developed that cut across states and regions, thereby promoting a globalization of the politics of refugee policy. For instance, from the second half of the 1980s and onward, European governments intensified consultations and efforts to harmonize asylum policies. Also the United States, Canada, and Australia were brought into the increasingly formalized system of consultations.[4] Nongovernmental organizations seeking to defend the rights of asylum-seekers or refugees are similarly organized on an international basis, for example, through umbrella organizations such as the European Consultations on Refugees and Exiles (ECRE) and Amnesty International. Electronic mail has had a revolutionary impact on the development of international solidarity networks to aid victims of persecution or human rights violations, including many refugees. Using such networks, local NGOs working, for instance, for refugees from Guatemala in Mexico can instantly tap in to their international networks, which link them to support groups in Europe, North America, and the rest of Latin America. Via computer discussions they exchange information, develop political campaigns, or plan work strategy. NGOs operating in the field of human rights or humanitarian assistance have been able to use this technological tool with great efficiency.

The International Refugee Regime

Much recent discussion of asylum has focused on the restrictive national policies instituted in Western Europe since the mid-1980s. Viewed in a longer historical perspective, however, we see that the statutory definition of *refugee* in international law has widened.[5] Between World Wars I and II, the refugee mandate of the League of Nations was temporary and limited to specific nationalities. There was a High Commissioner for refugees from Russia, later a few other nationalities were added, including German refugees in the 1930s. After World War II, by contrast, a universal concept of refugee was codified in the 1951 UN Convention on the Status of Refugees. *Refugee* was now defined with reference to a state of affairs ("persecution"), rather than the identity of a particular country. Clauses of the 1951 Convention, which limited its application to refugees from Europe, were nullified by the addition of a protocol in 1967, thereby completing the transformation from legal particularism to universalism—or from regional to global application.

In practice, the move to a global application occurred in a more hesitant and uneven manner. The first intergovernmental organizations established after World War II to assist refugees—The United Nations Relief and Rehabilitation Agency (UNRRA), superseded in 1947 by the International Refugee Organization (IRO)—were mandated to aid victims of war and upheavals in Europe only. When a massive refugee crisis developed in Asia in 1947, IRO refused to help. As a result, several million persons who were displaced by the partition of India in 1947 had to rely on the meager resources of their own governments and a few private charity organizations. The event for years poisoned relations between India and IRO's successor agency, the United Nations High Commissioner for Refugees (UNHCR). Only slightly more recognition was given to the Chinese who fled to Hong Kong after the Communist victory on the mainland in 1949. They did not receive official international assistance until 1957, when the United Nations authorized UNHCR to provide some support. Whereas political complications explain the Chinese case,[6] the neglect of India's refugees sprang from a relative indifference toward non-European victims of crisis at a time when Europe itself was devastated by war. The only large refugee populations outside Europe that were assisted by the emerging international refugee regime were the Palestinians and the Koreans. Both were part of conflicts that had strategic significance for the West, and separate aid agencies to care for them were established (respectively, the United Nations Relief for Palestine Refugees, later Relief and Works Agency for Palestine Refugees in the Near East, UNRWA, and the United Nations Korean Reconstruction Agency).

The Eurocentric orientation of the early refugee regime reflected the distribution of international power and the priority assigned to reconstruct and rehabilitate Europe after World War II. During the 1950s Europe remained the principal area of concern as the Cold War intensified and new refugee flows moved from East to West. Gradually, however, the decolonization process in Africa and Asia underscored the significance of conflicts elsewhere in the world. The infusion of new members in the United Nations made it possible in the early 1960s, and again in 1972, to pass resolutions that authorized UNHCR to assist a broad category of persons displaced by war, repression, and upheaval also outside Europe. The financial cost incurred as a result was largely born by Europe and North America. Apart from the humanitarian imperative, this was justified by political considerations: The West recognized that if left unassisted, large refugee populations could cause instability and create situations ripe for exploitation by radical or Communist forces. By the 1980s, virtually all UNHCR's activity occurred in the developing world.

The progressive globalization of an initially regionally focused regime thus reflected two structural developments during the second half of the twentieth century: the changing nature of the international system as post-colonial states were incorporated on terms of formal equality; and the overarching conflict between East and West, which globalized the strategic concerns of the opposing alliances. Accompanying these changes came a discourse in the United Nations that emphasized universal human rights and basic human needs. Both sets of values reinforced the universal legal concept of the 1951 Convention, which recognized that refugees had a claim to protection and assistance regardless of their geographic location.

The end of the Cold War led to new efforts to expand the scope of the international refugee regime. Already covering the entire globe, the regime could now expand only by intruding on the traditional domain of states. In 1992 the United Nations, emboldened to take a more active role in the post-Cold War World, formally reopened the question of internally displaced persons. Following a UN General Assembly resolution (46/182), which strengthened the UN's authority to intervene in humanitarian emergencies, the Secretary-General appointed a Special Representative to examine the needs and rights of internally displaced persons. The first report, issued in 1993, argued that internally displaced persons might need protection and assistance as much as refugees who had crossed an international border; in these cases the international community had an obligation to intervene, if necessary, to aid them.[7] There was no agreement on how to reconcile this with the UN principle of state sovereignty, but it was clear that collective action in practice would follow the configuration of state power: Weak, developing countries would most likely be the objects of intervention by the more powerful. If the international refugee regime were to expand in this way, one result would thus be greater inequality among states. Recognizing this, many developing countries in the United Nations opposed the move.

Causes of Refugee Flows

Wars and their aftermath have been principal causes of refugee flows in the twentieth century. Between World Wars I and II, Europe alone had around 9.5 million refugees, and they had twice that after World War II, if all displaced persons are included.[8] But also other forms of conflict caused displacement on a massive scale: The partition of India forced 14 million to move, and over 2 million Chinese fled to Taiwan and Hong Kong in the immediate aftermath of the Communist victory on the mainland. During the half century that followed, the events that generated a steadily growing global refugee population were of a similar character and can be divided into three main categories: wars, conflicts over the social order within states, and conflicts over how to define the base community that constituted the nation-state.

Some of these events, such as conflicts accompanying the decolonization in Africa and Asia, were part of a broader historical trend, which in retrospect becomes clear. In the 1970s and the 1980s, the process of state formation and modernization appeared to take a particularly violent turn as a series of local struggles over social order were caught up in the rivalry between the superpowers and became overdetermined by the Cold War. As the rivalry between the superpowers acquired a global scope it gave the local conflicts and related refugee consequences a common imprint. A pattern of violence and refugee flows, which interacted to create a self-reinforcing vicious cycle, appeared throughout the developing world. When the Cold War ended these conflicts mostly subsided or followed a local dynamic. Elsewhere, local conflict dynamics similarly prevailed, giving rise to a more disconnected and heterogenous pattern of refugee flows.

Refugee Movements and the Cold War

In Europe, the movement of people from the socialist Eastern bloc was considerable, despite the obstacles to exit. About 3.5 million Germans moved West before the Berlin Wall was built. The Hungarian uprising in 1956 made 200,000 persons leave, and 80,000 left in the aftermath of the Prague Spring of 1968.

The East-West flows were the result of social transformations of a revolutionary kind. This process was sharpened by the hostility between East and West, which also made it possible for the refugees to find ready asylum in the West. As implacable enemies of the revolution, the emigres helped to reinforce the refugee-producing cycle.

Outside Europe, a different pattern relating to state formation unfolded in the early post-war period.

Reorganization of Political Communities. In Africa, Asia, and the Middle East, refugee flows were initially related to decolonization. Two partitions (India and Palestine) displaced large populations and carried the seeds of further conflict, thus bringing about what partition, at best, had been designed to prevent.[9] In South Asia, the subsequent breakup of Pakistan (1971) caused further fragmentation. The Bangladeshi war of independence created a refugee population of unprecedented size and speed of formation. In the course of a few months, several million people streamed across the border to neighboring Indian states. Since they were fleeing from war as warfare—rather than its final outcome—the refugee situation was temporary. When secession was confirmed by Bangladeshi independence, most refugees returned. The pattern is typical for successful wars of decolonization and secession: The nature of the conflict contains the promise of a solution.

Although decolonization from European rule became a dominant historical trend in the period following World War II, similar challenges posed by aspiring nationalities within the new states generally failed. Until 1991, Bangladesh was a singular case of success. In the prevailing spirit of nationalism, however, many tried. The result was protracted and frequently recurring conflict that accounted for many of the refugee flows in Sub-Sahara Africa and South Asia in the postindependence period.

In South Asia's ethnically plural states, struggles over power and privilege tended to develop into questions of membership of the state itself. If a community were territorially concentrated and located on the geographic periphery of the state, conflict was likely to become a process of competitive state formation, with each group claiming exclusive membership. Autonomy-separatist conflicts developed in India's originally tribal northeastern region (Manipur, Mizoram, Nagaland) and in the northwest where separatist Sikhs in Punjab and, more recently, Muslims in Kashmir, fought central government forces. A difficult minority-majority relationship in Sri Lanka exploded in 1983, setting off a civil war that continues a decade later.

The refugee condition associated with protracted and unresolved struggles of this kind is fluid. People move back and forth between the homeland and asylum, depending upon the fluctuations of the conflict, their own engagement, and the available alternatives. Over time, the refugees tend to divide into three groups. The activist leaders and their followers remain in the vicinity of the conflict in order to pursue the struggle and—if neighboring states consent—form what we have called *refugee-warrior communities.*[10] Others migrate to settle elsewhere. The resource-rich tend to migrate long distances, seeking asylum or entering through other migration channels to establish themselves in high-income states. The resource-poor usually migrate locally. A third category appears as a floating mass of individuals biding their time and an uncertain future in refugee camps or improvised settlements. In South Asia, the pattern is exemplified by the Tamils of Sri Lanka and is identifiable in many conflict situations outside the region as well, of which the Palestinians probably constitute the most prominent case.[11]

Elsewhere in Asia, a different pattern of conflict evolved that caused major and mostly irreversible refugee flows.

Revolutionary Wars. In East and Southeast Asia, revolutionary Marxism became a powerful mobilizing ideology in the struggle for independence and social change. Class, not ethnic group, was the discourse of conflict, which also was fought with military force ranging from guerrillas to conventional armies. In China, the consolidation of the Communist party in 1949 made the losing Kuomintang retreat to their rear base in Taiwan, which became a refugee colony claiming to be the legitimate government of China. Over a million and a half arrived in the first wave. Once installed, however, the Nationalist regime accepted few additional refugees. Hong Kong became the principal alternative for those trying to leave the mainland. About 700,000 arrived between 1949 and 1951. Noting with alarm that the refugees were packed so tightly into the hillsides they seemed to "elbow each other off the precarious cliffs to which they cling," British authorities decided in 1950 that most new arrivals were illegal immigrants, subject to immediate deportation.[12] Apart from a small quota of legal migration, the policy of definitional exclusion was followed in subsequent years. During periods of great upheavals on the mainland, however, Hong Kong adopted a more liberal "touch base policy," whereby those who managed to get inside the crown colony were allowed to stay.

In relation to the size of the population, the outflow in the wake of the Communist victory in China was modest, equivalent to 4–5 persons per 1,000 or slightly less than the refugee flow from the more circumscribed French Revolution.[13] The reasons were not only the general prohibition of emigration laid down by the Communist government—which could be circumvented—but, apart from Taiwan, the lack of a place to go.

The significance of external patronage in securing asylum emerged more clearly three decades later when Vietnam was unified under a Communist regime. Persons closely identified with the *ancien régime* were evacuated as soon as the Communist troops entered Saigon in 1975; others fled on their own. They were relatively few—only 142,000 in the 1975–1977 period. As the revolution was consolidated, however, much larger social segments were affected and tried to escape. The minority ethnic Chinese constituted the merchant class and were doubly vulnerable. Being ordered to do agricultural work in the harsh New Economic Zones, many thousands left the country instead, with tacit encouragement from the Vietnamese authorities. In their wake followed a much broader outflow from various social segments who fled from both political oppression and economic austerity. Ex-soldiers and bureaucrats, professionals and peasants, fishermen and petty traders alike became "boat people." Over a five-year period starting in 1978, nearly half a million went to Southeast Asia and Hong Kong, another 260,000 ethnic Chinese resettled in China. Relative to the size of the population, it was an outflow rate of 1.4 percent, or over three times that of the Chinese revolution.

As it became clear that the Vietnamese revolution was irreversible, asylum became the equivalent of permanent relocation. Recognizing this, neighboring states refused for reasons of their own to receive the Vietnamese unless onward passage was guaranteed. At this point, the mechanism of the Vietnamese refugee migrations had more in common with those from Eastern Europe than from China. All revolutions have enemies that are the logical havens for those who escape, but the depth of U.S. involvement and defeat in Vietnam ensured a special engagement. The United States mobilized an international coalition, which by the end of the 1980s had enabled 1.3 million Indochinese, of which two-thirds were Vietnamese, to resettled in the Western industrialized countries. It was the first instance of large-scale, organized refugee resettlement from the developing world to the industrialized states

The 1980s. The Vietnam War engulfed neighboring Laos and set off a chain reaction of revolution, repression, and invasion in neighboring Cambodia that pushed up the global refugee count at the end of the 1970s. But also elsewhere, there were signs of a mounting refugee population. Almost simultaneously, revolutions and invasions sparked refugee flows in all the major regions of the developing world and focused the attention of the international community on the refugee phenomenon in a manner not seen since World War II.

Revolution and invasion in Afghanistan (1978–1979) provoked an immediate outflow of about 2 million; a decade of war later had brought the figure to 5 million. Revolution in Iran (1979) made a large segment of the Westernized middle class take up residence in Europe and the United States under various forms of refugee, immigration, or informal status. Invasion of Kampuchea (1979) brought about the collapse of a revolutionary system based on terror and sent half a million people fleeing across the border to Thailand. In the Western hemisphere, a sudden exodus of 125,000 persons who sailed from Cuba to U.S. shores dramatized that also the West could be affected directly. Although people had been leaving Cuba for the United States since the revolutionary coup in 1959, the uncontrolled nature and size of the "Marielitos" flow in 1980 caused profound concern in Washington.

There was no respite in the 1980s. Two major areas of sub-Saharan Africa developed into sustained refugee-producing areas. In the Horn of Africa, the Marxist revolutionary regime that had seized power in Ethiopia (1974) found itself fighting most of its own people as well as Somalia, which exploited its neighbor's predicament to press a long-standing irredentist claim. An uneasy peace prevailed in neighboring Sudan until the civil war between the northern and southern regions resumed in 1983. Drought and famine in 1984–1986 caused additional death and displacement. By 1987, over 1 million refugees were officially registered in the Horn; many more were internally displaced or unregistered.

In southern Africa, a conjuncture of events pointed toward war in the entire region. Being the only white government in sub-Saharan Africa by the end of the decade and facing the gathering momentum of a black liberation movement in its so-called trust territory of Namibia, Pretoria adopted an aggressive policy toward those neighboring states that could not be bought off. Simultaneously, Marxist-oriented regimes in neighboring Mozambique and Angola were irrevocably opposed to white rule in the region. In this confrontation, Pretoria supported the rebel movement in Mozambique, which originally had been sponsored by white-ruled Rhodesia; one of the most destructive wars in the entire region ensued. With equal determination, South Africa intervened in the civil war in Angola, where rival factions continued to compete for power after the Portuguese had left. The widening conflict in southern Africa left a refugee pattern similar to that in the Horn: a million and a half international refugees in the early 1980s and more internally displaced.

Also in Latin America, a refugee crisis was in evidence. Set off by repressive regimes in the Southern Cone countries in the early 1970s, the count mounted rapidly as the agrarian oligarchies of Central America succumbed to revolutionary struggles and vicious repression, especially in El Salvador and Guatemala. In the second half of the 1980s, perhaps 2.5 million people in Central America were displaced by war, many fleeing to neighboring countries and the United States. Only in Nicaragua was there a sizable return movement as most of the 200,000 who had fled when the violence brought on by the overthrow of the Somoza dictatorship went back. The proclamation of a revolutionary government in turn led to another outflow from the propertied classes who mainly found asylum in the United States.

Each of these conflicts had a distinct dynamic of its own. In Sub-Saharan Africa, for instance, the pace and nature of decolonization set the stage for postindependence politics, and the white-settler colonies left a particularly conflictual heritage. In Afghanistan, the traditional weakness of the central state accentuated the inability of the revolutionary government to deal with its local enemies, thereby making it more likely that the Soviet Union would intervene. In Central America, the United States had long pursued interventionist policies to shape the direction of social change and ensure its own influence. But above and beyond these particularities was a common element that gave coherence to the upheavals of the 1980s. The local conflict dynamics interacted with an especially severe phase of the Cold War, and each interaction in turn reinforced the large power rivalry in a more antagonistic direction. The refugee phenomenon was thus globalized in the sense that both the causes and manifestations were shaped by the same factor, that is, the logic of the Cold War.

The logic was apparent on different levels. Conflict over social change often came to be expressed in the dominant discourse of the time-revolutionary socialism versus liberal democracy. This served to link national struggles to the principal fault line of international power politics and paved the way for competitive intervention. Acting on the premise of a global competition, the large powers had increasingly moved to the periphery when the Cold War stabilized in Europe. Yet, some areas were deemed more "strategic" than others, and the time, place, and manner of intervention varied. These restraints became less operative in the 1980s.

The Soviet Union in the Brezhnev era followed a more overtly aggressive interventionist policy, using troops of its own (Afghanistan), or advisors combined with regular troops of client states (Cuban soldiers in Ethiopia and Angola). The United States under the Reagan Administration actively opposed the Soviet Union virtually anywhere in the world, although primarily through proxies or in so-called Low Intensity Conflicts (a policy institutionalized to the point of acquiring the acronym LIC).[14] Hence, arms supplies to Afghan factions fighting the Soviet Union were a means to inflict damage on the latter; tolerance or encouragement of Pretoria's role in Angola and Mozambique became an instrument for weakening Marxist regimes in these states and a bargaining chip to obtain Soviet withdrawal from the area. The logic of competitive intervention became so well established in the 1980s that the local arenas were simply referred to as "the regional conflicts," that is, of the Cold War. Only in South Asia did the nature of social change serve to isolate local conflict from East-West tension. Another factor was the structure of international relations, which acknowledged India as a major but independent-minded power in the region.

The wars of the Cold War followed a common pattern. In each case, local conflicts were magnified, as were death, destruction, and refugee flows. The nature and liberal supply of weapons ensured that destruction would be widespread and often indiscriminate (e.g., by the use of air power); and the logic of competitive intervention required that a gain by one side be offset by a commensurate strengthening of the other. For several years, both superpowers were able to provide the necessary increments to sustain the conflict. The costs were nevertheless substantial and in the end forced the Soviet Union to withdraw from Afghanistan (1989), a decisive step that accelerated the collapse of the Soviet system itself.

In its less extreme and more generalized form, superpower rivalry served to build up local clients or regimes regardless of their domestic legitimacy and repressive apparatus. The consequences can be traced in the movement of refugees from the violent "national security regimes" in South America, from the U.S.-supported regime of the Shah of Iran and the revolutionary reaction it invited, and from the Soviet Union's continuous rescue of socialism in Cuba.

Some of these refugees resettled in other regions or continents (mainly the Indochinese and the Iranians). Most remained in neighboring areas and many continued to actively participate in the conflict. In southern Africa, the Horn, Kampuchea, Afghanistan, and, to some extent, in Central America, displaced civilians represented the popular base of the guerrillas by providing labor, recruits, and political legitimacy. Although the precise relationship between the guerrillas and the civilian refugees varied, most were essentially "refugee-warrior" communities, of which the Palestinians constituted the prototypical case. Unlike the Palestinians, however, these communities served as important instruments for the interventionist policies of external powers. This could mean substantial benefits for the refugees in terms of generous relief assistance, but the downside was clear: The refugee-warrior communities became active participants in a cycle of conflict, intervention, and refugees.[15]

Welcome and Unwelcome Refugees. As a rule, refugees carry with them an element of the conflict from which they flee, whether voluntarily (as rebels engaging in revanchist politics), or involuntarily (as imputed by parties to the conflict). International asylum law recognized this early on by affirming that the act of granting asylum did not constitute a *casus belli.*[16] Contemporary legal codes likewise acknowledge the political element of the refugee condition by making it contingent upon "persecution" (1951 UN Convention). Persecution commonly is taken to imply a malevolent and deliberate act by a political agent.

The singular effect of the Cold War was not to politicize the refugee phenomenon, but to globalize this process and connect it to the dominant rivalry between the superpowers. Refugees became instruments of and parties to the Cold War, representing increments of power that were counted in the balance between East and West. In an age of mass politics and under the terms of ideological rivalry during the Cold War, refugees who crossed over to the West represented a political asset. In other periods refugees had been welcomed for their professional skills or political activism, their labor, or even their military power (as when entire armies with their camp followers defected). The classical refugees of the Cold War were valued for voting with their feet. Openly recognized in the West, the logic was implicit in the prohibition on exit in the East.[17]

In "the regional conflicts," refugee-warrior communities were welcomed as proxies in the superpower rivalry and often also in regional power struggles (e.g., the Khmer in the Thai-Vietnamese axis and the Afghans in the India-Pakistan equation).

The End of the Cold War

As the Cold War wound down, so did most of the "regional conflicts."[18] The collapse of Soviet socialism and subsequently the Soviet Union itself undermined the revolutionary left everywhere. The void created incentives for compromise at the local level and simultaneously offered the United States an opportunity to abandon foreign commitments that were controversial at home, inconclusive in the field, and, absent the Soviet

Union, of declining strategic value. Regional clients were either undercut or undertook parallel reforms, as happened in South Africa.

The pace and path of reconciliation had been demonstrated in El Salvador and Namibia already in 1991–1992. In both cases, a peace agreement was followed by international monitoring of demobilization and elections. Plans for economic reconstruction were laid and refugees started to return home. Early in 1993, Mozambique followed suit, and—after a period of much uncertainty and a considerable UN investment of money and human resources—Cambodia did as well. For the first time in over three decades, the Khmer people had in 1993 both peace and an elected government. In the Horn of Africa, the fall of Ethiopia's Marxist regime in 1991 permitted a peace settlement both in Eritrea and Ethiopia proper, permitting the UN to plan for an organized, large-scale return of refugees from the Sudan.

Elsewhere, the legacy of the Cold War dominated. Decades of violence and intrusive great power politics and a liberal supply of weapons had transformed local states and societies. Local factions had grown into well-armed, institutionalized, semi-autonomous entities that made up for their lack of legitimacy by the use of force, as in Afghanistan. Angola differed only in that the war had lasted longer, dating back to the violent struggle for decolonization in the mid-1960s. Despite the eventual withdrawal of foreign troops and general disengagement of external powers, neither country was at peace as the decade of the 1990s opened and the refugee situation remained fluid.

The Cold War, as noted, had been played out in the developing world as a consequence of the stability that over time had come to prevail in Europe, thereby limiting the possibilities for altering the status quo in the center of the conflict system. When that status quo suddenly collapsed, the simultaneous disintegration of a social system and an imperial structure caused a shift in the balance of violent conflict toward the old center—the industrialized North. The refugee flows moved accordingly.

The North. In and around the former Soviet Union, conflicts arose over national boundaries and ethnic communities in the Caucasus, Baltic States, and Central Asia. When turning violent, refugee flows generally followed a pattern associated with the reorganization of political communities. Russians moved to Russia, Armenians and Azeris crossed to join their own ethnic majorities in the war over Nagorno-Karabakh, although many Armenians also sought safety in Russia, ethnic Georgians trekked across the mountains from the break-away Abkhazian enclave to areas where they constituted a majority, and so on. Official Russian sources placed the total number of refugees and internally displaced at 1 million in early 1993. Of these, ethnic Russians returning from the republics were conservatively estimated at one-fourth. The other large groups were

Armenians (370,000) and Tajiks displaced within Tajikistan or to neighboring areas as a result of the civil war (400,000). Those displaced generally remained within the former Soviet Union and did not seek protection in the West, as European states had feared. Relief assistance was channeled through UNHCR and foreign NGOs working in the most disturbed areas in Central Asia and the Caucasus.[19]

In contrast to earlier East-West flows, which had served to disperse nationalities, these movements followed the principle of concentration. As ethnic origin became the defining principle of the nation-state, ethnic groups "unmixed" and minorities went "home." Similar relocations, only on a much larger scale, had occurred earlier in Europe.[20] When World War I brought down the Austrian-Hungarian Empire, perhaps 2 million Poles migrated to Poland, 1 million ethnic Germans moved to Germany, and hundreds of thousands of Magyars went to Hungary. In the shrinking Ottoman Empire a similar process started in the second half of the nineteenth century as non-Slavic Muslim populations were forced out of the Crimea and the Caucasus—later also from much of the Balkans—and headed for Anatolia. After the final imperial collapse, Bulgarians moved to Bulgaria, and Greece and Turkey agreed to a formal exchange of populations after the 1921 war between them.

Other ethnic groups fared worse. Some were expelled by brutal "ethnic cleansing" without having even a putative other "homeland"; others were rejected or were not welcomed in states ruled by their ethnic kin. These refugees became dispersed, as occurred with many refugees from the Balkans. One type was exemplified by the Kosovo-Albanians.

The ethnic Albanians from the Yugoslavian-, and later Serbian-ruled, Kosovo Province had sought political asylum in Europe since the late 1980s on the grounds that they were victims of Serbian nationalism. Although a relevant "homeland" of sorts existed in neighboring Albania, with which some of the Kosovo diaspora wanted to unite, the Kosovo-Albanians generally did not request, nor were they offered, refuge in Albania. It was hardly surprising: Albania was a poverty-stricken newly de-Stalinized country from where thousands of boat people had fled in 1991 after the Communist regime fell. However, Western European states for the most part rejected their asylum claims. Fearing that treatment of the Kosovo-Albanians would send signals to numerous dissatisfied ethnic groups elsewhere, European governments narrowed the gate to asylum.

The most pressing refugee problem in Europe, however, was caused by the protracted warfare and violent "ethnic cleansing" that accompanied the breakup of Yugoslavia. The first wave of refugees was brought on by the eight-month war between Serbia and Croatia after the latter's declaration of independence. Two familiar refugee patterns appeared. Minorities fled toward a safer "home" as violence unfolded in the ethnically mixed but disputed area of Krajina in Croatia. But also people who were not directly targeted fled from the fighting. When the war ended in January 1922, many returned, including Croatians who had gone to Western Europe.[21] In Bosnia-Herzegovina, the referendum in favor of independence on February 29, 1992, likewise signaled the outbreak of war. "Ethnic cleansing," initially and primarily directed against the Muslim minority but practiced by all parties, sent the survivors fleeing for safety in areas where they constituted majorities, or to states granting asylum.

Although there are no precise figures, it is clear that the refugees from the first major war in Europe since World War II were concentrated in their area of origin. Yet, a considerable number (almost half a million) was dispersed throughout Europe. By the end of 1993, the cumulative figures on refugees and displaced persons in the former Yugoslavia were as follows:

Within Croatia: 270,000 mainly from Bosnia-Herzegovina, of which an estimated 200,000 were Muslims; in addition, 246,000 remained internally displaced from the war in Croatia;
Within Serbia: 300,000 from Bosnia-Herzegovina and 160,000 from Croatia;
Within Bosnia-Herzegovina: 2.28 million besieged or internally displaced receiving relief assistance from the UNHCR;
Within Montenegro, Slovenia, and Macedonia: 117,000.[22]

Outside the Balkans, Western Europe was the principal destination. By mid-1992, European countries had an estimated 400,000 de facto refugees from the former Yugoslavia; a year later estimates had risen to 550,000. Most did not have formal refugee status but obtained various forms of temporary protection or were sponsored by relatives who had migrated earlier and formed communities of ex-Yugoslavians in several Western European countries. Only a few were resettled by UNHCR as "vulnerable cases." The largest concentration was in Germany (around 300,000 in 1993), the next largest concentrations were in Austria, Switzerland, and Sweden (50,000–70,000 each).[23]

The relatively restrictive policies toward Balkan War refugees stand in contrast to the welcome accorded thousands of refugees from Eastern Europe only a few decades earlier. In part, it reflected the trend toward restrictive asylum set off in the second half of the 1980s by economic recession and a sharp increase in the number of asylum-seekers from the developing world. The refugees from ex-Yugoslavia had the misfortune to arrive at a time when Western Europe was suffering its highest unemployment rate in decades. Fears that open borders and nationality disputes might produce huge numbers of refugees in post–Cold War Europe reinforced restrictive entry policies. The refugee was no longer seen as an exceptional occurrence that could be accommodated with relative ease.

By comparison with the Cold War pattern, the Western European response to Balkan refugees constituted a minimalist regime. There was no buildup of externally supported "refugee-warrior communities," and no support for refugees as ideological weapons in a larger conflict. Refugee policy had to be grounded primarily in humanitarian considerations. Behind this shift was a corresponding change in the foreign policy context. The European Community sought to limit its involvement to a UN-directed peacekeeping role and attempted mediation in ex-Yugoslavia. The conflict was viewed as too complex and, in the end, too marginal to the realities of power in the post–Cold War world to invite a more vigorous response. A large-scale program of humanitarian assistance was mounted, although critics feared it served to mask unwillingness to act more decisively to end the war.[24]

Although refugees from the war in Bosnia mostly were given temporary asylum in Europe, it was recognized that the stay probably would become permanent. Prospects for an eventual return were uncertain at best. A formal division of Bosnia along ethnic lines might set off new population movements, as seen in other cases of state partition. In the end, it seemed that Bosnian Muslims, in particular, would share the fate of other dispersed refugees in Europe—the Armenians and, for a long time, the Jews.

The South. Outside Europe, the end of the Cold War created prospects for more autonomous national development in the context of regional rather than global politics.[25] In much of Asia and Latin America, developments in the immediate post–Cold War world were of a kind that reduced refugee problems. Reconstruction and consolidation moved ahead in war-torn areas; in many other parts, prosperity increased and nonviolent forms of social and political change were consolidated. In the Middle East, the uncertainties of the new international order encouraged a brief international war (in the Persian Gulf, 1991); however, that also contributed to a historic peace settlement in the Palestinian conflict (1994). In much of sub-Saharan Africa, by contrast, the problems seemed systemic and deep-seated.

As the 1990s opened, problems of state formation and development reappeared in new and severe forms. War and near-anarchy prevailed in Somalia, Liberia, and Angola; ethnic massacres in Burundi were a repeat of 1972, only more were killed or driven into exile. The scale of Rwanda's ethnic genocide and mass refugee flows in 1994 was unprecedented in the region: Over half a million persons were killed, and at least twice that number fled to neighboring Zaire. Sudan continued to fluctuate between uneasy peace and civil war.

Africa's "weak state"—the central concept in political analysis of the region in the 1980s—had reappeared in the 1990s as the "failed state." Was the nation-state fundamentally an inappropriate framework for African development? asked long-standing observers of the region. Basil Davidson depicted the nation-state as an alien implant, rooted in colonial concepts of modernization. As "mere shells of a fragile and fallible civil society," the states crumble under stress and dissolve in "tribalism."[26] The stress factor itself, in this view, is more incidental.

In Liberia and Somalia, renewed conflict can be traced to the legacy of the Cold War. The disintegration of an international structure, which by means of competitive bidding had permitted a leader to establish the apparatus of a state and form an army, served as a catalyst. As external aid and legitimacy abruptly ended, tyranny gave way to "the specter of anarchy," as Aristide Zolberg wrote; warlords and their followers settled accounts in societies flush with weapons, and the refugee columns started to appear.[27] In semiarid regions, the physical environment and subsistence agriculture further shortened the path to catastrophe. If fighting disrupted the harvest in one season and the rains failed in the next, famine was probable. These were the ingredients of the Somalian disaster in 1991–1992.

Just as Yugoslavia had been a test case in Europe, Somalia became an early test case for how the post–Cold War world would respond to Africa's humanitarian emergencies. Viewed more narrowly in relation to the refugee question, the significance of the changing international context seems clear.

After being supported for years, first by the Soviet Union and then the United States, the Somali regime of General Siad Barre turned out to be a mere shell that fractured when external aid ceased. In its place came not another regime but clan warfare, chaos, and famine. At the height of the crisis in September 1992, around 3,000 persons were dying each day. Although internal displacement was considerable, relatively few became conventional refugees. By the end of 1992, about 300,000 persons of a total population of 6 million had struggled across the border to Kenya.

The Somalian disaster was met with a belated and uncertain response as regards both refugee aid and relief operations within the country. As has been well documented, the reason was not lack of early warning but failure to heed it in the UN and by the major powers.[28] This in turn reflected the international marginalization of previously strategic areas in the developing world. No longer connected to a dominant international structure of conflict, local strife appeared indeed as local to most of the outside world. Although technological developments made it possible to transmit globally almost instant images of the unfolding disaster, humanitarian concern had not reached the same level of global indivisibility. Without a patron to mobilize support on its behalf, Somalia could not compete with myriad other issues on the international agenda, and it could not energize the UN bureaucracy.[29] With slight variation, the pattern was repeated in the Rwanda disaster in 1994. The international community collectively denounced but did nothing else to stop the ethnic genocide until France, ready to assert its presence in a region of long-standing concern, intervened under a UN authorization.

Strategic devaluation probably had mixed consequences with respect to local conflict and its refugees. In Somalia, the struggle was at least contained in time and place; had it happened under the conditions of competitive interventions that characterized the Cold War it is easy to envisage a protracted conflict with mass outflows and establishment of refugee warrior communities. In Rwanda, however, the duration of the conflict was short, but the death toll and the refugee flows were nevertheless huge. The internal conflict between majority Hutu and minority Tutsi was caught up in a regional power struggle that had some of the same effect as the Cold War had in its time.

Uncertain Globalization

The violent conflicts that produce refugee flows are in themselves subject to influences from structural developments such as demographic growth and pressure on resources and the environment—all of which have acquired some global impact during the twentieth century. But the proximate causes of conflict are often decisive in shaping the nature and timing of its occurrence as well as the response of states to aid or not aid the refugees who result. Their response in turn affects the magnitude and direction of refugee flows, since, ultimately, a refugee cannot exist without a place of refuge.

As we have seen, the proximate causes of refugee flows during the second half of the twentieth century have varied in the extent to which they have been connected. The clearest cases are those linked to the decolonization process and the Cold War. In the 1980s, in particular, a series of local conflicts and associated refugee flows acquired a distinct Cold War imprint as they became drawn into and shaped by the superpower rivalry. The end of the Cold War meant that local conflict dynamics again came to prevail. Refugee flows generally underwent a strategic devaluation: Their political significance came to depend chiefly on the regional or local political context.

The de-linking of international refugee problems from a common political axis had several consequences. Humanitarian imperatives and, possibly, a general concern to maintain international order became the common ground for regulating refugee-producing conflicts and assisting its victims. Other reasons varied according to how individual states were affected. On the turbulent edge of the established Western states (as in the Balkans), a collective "peacekeeping" role in the midst of war was accompanied by liberal relief supplies but restrictive asylum. In marginalized areas of the developing world, collective intervention was possible, yet was typically late or hesitant (as in Somalia and, in modified form, in Rwanda). Arguably, the main advantage of these policies was that the situation could have been even worse in terms of deaths, destruction, and refugees if a competitive intervention of the 1980s-pattern had occurred.

Although the Cold War often "overdetermined" national struggles, local conflict dynamics tend to prevail in the post–Cold War world. This has important implications for the international refugee regime because it suggests that refugee flows are not likely to occur at the same time and in the same form. For instance, humanitarian emergencies in Somalia and Rwanda are independent of the political struggle between modernists and islamists in Algeria, or that between conservative elements in China and proponents of democratization. These conflicts may all produce major refugee flows, but since they are not structurally related the probability that they will occur simultaneously is rather low. Hence, the sense of crisis that struck the international refugee regime in the late 1970s and lasted into the 1980s and was generated by the simultaneous wars of the Cold War, is not likely to be repeated. Since the international refugee regime is less likely to be overwhelmed if refugee flows are diverse and spread out over time, there is reason to conclude that a global refugee crisis—which implies collective inability to respond—is an improbable scenario for the post–Cold War world.

In other respects the refugee phenomenon was shaped by contradictory developments in the last decades of the twentieth century. Technological developments and social networks established by previous migration have given refugees as well as migrants the means to move with increasing ease between and among continents. Since refugees are seen by receiving states as uninvited and unselected migrants, this possibility made several states restrict their asylum policies, especially the industrialized states. However, since they remained obliged by international law to recognize refugees, restrictions were accompanied by other efforts to prevent their geographic dispersion. This took the form *inter alia* of greater efforts to aid people in or near the country of origin.[30] If successful, this represents a regionalization or even localization of the refugee phenomenon.

Notes

1. Raymond Grew et al. (ed), "On the Prospect of Global History," in *Conceptualizing Global History,* Boulder: Westview Press, 1993, pp. 227–250.

2. Wang Gungwu, "Migration and Its Enemies," in *Conceptualizing Global History,* pp. 131–152.

3. After World War II, the initial policy of the Allied powers was to repatriate refugees and displaced persons to their country of nationality. That was followed by organized resettlement of 1.3 million persons, mainly to the Americas, Australia, and Israel. No similar large-scale dispersion of refugees across regions occurred until the late 1970s, when refugees from Indochina were resettled in Europe, Australia, and North America. A decade later, about 1 million persons had been resettled. Mixed flows of refugees and migrants from the Caribbean and Central America to the United States have been a more continuous phenomenon, although intensifying during periods of strife as in Central America in the 1970s and 1980s. Given the geographic proximity of sending and receiving countries, these are in some respect intraregional movements. The interregional distribution by the early 1990s is indicated by the following figures: In 1993, Africa had an estimated 7.4 million refugees, although less than 100,000 Africans that year had applied for asylum in the United States, Canada, and Europe taken together. Asia had around 5.7 million refugees, although some 150,000 had lodged asylum applications in Europe and North America, the equivalent figures for Latin America were 130,000 and 91,700. These figures do not include organized resettlement across regions, of which the United States' program remained the principal one (around 119,000 were admitted as refugees in 1993, of which three-quarters came from the former Soviet Union and Vietnam. Sources: *Populations of Concern to UNHCR,* Geneva: UNHCR, 1993 and *World Refugee Survey, 1994,* Washington, D.C.: U.S. Committee for Refugees.

4. Within the growing literature on this subject, especially useful are Daniel Joly, "The Porous Dam: European Harmonization on Asylum in the Nineties," *International Journal of Refugee Law,* vol. 6, no. 2 (1994) and Charles B. Keely and Sharon Stanton Russell, "Responses of Industrial Countries to Asylum-Seekers," *Journal of International Affairs,* vol. 47, no. 2 (1994).

5. For a recent analysis of institutional developments, see Gil Loescher, *Beyond Charity: International Cooperation and the Global Refugee Problem,* New York: Oxford University Press, 1993. The standard older work is Louise W. Holborn, *Refugees: A Problem of Our Time, the Work of the High Commissioner for Refugees, 1951–1972,* Metuchen, N.J.: Scarecrow Press, 1975. The principal recent legal studies are Guy S. Goodwin-Gill, *The Refugee in International Law,* Oxford: Clarendon Press, 1983 and James Hathaway, *The Law of Refugee Status,* Toronto: Butterworth, 1991.

6. At the time, UNHCR was only mandated to assist "refugees" as defined in the UN Convention. To aid Chinese refugees in Hong Kong would imply that they were victims of persecution. This would be a tacit recognition of the mainland Chinese regime since the refugees in question clearly did not flee from the Chinese regime represented in the UN. Taiwan and its allies in the UN blocked aid until the UN General Assembly in 1957 found a formula to circumvent the issue by authorizing UNHCR to use its "good offices" regardless of the status of the beneficiaries.

7. United Nations, *Human Rights, Mass Exoduses, and Displaced Persons,* New York: United Nations, E/CM.4/1993/35. The special representative, Francis Deng, also discussed the question in *Protecting the Dispossessed,* Washington, D.C.: Brookings Institution, 1993.

8. Michael Marrus, *The Unwanted,* Oxford: Oxford University Press, 1985 and Eugene M. Kulisher, *Europe on the Move: War and Population Changes, 1917–1947,*

New York: Columbia University Press, 1948. Leslie Page Mooch, *Moving Europeans: Migration in Western Europe Since 1650,* Bloomington: Indiana University Press, 1992, uses the higher figure of 30 million (p. 162).

9. For India, see C. H. Philips and M. D. Wainwright, eds., *The Partition of India,* London: Allen & Unwin, 1970. Recent research on the partition of Palestine is presented by Benny Morris in *The Birth of the Palestinian Refugee Problem, 1947–1949,* Cambridge: Cambridge University Press, 1987.

10. The term was originally developed with reference to the Afghan refugees in Pakistan and is elaborated in Aristide Zolberg, Astri Suhrke, and Sergio Aguyao, *Escape from Violence: Conflict and Refugees in the Developing World,* New York: Oxford University Press, 1989.

11. For a dispassionate account of the Palestinian case, see Laurie A. Brandt, *The Palestinians in the Arab World,* New York: 1988.

12. Government of Hong Kong, *Annual Report,* 1953, p. 11.

13. Based on a population of 580 million as given in the 1954 census.

14. Michael T. Klare and Peter Kornbluh, *Low-Intensity Warfare: Counterinsurgency, Proinsurgency and Antiterrorism in the Eighties,* New York: 1988. See also Fred Halliday, *Soviet Policy in the Arc of Crisis,* Washington, D.C.: Institute for Policy Studies, 1981.

15. See, e.g., Linda Mason and Roger Brown, *Rice, Rivalry, and Politics: Managing Cambodian Relief,* Notre Dame, Ind.: University of Notre Dame Press, 1983 and Helga Baitenmann, "NGOs and the Afghan War," *Third World Quarterly,* 12:1 (1990):62–85.

16. Eduardo Arboleda, "Refugee Definition in Africa and Latin America: The Lessons of Pragmatism," *International Journal of Refugee Law* 3:2 (April 1991):185–207; Guy S. Goodwin-Gill, *The Refugee in International Law,* Oxford: Clarendon Press, 1983.

17. This was not the only reason. Barriers to exit were not unknown in imperial China and czarist Russia. See Alan Dowty, *Closed Borders: The Contempory Assault on Freedom of Movement,* New Haven: Yale University Press, 1987.

18. See Anthony Lake, ed., *After the Wars,* Washington, D.C.: Overseas Development Council, 1990 and Astri Suhrke, "A Crisis Diminished: Refugees in the Developing World," *International Journal* (Toronto) 48(spring 1993):214–239.

19. Rogers Brubaker, "Political Dimensions of Migration From and Among Soviet Successor States," in Myron Weiner, ed., *International Migration and Security,* Boulder: Westview, 1993, pp. 39–64; Daniel Heradstveit, "Flyktningar i den tidlegare Sovjetunionen," in Astri Suhrke and Svein Gjerdåker, eds., *Dagens folkevandringer—berörer de oss?* Oslo: Cappelen, 1993.

20. Walter Adams, "Extent and Nature of the World Refugee Problem," *Annals of the American Academy of Political and Social Sciences* 203(1939):26–36.

21. This and other figures for the section on the former Yugoslavia are based on UNHCR sources (Geneva), the monthly bulletin of the External Affairs Division of the UNHCR in Zagreb, entitled, *Information Notes on Former Yugoslavia,* and interviews in October 1993 in Zagreb with the UNHCR, the Croatian Office for Displaced Persons, and representatives of the Scandinavian diplomatic and consular missions.

22. UNHCR (Zagreb), *Information Notes,* October 3, 1993.

23. "Survey of Implementation of Temporary Protection," memo., UNHCR (Geneva), July 1993.

24. Rosalyn Higgins, "The New United Nations and Former Yugoslavia," *International Affairs* (London) 69:3(1993):465–483.

25. Jorge Castañeda, "Latin America and the End of the Cold War," *World Policy Journal* 7:3(1990):469–492.

26. Basil Davidson, *The Black Man's Burden,* London: James Currey, 1992.

27. Aristide Zolberg, "The Specter of Anarchy," *Dissent* 39(summer 1992):303–311.

28. U.S. House of Representatives, Select Committee on Hunger, *Humanitarian Intervention: A Review of Theory and Practice,* Hearings, 102nd. Cong., 2nd. sess., September 25, 1992, Washington, D.C.: GPO.

29. For a UN insider's indictment, see Mohamed Sahnoun, *Somalia: The Missed Opportunities,* Washington, D.C.: United States Institute of Peace Press, 1994.

30. See, e.g., *Reception in the Region of Origin.* Intergovernmental Consultations on Asylum, Refugee, and Migration Policies in Europe, North America, and Australia. Working Paper. Geneva: IGC Secretariat, September 1994.

9

Travel, Migration, and Images of Social Life

Mike Featherstone

Robert Park once remarked that human beings, like the higher types of animals—"everything above the oyster, in fact—are made for locomotion and action."

—(1923, p. 157, quoted in G. Suttles, *Kamikaze Biker,* 1991, p. xi)

All I ask is heaven above and the road before me.

—(The Vagabond in Vaughan Williams' *Songs of Travel*)

History is always written from a sedentary point of view and in the name of a unitary State apparatus, at least a possible one, even when the topic is nomads. What is lacking is a Nomadology, the opposite of a history.

—(G. Deleuze and F. Guattari, *A Thousand Plateaus,* 1987, p. 23)

L'etranger te permet d'etre toi-meme, en faisant, de toi, un etranger.

—(Jabes, 1989, p. 9; quoted in I. Chambers, *Migrancy, Culture, and Identity,* 1994, p. 12)

I hate travelling and explorers.

—(C. Levi-Strauss, *Tristes Tropiques,* 1976 p. 15)

In the literature on postmodernism there is a tendency to criticize notions of fixed identity and celebrate disorder, syncretism, and hybridity. For some, the latter qualities are assumed to be in the nature of social life—somehow, despite the "antifoundational" rhetoric, a more basic and fundamental aspect of culture, which became occluded. Alternatively, there is a hidden historical narrative in which the present phase is assumed to be distinct from the past—something that in its most inflated form is presented as a new age, postmodernity. In both cases there is the assumption that many of our existing models can no longer adequately handle the increasing complexity and fluidity of contemporary life. They are criticized for relying on, or seeking to establish, universal categories, unified identities and systemic models. In contrast to this perceived rigidity and inflexibility, in which theory seeks to speak for and about everyone everywhere, postmodern theories emphasize our limited horizons and the integrity of all the varieties of local knowledge.

Of particular interest in this context is the frequent use of metaphors of movement and marginality. There are references to travel, nomadism, migrancy, border-crossings, and living on the borders. Nomadism and migrancy are seen not only as characteristics of the contemporary global condition but as central to language. I. Chambers (1990, 1994), for example, refers to the nomadic experience of language, which ceases to be an instrument of precision and clarity. Rather thought wanders and migrates: Instead of having a fixed base or home, it dwells in a mobile habitat that produces discontinuities and fragmented experiences. The nomad has become an important category in this type of cultural studies literature. T. H. Gabriel (1990, p. 396) reminds us that the nomadic way of life and art forms have two main aspects. First, "the fundamental ideal that all life, experience and existence is without frontiers and boundaries." Second, "the foundational idea of not glorying fulfilment in terms of territory and resources." The temporary existence of the nomad involves a rejection of the state apparati and state laws. It is also assumed that a wandering life produces a wandering aesthetics, with a constant shift of form and content.

The theorists who have been particularly influential in this context are G. Deleuze and F. Guattari (1983, 1987), not only through their discussions of "nomadic thought" and "nomadic art" but through their general critique of fixed categories and identities. Deleuze and Guattari's celebration of a return to precognitive forms of experience and their concept of "flows," have been particularly influential on a younger generation of theorists in cultural studies. This is found in some of the literature on "the internet" which has been influenced by their notions of dispersed power, rhizomes, and flows. From one perspective Deleuze and Guattari can be seen as the latest in a tradition of intellectual and artistic thought, which although influenced by the philosophies of Bergson and Nietzsche with their valuation of immediate experience over form, also draws upon the transgressive avant-garde and bohemian impulses that can be found in the tradition of artistic modernism since the nineteenth century. This tradition has often sought to provide a critique of the achievements and lifestyles of modernity and has strong sympathies for the outsider. The bohemian, for example, identified strongly with the wandering life of the gypsies, Murger's novel and Bizet's opera *Carmen* being key influences in the formation of the bohemian mythology in the mid-nineteenth century (Pels and Crebas, 1988). Yet there are clearly antecedents that can be traced back a long way. The increasing valuation of travel as experience, as in the case of educative self-formative projects (*Bildungsprozess*) can be found, for example, in the Grand Tour in the Western tradition, which came into prominence in the eighteenth century. This notion of travel as experience can be traced back at least as far as the Renaissance and Middle Ages with the valuation of the life of the traveling scholar, artist, and vagabond. This can also be linked into older notions of the heroic quest and life as a spiritual/creative journey (religious and secular forms of pilgrimage).[1] Nomadic themes and experiences, then, have often been valued among artists and intellectuals and the growing legions of bohemians and other camp followers, who since the nineteenth century have sought to imitate their lifestyles, and have developed an interest in the aestheticization of life.

The linkage between mobility and the regenerative powers of travel is a powerful theme in Western culture, especially in art and literature. Travel has often been regarded as aiding the decentering of habitual categories, a form of playing with cultural disorder, something that can also be found in postmodern theory. Although postmodernism can be seen to be a continuation of these neoromantic themes there are further aspects of mobility in contemporary life that it, along with postcolonial theory, draws attention to. The first relates to the increasing flows of people around the world: the numbers of sojourners, refugees, and migrant workers means that "the other" is no longer something to be searched out in exotic locations in the distant parts of the world by adventurers, literary travelers, and tourists. The others work and live alongside us in the metropolitan areas. In effect "the rest are in the West." The second aspect relates to the flows of information and images that also further the process of global compression. We no longer need to travel to see and understand the other; the images flow into our living rooms and the problem ceases to be one of access to limited information about the other, rather it becomes a problem of selection, of managing and ordering the overload of information. The development of the new information technology in the direction of virtual reality and cyberspace have added to this problem through the potential, which will soon be available, to access all the information and images in human history. In addition to images and information about the other, the technology also has the potential to increase the dialogue with the other: The various others around the world can now speak back to the West and dispute its various accounts, symbolic hierarchies, and universalist claims. Ultimately, it is argued, we face a world of not just mobile subjects, but mobile objects; or rather a world in which the distinction between subjects and objects becomes narrowed and eclipsed as they both become joined and dispersed in an increasingly fluid informational field (Lash and Urry, 1993).

We therefore have a certain amount of category turmoil, because notions of mobility, movement, and border-crossing are used to confront and decenter relatively established taxonomies, canons, and symbolic hierarchies. In its most heightened form this can be found in the discipline cluster of cultural studies (see Grossberg, Nelson, and Triechler, 1992), but it is also to be found in the social sciences in anthropology (Clifford and Marcus, 1986; Clifford, 1988), political theory (Connolly, 1994), sociology (Game, 1991), psychology (Shotter, 1993), geography (Soja, 1989), women's studies (Nicholson, 1990), and business studies (Clegg, 1989), as the implications of questions of cultural complexity, which are gathered under the catch-all term *postmodernism,* continue to be explored.

If we seek to investigate the place of mobility in social life we therefore cannot ignore the ways in which it has been represented culturally and the ways in which metaphors of travel and movement form an important part of the cultural tradition of modernism (Van Den Abbeele, 1992). This suggests we need to investigate the framing capacity of these metaphors and their ability to not only direct our gaze but form particular images of the world. In effect we need to investigate the process of theory-building not only in terms of the current phase, but also in terms of the formation of images of social life in the past. Why, for example, does sociology pay so little attention to mobility and migration? Why did it for so long, and still today in some quarters, perpetuate an image of sedentary Europe and the notion that traditional societies were made up of bounded, settled *Gemeinschaften?* The danger of confining sociology to the study of modernity, as some would advocate, is that it confines the premodern to the status of an inchoate traditional society. In effect it confirms all the limitations of what Elias (1987a) has referred to as "the retreat of sociologists into the present."

Society and the Settled Image of Social Life

One of the key terms in sociology is *society.* Yet it is a term that has not always been subject to close scrutiny. In R. Nisbet's (1967) influential *The Sociological Tradition,* whereas *community, authority, status, the sacred,* and *alienation* make it into the list of the key unit-ideas of sociology, there is no place for *society.* This is because Nisbet (1967, p. 5) informs us that such ideas must be *distinctive,* they must help to differentiate one discipline from another and ideas "like 'individual,' 'society,' 'order' are useless here. . . . for these are elements of *all* the disciplines of social thought." Yet perhaps Nisbet exaggerates the universal validity of these ideas with the assumption that they are so essential and fundamental that they can be taken for granted and need not be subjected to analysis. Such ideas have a history: They come into being and may very well fade away. Such at least would seem to be the implications of the recent arguments that we are now witnessing "the end of the social" (Touraine, 1986; Baudrillard, 1993)—arguments that are often made without specific reference to globalization. In Baudrillard's case, for example, it is the development of the commodity-form that has led to a superabundance of commodity-signs in today's consumer cultures, allied with technological developments, in particular the mass media, which has increased the capacity to produce simulations. The "derealization of the real," is seen as producing social fragmentation and threatening normativity and social structures. In effect the solid base of the social bond in norm-reinforcing face-to-face social interactions has been removed in a general attenuation of social life. For Touraine (1986) the process of movement into the postindustrial society need not be seen as a totally negative one because it leads to a greater capacity for action. In effect politics, long suppressed in the sociological worldview to a derivative of the social, is resurrected with the fragmentation of long-existing social structures and by the increasing opportunity and capacity for individuals, collectivities, and social movements to act.

Although Nisbet, as mentioned previously, is reluctant to explore the history of the concept *society,* he does make the telling point that "the referent of 'social' was almost invariably the communal. *Communitas,* not *societas* with its more impersonal connotations, is the real etymological source of the sociological use of the word 'social' in his studies of personality, kinship, economy, and polity" (Nisbet, 1967, p. 56). This is evident in the writings of one of the key figures in the establishment of sociology, Auguste Comte, whose view of social life was very much dominated by the goal of devising new institutional forms that would replace traditional modes of communal order. His views should be seen in the context of the conservative reaction to the French Revolution, out of which sociology was born. This also entailed a reaction to the optimism of the Enlightenment with its commitment to action and progress, which led to a revival of interest in traditional forms of order such as the medieval manor and the village. Durkheim followed Comte in regarding society as community writ large. Durkheim is, of course, the sociologist *par excellence,* who stressed the power of society and the reality of the social. His concepts of the collective conscience, the sacred, and the social bond, stress the common beliefs and sentiments that are held to further social integration. Society was conceived as a bounded entity that was usually analyzed at a high level of abstraction. If a broader understanding of the particularities of a given society were needed then it could be compared with another society. Societies were conceived as the basic units of social life, and to understand social life entailed the use of a repertoire of societal concepts.

The social was seen as more fundamental to social life than the polity, indeed in the social science division of labor that was emerging, there was a marked hostility to political science with its emphasis upon power and action, nationalism, and internationalism. As we will see, whereas the focus of sociology has been predominantly on the internal relations of (nation-state) societies, the value position of sociologists has often been antinationalist-coupled in some cases with an internationalist attachment to the notion of humanity. For some sociologists nationalism and warfare belonged to an earlier stage of development now rapidly becoming surpassed (e.g., Spencer's sequence of movement from military to industrial societies); that is until the cataclysmic event of World War I caused some to rethink their categories. Society, then, became regarded as the generic and fundamental unit of social life and in this sense did not need a history because history was in effect conceived as the development of society.

At the same time, we need to focus upon the relation of society to space as well as time. In short, where is "the where" of society? Part of the answer may come from the implicit assumption of Comte and Durkheim that society is community writ large. It could be added that if society is not integrated and prey to the social disorganization of modernity, then it should be integrated, and whether the mode of integration is to come from corporate groupings (Durkheim) or socialism (Tonnies), such integration is imperative. Society, then should occupy a single bounded space with an integrated social structure and culture. Important in this context is F. Tonnies's (1955) influential *Gemeinschaft und Gesellschaft*,[2] in which we are nominally presented with two fundamental ideal types of social life. Yet it is clear that he regarded community and association as forming a developmental sequence and that his sympathies lie with *Gemeinschaft*. Tonnies's depiction of *Gesellschaft* as atomized secondary relationships, social disintegration, and cultural fragmentation is largely a negative one, constructed from the perspective of community. Tonnies's views here were influenced by the late nineteenth century Nietzsche revival in Germany, especially by *The Birth of Tragedy*, with its argument for a new Dionysian age (Liebersohn, 1988). Tonnies's image of *Gemeinschaft* drew upon an idealized picture of medieval Germany in which the family household was the basic unit with the strength of blood and kinship ties drawing people together into larger village and regional units. As we will see, this is very much an image of a settled place with a common culture.

This image of the traditional community with its high level of normative integration and order, which has been so influential in constructing the image of society, is of course highly nostalgic. Its vision of prior harmony and simplicity presents a picture of a fall from grace that resonated with the popularity of depictions of childhood as a phase of lost innocence, which became popular in the wake of the Romantic movements of the nineteenth century. It reduced premodern societies to flatness and immobility. That societies might be able to adequately exist without a high level of normative integration and common values is hardly considered.

Tonnies (1955, p. 261) emphasizes that *Gemeinschaft* is based upon a consensus of wills and concord provided by common folkways, mores, and religion, clearly has little room for power struggles, violence, and war. Features that are central to the investigations of preindustrial social life are provided by Norbert Elias, Le Goff, Raymond Williams, and others. Elias (1978/1982), for example, emphasizes the slow process of the taming of violent impulses as warriors were gradually induced to become courtiers as part of the state formation process. His account of everyday life is one in which those with smaller, weaker, less trained bodies (women and children) were prey to the less constrained, violent impulses of the more powerful (adults and men, especially specialists in violence such as warriors). A further nonnostalgic account, which dissolves the harmonious depiction of "traditional society" is provided by Raymond Williams (1975), who is scathing about the constant series of references to the "organic communities" of Old England, which successive generations see as imperiled and dying out; (see also Pearson's [1983] critique of depictions of a golden age of family values, which are constructed to make a sharp contrast to the alleged disorderly and violent present).

In addition to neglecting violence, conflict, and war this harmonious communal image of social life gives little attention to mobility: not just the displacements of people through warfare, but the more routine movements of wayfarers, migrant workers, pilgrims, travelers, beggars, and others (Jusserand, 1973). In contrast to the harmonious village in the mind where everyone lived and died within the confines of a settled place, Moch (1992, p. 1) argues

> Our image of a sedentary Europe . . . is seriously flawed. People were on the move; and where and why they traveled tells us a good bit about the past and about the pressures and processes that produced the world with which we are familiar. Human movement is connected to every level of life in western Europe—from the intimacy of family decisions about how cash will be earned to the global scale, where it reflects Europe's place in the world economy. Migration, in short, connects the changes in European history with the lives of men and women in the past.

Western Europe is, of course, not the world and we should be aware that the peculiarities of its migration pattern were linked to the family structure, which not only encouraged partner-centered marriage and the setting up of separate households, but encouraged a phase of independent youth in which young people (especially men) traveled over long distances to work. This contrasted with the pattern in Southern and Southeastern Europe, and in many other parts of the world, where the young men remained in the family of origin before and after marriage (see Mitterauer, 1992, p. 22). The main point to emphasize, however, is that the model of society developed by sociologists, which drew largely upon Western European experience, ignored mobility in its depiction of society as overintegrated and settled, an image that drew upon a nostalgic construction of community-based preindustrial society depicted as the polar opposite of modernity, with the latter perceived as entailing relentless change and social disorder.

This model assumes that societies reproduce themselves through a common set of values that induce a normative consensus. It has been heavily criticized in both its Parsonian and neo-Marxist variants by N. Abercrombie, S. Hill, and B. S. Turner in their book *The Dominant Ideology Thesis* (1980). They find little evidence of a shared value system or a dominant ideology in either feudalism, market capitalism, or late capitalism. The assumption that a common culture is the necessary social cement that makes social life possible has also been influential in anthropology, with the myth of the isolated integrated tribal society, which will be discussed shortly (see Featherstone, 1991a, pp. 131ff). In both cases the image of social life is of a bounded entity with a high level of social and cultural integration, models that assume that society has a high degree of functional interdependence of its various parts as well as a high degree of unity and independence vis à vis other societies. There is little sense of power relations, conflicts, and hybridity. There is little sense of leakages of people and culture: In effect all the elements of social and cultural life hang together to the extent that there are few cultural ambiguities or problems of conflicting or double identities. Sociology in its pursuit of the typical, average, or normal has generally had little interest in the idiosyncratic and the exceptional. If there are inequalities, then the problem becomes how are they reproduced and transmitted across the generations, something that leads to a more general concern with behavior as opposed to action. This has been emphasised by Lasch (1991, p. 135), who in a discussion of nostalgia argues

> literary representations of small town-life often fall into a kind of sociological style of thought, concerning themselves with the repetitive cycle of births, marriages and deaths. In other words, they concern themselves with behaviour as opposed to action. As Arendt has shown, the concept of behaviour is closely linked, in turn, to the concept of society, since the social realm is distinguished from the political by the absence of conscious determination, the tenacity of customs and rituals the original significance of which has been lost to memory, and the accumulated weight of habits highly resistant to change. In the reaction against eighteenth century liberalism, "society" became a rallying cry for those who condemned revolution on the grounds that deep-seated habits and prejudices could not be altered overnight, at least not

> without causing irreparable harm. For conservatives and socialists alike the discovery of society implied a devaluation of politics.

It has also been argued that the academic division of labor, which became established in the social sciences in the nineteenth century, resulted in sociology ceding not only the analysis of action and the state to politics but international relations as well (Wallerstein, 1987). With regard to the international field perhaps this view is a little too oversimplified; it would seem to apply best to international politics, for it ignores the tradition that developed in European sociology (largely French influenced), which focused upon humanity. Saint-Simon, Comte, and Durkheim, in addition to their focus upon society, were in their various ways aware of the linkages between industrialization and what we now call globalization (Turner, 1990a). In effect they were concerned about the ways in which the social disorganization and individualism that accompanied industrialization could be curbed by the development of a new set of moral bonds that would have universal validity. The tension between the societal and global focus of analysis emerged most noticeably in Durkheim's sociology. On the one hand he explored the possibility of new modes of moral individualism, which could become in effect a new religion that would be the sole common denominator for a highly differentiated humanity (Durkheim, 1969). On the other hand his concern with social order and solidarity, it has been argued, was influenced by the nationalist sentiments that increased after the 1870 French defeat in the Franco-Prussian War; in this context it has been suggested that the potential for both nationalism to be regarded as a source for the *conscience collective* and the nation as a source for the sacred in the modern world, became important themes running throughout his mature work (Turner, 1990a, p. 347).

Indeed, his discussion of the powerful emotional bonding between people and the resilience of the sacred in the modern world would seem to have continuing relevance for the understanding of the contemporary resurgence of nationalism, new religious movements, and even aspects of consumer culture (Featherstone, 1991a, ch 8; Alexander, 1988). At the same time Durkheim took seriously the moral and cultural mission of intellectuals to find some new means of ordering social life and regulating the relations between societies, hence his focus on humanity. Yet this emphasis upon humanity and the global dimension was not accompanied by a sociology of the emergent post- or suprasocietal entities, this does not seem to have been a concern of Durkheim's. Rather the focus was on the moral and cultural levels, with the emphasis given to the cultivation of new forms of solidarity that would enable modes of common identification between different people and lessen xenophobia as well as egoism and selfish individualism. Hence there is a tension within the work of Durkheim between the focus upon society as the basic unit of social life and the delineation of its mechanisms for normative and moral regulation, and the focus upon humanity driven by the need to discover new types of moral integration that will supersede the loyalties generated by nation-state societies in the phase of intensified globalization and national rivalries that occurred in the late nineteenth and early twentieth centuries.

It has been argued that this tension that was evident within the major classical sociologists has ceased to operate among their successors. W. E. Moore (1966), for example, in making a plea for the revival of this broader focus, criticizes the Americanization of sociology for its narrow focus upon society, the unstated subtext of which, as I have argued, is the bounded nation-state. The critique of this focus upon society as the final unit of social life in which it is regarded as the basic generic category of sociology has been elaborated by F. Tenbruck. He argues that "sociology tends to suggest the idea of societies as entities, requiring their study as *sui generis* objects and conceives of their structure as merely internal. In this way it establishes an artificial object that only admits of a one-sided selection, consideration and explanation of fact" (Tenbruck, 1994, p. 78). Concepts like *subsystem, subcultures, levels,* and *dimensions* remain within this perspective of the dominance of society as an integrated holistic entity. Likewise the general categories frequently used within sociology such as *structure, differentiation,* and *complexity* are assumed to be general variables that operate in all times and places.

This focus upon the intrasocietal dimension leads to a neglect of inter- and transsocietal processes such as: the reciprocal influences of societies on each other; the religious, political, economic, and cultural processes that occur across boundaries; the flows of migrants, exiles, and refugees; and military, cultural, and economic expansion. Where aspects of the above phenomena are studied, the tendency within sociology is to see them from the perspective of their intrasocietal linkages and effects for example, migrants are examined from the perspective of assimilation and integration into the host society. When social change is considered, the tendency is to focus upon the internal constitution of societies that are assumed to parallel each other in terms of their major structural mechanisms that produce change. Hence theories of modernization are based upon the assumptions that societies change along common lines of internal development. From this perspective differences between countries are just different states of a process that is seen everywhere as directed and straining toward some notion of normal development (for a critique of the notion of development see Tenbruck, 1990). Yet this misses the way in which European modernization arose in unique conditions of a network, or figuration, of interrelated nation-state societies, which from their early stages of formation were bound together in interdependencies and power struggles. Needless to say the particularities of this historically unique reference group can hardly be assumed to be replicable in other times and places.

Following Weber, Tenbruck emphasizes that societies are always shaped by the external situation.[3] Important here is the permanent preparedness for war and defense of borders. Even those societies that have sought to maintain isolation such as Tokugawa Japan have had to go to great efforts in terms of military preparedness and surveillance to regulate their inhabitants and in order to manipulate the "valve" through which interchanges with outsiders in trade, warfare, migration, and so on, could occur. Indeed it is not possible to understand the development of Japanese society without paying attention to the long-term relationship with China as its major significant other. The cultural borrowings and syncretisms that have resulted from this process, as we shall see shortly in our discussion of culture, cannot but put a big question mark against the long-held notions of culture within sociology and anthropology that emphasize organic or aesthetic unity.

This suggests that sociology needs to adopt not only a relational understanding of the shifting place of what have come to be known as "societies" within their particular reference groups but also a long-term perspective that considers societies as temporary phenomena. Societies then as processual entities should be considered as always in the process of formation and deformation: They do not always have to exist for social relations to take place, they come into being and fade away—perspectives that one can glean from the writings of Weber, Simmel, and Elias. But it is not just societies that are in the process of formation and deformation, it is also the larger reference group within which they are born, grow, and change that is significant. This is a process that Weber and Elias were clearly aware of through their focus upon the state and the power balances between nation-states. Indeed they can hardly be considered sociological imperialists through their capacity to shift from a sociological frame of reference to discuss what some would wish to separate out as political, economic, and (in Elias's case) psychological data, from a perspective that was always sensitive to historical particularities. Hence their mode of analysis was always pointing toward the global, the sense that all the nation-states and other forms of association in the world would become increasingly bound together in power struggles and interdependencies. As Elias indicates in his synopsis to *The Civilizing Process* (1982) the creation of larger nation-states and blocs and the nature of the power balances, interdependencies, and linkages between and across them will influence the types of identity formation and personality structure that develop in various parts of the world.

It is only relatively recently and in response to the current phase of intensified global competition and interdependencies that we have started to think that there might be a sociological problem here: how to develop a series of concepts that are adequate to understand this process. Concepts that in the first place are not based upon the assumptions of the set gathered together under the master concept society, so that the perspective of those who talk about world society, as some form of emergent great unifier modelled on the nation-state, is rejected. Second concepts that are sensitive to the cultural and social dimensions of these processes and do not reduce them to derivations from, or reactions to, the economic. The process of globalization, then, can be understood as the increasing extension of the reference group of societies, which are established in a process of contact that necessarily forms a world, however inchoate and limited that world might be when compared to the finite known world that we inhabit. This larger trans- and suprasocietal process forms the context within which societies are able to develop. The process of state formation in Europe, for example, produced a series of power struggles, rivalries, alliances, and elimination contests. The competition for additional power resources to draw upon and use in these struggles increasingly became widened to take in the whole world. It should be added that the development of modernity cannot be understood in isolation from this process, despite the tendencies to conceive it in terms of the unfolding of an inner logic that is immanent to society. I will return to a discussion of modernity shortly, after considering the images of culture and society that have been developed within anthropology.

Cultural Integration and Rootedness

Anthropology since its inception has always sought to talk about the characteristics of "man" in general, (or "humanity," as this remaining connection to philosophical anthropology is depicted today). At the same time it has sought to be sensitive to the particularities of the tribal collectivity addressed. An assumption, influenced by German romanticism and late nineteenth century hermeneutics (for example Dilthey who influenced Boas), has been that tribes possess distinctive cultures that form unique complexes that need to be interpreted in their own terms. The assumed isolation of the tribal societies that were scattered around the distant parts of the world before they were "discovered" by Europeans and North Americans, is assumed to lessen the problem of "contamination" and preserve in a purer form the unique features that can be assumed to cohere into an integrated whole. The term *culture* is often used to apply to the totality encompassing social and cultural life; in this sense culture has often been used to refer to "the whole way of life," of a people.[4] The distinctiveness of the cultural practices of different peoples has been linked to the construction of the other culture as "strange," and the representation of the anthropologist as a "merchant of astonishment," who dips into the world-showcase of cultures to titillate our sensibilities (Friedman, 1987).

This notion of a culture as a unique separate totality in which all the various intricate and bizarre parts fit together to make a unified whole is, for example, found in the work of Ruth Benedict. Benedict (1934) was influenced by the work of Boas with his assumptions that the main creative force of culture is the tendency toward consistency, which in turn derives from the drive for emotional consistency (Hatch, 1973, p. 81). The differences between cultures is conceived as similar to the differences between people. A culture is a combination of elements within an overall distinguishing pattern of organization that effectively makes each cultural configuration singular and incommensurable. This orientation to culture is captured in the following remarks from *The Chrysanthemum and the Sword:*

> As a cultural anthropologist also I started from the premise that the most isolated bits of behaviour have some systematic relation to each other. I took seriously the way hundreds of details fall into over-all patterns. A human society must make for itself some design for living. It approves certain ways of meeting situations, certain ways of sizing them up. People in that society regard these solutions as foundations of the universe. They integrate them, no matter what the difficulties. Men who have accepted a system of values by which to live cannot without courting inefficiency and chaos keep for long a fenced-off portion of their lives where they think and behave according to a contrary set of values. They try to bring about more conformity. They provide themselves with some common rationale and some common motivations. Some degree of consistency is necessary or the whole scheme falls to pieces (Benedict, 1946, p. 12).

Benedict's assumptions about the unity and separateness of cultures meet with little sympathy from many contemporary anthropologists, who are more sensitive to disunities, fragmentation, contestation, pluralism, and the processual nature of culture.[5] As Eric Wolff (1990) informs us, "anthropology has treated signification mainly in terms of encompassing cultural unities such as patterns, configurations, ethos, eidos, epistemes, paradigms, cultural structures." The tendency has been for these unities to be conceived as the outcomes of processes of logico-aesthetic integration. Here the assumption is that there is some underlying logical or aesthetic force at work in the drive toward integration and reintegration; it is as if these cognitive processes were guided by a *telos* all their own. This perspective, which assumes the replication of uniformity, misses the problem of "the organization of diversity." The assumption that there is some inherent patterning to culture, then, is not only difficult to apply to open as opposed to closed societies, or pluralistic and differentiated as opposed to unified societies.

There is an important sense Wolff (1990) reminds us, in referring to the work of Wallace (1970), that all societies are, in a radical sense, plural societies. They are composed of the diverse cognitive perspectives of men, women, and children, males and females, masters and slaves, warriors and priests, all of which will have different models of social life. This echoes the views of feminist anthropologists that men and women do not share the same cultural understandings. It is wrong to assume that such divergent perspectives will somehow be harmoniously integrated within some overarching framework driven by a cultural logic. Rather we need to ask the questions which groups will want to represent the social world as coherent and consistent? and why and how do they seek to develop and proliferate their particular representations of the world? We need to investigate the reasons why cultural specialists (priests, artists, intellectuals, academics, and cultural intermediaries) seek at various times to produce models of social life that emphasize consistency and at other times (e.g., the current wave of interest in postmodernism) develop theories that stress disunity and disorder (see Featherstone, 1991). The shift in the perception of the social world as relatively integrated and centered to one in which the foundations are cracked and "the centre cannot hold," may well be related to shifts in the power balances and interdependencies of various groups of cultural specialists both in terms of their internal outsider-established struggles and their more general relations to other more powerful and less powerful groups who offer them employment, protection, admiration, endorsement, and even indifference and contempt, as masters and publics. When establishments become destabilized the selectivity of the particular view of the world and their conceptual apparatus becomes apparent as its particularity, as opposed to universality, emerges when it is ranged alongside the alternative schemata that are busy surfacing and being resurrected. Hence as Wolff (1990) reminds us, power should never be conceived as external to signification, as something that only comes in afterward, for power essentially inhabits meaning. Here we should also mention the approach of Norbert Elias (1987a), who argues for a process-sociology, which, through focusing upon changes over time, becomes sensitive to the formation and deformation of bodies of knowledge in the shifting interdependencies and balances of power between various social groups.

A further problem with the unified vision of culture is highlighted by Renato Rosaldo (1993, pp. 91ff). This is the tendency to present culture at one pole of a stark Manichaean choice between order and chaos. Culture, then, is often presented as a necessary corrective, normative regulation to underlying violence and selfish egoism. Influential contemporary anthropologists such as Geertz and Turner, he argues, inherit this position from Durkheim. For Rosaldo, the basic problem with Durkheim's sociology is that it is built upon the twin imperatives of integration and regulation that keep at bay a "what-would-happen-if" vision of chaos, which is rarely articulated. In effect Durkheim leaves little room between order and chaos, and has little sense that people can live with ambiguity, uncertainty, spontaneity, and improvisation. It is possible to regard Durkheim's concern to develop an univocal theory of society as part of a more general movement within modernity to produce a systematic and ordered vision of the world that eliminates ambiguity (Levine, 1985). Foucault's work points to the development of the human sciences as part of a project to order, dissect, and regulate human social life.

Yet however suspicious we should be about the concept of postmodernity read as an epochal break, we should be aware that both the theories and models it develops and the features of the contemporary world it constructs as evidence of new tendencies in social life direct our attention toward the question of the extent to which disorder has always been a feature of social life and the degree to which order/disorder varies in different parts of history and places in the world. It would seem hard to dispute that human social life depends upon the use of symbols, with which the world is not only structured but demarcated and classified in taken-for-granted evaluative ways. Classification entails the use of boundaries, which, although taken for granted as we move through the everyday world, vary in their degree of absoluteness, rigidity, and tolerance of ambiguity (see Zerubavel, 1991). What would seem to fit with the arguments of those who suggest that we are moving into a new era of postmodernity, is the assumption that we are seeing a generation of global conditions in which certain groups of people are becoming involved in situations demanding more flexible classifications, situations in which it is not possible to refer to one set of overriding cultural rules that can arbitrate without ambiguity. This is not to suggest that we live in societies with an open public sphere with equal access for participants; far from it. Rather it is to argue that more people are seeking access to public platform and demanding citizen rights for minorities and outsider groups. The politics of multiculturalism demands a certain degree of respect and tolerance, not without its own aporias (Taylor, 1992), and something that leads to a questioning of the modes of the classification and categorization devices of other groups. It can also be argued that this deconstructive mood with its sensibility to ambiguity and fluidity is not just a recent postmodern phenomenon, but that it has a long history encompassing modernity and premodern times (Featherstone, 1991a, ch. 5). Within modernity it is certainly possible to link its development to the rise of various artistic and intellectual movements in Europe in the nineteenth and twentieth centuries, which later became known as modernism, that mounted a cultural critique against the project of order I have discussed.

The argument for a greater reflexivity in the construction of tribal life as societies and cultures has developed around the close scrutiny of the practice of ethnography. Here the ethnographer ceases to be permitted to remain invisible, but the whole process of interpretation and construction of categories is subjected to a critique that emphasizes that ethnography is essentially a mode of writing culture, which is constrained by literary devices, tropes, and metaphors that act in the text to produce the effect of unity and a closed narrative. This postmodern turn in anthropology can be found in the writings of J. Clifford (1988), J. Clifford and G. Marcus (1986), G. Marcus and M. M. J. Fisher (1986), G. Marcus (1992b), V. Crapanzo (1980, 1992), M. Taussig (1980, 1987), and others. Marcus and Fischer (1986), for example, identify their project as driven by the "crisis of representation," which highlights the problem of adequately depicting cultural differences. In this they have sought to build on the writings of E. W. Said (1978), H. White (1973), and others who question the possibility of the adequate recovery of another culture—the "salvage paradigm," so long influential in anthropology. The model of culture that has operated since E. B. Tylor's famous definition of culture as "that complex whole," not only suggests an organic or mechanical image of culture, it also is premised upon the assumption of "the existence of an initially unperceived coherence, a surprising meaningfulness, a covert rationality" (Thornton, 1992, p. 22). The aim here is to bring to the surface the rhetorical devices that are used to construct this idealized image of society and culture that gives the anthropologist the sense of a coherent reality that he or she has the authority to capture and distill (this can apply equally to history, and in addition to White [1973], we should point to the work of Bann [1984]).

Instead of the genre convention of realism with its intention to totalize and represent the reality of a whole world or form of life, Marcus and Fischer (1986, p. 23) favor a more experimental approach in which a number of rhetorical devices are used to create a text that is intentionally and openly incomplete. Such texts lay bare their own processes of construction and reveal the various elements that were brought into and excluded from the final frame. Crapanzo (1980), for example, in his *Tuhami: Portrait of a Moroccan,* refuses to produce a unified narrative and sense of cultural coherence. The book departs from the traditional life-history framework by self-consciously using modernist techniques to present the edited transcripts of interview as a puzzle, requiring the reader's interpretation. He holds back the authority of the ethnographer by deliberately manipulating form to capture mood, fantasy, and emotion to produce a fragmented, almost surrealist, text (see discussion in Marcus and Fischer, 1986, pp. 71ff).

The use of such devices is hardly new, and they have clearly a modernist rather than postmodernist origin. This is emphasized by Clifford (1988), who discusses surrealism's impact on anthropology, with its valuation of an aesthetics of fragments, unexpected juxtapositions, and the mixing of the unconscious, dream images, and extraordinary experiences with mundane everyday life. Of particular interest in this context are those French ethnographers who were influenced by the College de Sociologie, a loose informal grouping of intellectuals that developed in Paris in the 1930s around the work of Bataille (see Richardson, 1992). They developed a neo-Durkheimian interest in the sacred, combined with ritual expressions of transgression, excess, and sacrifice. In effect, it was argued: Cultures should not be seen as unified, rather they are deeply ambivalent in structure. Cultures include instructions on both the rule *and* the transgression. Marcel Griaule, one of this group, argued that the enthnographic surrealist should delight in cultural impurities and disturbing syncretisms (Clifford, 1988, p. 131). Michel Leiras, another member of the group, became preoccupied with the problem of the appropriate narrative form for the material he was collecting, which eventually led to *L'Afrique fantome,* an open-ended "anti-book" that was a series of entries composed of facts and images that he refused to unify by letting his imagination work over them. His advice to the reader read "Warning this book is unreadable" (cited in Clifford, 1988, p. 167).

Surrealism, then, used techniques of collage, cutting, and assemblage, with the cuts left visible and not blended into a unified representation. It sought to destabilize the authority of the artist/scientist/narrator and the myth of the gifted special person who could bring back for us more fundamental knowledge of reality. The confident monologue of the singular voice gives way to an inchoate polyphony. It is also interesting to note that Walter Benjamin (1982), who labored on his massive *Das Passagen-werk,* a surrealist-inspired fragmentary account of the rise of mass culture and consumer dreamworlds in mid-nineteenth century Paris, frequented the College de Sociologie in the late 1930s. Benjamin's writings have been particularly influential among postmodern theorists and have also been used in ethnography (e.g., Taussig, 1980, 1987). I might add wryly that the opposition to strong conceptual unities and preference for weaker frames, which are somehow held to be nearer to unmediated life itself, has long been a tradition within artistic and intellectual movements (such as *Lebensphilosophie* around the turn of the century, see the discussion of its relevance to Georg Simmel's writings in Featherstone, 1991b). The tradition reappeared in the postmodernism of the 1960s, where one only has to think of the nonaction films of Andy Warhol, such as *Sleep* (1963; a six-hour film of a man sleeping), and *Mario Banana* (1964; a male transvestite eating a banana). For a discussion of these films, see O'Pray, 1989. Its reverence for the unmediated particularity of life, or the re-presenting of cultural representations without commentary, points toward an inherent tension within the social sciences. That is, on the one hand the pressure to generalize, to construct general theories that have the most possible universal relevance, and on the other hand, the tendency to particularize, to do justice to the assumed unique singularity of people, institutions, and culture and to break down even further the alleged identities of these particularities to reveal the multiple voices and conflicting perspectives that inhabit them.

Before I leave the discussion of the assumption of cultural integration in anthropology it is worth raising the question, "what does the notion of an integral tribal society with a separate culture do for us?" One answer is given by Baudrillard (1993), who comments on the tremendous fuss made of the discovery of an unknown tribe in the Philippines. His argument is that the reason that every effort was made to keep them isolated from contact in a sort of reservation (unknown to the tribe) is that as we become increasingly sucked into a simulational culture and mourn the loss of the real; the existence of a set of "real" human beings somewhere on earth makes us feel more human (again).

It has been suggested that after Malinowski, anthropology tended to focus upon the village as a bounded site of residence, effectively using the rhetorical device of synecdoche, in which a part (the village) could be taken to represent the whole (the culture) (Clifford, 1992). The focus is on the village as a place of local dwelling. Any notion of movement or mobility tends to be restricted to the village and surrounding area constructed as "the field." Yet according to Clifford (1992, p. 100) this misses a number of factors that slip out of the account constructed. In the first place, there are the means of transport and communication—the boat, the car, the telephone—that link the village to the outside world. Second, there is the relationship with the capital city and the national context—the places the ethnographer has to visit in order to get permission to visit the village. Third, there is the university home of the researcher and all the sorts of comings and goings in and out of the field by both natives and researchers that take place with relative ease in the contemporary world. In addition the central role of "the informant," which has often been occluded and undertheorized in the past, needs to be made more central. In doing so, we should not think of the informant as a passive writer/inscriber who resides in the field, but as a traveler too. It is therefore far from adequate to localize nonwestern people as "natives," by freezing part of their lives and using it to represent the whole. This static depiction of native peoples confined to their local areas is very much a fiction. Indeed A. Appadurai (1988, p. 37) uses the stronger term *incarcerated* and goes on to reminds us "Natives, people confined to and by the places to which they belong, groups unsullied by contact with a larger world have probably never existed" (Appadurai, 1988, p. 39).

Yet if it is a fiction, it is a very powerful one that has become deeply entrenched in social life, and we need to inquire into the process of its formation. Here it should be understood as related to two parallel processes. The first is the "discovery" of native peoples with the opening up of the New World from the sixteenth century onward and the problems this made for existing systems of classification. If this process of colonialism and the development of mercantile capitalism opened up a phase of greater travel, mobility, and mixing of peoples, goods, and categories, then it should also be stood alongside a second process, the development of the nation. It can be argued that the formulation of the people in a territorial area into a nation was a part of the state-formation process, which gathered impetus with the intensification of rivalries as states became drawn together into a tighter figuration through war, colonial expansion, and economic competition. In the late eighteenth and nineteenth centuries artists and intellectuals rediscovered and invented ethnic histories and national traditions that helped to develop a national identity (see Burke, 1978). This may well have helped to formulate the organic metaphor of culture as something integrated, bounded, and distinct. National identities have emphasized blood and soil. They have also drawn upon arborescent metaphors of rootedness. Keith Thomas (1983, p. 220) has traced the history of the oak tree as an emblem of the British people (see Malkki, 1992, p. 27). National identities by their emphasis upon natural metaphors of roots, soil, motherland, and fatherland have provided not only a sense of rootedness but also of exclusivity—it is only possible to belong to one national genealogical tree.[6] These brief remarks would suggest that it is possible to reconstruct the formation of sedentary metaphors in the territorialization of our identities alongside the growth of the nation-state and the development of assumptions about the rights and obligations of citizens and subjects. The notion of the nation as "homeland," of the home as a place of residence from which one ventures out, but always seeks to return, is a powerful related metaphor, as is the opposite notion that modernity induces an unhappy state of "homelessness," which will be discussed later.

There is not the space to discuss here the important question of the relationship between the process of the generation of strong national identities in the phase of intensified competition between nation-states after 1870, which produced strong images of nations as "imagined communities," each with its own homeland and heritage, and migration. The "great swarmings," the intensified migration of the period 1880–1920, was also a phase in which nation-states developed panics about immigration crises and the need to construct strong boundaries and identities (see Aristide Zolberg's chapter in this volume). Heated debates took place within the United States in the late nineteenth century about the merits of the assimilation model versus more plural models of tolerance to ethnic diversity (Lasch, 1991). The phase of intensified mobility was therefore also a phase of concern about home and identity; yet it is difficult to encounter positive images of the mobility and migration, although they doubtless exist. The various countercultural currents of modernity, such as artistic modernism, bohemias, and so on, with their interest in travel and the outsider, and the tales of migrants, slaves, and refugees would provide some sources.

The relationship between travel and home is, therefore, a complex relational one. Certain peoples have also developed alongside the formation of the nation-state various positive and negative depictions of travel and the degree of boundedness and closure of the nation-state. The Portuguese, for example, ever since the exploratory voyages of the fifteenth and sixteenth centuries, developed a much greater sense of the world than the nation-state as their spatial unit. The term *saudade,* roughly translated as longing or nostalgia, has for the Portuguese long been associated with unending wanderlust (Feldman-Bianco, 1992). It points to the double sense of a concern with travel and wandering but also to the collective memory of Portugal as an imagined community. Other parts of the world may well share this sense of national identity as movement and mobility, as Wang Gungwu (1993) has argued is the case with Southeast Asia. This is in marked contrast to East Asia, where mobility and migration are seen as limited and marginal in the context of a static agrarian society reinforced by Confucian pietism and bureaucratic structures. It would be interesting to reconstruct aspects of the national identities of various Western nations in the light of these remarks. For a preliminary contrast between the United States and Sweden in terms of their attitudes toward the lure of "the road" based upon road movies, see R. Eyreman and O. Lofgren, 1995).

A further point needs to be made before I turn to modernity. This is the assumption that communities (tribal or preindustrial), societies, or nations are spatially separated entities. This notion, as I mentioned earlier, misses the grounds within which these entities are situated. In effect their identities are formed in a figuration of communities or societies. Yet the danger with this approach is that it assumes a fixed level of coherence and identity formation of the basic units. This is also the case when nation-states are conceived as actors on the international stage, with one state engaging another. As A. Bergson (1990) has pointed out in a critique of Wallerstein's work there is a methodological individualist attitude evident in his assumption that nation-states acquire their properties prior to their participation in the world-system. In effect they seem "born whole."

Yet nation-states only developed within a figuration that acted as a ground and constraint to their actions. All sorts of contacts were occurring between nascent proto-nation-states through the church, dynastic ties, and other forms of association, which helped to develop a cultural complex of interchanges and transactions, which acted as a developing field or ground within which nation-states could begin to form their identities. For the vast majority of nation-states that emerged in the nineteenth and twentieth centuries this international cultural complex, or transnational field, formed a gradually extending world whose significance became increasingly salient with the intensification of contact. The space within which local communities, societies, and nation-states developed then has always been hierarchically interconnected through the power balances and interdependencies that were unavoidably developing alongside the very formation of these entities. In the same way as I cautioned to be suspicious of the use of the term *tradition,* it should be apparent that we should also be cautious about the positing of a primeval state of autonomy of peoples, communities, or societies that was violated by the development of modernity, capitalism, or colonialism. As A. Gupta and J. Ferguson (1992, p. 8) remark, "Instead of assuming the autonomy of the primeval community, we need to examine how it was formed *as a community* in the first place."

To be aware of the construction of local communities, societies, and nation-states as sedentary homelands does not mean that we should switch to the opposite assumption that the normal condition of human beings is, or should be, one in which everyone is a nomad or a traveller. Rather we need to develop theories of culture that do justice to its processual and relational aspects. We need to inquire into the grounds for the formation of images of the world as a hybrid motion of displaced nomads as well as the persistence of images of localities as integrated and settled communities. The challenge to theorizing today is how to construct theories of communal living in localities that do not merely represent sedentariness as the norm but seek to consider its various modalities, including displacements into images of imaginary homes/homelands. Such theories need to also take into account the ways in which those inhabitants who engage in various modes of travel manage to construct and live out their various affiliations and identities.[7]

Global Modernities

Today the term *modernity* is widely used in the social sciences. There are many reasons for this: the inability of other terms such as *capitalism* to cover all aspects of contemporary social life that accompanied the decline of interest in the various forms of Marxism and neo-Marxism since the 1980s; the growth of interest in postmodernism, which tends to circumscribe modernity by pointing to its limits and directs our attention back to the question of what it was; the upsurge of interest in culture and the nature of contemporary and modern experience. From a sociological perspective *modernity* is usually defined as "a post-traditional order" (Giddens, 1991, p. 2). Its main features include: first, industrialism based upon machine production; second, capitalism based upon commodity production and the commodification of labor power; third, a massive increase in organizational power based upon the surveillance of populations; fourth, the control of the means of violence and the industrialization of war; fifth, the development of the nation-state, the basic referent for what we call "society" (Giddens, 1992, pp. 15ff; 1991, pp. 10ff; for a slightly different list, see Hall, 1992a; Turner, 1990b). For Giddens these factors help to generate the characteristic sense of dynamism in modern institutions, the sense that the modern world is a runaway world. This is based upon the separation of time and space, which means that activities are no longer confined to place and that simultaneous communication can take place over distance; the disembedding of social institutions from tradition through the use of abstract systems and media such as money; and the increasing use of reflexive knowledge.

Giddens concentrates on the institutional dimension of modernity and he gives little attention to the cultural dimension. He does (1991, pp. 137ff), however, suggests that two images of modernity have dominated sociological literature: The first, taken from Weber, is that of "the iron cage," bureaucratization of life, and the second, taken from Marx, is that of modernity as a monster, which, although irrational in the form of capitalism, can be in principle tamed. Against these Giddens proposes his own image of the "juggernaut—a runaway engine of enormous power which collectively as human beings, we can drive to some extent but which also threatens to rush out of our control and which could rend itself asunder." Common to all three images is the assumption that there is a singular modernity that de-traditionalizes the world. In effect the basic mechanisms that bring about modernity will produce more or less similar effects throughout the world. Culture will follow and adapt to these more basic economic, political, and institutional processes.

The relationship between the various aspects of modernity is very complex. On the one hand, there is the question of the validity of dilineating modernity in terms of a number of key dimensions (social, economic, political, and cultural), which are analyzed separately and then shown to interlink (see, for example, Hall, 1992a). As Elias (1984) reminds us, we cannot assume this division of social life into separate spheres each with their separate discipline to be in the nature of things; rather they should be seen as emergent categories that depend upon a process of formation. Elias examines the growth of economics in the eighteenth century as the first science of society that was premised upon the emergence of a distinctive economic sphere that in turn depended upon the accumulation of both the numbers and the power potential of economic specialists.

The second point relates to the relationship between the institutional and cultural dimensions of modernity. Although the distinctions between the two aspects are not always easy to make, B. Tibi (1995), for example, would see the institutional dimension in terms of the characteristics outlined by Giddens (1990, 1991), which I have already discussed, and the cultural complex as the unfinished project of modernity as described by J. Habermas (1990). Giddens assumes the former to be eminently globalizable, indeed he assumes that modernity produces globalization in a manner that does not take into account the independent force of cultural factors in this process and does not see that in important respects the imputed causality could be reversed and globalization could be seen to produce modernity (see Robertson, 1992a, 1992b for this argument). Habermas's project of modernity entails the realization of the Enlightenment vision of a good society in which not only traditional dogmatic authority structures have been criticized and abolished but the negative aspects of modern science, technology, and instrumental rationality (the domination of nature and the domination of man by man, which are in effect the "dark side" of the Enlightenment) have been curbed and held in check by an active public of reflexive and responsible people.

Whereas Tibi (1985) and many others have detected the Eurocentric nature of Habermas's depiction, the same could also be said for Giddens in terms of his assumptions about the experiential, cultural, and subjective changes in modern life that allegedly follow from the accelerated institutional changes as we move into "high modernity." In addition Giddens shows little sensitivity to the culture/power complex, the ways in which the various images of "the other" and the West, which became generated through the process of colonialism, operate within the expanding global figuration of nation-states, proto-nation-states, and other collectivities and how they led to a selective appropriation of modernity. Not only was there a series of different entry points into modernity (Therborn, 1995), there was also a series of different projects developed as well as demands for selective appropriation of the institutional parameters. Tibi (1985), for example, has referred to the contemporary Muslim dilemma as the "Islamic dream of semi-modernity." It has even been suggested that "the signifier 'modern' should be regarded as a regional term peculiar to the West."

For all of Giddens's discussions of time-space, the spatial dimension of modernity is underplayed. As I will emphasize later, we need to ask the question of the spatial dimension of modernity, or "where is modernity?" not just in terms of some superior logic emanating from the Western center (versions of Weber's rationalization thesis) but in terms of the spatial relationship of the non-West to the West. Modernity, then should not be seen exclusively in temporal terms, as an epoch, but in spatial and relational terms too; terms that entailed power relationships in the very construction and implementation of the set of categories that are now only coming to the surface as the non-West accumulates the power resources to speak back and be listened to in the West. As I have emphasized, postmodern and postcolonial theories are symptoms of this process that point to this shift in power balances. To dismiss them as hypostatized, temporal, or epochal categories (e.g., postmodernity) is to miss this important cultural dimension of the process.

As we will shortly see this is very much a view from the Western center, which discounts the possibility that despite the integrating and unifying tendencies, there could be the development of global modernit*ies*, in the plural, and that there could also be many projects of modernity (to play off one of Habermas's phrases), which are yet to be completed. In short we need to attend to the spatial dimension of modernity and its particular cultural embedment in the West. The process of separation of the West from the rest of the world and the subsequent attempt to impose its version of modernity onto the rest of the world suggests a movement from the belief in the West's capacity to hierarchize and order flows of communication and people, to one in which mixing, movement, and dislocation become the norm, as the interchange between the rest and the West can no longer be regulated. But perhaps it is wrong to conceive these two aspects as merely sequential stages: Perhaps they should be understood as long copresent within the development of Western modernity.

The first image of modernity is one of order and entails the progressive control, domination, and regulation of the natural and social worlds through the application of rational knowledge. In this image the Enlightenment faith in science and technology is seen as flawed, for instead of delivering the good society and human happiness, the secret inner logic of history is a narrative of the fall, one that points to the realization of a dystopia rather than a utopia. This has been a particularly strong theme in German social thought and those influenced by Nietzsche's writings. Weber's vision of the refeudalization of social relationships and the bureaucratization of the world, in which machinelike routines govern human beings and drive out all creativity, is echoed in Horkheimer and Adorno's image of "a totally administered world." This also resonates with Foucault's emphasis on the application of knowledge from the human sciences to produce increasing surveillance, panopticism, and discipline.[8]

Zygmunt Bauman (1991) has likewise emphasized that a central feature of modernity is the production of order, yet he points to the limits of this process and our inability to complete the project. Modernity is a time when the ordering of nature, the social world, and the self and the connections between all three, are reflected upon. Yet the quest for order needs to feed off the notion of the opposite of order: chaos. This is the sense that we are threatened by incoherence, incongruity, irrationality, ambiguity, contingency, polysemy, confusion, and ambivalence; in effect modern existence is saturated by a "without us the deluge," feeling as we strive for control (Bauman, 1991, p. 7). Modern consciousness is governed by the urge to extend outward, to map and classify, which means it has to discover or reveal ever new layers of chaos beneath its constructed order to feed its Sisyphean restlessness. In effect Bauman is reading modernity from the point of view of postmodern theory in teasing out its inherent limits and contradictions. Bauman's reflections are helpful here in drawing attention to the ways in which our two images of modernity as order and chaos are linked.

If the first image emphasizes the dark side of enlightenment and reason to present an image of modernity as fixed, static, and closed, the second image emphasizes modernity as continual change driven by the need to deal with the disorder that it both seeks out and generates. This second image has modernity producing endless disruption and social disorganization as it passifies and controls nature for human purposes and tears down the old structures of social life to make way for the new. It is a heroic Promethian image of human life captured by Goethe in *Faust,* Part 2, where the social and physical landscape is transformed in the name of progress (see Berman, 1982). This image became particularly influential in social thought in Germany and the United States in the late nineteenth and early twentieth centuries as both countries experienced rapid industrialization and the expansion of cities such as Berlin and Chicago into metropolises. The picture presented of Chicago by Robert Park and his group of associates, who became known as the Chicago School of Sociology, was one of a constant inflow of immigrants who had to be processed by the city. The model of the city was based upon human ecology and stressed competition for territory and constant movement as the city expanded and pulled in more migrants whose assimilation process entailed spatial movement through the city natural areas to accompany their movement through life time. Hence social disorganization (the slum, crime, delinquency, the hobo) was seen as a necessary part of the dynamics of modern urban life. Park's notion of modern urban life was influenced by the time he spent during the last decade of the nineteenth century working with Georg Simmel in Berlin, a city that experienced a parallel phase of rapid growth.

It is from Simmel that we can start to build a picture of the experiential and cultural dimensions of modernity. Simmel's writings on money and the metropolis are well known, and it has been argued that he developed a nonnostalgic approach to modern life that made him "the first sociologist of modernity" (Frisby, 1983, 1985).[9] Simmel emphasized the fragmentary dynamic nature of modern life as people in large cities were bombarded by a range of impressions and sensations that threatened to overwhelm them. This could lead to neurasthenia, a defense against which was the blasé attitude of the urbanite, which Simmel speaks of in his famous essay on the metropolis and mental life. It is this battle with the dissolution of fixed contents to discover some capacity to adequately unify, frame, or form the excess of fluidity and motion that is central to modern life. As Simmel (1923, quoted in Frisby, 1985, p. 46) remarks, "the essence of modernity as such is psychologism, the experiencing [das Erleben] and interpretation of the world in terms of the reaction of our inner life and indeed as an inner world, the dissolution of fixed contents in the fluid element of the soul, from which all that is substantive is filtered and whose forms are merely forms of motion."

Although the linkage between fluidity and motion with modernity is something we will return to shortly, it is worth emphasizing that there is a further aspect of modern culture that can be drawn from Simmel's work: the tragic accumulation of culture. The accumulation of objective culture, the production of knowledge in various media, has expanded tremendously in modern times and is beyond the capacity of individuals to assimilate into their subjective cultures. In Goethe's time perhaps there was a better balance between subjective and objective culture, but Simmel holds that this is something we have lost. In modernity, therefore, we are left with a sense of cultural fragmentation and an overoptioned life in which we have an absence of certainty and guidelines. Hence any selection becomes a wager on a particular body of culture that we hope will provide *the* ultimate meaningful framework for our lives. The fragmentation of experience in our everyday lives in the streets of the metropolis is therefore mirrored by the fragmentation of the knowledge base that we endlessly traverse in an effort to find some lasting and justifiable perspective to give a more than fleeting coherence to our lives. This specifically modern experience of temporality is particularly evident in the phenomenon of fashion. The constant parade of new fashions provides a permanent sense of change in which the new styles provide shocks and an accelerated sense of the tempo of life (see Simmel, 1995; Lichtblau, 1995).

Simmel was not of course the first person to attempt to chart the aporias of modern culture, and it would seem his interest in charting the sense of the transitory experience of modernity and "the aestheticization of everyday life" (see Featherstone, 1991a, ch. 5) builds upon some of the motifs that are to be found in the writings of Baudelaire, who is generally credited with introducing the concept of *modernite.* For Baudelaire (1972) the key feature of the experience of modern life was the sense of "newness." The fact that modern societies produced an endless parade of commodities, buildings, fashions, social types, and cultural movements, and that they were all destined to be rapidly replaced by others, reinforced the sense of the transitoriness of the present moment (see Benjamin, 1973; Frisby, 1985; Osborne, 1992). The *flaneur,* or stroller, in the public spaces of the large cities was able to experience these kaleidoscopic images and fragments whose novelty, immediacy, and vividness, coupled with their fleeting nature and often strange juxtaposition, provided a range of aesthetic sensations and experiences (see Mazlish, 1994, for a discussion). Baudelaire is sometimes regarded as the founder of artistic modernism, which emerged in reaction to classicism and romanticism. Modernism not only sought to capture the fragmentary quality of modern life in all its everyday banality and ugliness, it also became associated with countercultural and transgressive impulses that developed the bohemian critique of the bourgeois lifestyle. Modernism also became associated with formal innovations and strong avant-gardist impulses. I have already mentioned how the sensitivity to the problem of representation and more complex notions of unity found in modernism have been taken up in the various adaptations of postmodernism in sociology, anthropology, and cultural studies. Walter Benjamin (1973) devoted considerable space to the analysis of Baudelaire's Paris and the birth of mass consumer culture and also showed a methodological sensitivity in the use of modernist, as opposed to realist, modes of representation (e.g., montage, juxtaposition) in his writings (see Buck-Morss, 1989).[10]

If we wish to understand the culture of modernity, then we need to consider both the impulse to generate a culture of order through the colonization and domestication of the world defined as disorder and the critique of this ordering impulse through the celebration of the ability to live with disorder, fragmentation, and mixing, which is to be found in modernism. The first approach not only seeks to oppose chaos with order (Bauman, 1991) it also seeks to oppose mixing and hybridization with separation and purification with a view to the creation of strict classifications (Latour, 1993). The second approach develops an interest into the types of experience and ways of life that develop in the modern city and seeks to grapple with the problem of representation, to enable them to be adequately expressed in artistic terms, or made intelligible through a theoretical discourse. Hence the growth of artistic modernism and the culture of modernity are (unsurprisingly) inextricably linked.

Yet it can be argued that the sense of cultural disorder, the overload of sensory impressions and sign-play, cannot be confined to modernity—

they have forerunners in the upside-down world and sign-play of the carnivals and fairs of the Middle Ages (Featherstone, 1991a, ch. 5).[11] The consumer culture sign-play and spectacles can also be traced back to the designs of the seventeenth-century European absolutist state (most notably Spain) to produce the aestheticization and spectacles that became known as the culture of the baroque (Maravall, 1986). It may well be possible to discover a similar sensitivity to sign-play, the mixing of codes, fleeting impressions, and a concern with aestheticization, style, and fashion in the "floating worlds" of cities such as Edo and Kyoto, which developed in Tokogawa Japan between the seventeenth and the nineteenth centuries. If, then, we attempt to break down some of the elements of the experience of modernity that were associated with the problematic of cultural modernism, we may well find that they existed, albeit in different forms, in other times and places.

The nascent consumer cultures that developed in the modern European cities, such as eighteenth-century London and nineteenth-century Paris and Berlin, were places into which commodities, new exotic goods, information, and people from various parts of the world flowed. They were places of social and cultural mixing, generated as much by their capacity to take in things from the outside, be it their own national hinterlands or the world at large, as through the working out of an internal dynamic of restless modernity. Yet most accounts of modernity have focused upon its chronological unfolding and particular experiential and cultural qualities, either without reference to spatial location, other than a vague or unstated assumption that it took place in the West (understandable when one considers the writers and audiences), or in European cities or nation-states. There is little sense of the relational basis of this process through the formation of relationships between the West and other parts of the world. For example, the collection of essays entitled *The Culture of Capital: Art, Power, and the Nineteenth Century Middle Class* (Seed and Wolff, 1988) focuses largely on the city of Manchester's art and class structure, without reference to the countries from whence the cotton came or the colonial and trade relations that tied Manchester (the place we are taught in history was the first industrial capitalist city) into a world.[12] It is therefore important to consider the spatial dimension of modernity in terms of the process of globalization that developed in parallel to it. But first we must return briefly to consider the experience of modernity.

The *flaneur,* the stroller or idler in the big cities described by Baudelaire, Benjamin, and Simmel, enjoyed the immersion in the crowd, the variety of faces, body types, and fashions as well as the flood of images in the advertising holdings, billboards, window displays, department stores, exhibitions, and world fairs that made up the urban landscape. He or she experienced a sense of mixing and sign-play, as formerly sealed apart categories of people and culture were juxtaposed, setting off half-remembered memories and allegories. The flaneur usually moved around a known urban world, yet one in which the shock of new encounters, was potentially present, as the dynamic of modernity brought in new things, people, and places, as the old and present were torn down to make way for the new. The flaneur experienced swings between the immersion in the immediacy of life and the distanced voyeuristic contemplation of it from a seemingly invisible perspective as people moved around among others who also adopted the "distanced," blasé attitude that acted as a defense against overstimulation (neurasthenia). The flaneur was a traveler, albeit of a limited sort, who played with the idea of genuine experience and its aesthetic recovery.

Travel can be understood as paradigmatic of experience, and we should remember that the root of the word *experience* is *per*, which means to try, to test, to risk. Travel, of course, can be routine and mundane, or something to be endured as an impediment until one is settled back at home. Seneca, for example, saw Roman travel as distracted wandering and held that it was better to stay at home. It has been argued that it was not until modern times that travel was celebrated as a voyage of self-discovery (Leed, 1991, p. 7). Yet it is too simple to see the experiential side of travel and the pleasures of discovery and new sensations as a product of modernity, for it is possible to reverse the relationship and argue that what we regard as the experience of modernity is something that was experienced in premodern times by travelers. This is the argument of Leed (1991, pp. 6–7), who addresses the question, "How do the transformations of travel produce in the mind of the traveler, a certain mentality that has often been termed 'modern,' post-Renaissance, but that is as old as civilized travel?" Travel, then thrusts the new into the middle of life, it opens up life to contingency and creates "exotica" (matter out of place).

Hence it can be argued that travel is closely bound to the notion of modernity. The Renaissance voyages that took place beginning in the sixteenth century enabled Europeans to encounter people of different ethnicities and encouraged them to make comparisons between themselves and others. The encounters and comparisons helped to change the self-image of Europeans from being a periphery to ancient centers to one of being a center in its own right, which was at the cutting edge of the "modern" (Leed, 1991, p. 21). This increasing contact helped to generate the production and exchange of differences. As T. Todorov (1984, p. 49) reminds us the discovery of the New World saw the production of two apparently contradictory myths, one whereby the "other" is a "noble savage," and one whereby he is a "dirty dog," a potential slave.[13] Columbus effectively imposed his own values upon alterity and did not seek to know the other on its own terms. Yet the treasures and specimens, the plants, animals, and people Columbus sent back to Spain and the various accounts of the voyages had a profound impact upon the existing bodies of knowledge and modes of classification. It has been argued by A. Grafton (1992) that between 1550 and 1650 there was a move on the part of Western thinkers away from assuming that they could find all important truths in ancient books, toward empirical knowledge. The ancient view of a coherent and ordered universe now ran up against countless inconvenient facts. Francis Bacon's *Great Instauration* (1620) sought to produce knowledge that no longer relied upon the ancient authorities. He used a wealth of information from the various voyages and argued that we should test out theories and establish knowledge on the basis of experiment and observation. The title page of the book shows a ship sailing past classical columns, which represent the Pillars of Hercules, the ancient limits of navigation and knowledge. Against those who would caution not to go too far, Bacon urged his readers "too far is not enough" (Grafton, 1992, p. 198).[14]

A consequence of this process was that differences in space became associated with differences in time. This temporalization of difference was used to produce an evolutionary hierarchy. This allowed Europeans to produce a moral justification for the exploitation, now seen as a necessary *Bildungsprozess,* which was imperative for those designated children or "minors" to go through if they were ever to develop and attain enlightenment. It was this confinement of other cultures to past history, to lower stages on the same ladder of history, that enhanced the sense of the threshold of advancing presentness of the European nations, a sense of modernity that in actuality developed out of the occluded spatial encounters with nonwestern others.

It is of course this sense of a unified humankind converging on the common path beaten by the advancing Western modernity that became heavily criticized by elements of artistic modernism, with its sympathies for those who were the victims of this process. I have already discussed the ways in which anthropological and other theories adopted some of the techniques of artistic modernism, such as collage and montage, to produce a sense of a more complex multivocal process in which the boundedness of the locality is deconstructed. Yet it is different again when not only are the others' perspectives and voices considered alongside those of the anthropologist/writer to problematize the process of cultural formation, but theories of modernity are produced from different parts of the world that dispute the Western account. When it is a part of the world like Japan and East Asia, which are rapidly gaining power potential in the shifting global balance of power, then we can assume that in the future this could lead to a revision of the long-established conceptual set: tradition and modernity, to which we can now add postmodernity.[15] European colonialism therefore played an important role in the spatial totalization of Western modernity,[16] which resulted in modernity providing the standpoint for historical totalization, the standpoint from which all other cultures were to be judged and hierarchically ordered (see Osborne, 1992).

Modernization theory merely represents a continuation of this logic, with progress now defined as Americanization to replace Europeanization, in tune with the shifting global balance of power in the second half of the twentieth century. But this post-World War II era also began a phase of decolonialism and the growth in the global power of the non-West, which ushered in a process of the relativization of the modern world. That is, the modern world was revealed to be the Western world and to be only a world among many worlds, which began a process of re-forming the various "we-images" and "they-images" of Western and other nations. As Sakai (1989, p. 106) remarks:

> What this simple but undeniable recognition pointed to was that history was not only temporal or chronological but also spatial and relational. The condition for the possibility of conceiving of history as a linear and evolutionary series of incidents lay in its not as yet thematized relation to other histories, other *coexisting* temporalities. Whereas monistic history . . . did not know its implicit reliance on other histories and thought itself autonomous and total, "world" history conceived of itself as the spatial relations of histories. In world history, therefore, one could not think of history exclusively in those terms which referred back only to that same history; monistic history could not deal with the world as it was apprehended in world history since the world is primarily a sphere of heterogeneity and others.

It is the series of challenges in the various dimensions of international and transnational contact between nation-states, not a benevolent gesture on the part of the more powerful Western nations, which results in a shift in the fantasy base of the we- and they-images. This inaugurates a process of enforced listening for the Western nations. Modernity, then, began as a process of the self-recognition of Europe in which the Orient and other parts of the world became confined to an image of premodern traditionalism. The spatial expansion of Europe through colonialism, with the resultant inflow of goods, people, and information, helped to produce various modes of mixing and disorder within a range of social and cultural life forms and practices, which helped to generate an enhanced sense of the new, presentness, and the transitory nature of time. A disorder and mixing, which in one area of cultural life, became reconstituted as a new symbolic hierarchy in which the various peoples of the world were rank-ordered as part of an assumed universal evolutionary history. This aspect of the project of modernity becomes relativized through two main factors: first, the shifts in the global balance of power away from the West in the second half of the twentieth century; second, the increased intensity of transnational flows of commodities, people, images, and information that are bypassing the boundaries of the nation-states (Lash and Urry, 1993). It is this latter aspect, in particular the intensification of global migration, that is producing intensified contacts that are undermining the once-secure fantasy-based we- and they-images and changing the nature of identity formation to the extent that categories of people are emerging who live more mobile lives and are at ease with more fluid identities. It is this process of mobility and migrancy, now labeled postmodern by some, that is held to be both the methodological key and the actuality of the contemporary world.

Notes

1. This is, of course, largely a male ideal. As Janet Wolff (1993) reminds us it is men who have predominantly traveled and women have remained at home.

2. The first edition of the book appeared in 1887. The book has been referred to as "the founding charter of modern sociology" (Lasch, 1991, p. 139). It has been particularly influential in structuring the contrasts between tradition and modernity, community and urban life, which have been influential in the development of sociology in the United States (especially the Chicago School). In addition it has been regarded as one major source of Talcott Parson's "pattern variables."

3. Tenbruck's perspective has also been influenced by Simmel, who like Weber, argued against those who sought to understand social life from idealized comprehensive concepts such as society, seeing the latter as having the role of a preliminary "emergency shelter," which should soon be discarded. For Simmel our focus of attention should be on the forms of sociation and interactions between individuals (see Frisby and Sayer, 1986, pp. 54ff). For a discussion of Tenbruck's ideas in the context of a critique of the comparative method see Axtman, 1993.

4. For a discussion of the different uses of the term *culture* in anthropology, see Boon, 1973. The notion of culture as "the whole way of life," of a people was formulated by Raymond Williams (1981) and has been influential in the field of cultural studies (see G. Turner, 1990).

5. Benedict's (1946) book has been subjected to a strong critique by the current generation of Japanese Studies scholars. Not only do they follow many of the assumptions about fragmentation and pluralism associated with postmodernism that I have discussed, they also refuse to see these changes as just a product of a post-1960s consumer culture. Hence the supposed ethnic and cultural homogenity of Japan is now being challenged as social movements and scholars alike rediscover, and are able to voice their views, on the outsiders allegedly incorporated and blended into Japaneseness. This is not to say that *Nihonjinron* (Japanese exclusiveness) has ceased to be the most powerful national image in Japan—far from it. Rather it is to suggest that groups like the Okinawans and the Ainu as well as long-resident groups such as the Koreans are now discovering their public voice, suggesting a slight shift in the established/outsiders power balance.

6. Deleuze and Guattari (1987, p. 18) remark, "It is odd how the tree has dominated Western reality and all of Western thought, from botany to biology and anatomy, but also gnosiology, theology, ontology, all of philosophy. . . . : the root-foundation, *Grund, racine, fondement.* The West has a special relation to the forest and deforestation . . ." (cited in Malkki, 1992, p. 28). The place of the forest in German intellectual thought and popular culture is particularly important.

7. The problems of multiple identifications in the contemporary world, which are to be found in the remotest areas, are captured in the film *Black Harvest* (Robin Anderson/Bob Connolly, 1992), which follows the initial success and eventual failure of a half-Australian businessman/half-New Guinea tribesman to organize a tribe to raise a crop of coffee.

8. In Foucault's case it is the increase in population pressure that encourages the state to regulate and control the excess of bodies. It is interesting to note that in his *Madness and Civilization* (1971) he romantically draws a positive picture of the premodern madman who is free to wander and intervene in social life without the threat of incarceration or treatment, both of which emerge with modernity. Influenced by Nietzsche, his image of the premodern is one of individuality, difference, and mobility, with the modern life being engulfed by an increasingly homogenized mass of narrowly individuated people whose real differences are minimal. Weber's and Adorno's writings also show similar traces of Nietzsche's influence.

9. As we have already mentioned the loss of *Gemeinschaft* was an important theme not only in the writings of Tonnies and other German sociologists but in literature and the humanities as well. Yet Tonnies was not just harking back to a traditional *Gemeinschaft.* His image of modern society, *Gesellschaft,* emphasizes that its very transitoriness and newness meant that modern society could not be considered as a fixed end state. In effect *Gesellschaft* itself should be considered as only a transitional and superficial phenomenon (Frisby, 1985, p. 13). Tonnies did not use the term *postmodern,* although like other German theorists influenced by the Hegelian and Marxist traditions he could envisage something beyond the modern. This something typically entailed an *Aufhebung* of capitalist modernity, which sought to use technological developments to create some form of communal living that provided social and moral integration and realization of freedom and individuality.

10. The use of the term *modern* can be traced back, much further than nineteenth century metropolises, or the eighteenth century Enlightenment, or the early eighteenth century "battle of the books," the quarrel between the Ancients and the Moderns. The term *modern,* Habermas (1981) reminds us, derives from the late fifth century Latin term *modernus,* which was used to demarcate a Christian present from a pagan past (Smart, 1990, p. 17). In this context it points to a break in continuity, to the emergence of something new. Here we find that modern would seem to suggest the destabilization of old categories and the sense of a new start or new era. Vattimo (1988) suggests that modernity's key notion of progress was a secularization of the Judaic-Christian notions of salvation and redemption. Postmodernity entails the abandonment of this belief in development and perfectibility through scientific and technological progress.

11. It has been argued that the sign-play and cultural fragmentation that some want to see as a central feature of postmodernism is very much evident in the de-

pictions of *modernite,* which we find in the accounts of the experience of the modern city in the writings of Benjamin, Baudelaire, and Simmel (Featherstone, 1991, ch. 5). From this perspective there are strong continuities between modernism and postmodernism, as Lyotard has argued. See the oft-quoted remark of Lyotard (1984, p. 79) that postmodernism "is not modernism at its end but in the nascent state, and this state is constant," which points to the transitoriness of the new and the avant-garde impulses that are characteristic of artistic modernism (see also Frisby, 1985; Lichtblau, 1995). However, this stance gives insufficient emphasis to the "end of history" arguments in postmodern theory in which although there is an endless parade of styles and images, these are merely replays of images taken from the imaginary museum of cultures and histories (for a version of this perspective, see Vattimo, 1988).

12. This is not to belittle the book, it is a work of fine scholarship. Rather it is to suggest that it represents perhaps the end point of a particular approach to history that would conceive social, cultural, or local history in strictly local terms with the cutoff boundary being the locality or nation-state. What does seem to be apparent is that the movement toward postcolonial theory, world-systems theory, and postmodernism, which gathered pace during the 1980s, has expanded the frame of reference toward the global and encouraged a more relational focus. A book published only four years later by Catherine Hall (1992), *White, Male, and Middle Class* not only focuses on gender relations like the Seed and Wolff collection, but also considers the way in which English identities have been rooted in imperial power. In this context one could also mention that an essay from the founder of world-systems theory, Immanuel Wallerstein (1990), who has attacked the narrow focus upon the nation-state, begins with a citation from Sidney Mintz's writings on sugar, *The Power of Sweetness and the Sweetness of Power* (1988). One could envisage a similar book on cotton, which focuses on the relations between Manchester capitalism and imperialist presence in the Indian subcontinent and other colonies. Or, rather, we should add that this and similar topics (chocolate, tea, etc.) are being addressed as student projects on cultural studies and communications courses. We could also mention Said's (1993) *Culture and Imperialism,* with its relational interpretation of Jane Austen's novels that highlights the rare occluded references she makes to the colonial source of the wealth on which the eighteenth-century English country house society was based. In effect the premises and categories of taken-for-granted worlds are challenged by these types of analyses.

13. See P. Gilroy (1994) for an account of the implications of the actual slave trade and the shipping of millions of blacks across the Atlantic, which emphasizes the hybrid nature of cultural identity and argues that the enforced black migrations developed a counterculture to modernity. This fact is intrinsic to modernity but is invariably left out of conventional accounts that readily take modernity self-image as a starting point and have little conception of the integral rather than aberrant nature of slavery, the "dark side of modernity."

14. Bacon is presented as one of the key figures in the development of modern science in Horkheimer and Adorno's (1972) *Dialectic of Enlightenment.* He is seen as obsessed by the scientistic vision of dominating nature and controlling the world through scientific knowledge. In common with other members of the Frankfurt School, Horkheimer and Adorno largely concentrate on the "internal,"

i.e., capitalist, modernity narrative of the domination of instrumental reason and do not focus on the place in this process of the West's relationship to others.

15. Here we should attempt to think through a set of categories that includes the various possible meanings of the "Japanization of the West" and not just the "modernization of Japan" (Miyoshi and Harootunian, 1989).

16. Sociology has long neglected the analysis of the colonies. There is little sense of the relational dependence of Western societies on colonies in accounts of the formation of modernity (among the exceptions are King, 1990, 1995; Hall, 1992c). In *The Sociology of the Colonies,* Maunier (1949, p. xi) takes a typically top-down, nation-state–inspired perspective when he argues "The contact of groups or of peoples becomes a contact of civilizations, or of cultural spheres, when it occurs between communities which have not the same form, the same constitution, the same laws: which are therefore not on the same rung of the social ladder. If they are obliged to live together, their problem is how best to pass from diversity to uniformity, to reconcile difference and resemblance, to start from isolation and arrive at fusion. Assimilation or adaption marks the path to unification."

References

Abercrombie, N., S. Hill, and B. S. Turner. (1980) *The Dominant Ideology Thesis.* London: Allen and Unwin.

Appadurai, A. (1988) "Putting Hierarchy in Its Place," *Cultural Anthropology* 3(1).

Axtman, R. (1993) "Society, Globalization, and the Comparative Method," *History of the Human Sciences* 6(2).

Bann, S. (1984) *The Clothing of Clio.* Cambridge: Cambridge University Press.

Baudelaire, C. (1972) "The Painter of Modern Life," in *Selected Writings on Art and Literature.* Harmondsworth, Engl.: Penguin.

Baudrillard, J. (1993) *Symbolic Exchange and Death.* London: Sage.

Bauman, Z. (1991) *Modernity and Ambivalence.* Oxford: Polity.

Benedict, R. (1934) *Patterns of Culture.* Boston: Houghton Mifflin.

Benedict, R. (1946) *The Chrysanthemum and the Sword.* Boston: Houghton Mifflin.

Benjamin, W. (1973) *Charles Baudelaire: A Lyric Poet in the Era of High Capitalism.* London: New Left Books.

Benjamin, W. (1982) *Das Passagen-Werk.* 2 vols. Frankfurt: Suhrkamp.

Bergesen, A. (1990) "Turning World-System Theory on its Head," in M. Featherstone, ed., *Global Culture.* London: Sage.

Berman, M. (1982) *All That Is Solid Melts into Air.* New York: Simon and Schuster.

Boon, J. (1973) "Further Operations of Culture in Anthropology," in L. Schneider and C. Bonjean, eds., *The Idea of Culture in the Social Sciences.* Cambridge: Cambridge University Press.

Buck-Morss, S. (1989) *Dialectic of Seeing: Walter Benjamin and the Arcades Project.* Cambridge, Mass.: MIT Press.

Burke, P. (1978) *Popular Culture in Early Modern Europe.* London: Temple Smith.

Chambers, I. (1990) *Border Dialogues: Journeys in Postmodernity.* London: Routledge.

Chambers, I. (1994) *Migrancy, Culture, and Identity.* London: Routledge.

Clegg, S. (1989) *Frameworks of Power.* London: Sage.

Clifford, J. (1988) *The Predicament of Culture.* Cambridge, Mass.: Harvard University Press.
Clifford, J. (1992) "Traveling Cultures," in L. Grossberg, C. Nelson, and P. Triechler, eds., *Cultural Studies.* London: Routledge.
Clifford, J., and G. Marcus, eds. (1986) *Writing Culture.* Berkeley: California University Press.
Connolly, W. (1994) "Tocqueville, Territory, and Violence," *Theory, Culture, and Society* 11(1).
Crapanzo, V. (1980) *Tuhami: Portrait of a Moroccan.* Chicago: Chicago University Press.
Crapanzo, V. (1992) *Hermes' Dilemma and Hamlet's Desire: On the Epistemology of Interpretation.* Cambridge, Mass.: Harvard University Press.
Deleuze, G., and F. Guattari. (1983) *Anti-Oedipus.* Minneapolis: Minnesota University Press.
Deleuze, G., and F. Guattari. (1987) *A Thousand Plateaus: Capitalism and Schizophrenia.* Minneapolis: Minnesota University Press.
Derrida, J. (1979) "Living on Border Lines," in H. Bloom, ed., *Deconstruction and Criticism.* London: Routledge.
de Swaan, B. (1994) "The Sociological Study of Transnational Society," Amsterdam School voor Sociaalwetenschappelijk Onderzoek, mimeo.
Durkheim, E. (1969) "Individualism and the Intellectuals," *Political Studies* 17.
Elias, N. (1978/1982) *The Civilizing Process.* 2 Vols. Oxford: Blackwell.
Elias, N. (1984) "On the Sociogenesis of Sociology," *Sociologisch Tijdschrift* 11(1).
Eyerman, R., and O. Lofgren. (1995) "Road Movies," *Theory, Culture, and Society* 12(1).
Featherstone, M. (1991a) *Postmodernism and Consumer Culture.* London: Sage.
Featherstone, M. (1991b) "Georg Simmel: An Introduction," *Theory, Culture, and Society* 8(3).
Featherstone, M. (1993a) "Global and Local Cultures," in J. Bird and G. Robertson, eds., *Mapping the Futures, Local Cultures, Global Change.* New York: Routledge.
Featherstone, M. (1993b) "Cultural Production, Consumption, and the Development of the Cultural Sphere," in R. Munch and N. Smelser, eds., *Theory of Culture.* Berkeley: California University Press.
Featherstone, M., and S. Lash. (1995) "Globalization, Modernity, and the Spatialization of Social Theory," in M. Featherstone, S. Lash, and R. Robertson, eds., *Global Modernities.* London: Sage.
Feldman-Bianco, Bella. (1992) "Multiple Layers of Time and Space: The Construction of Class, Ethnicity, and Nationalism among Portuguese Immigrants," in N. G. Schiller, L. Basch, and C. Blanc-Szanton, eds., *Towards a Transnational Perspective on Migration: Race, Class, Ethnicity, and Nationalism Reconsidered. Annals of the New York Academy of Science,* vol. 645. New York: New York Academy of Sciences.
Foucault, M. (1971) *Madness and Civilization.* London: Tavistock.
Friedman, J. (1987) "Prolegomena to the Adventures of Phallus in Blunderland: An Anti-Anti Discourse," *Culture and History* 1(1).
Frisby, D. (1985) *Fragments of Modernity.* Oxford: Polity Press.
Frisby, D., and D. Sayer. (1986) *Society.* London: Tavistock.

Gabriel, T. H. (1990) "Thoughts on Nomadic Aesthetics and the Black Independent Cinema: Traces of a Journey," in R. Ferguson, M. Gever, T. T. Minh-ha, and C. West, eds., *Out There: Marginalization and Contemporary Culture.* Cambridge, Mass.: MIT Press.

Game, A. (1991) *Undoing the Social.* Milton Keynes, Engl.: Open University Press.

Giddens, A. (1990) *The Consequences of Modernity.* Oxford: Polity Press.

Giddens, A. (1991) *Modernity and Self-Identity.* Oxford: Polity Press.

Gilroy, P. (1994) *The Black Atlantic.* London: Verso.

Grafton, A. (1992) *New Worlds, Ancient Texts: The Power and Shock of Discovery.* Cambridge, Mass.: Harvard University Press.

Grossberg, L., C. Nelson., and P. Triechler, eds. (1992) *Cultural Studies.* London: Routledge.

Gupta, A., and J. Ferguson. (1992) "Beyond 'Culture': Space, Identity, and the Politics of Difference," *Cultural Anthropology* 7:6–23.

Habermas, J. (1990) *The Philosophical Discourse of Modernity.* Oxford: Polity.

Hall, C. (1992) *White, Male, and Middle Class.* Oxford: Polity.

Hall, S. (1992a) "Introduction," to S. Hall and B. Gieben, eds., *Formation of Modernity.* Oxford: Polity Press.

Hall, S. (1992b) "The Question of Cultural Identity," in S. Hall, D. Held, and T. McGrew, eds., *Modernity and Its Futures.* Oxford: Polity Press.

Hall, S. (1992c) "The Rest and the West: Discourse and Power," in S. Hall and B. Gieben, eds., *Formation of Modernity.* Oxford: Polity Press.

Hatch, E. (1973) *Theories of Culture.* New York: Columbia University Press.

Horkheimer, M., and T. Adorno. (1972) *Dialectic of Enlightenment.* New York: Herder and Herder.

Jusserand, J. J. (1973) *English Wayfaring Life in the Middle Ages.* Boston: Milford House.

King, A. D. (1990) *Global Cities.* London: Routledge.

King, A. D. (1995) "The Times and Spaces of Modernity (or Who Needs Postmodernism?)," in M. Featherstone, S. Lash, and R. Robertson, eds., *Global Modernities.* London: Sage.

Kuper, A. (1988) *The Invention of Primitive Society.* London: Routledge.

Lasch, C. (1991) *The True and Only Heaven: Progress and Its Critics.* New York: Norton.

Lash, S. and J. Urry. (1993) *Economies of Signs and Spaces.* London: Sage.

Latour, B. (1993) *We Have Never Been Modern.* London: Harvester.

Leed, E. J. (1991) *The Mind of the Traveler.* New York: Basic Books.

Levine, D. (1985) *The Flight from Ambiguity.* Chicago: Chicago University Press.

Lévi-Strauss, C. (1976) *Tristes Tropiques.* Harmondsworth: Penguin.

Lichtblau, K. (1995) "Sociology and the Diagnosis of the Times: Or the Reflexivity of Modernity," *Theory, Culture, and Society* 12(1).

Liebersohn, H. (1988) *Fate and Utopia in German Sociology 1870–1923.* Cambridge, Mass.: MIT Press.

Malkki, Liisa. (1992) "National Geographic: The Rooting of Peoples and the Territorialization of National Identity Among Scholars and Refugees," *Cultural Anthropology* 7:24–44.

Maravall, J. A. (1986) *Culture of the Baroque.* Manchester: Manchester University Press.

Marcus, G., ed. (1992) *Rereading Cultural Anthropology.* Durham, N.C.: Duke University Press.
Marcus, G., and M. M. J. Fischer. (1986) *Anthropology as Cultural Critique.* Chicago: Chicago University Press.
Mazlish, B. (1994) "The Flaneur: From Spectator to Representation," in K. Tester, ed., *The Flaneur.* London: Routledge.
Mintz, S. (1988) *The Power of Sweetness and the Sweetness of Power.* 8th Duiker Lecture. Deventer, Netherlands: Van Loghum Slaterus.
Mitterauer, M. (1992) *A History of Youth.* Oxford: Blackwell.
Miyoshi, M. (1989) "Against the Native Grain: The Japanese Novel and the Postmodern West," in H. Harootunian and M. Myoshi, eds., *Postmodernism and Japan.* Durham, N.C.: Duke University Press.
Miyoshi, M., and H. Harootunian. (1989) "Introduction," in H. Harootunian and M. Myoshi, eds., *Postmodernism and Japan.* Durham, N.C.: Duke University Press.
Moore, W. E. (1966) "Global Sociology: The World as a Singular System," *American Journal of Sociology* 71(5).
Nicholson, L. J., ed. (1990) *Feminism/Postmodernism.* London: Routledge.
Nisbet, R. (1967) *The Sociological Tradition.* London: Heinemann.
Osborne, P. (1992) "Modernity Is a Qualitative, Not a Chronological Category," in F. Barker, P. Hulme, and M. Iverson, eds., *Postmodernism and the Re-reading of Modernity.* Manchester: Manchester University Press.
Pels, D., and A. Crebas. (1988) "Carmen or the Invention of a New Feminine Myth," *Theory, Culture, and Society* 5(4). Reprinted in M. Featherstone, M. Hepworth, and B. S. Turner, eds., *The Body: Social Process and Cultural Theory.* London: Sage.
Richardson, M. (1992) "The Sacred and the College de Sociologie," *Theory, Culture, and Society* 9(3).
Robertson, R. (1992a) *Globalization.* London: Sage.
Robertson, R. (1992b) "Globality and Modernity," *Theory, Culture, and Society* 9(2).
Rosaldo, R. (1993) *Culture and Truth: The Remaking of Social Analysis.* London: Routledge.
Said, E. W. (1978) *Orientalism.* Harmondsworth, Engl.: Penguin.
Said, E. W. (1993) *Culture and Imperialism.* New York: Vintage.
Sakai, N. (1989) "Modernity and Its Critique: The Problem of Universalism and Particularism," in H. Harootunian and M. Myoshi, eds., *Postmodernism and Japan.* Durham, N.C.: Duke University Press.
Seed, J., and J. Wolff, eds., (1988) *The Culture of Capital: Art, Power, and the Nineteenth-Century Middle Class.* Manchester: Manchester University Press.
Shotter, J. (1993) *Cultural Politics of Everyday Life.* Milton Keynes, Engl.: Open University Press.
Simmel, G. (1923) "Rodin," in *Philosophische Kultur.* 3rd Edition. Potsdam, Germ.
Simmel, G. (1995) "Fashion," in D. Frisby and M. Featherstone, eds., *Simmel on Culture.* London: Sage.
Smart, B. (1990) "Modernity, Postmodernity, and the Present," in B. S. Turner, ed., *Theories of Modernity and Postmodernity.* London: Sage.
Soja, E. (1989) *Postmodern Geographies.* London: Verso.
Suttles, G. (1991) "Preface," to *Kamikaze Biker.* Chicago: Chicago University Press.

Taussig, M. (1980) *The Devil and Commodity Fetishism in South America.* Chapel Hill: North Carolina University Press.
Taussig, M. (1987) *Shamanism, Colonialism, and the Wild Man: A Study of Terror and Healing.* Chicago: Chicago University Press.
Taylor, C. (1992) *The Politics of Multiculturalism.* Princeton: Princeton University Press.
Tenbruck, F. (1990) "The Dream of a Secular Ecumene: The Meaning and Politics of Development," in M. Featherstone, ed., *Global Culture.* London: Sage.
Tenbruck, F. (1994) "History of Society or Universal History," *Theory, Culture, and Society* 11(1).
Therborn, G. (1995) "Routes To/Through Modernity," in M. Featherstone, S. Lash, and R. Robertson, eds., *Global Modernities.* London: Sage.
Thomas, K. (1983) *Man and the Natural World.* Harmondsworth, Engl.: Allen Lane.
Thornton, R. J. (1992) "The Rhetoric of Ethnographic Holism," in G. Marcus, ed., *Rereading Cultural Anthropology.* Durham, N.C.: Duke University Press.
Tibi, B. (1995) "Culture and Knowledge: The Politics of Islamisation of Knowledge as a Postmodern Project? The Fundamentalist Claim to De-Westernisation," *Theory, Culture, and Society* 12(1).
Todorov, T. (1984) *The Conquest of America.* New York: Harper.
Todorov, T. (1989) *Nous et les Autres.* Paris: Seuil.
Tonnies, F. (1955) *Community and Association.* London: Routledge.
Touraine, A. (1986) *Le Retour de l'Acteur.* Paris.
Turner, B. S. (1990a) "Two Faces of Sociology: Global or National," in M. Featherstone, ed., *Global Culture.* London: Sage.
Turner, B. S., ed. (1990b) "Introduction," to B. S. Turner, ed., *Theories of Modernity and Postmodernity.* London: Sage.
Turner, G. (1990) *British Cultural Studies.* London: Unwin & Hyman.
Van den Abeele, G. (1992) *Travel as Metaphor.* Minneapolis: Minnesota University Press.
Vattimo, G. (1988) *The End of History.* Oxford: Polity.
Wallace, A. F. C. (1970) *Culture and Personality.* New York.
Wallerstein, I. (1987) "World-Systems Analysis," in A. Giddens and J. Turner, eds., *Social Theory Today.* Oxford: Polity Press, pp. 309–324.
Wallerstein, I. (1990) "Culture as the Ideological Battleground of the Modern World-System," in M. Featherstone, ed., *Global Culture.* London: Sage.
Wang, Gungwu. (1993) "Migration and Its Enemies," in B. Mazlish and R. Buultjens, eds., *Conceptualizing Global History.* Boulder: Westview Press.
White, H. (1973) *Metahistory.* Baltimore: Johns Hopkins University Press.
Williams, R. (1973) *The Countryside and the City.* London: Chatto and Windus.
Williams, R. (1981) *Culture.* London: Fontana.
Wolff, Eric R. (1990) "Distinguished Lecture: Facing Power—Old Insights, New Questions," *American Anthropologist* 92(3).
Wolff, J. (1993) "On the Road Again: Metaphors of Travel in Cultural Criticism," *Cultural Studies* 7(2).
Zerubavel, E. (1991) *The Fine Line: Making Distinctions in Everyday Life.* Chicago: Chicago University Press.

10

Global Movements, Global Walls: Responses to Migration, 1885–1925

Aristide R. Zolberg

In the final decades of the long nineteenth century, a concatenation of worldwide changes associated with the globalization of capitalism induced a sudden and massive increase in the number of people on the move worldwide and in the distances they covered. Propelled by necessity and drawn by opportunity, the uprooted originated from every corner of the globe and migrated wherever land or work might be available, mostly to the United States or one of the other countries controlled by settlers of European stock, but increasingly also to the more developed parts of Europe itself. Despite their desirability to employers as cheap labor, the steadily more disparate newcomers came to be perceived by many as a threat to cultural integrity and political stability. Already in the throes of growing domestic and international tensions, the receivers also saw themselves beset by an unprecedented "immigration crisis."

The legacy of a much less mobile epoch, existing mechanisms for controlling the movement of people across international borders, were inadequate to stem the tide; and even where immigration was generally welcome, the vastly increased numbers to be dealt with and their extraordinary diversity surpassed the capacity of the institutions developed earlier to manage the incorporation of newcomers. Under pressure to act more effectively, each of the receiving states was challenged to devise new regulatory mechanisms for controlling admission, not only into the territory but also into the society and the state, conceived as a body politic.

Albeit driven primarily by domestic considerations, decisionmakers were fully aware of the interconnectedness of the disparate migration streams and believed enhanced border control was imperative because the closing of doors elsewhere increased pressure on their own borders. As in the arms race, which originated around the same time, the fear of acting too late to keep out unwanted immigrants triggered anticipatory moves and thereby determined an upward spiral of restriction. Although it would be too much to speak of concertation among the states in question, the new policies were thus highly *interactive,* and the dynamics involved were thus simultaneously national and international.

In this manner, the aggregate actions of individual states—with some variation in timing and degree of closure—resulted in the formation of a *restrictive international immigration regime,* tending toward *zero immigration* as its baseline. The most visible consequence of these developments was a drastic reduction of immigration into the world's affluent countries, and since this constituted a large part of ongoing flows, of international migration more generally. Concurrently, global mobility was reduced further by the draconian regulations the European powers imposed on the outward movement of the colonial peoples who came under their control in Asia, Africa, and the Caribbean.[1] Moreover, from the 1920s onward there arose in Europe a number of new authoritarian regimes that restricted the exit of their citizens for economic and political reasons.[2] An important consequence of restrictions on exit and entry was the near-impossibility for persecuted groups to secure asylum abroad and concomitantly the legitimation of their persecution as people who were demonstrably undesirable because nobody wanted them.[3]

Epochal Changes

The final decades of the nineteenth century constituted a moment of perceptible globalization of the economic, strategic, and cultural spheres. For the first time, the earth was linked by way of transcontinental railroad networks and transoceanic steamship lines into a single web of mass transportation; and the combination of rapidly spreading literacy, with cheap printing, enhanced by the telegraph and photography, concurrently produced an integrated sphere of worldwide communication, fostering the emergence of rudimentary elements of a genuinely global culture. But at the same time, the unevenness of world conditions was accentuated, with a growing gap between a small group of capital-rich, technologically advanced, and concomitantly strategically powerful countries, European or of European origin plus Japan and the rest.[4] Internal conditions among the latter were henceforth largely determined by the transnational economic, social, cultural, and political processes generated by the leading countries, all of which also engaged in colonial expansion.[5]

Although most of the leading countries were becoming liberal democracies, with governments accountable to broadly based representative bodies, this was combined with an expanding and more centralized state apparatus, giving the state a much greater capacity for internal and external intervention.[6] Economic competition among the leading states in a worldwide arena, under conditions of accentuated economic fluctuations whose effects were concomitantly worldwide, resulted in the reorganization of the global economy into neomercantilist segments. These rivalries interacted with the evolution of three of the world's states—the United Kingdom, the Russian Empire, and the United States—into a new breed of superpowers, either by virtue of continental size and commensurately large population, or by virtue of an extensive maritime empire. The strategic chessboard also expanded to encompass what were from the European perspective marginal regions, particularly the Pacific. Undermining the century-old Concert of Europe, these developments rendered international conflict more likely; and once it erupted, the processes it unleashed further exacerbated global dislocations.

There were also epochal changes in the demographic sphere, aptly summarized by Barraclough's phrase, "the dwarfing of Europe."[7] Completing the revolution they had begun to experience in the eighteenth century, the industrialized countries entered a phase of much slower growth, which afforded them a population structure that was more efficient in relation to the new economic dynamics. Leading the way with regard to the demographic revolution, France reached a stable population level around 1850; but whereas this was long viewed as an exceptional state of affairs, England began to experience a fertility decline in 1890, Switzerland, in 1905, and Germany, in 1910. In the previous century and a half Western populations had grown at a more rapid rate than the rest, but the difference was now reversed, and subsequently widened further. Consequently, Europe's proportion of world population reached its historical maximum around World War I, and the United States's and Japan's did so a few decades later.[8] This development attracted considerable attention because it entailed a dramatic shift in the relative importance of white and colored populations, precisely at a time when "racial" differences were being essentialized. For contemporaneous elites, this ominous phenomenon reenacted at the international level the inability of European ruling strata to maintain their demographic strength within their own societies. In a world sharply divided between haves and have-nots and a time when population size was reckoned as a vital component of international power, the decreasing fertility of the haves came to be viewed as a dangerous form of unilateral disarmament.[9]

Rapid population expansion in the world at large was expected to produce a Malthusian crisis of subsistence, for which the only remedy would be migration. By 1900, Barraclough suggests, there was an "almost neurotic awareness of this process," expressed most egregiously by way of warnings regarding "the yellow peril."[10] Although this was attributable in large measure to a projection of widespread racist phantasms regarding Asia, which will be discussed later on, the belief that economic development occasioned massive uprooting was hardly irrational, but rather a sound extrapolation of ongoing Western experience, which was consecrated by E. G. Ravenstein in his classic 1885 presentation to the fellows of the Royal Statistical Society as one of the fundamental laws of migration.[11]

The expansion of population movements was vastly facilitated by the development of an integrated worldwide network of rapid and inexpensive mass transportation. It did so in several complementary ways: not only by providing the facilities for draining rural regions whose population hitherto experienced only very local mobility as well as by opening up new regions for capitalist development but also by providing a dynamic economic sector that generated considerable demand for precisely the sort of labor displaced rural populations might carry out. For the period under consideration, this development was especially dramatic among the late developers in Europe as well as among the overseas countries. For example, whereas by this time the United Kingdom reached a plateau, with the total railroad network in service growing only from 21,558 km in 1871 to 32,623 in 1913, in Austria-Hungary it soared from 6,112 to 22,981, in Russia, from 10,731 to 62,300, in Norway, from 359 to 3,085, and in Italy from 6,429 to 18,873.[12] On the receiving side, the U.S. total grew from 85,170 km in 1870 to 386,714 in 1910; but Canada experienced an even more dramatic growth, from a mere 4,211 in 1870 to 39,799 in 1910, and that rate of expansion was in turn surpassed by latecomers such as Argentina (from 732 to 27,713) and Brazil (from 745 to 21,326). Once again, similar processes took place in Asia and Africa.

The other major element in the network was the steamship. Although the use of steam in navigation originated at the beginning of the nineteenth century, and in fact preceded the railroad, its application to mass transportation came somewhat later. The major turning point in ocean-crossing occurred in the 1860s, as the result of the replacement of the wheel by the screw and of wood by iron—lighter, more lasting, and easier to repair—which together facilitated the building of much larger and faster ships.[13] Steam rapidly took over; for example, in 1860 it accounted for 31.5 percent of passenger traffic arriving in New York, by 1865, over half, and in 1870, over 90 percent. In 1856, transatlantic sailing vessels carried on the average 247 passengers, as against 232 for steam; but in 1870 the relationship was reversed, 153 as against 385; and by the 1880s, as many as 1,500 persons were occasionally packed into a single vessel.[14] Competition ensured the triumph of speed, since greater speed made possible more frequent sailings for each vessel. In 1871 the fastest vessel made the crossing in eight to ten days, carrying a crew of 130 plus 200 cabin passengers and 1,000 more in steerage; but the average was still ten to twelve days; in 1889–1890 the Hamburg-America's vessels set a new record of seven days from Southampton to New York, which was bested seven years later by the Norddeutsche Lloyd. The shipping industry expanded spectacularly: As of 1873, seventeen companies were operating 173 ships totaling over 500,000 tons between New York and Europe, with the largest ship around 4,000 tons; but by 1914, Hamburg-America alone operated 442 ships with 1.4 million tons, and the largest ship was over 50,000 tons.

Although the expansion of shipping capacity was a response to growing demand, it also contributed to the expansion of emigration, in that the companies actively promoted their services and recruited passengers, much as was the case earlier with regard to northwestern Europe, but on a commensurately much larger scale. In particular, the Hamburg-America Line developed a network of agents in Russia and Eastern Europe from the 1870s, and helped stimulate the great Jewish emigration. In the fall of 1894, in collaboration with the city of Hamburg, they built new port facilities, complete transient facilities for emigrants arriving by rail from neighboring regions of the Czarist and Austro-Hungarian empires, including churches and synagogues. Altogether, of the 1.8 million who left Austria between 1870 and 1910, 1.3 million used Hamburg or Bremen.[15] Shipping lines, like railroads, also helped to develop markets by moving closer to places of origin, and both were integrated into well-established itineraries. For example, a German observer noted that the recently developed rail and steamship networks allowed an Italian to get to North or South America for less than the rail fare to East Prussia. Traffic specialization also contributed to the institutionalization of specific currents. For the Iberian Peninsula in relation to South America as well, "migration accelerated as passenger ships became larger and chains of information grew stronger."[16]

Although it is difficult to find reliable long chronological series regarding cost, there is no doubt of an appreciable secular decrease. On the New York run, the steerage price was about $40 in 1870 but down around $20 around the turn of the century, dipping lower in years of depression such as 1894, when the fare from Ireland fell to $8.75.[17] Much of this was financed by remittances and prepaid tickets sent home from overseas; although this was already a well-established phenomenon in the middle third of the nineteenth century, the enlargement and diversification of the immigrant communities had further amplifying effects. For example, in the period 1905–1914, an estimated one-third of Norwegian males and two-fifths of the females crossed to America on prepaid tickets.[18]

The processes determining the massive uprooting itself were identified by Marx early on as "the great transformation," a term that provides the title of Karl Polanyi's classic analysis of the rise and fall of the market economy.[19] Whereas over the long term, the transformation of an agrarian society into an industrial one might enable a given territory to sustain a much larger population and at a higher general standard of living, the catastrophic impact of the transition on the countryside left many people with no alternative but to leave home.[20] Overall, but with considerable local variation in timing and extent, improvements in the production and distribution of food brought about a decrease in the death rate, and thereby underwrote population growth; but since the larger population shared finite land resources, the proportion of landless laborers increased. Concurrently, however, the changes that rocked the countryside dramatically reduced and narrowed the population's sources of income. As land became more concentrated and production more specialized, particularly with the introduction of sugar beet as a leading crop of northwestern Europe, farmers found the traditional system of service based on an annual contract providing for housing as well as wages economically burdensome; for example, between 1895 and 1907, the number of servants (in distinction from wageworkers) employed in agriculture within Germany fell by 20 percent. With the shift to short-term wage work, social ties and shared interests binding landlords to workers were severed, leaving large numbers without housing or sustenance. The presence of a greater rural population also rendered crop failures more devastating. And finally, as capital moved to urban sites and fled some regions altogether, the European countryside was deindustrialized; chances for village work disappeared and the pay rates for rural goods declined, reducing the ability of country workers to get by in the local cottage economy.

These transformations led to the easing of prevailing legal and administrative barriers to internal movement and to emigration, and in many instances emigration came to be viewed as a welcome solution to new problems. It should be remembered that during the period of absolutism and mercantilism, which coincided by and large with an epoch of slow population growth (or even of decline), subjects and the services they were capable of performing were in effect part of the sovereign's domain; unauthorized departure was a form of treason and punishable as such—including often retaliation against relations who remained behind. Albeit not effectively enforced in all cases, this constituted a significant deterrent, especially for those with property to lose.[21] The right of citizens to leave their country freely (and to return) was proclaimed in the French Declaration of the Rights of Man, but became practically relevant only in the late 1820s, when Britain relinquished long-standing prohibitions against the emigration of skilled subjects, which had been reinforced in the wake of the American revolution, as part of the removal of barriers to market forces in keeping with the principles of the new political economy. At this time, emigration was discovered to be a cost-effective substitute for poor relief as well as a safety valve for social unrest at home, particularly in the troublesome Irish periphery. Proceeding by trial and error,

Britain hit upon a dual solution—self-sustaining emigration, which flowed mostly to the United States, and subsidized emigration to man imperial undertakings, mostly to Canada (where Englishmen were needed as a counterweight to French Canadians) and Australia. The Swiss cantons, the German principalities, the Low Countries, and the Scandinavian kingdoms followed suit in the middle third of the century. However, France deviated from the general trend: Because of its precocious achievement of demographic stability, the state maintained a mercantilist stance toward population, discouraging emigration (except to settle Algeria) and encouraging foreign settlement.

In the classic formulation, "push" forces were combined with the "pull" of demand generated by the vigorously growing agroindustrial and industrial sectors. Eschewing traditional craftsmen and women, employers were eager for less-skilled, less-expensive, more docile, and more disposable labor. Migrants from less-developed regions, within the state itself—as in the case of Ireland in relation to the United Kingdom or Bretons in France—or abroad were especially convenient for these purposes.[22]

Expansion, Diversification, and Globalization of the Migration System

Arising early among the nations of northwestern Europe, industrialization fostered the great transatlantic migration of the middle decades of the nineteenth century, in later decades this process continued to stimulate steadily larger emigration from the original group, but also began to engulf the southern and eastern latecomers, propelling their swelling populations in search of work, at home or abroad. Latecomers followed suit with regard to emigration policy as well: For example, Spain maintained tight legal restrictions on exit through the 1850s, then relaxed them somewhat, and by 1903 passports and governmental permission were no longer required at all.[23] Although the largest movements were transoceanic, including South America as well as North America and the English-speaking dominions in the Pacific, there were also sizeable flows into the economically advanced European countries. In the latter decades of the nineteenth century, there were sizeable flows of Russian Poles to Germany, Flemish Belgians and Italians to France, Swedes to Denmark, and later Finns to Sweden, and Italians to Switzerland.

In the brief span of time when they operated nearly unfettered in the absence of any significant restrictions on entry—except for the enactment of barriers to the movement of Asians into "white" countries, to be discussed later—the nexus of factors considered induced a vast expansion of international migrations to unprecedented and hitherto truly inconceivable levels. Most spectacularly visible, in the Atlantic region as a whole (including both within Europe and overseas) the combined international flows grew fourfold within a forty year period, from 2.7 million for the 1871–1880 decade to over 11 million in 1901–1910.[24] Overseas migration to the major receivers alone (Argentina, Brazil, Canada, and the United States) expanded in the same span by an even more dramatic fivefold factor, from 2.6 million to 12.9 million. Although repatriation (or return migration) increased in this period as well and undoubtedly constituted a growing share of the total, this matters little for present purposes, in that the perception of the receivers regarding the magnitude of immigration was governed, then as now, entirely by gross immigration figures.

Concurrently, the composition of immigration changed markedly as well. With regard to overseas Atlantic movement, at the beginning of the period under consideration the leading contributors were Britain (27 percent of the total), Germany, Ireland, and the Scandinavian group; but on the eve of World War I Britain had fallen to second place (23 percent of the total), with Italy now well ahead of the pack (33 percent), and Austro-Hungary and Spain in the lead quartet. On the basis of their relative contribution to overseas movement (decennial intercontinental emigration in proportion to national population), in 1871–1880, the top four European emigration countries were Ireland, Britain, Norway, and Portugal, whereas in 1913 they were Italy, Portugal, Spain, and Britain; and although the annual rate of emigration for first-place Ireland in 1871–1880 was 661 per 100,000 inhabitants, for Italy in 1913 it was nearly three times higher, 1,630 per 100,000. In fact, all four leaders at that time had an emigration rate above 1,000 per 100,000.[25]

Similar forces were already at work in various parts of what would later be called the "Third World" as well, largely as the result of more intrusive penetration by the industrializing countries, which between 1876 and 1915 appropriated one-quarter of the globe's land surface, but also as a consequence of indigenous attempts to catch up. Some of the flows followed well-established paths, others were entirely new.

An outstanding component of the new migration epoch was the organization of massive population transfers by European colonial governments. These were not only important in themselves but contributed to the globalization of movement by normalizing uprooting in various regions; beyond this, they entailed the establishment of administrative and transportation links between different colonies as well as the implantation of migrant communities among them, which subsequently facilitated self-propelled movement.

As is well known, sugar production was closely linked with the importation of African slaves to the New World because of its technical requirements of a massive input of specialized, disciplined labor;[26] and when the trade was abolished, substitutes were recruited in South and East Asia.

The other colonial commodities for which an expanding demand was stimulated by the increasingly populous and affluent Europe of the industrial revolution—including fibers (cotton, sisal), lubricants (palm oil), stimulants (coffee, tea, cocoa), and last but not least hevea (natural rubber)—were also produced mostly in plantations owned and operated by whites with third world labor, often imported from some other region and usually involving some element of bondage or coercion.[27] Colonial labor was imported throughout the plantation belt, wherever an adequate supply could not be secured locally, either because the indigenous populations could not be mobilized into a labor force by money wages or by force, or because of the sheer insufficiency of numbers. There are also indications that imported workers were *preferred* to natives as plantations workers, because it was easier to control displaced persons—who concomitantly acquired a reputation for greater "docility," which immigrant workers worldwide tend to share—and were easier to dispose of when no longer needed.

A major case in point was the Indian subcontinent. Already in the late eighteenth century, the European trading companies operating in South Asia recruited Indians as indentured workers, or even outright slaves, to operate newly launched sugar plantations in various Indian Ocean islands, such as Mauritius and Réunion; early on, the Dutch also imported Indians to Indonesia. In the late 1830s, facing the prospect of emancipation of their slaves, British planters in the West Indies naturally turned to the Indian subcontinent for substitutes; around the same time, Indian labor was also sought for plantations in Southeast Asia, particularly Burma and Malaya. Others followed suit. The growing demand was matched by a growing supply, as British trade policy deliberately induced the deindustrialization of India, and the commercialization of land and the turn to capitalist agriculture wrought effects similar to those noted for Europe. Certain Indian districts were thoroughly reorganized to meet the exigencies of the labor trade: Irrigated rice was grown for export to plantation dependencies, and the colonial government adopted land policies favoring consolidation in private hands, which fostered the formation of a landless class, more prone to emigration. Most of the recruits were untouchables, or members of the non-Brahman lower classes of peasantry.[28] Political considerations entered into play as well. Having determined on the policy of "shoveling out the poor" to deal with mounting "social problems" within the United Kingdom, the British authorities applied it to India as well, particularly in the wake of the 1857 Mutiny.

Initially, the exportation of Indian contract workers was limited to the British Empire itself, initially mostly to sugar plantations of the Indian Ocean (Mauritius) and the Caribbean, and later to others in Southeast Asia (Malaya, Burma), and regulated by colonial governments at both ends of the journey; but when the supply exceeded the Empire's demand, Britain also exported Indians to other European possessions.[29]

These vast movements entailed a complex delivery system. At the apex in India was an elite of subagents, usually middlemen minorities such as Jews, Armenians, Indian Christians, or Eurasians. They in turn sent out recruiters—subagents, knowledgeable about local conditions, who operated by offering advances to settle debts, provide a going away feast, and purchase the ticket. East Indians sent to plantations in Mauritius and Guyana were drawn initially from the hill-dwelling populations, known as *danghar.* In the 1870s these also took part in the migration to the tea plantations of Assam and Bhutan. Afterward, recruiters turned to the population of the "presidency" towns—Bombay, Madras, Calcutta—and eventually South India, so much so that workers were often referred to as "Malabars." Laborers for Ceylon (Sri Lanka), Burma, Malaya, and Natal were mostly Tamil-speakers.

Altogether, approximately 1 million Indian contract workers were shipped outside of Asia from 1834 to 1916; but this represented but a small fraction of the subcontinent's total labor emigration, with estimates for the period 1834–1937 ranging from about 31 million to as high as 45 million, including over 4 million to Malaya alone. Although the workers saw themselves in the main as sojourners rather than emigrants, there were sizeable residues of permanent settlement. As of 1945, populations of East Indian origin numbered about 1 million in Burma; 750,000 each in Ceylon and Malaya; 300,000 each in Mauritius, Trinidad, and Guyana; and 100,000 each in Fiji and Natal.[30] Although none of the organized labor supply networks were directed toward North America, around the turn of the century Indians began appearing in British Columbia and California. Some 7,000 arrivals were recorded in the United States before Indians were excluded in 1917.

Southeast Asia had long been the domain of Chinese trading colonies and concomitant migrations.[31] Although the Chinese state's decision in the fifteenth century to throttle foreign commerce and create an unpopulated no-man's-land along the coast to prevent foreign contact with the Han population stemmed out-migration, labor continued to be exported by the Portuguese through Macao, and the Dutch East India Company captured Chinese along the China coast in order to populate its headquarter plantation in Batavia. Eager to procure labor for their expanding plantations (Malaya, Dutch East Indies) that were producing tropical commodities for the world market, at the end of the "Opium Wars" (1839–1842, 1856–1860), the Europeans insisted on including in the treaties they dictated provisions removing barriers to emigration and allowing foreign entrepreneurs to operate freely in the "Treaty ports." This facilitated the launching of a "coolie" trade, which combined Chinese and

European entrepreneurs into an extensive network of labor recruitment and shipping.[32] The supply was assured by growing rural poverty, attributable on the one hand to a spurt of population growth, leading to competition for scarce land and hence higher rents—as in Ireland or in India; and on the other to an increase in the size of the Chinese upper class, leading to a greater squeeze on the peasantry.[33]

Long the center of trade with Southeast Asia, Quanzhou, in Fujian (Fukien) Province, was also the fountainhead of nineteenth-century emigration to Malaya and neighboring countries. Most of the America-bound Chinese originated instead around Guangzhou (Canton), the capital of Guangdong (Kwangtung) Province, which had a long history as China's main port open to foreign commerce. Bearing the brunt of the concessions China was forced to make in the wake of the "Opium Wars," the region's population experienced dramatic downward mobility, with many driven to accept labor contracts abroad, both as free passengers and as "credit-ticket" indentured labor. Over the next decades emigration was further stimulated by a series of violent political upheavals, including the Taiping Rebellion, the Bendi-Keija [Hakka] ethnic conflict, and the Red Turban uprisings.[34]

Availing themselves of these opportunities, in the late 1840s British and American entrepreneurs organized new Chinese migrations across the Pacific to South and North America. Given subsequent developments, it is noteworthy that at the time, U.S. diplomats in China were concerned over competition resulting from the increased use of Chinese labor on West Indian plantations; hence they advocated presidential intervention to prevent the use of U.S. shipping in furthering such emigration, and in keeping with this, in 1858 the Congress called for a condemnation of the "coolie trade" as "a matter of humanity and policy."[35] However the attorney general ruled the following year that the United States did not have that authority; accordingly, a law was enacted in 1862 merely prohibiting the coolie trade by U.S. citizens in U.S. vessels. The measure was ambiguous, however, because it was not designed to block voluntary emigration, or to prevent U.S. vessels from carrying "voluntary" emigration, most of which was in fact founded on debt bondage.[36]

Indeed, six years later, Washington actively intervened to further expand the traffic. This episode is worth considering in some detail, because it highlights the determinative role of the United States in fostering a migration that even then evoked considerable opposition, and which was widely viewed as a malevolent "invasion" engineered by Oriental cunning. Throughout the first half of the nineteenth century, ongoing dynamics provided the United States with an ample supply of European immigrants, with no need for positive policy intervention; however, in the face of a manpower shortage induced by the Civil War, Secretary of State

Seward (of Alaska fame) secured the enactment of a law designed to facilitate the recruitment of labor from hitherto untapped regions by financing their transportation and concomitantly authorizing labor contracts, enforceable in U.S. courts, that would make such ventures profitable. The measure led to the establishment of a quasi-official recruiting agency, the American Emigration Company. Although the company was oriented mostly to Europe, an attempt was made to import Chinese workers as well; however, this was discouraged by the U.S. Commissioner for Immigration on the grounds that it was contrary to the interests of the United States to introduce "new races bound to service and labor" and was contrary to established laws.[37] When an attempt was made to enhance profitability by imposing penal sanctions on workers who violated their contract, the law was denounced as licensing a new form of bondage. Opponents explicitly charged that European contract workers would be no better off than Chinese "coolies." Accordingly, the law was repealed in March 1868.

Concurrently, Seward imposed on a reluctant Chinese government a treaty designed explicitly to facilitate the massive procurement of labor.[38] The document asserted the right of the Chinese to expatriate themselves and to immigrate freely into the United States, but specified that the right of entry should not be construed to entail the right to acquire U.S. citizenship by way of naturalization. Seward evidently envisaged future arrivals as sojourners rather than immigrants—in today's parlance, guest workers. The treaty led to a rapid escalation of Chinese arrivals, from an annual average of 4,300 for the 1861–1867 period to successive highs of 15,740 in 1870, 20,292 in 1873, and 22,781 in 1876.

Thanks to the completion of the transcontinental railroad in 1869, Chinese labor could be moved inland and came to be thought of as a national asset. For example, after initially deriding the Burlingame treaty, the editor of *The Nation* subsequently welcomed it, explaining in July 1869 that prejudice and prohibitory legislation notwithstanding, U.S. capital would continue to seek Chinese workers because they "will work harder and for less wages, and are more tractable" than Irish or Germans.[39] In the South, where reconstruction afforded blacks unprecedented rights, the Chinese were touted by entrepreneurs as a "docile and thrifty" substitute; the one drawback, however, was that they would not go in debt to the proprietor and hence could not be retained after their contract expired.[40] The promoters of a Chinese Labor Convention held in Memphis in July 1869, spoke of bringing in several hundred thousand workers to the cotton fields; and the following year several hundred Chinese were recruited for work on the Alabama-Chattanooga railroad. However, the importers were hampered by prohibitions on the coolie trade and further failed to raise the needed capital; moreover, to impede competition, in 1870 the

British authorities in Hong Kong prohibited the export of Chinese labor outside the British colonies. More fundamentally, in the absence of effective instruments of coercion, the Chinese turned out to be much less "docile" than anticipated; and southern planters soon discovered the possibility of exploiting black sharecroppers.[41]

Chinese labor came to be used in the industrial sector as well. As early as 1853, in the face of the apparent reluctance of European immigrants to settle in the south, the Eddyville Iron Works in Kentucky engaged twenty Chinese "coolies" as iron workers. In California, after the transcontinental railroad was completed in 1869, Chinese workers facilitated the rapid industrialization of the mining sector. One year later, a contingent of seventy-five Chinese shoemakers were brought all the way from San Francisco to North Adams, Massachusetts, under a three-year contract, to break a strike staged by mostly Irish and French Canadian Knights of St. Crispin; later in the year, two carloads were brought for the same purpose to the Passaic Steam Laundry in New Jersey; and a similar episode was reenacted two years later at a cutlery in Beaver Falls, Pennsylvania.[42] Although the practice remained limited because of its high cost and was abandoned altogether following the crash of 1873, it propelled Chinese immigration to the fore as a central grievance of organized labor.

Although the Chinese migrations probably constituted the largest of all the extra-European flows during this period, there are no reliable comprehensive estimates. Immigration data for the United States must be taken as indicative only, because legal prohibitions reduced *recorded* immigration, but contemporaneous accounts suggest there were many surreptitious landings, both in the United States and Mexico. Recorded arrivals from Asia reached a first peak of 39,629 in 1882, of whom 39,579 originated in China; the following year, following the enactment of restrictive legislation, admissions fell to 8,031 and subsequently to 3,363, a level never exceeded again until after World War II.[43] Altogether, 322,000 Chinese arrivals were recorded for the 1848–1882 period. Contrary to the conventional historiography that contrasts Chinese "sojourners" with European "immigrants," the crude rate of return of during the period of free movement (1848–1882) was 47 percent, comparable to many European groups such as Italians (albeit for a slightly later period).[44] As of the early 1870s, the Chinese constituted about 9 percent of California's total population; but as nearly all of them were adult males, they amounted to one-fifth of the economically active and one-fourth of all wage earners.[45] Some 90,000 Chinese were shipped to Peru in 1849–1874, mostly by way of Macao, others by way of Hong Kong to British Columbia to build the Canadian Pacific. But over the period under consideration, some 15 million Chinese migrated to Southeast Asia, mostly by way of Singapore, both as contract workers and as permanent settlers.[46]

Whereas Chinese transpacific migrations illustrate the consequences of that country's dependent status within the global economy, the case of Japan illustrates how a successful attempt by a late developer to catch up also stimulated massive emigration. In short, the Japanese government's modernization from above after the Meji Restoration (1868) fostered conditions similar to those of the European "Great Transformation," which similarly led the government to abandon its traditional policy and instead encourage emigration as a safety valve and source of public income.[47] By the turn of the twentieth century, Japanese workers constituted two-thirds of the sugar plantation workforce in Hawaii. But after they engaged in strikes, the Sugar Planters' Association took advantage of the U.S. missionary network to organize the recruitment of Korean substitutes. However, when Japan gained the upper hand in Korea, emigration was severely restricted so as to maintain an adequate supply of labor locally for Japanese enterprises. In 1907, to forestall a congressional attempt to exclude Japanese along with Chinese, President Theordore Roosevelt secured the cooperation of the Japanese authorities in a "gentlemen's agreement" whereby they prohibited further emigration to the United States. Altogether, some 400,000 Japanese arrivals were recorded in the United States, including Hawaii, between 1885 and 1924, when they were excluded along with all other Asians.

European expansion also generated large-scale African migrations. Despite its abolition by Britain and the United States as well as a few others at the beginning of the nineteenth century, the slave trade continued to expand, and exports of human beings from Africa reached an all-time peak in the 1840s.[48] The trade would have undoubtedly grown further in response to soaring demand for plantation-produced commodities, particularly sugar, had it not been for concerted international action, which effectively extinguished it from the European-dominated world in the 1870s. Although some attempts were made to recruit Africans as indentured workers, particularly in the West Indies, British ventures to that effect were denounced by other states as illegitimate: In effect, Africans were so markedly identified with slavery that they were not acceptable as *substitutes* for slaves. Moreover, at the time, Africans, in contrast with Asians, were not yet subject to the uprooting effects of capitalist transformations and hence were not driven to sell their labor for wages.

This also posed problems for the economic development of African colonies. Plantations and mines could be launched only after populations were "pacified," that is, when the Europeans acquired a sufficient degree of control over the populations in question to reduce their self-sufficiency and tax them, either in the form of required labor or in cash, which obligated them to work for wages or to produce commodities for the market. In parts of West Africa, some export crops grown elsewhere on plantations or estates, notably cocoa and coffee, were eventually produced instead by local Africans on a smallholder basis, but often with a large input of labor from neighboring colonies (e.g., "Mossi" workers from Burkina Faso (then Upper Volta) in Ghana and Côte d'Ivoire).

In southern Africa, the discovery of gold and diamond deposits promised such enormous profits that ways were quickly found to secure an adequate labor supply. Elaborated on a trial and error basis, the measures devised resulted in a highly integrated transnational politicoeconomic system, with migrations as a key component.[49] By 1876 gold-mining was organized on a large scale, combining white diggers who monopolized the higher-paid jobs and African laborers brought in under contract for short periods of about three months, later extended to between six and eighteen months. In the diamond fields, the African workers were confined to residential compounds for their contract period, to stop the illicit sale of diamonds and to control desertion; this was subsequently adopted in the gold mines as well. In the face of a labor shortage, around the turn of the twentieth century, the mines imported Chinese "coolies" as well; however, the practice was stopped in 1907 following a strike of white workers. The massive use of migrant workers in turn stimulated a demand for provisions, for which production labor was required as well. The supply was enlarged by expropriating Africans from their lands and confining them to native reserves that impeded economic self-sufficiency as well as by excluding them from the production of most cash crops while subjecting them to taxes and labor obligations. In the face of growing demand, the domain of recruitment expanded beyond South Africa to as far away as Nyasaland (Malawi) and Mozambique, where the Portuguese authorities imposed forced labor to generate manpower exports for which South Africa compensated them in gold. Similar systems were developed in Southern Rhodesia (now Zimbabwe), Southwest Africa (Namibia), and Angola.

Building the Great Wall

Ironically, although the vast expansion of international migrations in the final decades of the nineteenth century was largely rooted in the affluent states' soaring demand for labor, at home or in their colonies, as well as in the worldwide impact of the market forces they unleashed, the receivers quickly came to see themselves as victims of an alien invasion. In response, they institutionalized more effective border controls and imposed severe limits on entry for purposes of permanent settlement. Although the new policy orientation was clearly visible as early as the 1880s, it took nearly a quarter of a century for the restrictionists to achieve their objectives, partly because of opposition, partly because of the sheer difficulty of devising effective measures. In the intervening period international migration continued to expand, so that the historical peak was reached in most receiving countries well after attempts were launched to limit entry—a fact that exacerbated the sense of "crisis." World War I and the Soviet Revolution prompted a further reinforcement of controls and restrictions on grounds of national security. By the 1920s most states had erected solid walls, with narrow gates to let in specific categories.

Struggles over the determination of immigration policy straddled two distinct axes of concern and interest, the one essentially economic, the other "moral," or political. In the economic sphere, immigration pitted large manufacturers who relied on massive inputs of unskilled labor against more traditional craftsmen and native workers, who feared deskilling and displacement and believed the availability of foreign workers gave "capitalists" an unfair advantage. From the perspective of labor, in particular, limits on immigration constituted a a legitimate form of "protection," which paralleled the tariffs being imposed even then on foreign manufactured goods. Matters were made worse by the fact that once networks were established, the supply of foreign workers grew somewhat independently of the level of the demand.

The "moral," or political, dimension pertained to an assessment of the putative impact of immigration on the "integrity" of the nation, anchored in "scientific" and popular understandings of culture and psychology. As shaped by nationalism and imperial rivalries, these involved prejudicial stereotypes regarding the "character" of particular groups and their suitability for membership in the receiving nation. Paradoxically, the very qualities that made immigrants especially fit for their assigned role in the receiving country's economy—their "brute strength," "simplicity," and "docility"—rendered them unsuitable for inclusion. Moreover, their apparent willingness to accept living conditions below the publicly approved standard of the receiving countries functioned as a self-fulfilling prophecy: In effect, they became the inferior beings they were imagined to be.

Accordingly, ruling elites tended to be split—and in some cases, genuinely ambivalent—on the issue of immigration. For example, Max Weber sharply criticized the landlords of eastern Germany, who in the course of their transformation into capitalist entrepreneurs replaced quasi-servile farm dependents with hired Polish help. Speaking as a nationalist, he concluded the study he conducted on behalf of the *Verein für Socialpolitik* in 1892 by pointing out that Poles might be good for capitalism, but were bad for Germany, in that the increase in a Catholic and non-German-speaking population constituted a major obstacle to national integration. Accordingly, he recommended measures to prevent their permanent settlement.[50]

In the United States, similar objections had been voiced in the late eighteenth century about Germans, and later on about the Irish, peoples who were considered atavistically unfit for life in a republic. The arrival of the Chinese precipitated even more acute concerns. In California, they naturally provoked the hostility of white miners and later American or European immigrant workers. White small businessmen also joined the exclusionist camp, leaving the railroad and mining "monopolists" as the only advocates of the Chinese.[51] However, they were soon joined by agricultural entrepreneurs who discovered California's vocation as a produce cornucopia for the expanding nationwide consumer market, for which a massive supply of cheap "stoop" labor was required; as of 1886, the bulk of California's farm labor was Chinese, and the state's farmers steadfastly opposed exclusion.[52]

Nevertheless, anti-Chinese sentiment made rapid strides among the general public, whose prejudices were rooted in traditional Christian attitudes toward heathens and exacerbated by well-publicized events, such as the massacres of U.S. missionaries in Tientsin (1868), a coolie revolt in Peru (1870), and the outbreak of a famine (1879), which raised the specter of the United States being swamped by a tidal wave of starving humanity vastly larger even than that of the Irish of the preceding generation.[53] In 1875, at the initiative of President Grant, Congress enacted a law to exclude Chinese brought by "headmen" against their will, singling out women imported for "lewd and shameful purposes" as the worst segment. This constituted a major turning point in U.S. immigration policy, because it was the first national measure to control admissions directly. In 1880, a mere twelve years after imposing on China a treaty to foster the export of labor, the United States dictated the terms of a modification of that treaty whereby it could decide one-sidedly to restrict Chinese immigration; and two years later the importation of Chinese contract labor was prohibited for a ten-year period. The measure was renewed several times and eventually extended to encompass the new U.S. possessions in the Pacific.

Beyond its deterrent effect, the 1882 law established a presumption that any Chinese seeking to enter were "coolies," and that those who were in the United States were there illegally. All persons of Chinese origin, including those who were U.S. citizens by virtue of birth, were henceforth subject to harassing identity checks and liable to deportation unless able to produce a certificate that proved they were *not* coolies, or proof of U.S. birth. The states piled up discriminatory laws designed to deprive the Chinese of their means of livelihood, restrict their social mobility, and deny them political power.[54] Besides their ineligibility for naturalization, which was upheld by the Supreme Court in 1922 as applying also to Japanese, and in 1923 to Indians, Asians faced obstacles such as the

California prohibitions on the use of certain types of nets for commercial fishing and on establishing laundries in wooden buildings, and its 1913 land law, which prohibited "aliens ineligible to citizenship" from buying agricultural land or leasing it for more than three years. There were also half-hearted efforts to return Chinese workers to their homeland, paralleling efforts earlier in the century to return freed slaves to Africa.

The movement to exclude the Chinese quickly brought their immigration to a virtual halt. However, it failed to reduce the flow of peoples of color into the country because, as Mary Coolidge observed in 1909, "The history of general labor in California since about 1886 is the story of efforts to find substitutes for the vanishing Chinese."[55] Farmers and ranchers first turned to Japanese and Filipinos, whose experience as groups initially wooed and later excluded, largely paralleled that of their predecessors; but as the influx of U.S. capital into mining, farming, and transportation transformed Mexico's hitherto isolated northern states into "the Border," a permanent solution emerged.[56]

The federal laws enacted in the 1880s with regard to European immigration were merely culled from the existing corpus of state and local measures directed against the entry of persons deemed incapable of supporting themselves by reason of physical or mental disability or morally unfit as indicated by a previous criminal record.[57] Given the apparently inexhaustible pool of immigrants, business no longer objected to these regulations, which in fact screened out those unable or unwilling to function in a mature capitalist society. In 1885, organized labor gained sufficient strength to secure enactment of a prohibition of immigration under prearranged contract, which had been notoriously used to recruit strikebreakers; but by all reports this had little impact because employers enlisted replacement workers after they landed instead.

Around the turn of the century, a steady flow of disposable and cheap unskilled labor, ethnically distinct from indigenous workers—mostly the descendants of earlier waves of immigrants from northwestern Europe—accorded well with the requirements of the manufacturing sector, which was rapidly shifting from craft methods toward mass production, while simultaneously seeking to prevent labor from improving its bargaining position by way of collective action. However, once again, the very attributes that rendered the newcomers suitable as cheap labor were viewed by many as politically problematic. Their linguistic and religious distance from the hegemonic anglo-germanic, Protestant culture, was expected to make their assimilation into the mainstream more difficult; this was compounded by the sheer mass of newcomers, as well as by the fact that many of them saw themselves as temporary migrants, with little incentive or opportunity to adopt U.S. ways.

The movement to restrict general immigration was initiated by traditional social elites and quickly gained widespread support among what would be termed later the *silent majority.* Concurrently, organized labor, with support from an emerging group of professional economists, also advocated limits as a sine qua non for improving the situation of the American working class. Thus, the immigration debate fostered opposing coalitions of strange bedfellows, cutting across the right-left continuum: The growing restrictionist movement, which included "WASP" social and intellectual elites, organized labor, and populist political forces that encompassed the South as a whole and rural constituencies throughout the country, was opposed by organized capitalists, together with the Catholic Church, Jewish organizations, and urban political machines.

The basic reorientation of the U.S. immigration policy took place in 1896, when both houses of Congress approved a proposal imposing a literacy requirement, designed to reduce total incoming numbers and effect an ethnic selection by barring the bulk of arrivals from Southern and Eastern Europe, where schooling was rarely available. However, the measure was vetoed by President Cleveland, and the tug-of-war was reenacted several times until a literacy law was finally passed in 1917 over Woodrow Wilson's two successive vetoes. Although war-induced xenophobia was undoubtedly a contributing factor, by this time there was a consensus, shared by politically progressive groups, that a continued massive inflow of poor strangers was undesirable.

However, as soon as shipping returned to normal in 1919, numbers rapidly escalated and gave every indication of soon exceeding prewar peaks. Concurrently, the anti-immigration camp was further reinforced by the fear of revolutionary contagion and a yearning for a return to "normalcy" as well as postwar economic doldrums. The widely supported determination to close the door can be understood as part of a wide array of regime-maintenance undertakings of the period, including stepped up repression of radicalism, national prohibition of aloholic beverages, mandatory segregation throughout the South, and social discrimination against Catholics and Jews in elite institutions. Concurrently, elites adopted a firmly assimilationist stance toward recent immigrants and their descendants.[58]

Spurred on by favorable prospects, the restrictionists expanded their objectives to include a ban on all immigration from Asia as well as first a temporary, and subsequently a *permanent,* annual limit on the number of admissions from Europe, coupled with allocation of these numbers in a manner designed to restore the ethnic profile that prevailed *before* the latest wave arrived. Completed in 1924, the policy reduced immigration from Europe from about 1 million a year to 150,000.

The innovative mechanisms devised to implement the new system were as significant as the policy itself. Hitherto, the policing of immigration was essentially conceived in terms of inspection at the border, as reflected in the construction of a huge processing station at Ellis Island in the early 1900s. However, the adoption of quotas wreaked havoc with ongoing practices, creating considerable duress for the immigrants, who might find the quota filled by the time they arrived in the United States, but also difficulties for the shippers and the U.S. authorities, who would have to dispose of the unauthorized excess. It thus became quickly evident that efficient operation of the new system required distribution of entry permits in advance of embarkation, which in turn mandated an extensive U.S. immigration bureaucracy abroad. This was established by the Rogers Act of 1924, which professionalized the U.S. consular service and charged it among other things with the task of attributing immigration visas. Once this bureaucracy was in place, the complex verification procedures—which included in addition to the literacy test a variety of police checks, medical inspection, determination of financial responsibility, and a political interview—could be carried out abroad as prerequisites for obtaining the visa. The expanded consular service also made it possible for the United States to impose notoriously demanding requirements on temporary visitors, thereby reducing the likelihood that such visits would constitute a significant source of illegal immigration by overstaying.

The adoption of "remote control" was of course facilitated by the fact that direct access to the United States from outside the North American continent was possible only by ship, and that such a vessel constitutes a closed container, which one cannot enter or leave once under way.[59] Easily applicable to air travel, it constituted a strikingly precocious adaptation of the concept of the transformation of territorial space in the age of global history.

Once again, however, the efforts to stem ongoing flows were accompanied by actions that stimulated the onset of others. World War I enhanced the demand for U.S. goods, but simultaneously occasioned a labor shortage, as transatlantic immigration ground to an abrupt halt and subsequently because U.S. males were drafted for military service. Accordingly, employers secured measures that exonerated workers from neighboring countries from the new literacy requirements as well as from the prohibition against contract labor. The sources included Mexico, where many were being uprooted by revolutionary upheavals; Quebec, which had long provided migrant labor for the New England lumber industry and its factories; and the English-speaking islands of the Caribbean. Although according to the racialist theories that justified the exclusion of Asians and the draconian restrictions on Eastern and Southern Europeans, all these groups were undesirable, the exceptional wartime arrangements were in effect institutionalized in the 1920s by exempting independent countries of the Western Hemisphere from the immigration ceiling and quota system that governed flows from Europe.[60]

Beyond this, in response to pressures from agricultural interests, immigration authorities condoned the practice of unregulated movement across the U.S.-Mexican border, and cooperated with employers to ensure an adequate supply of labor when demand was high as well as to dispose of the workers when no longer needed. The resulting dualism of a well-regulated main gate and an informally managed backdoor became a permanent feature of U.S. immigration that still prevails today. Combined with renewed exceptional measures to tap neighboring parts of the "south" in wartime or to provide temporary workers for particular sectors, these practices contributed to the formation of extensive self-sustaining migratory networks throughout the region.

The experience of the other English-speaking overseas countries largely paralleled that of the United States. In relation to population size, on the eve of World War I immigration was a much larger phenomenon in Canada than in the United States. Still the historical maximum for a single year, the 400,870 arrivals recorded in 1913 amounted to 5 percent of the country's population—over three times the highest level in relation to population achieved in the United States (1907). Unlike in the United States, until late in the nineteenth century immigration to Canada was tightly controlled by way of passenger regulations as well as land and settlement policies, designed in London to favor British immigrants of a class suited to the role of imperial guardianship. Immigration was seen as a critical mechanism for overcoming the demographic superiority of the French Canadians, and hence their political weight in the dawning democratic age. However, in the absence of industrial development, Canada functioned largely as a way station to the United States.[61] Around the turn of the twentieth century, in the face of a continuing shortage of agriculturally oriented immigrants from the United Kingdom as well as of French-Canadian demands for equal status as a "founding nation," the preference system was broadened to include French-speaking Europeans and other national groups committed to agriculture (e.g., Ukrainians) as well as economically qualified U.S. citizens; blacks and Asians were firmly excluded. The Chinese were dealt with summarily; but Indians, who trickled into British Columbia around the turn of the twentieth century, were difficult to keep out because as British subjects, they had the right to travel freely to other parts of the empire. However, in 1908 the restrictionists achieved their objective by devising a law that barred immigrants who did not come by "continuous journey" from their country of origin.[62]

Immigration from Europe finally soared in the 1890s, when U.S. migration to Canada briefly outweighed the southward movement. After World

War I, the problem was no longer how to secure suitable immigrants, but how to keep out the mass of undesirables deflected toward Canada by U.S. restrictions. The solution here also included an annual cap on immigration and a system of preferences that deterred Southern and Eastern Europeans. Consequently, in the period 1921–1931 the contribution of immigration to Canadian population growth was only half as large as that of births, and in the following decade, less than one-tenth.

Similarly, Australia positively encouraged British immigration while restricting the admission of Eastern and Southern Europeans and excluding nonwhites.[63] The policy's success is reflected in the fact that as of 1947, 95 percent of the country's 7.6 million were of the preferred stock, of whom 88 percent were British or Irish; one percent was Aborigine, leaving only 4 percent as the contribution of less-desirable immigration. Canada and Australia also adopted the "remote control" system developed in the United States.

Although the specter of the "yellow peril" was evoked in Europe as well, a more directly threatening invasion was at hand—the massive westward exodus of the Jews from Eastern Europe.[64] During the heated debates on legislation to restrict immigration that raged in England around the turn of the twentieth century, the Chinese were referred to as the truest of aliens, but the Jews differed only "as a matter of degree."[65] Within the prevailing frameworks of racialist ideology, many parallels were drawn between the two groups. As the globe became more integrated and the worldwide stream of migration brought hitherto invisible men to its very center, both figured in mythical conspiracies depicted in such fictions as "The Protocol of the Elders of Zion" and Sax Rohmer's popular Fu Manchu novels. Having mastered mysterious mental processes or accumulated esoteric knowledge consigned in arcane texts, the Chinese and the Jews were thought to have the power to hypnotize ordinary beings into becoming subservient instruments of their will, or to enslave them with the bait of gold or opium, using them to operate malevolent transnational networks of illegitimate gain that national authorities were helpless to resist. Both groups were also associated with filth and contagious disease, particularly cholera, which still perennially reappeared in Europe by way of shipping routes, and hence was associated with migration.[66]

By and large, the massive migration of the Jews from Eastern Europe was stimulated by economic factors associated with the "great transformation" already noted, which undermined their traditional roles as trade intermediaries, craftsmen, and small manufacturers; although this population was generally poor, philanthropic assistance from fellow Jews in the receiving countries made it easier for them to emigrate. In newly independent Rumania and in the Czarist Empire, the exodus was accelerated and magnified by new discriminatory measures and outright violence, in the face of which Western-based Jewish organizations secured the lifting of prohibitions on exit. Although the preferred destination was the United States, there were also smaller streams to various European countries, Canada, and Latin America. Everywhere, the arrival of East European Jews precipitated hostile reactions, manifested by way of a more political form of anti-Semitism—the Dreyfus Affair in France, the electoral campaigns of Karl Lueger in Vienna—as well as efforts to bar their entry.[67] That they were not excluded as quickly or as thoroughly as the Chinese, despite widespread fearful hostility, is attributable to the presence within the receiving countries of well-established Jewish communities that had managed to achieve relatively high status and wielded some economic and political power.

In England, *immigrant* became synonymous with *Jew*. As in France and Central Europe, anti-Semitism was readily exploited by the emerging nationalist Right. Invoking the 1882 U.S. legislation against the Chinese and other "unfit groups" as their warrant, from the mid-1880s on a spate of nationalist associations undertook to fight the "alien invasion," which, they argued, weakened the core of the empire at a time of expanding responsibility. In his Unionist campaign of 1892, Joseph Chamberlain endorsed restriction with the expressed purpose of diverting working-class support from the Home-Rule Liberals. Although the leading theme of the English campaign was the threat of "declining quality," immigration was also opposed on economic grounds, particularly during the 1894 depression, when the Trade Union Congress (TUC) endorsed restriction on the grounds that the immigrant-based mass-production garment industry undermined the traditional trades. Later, however, the TUC reversed its stance on the grounds that the issue was a red herring designed to detract attention from the working class's real problems. Although an Aliens bill was first proposed in 1894, the Liberals opposed it steadily as an unwarranted interference with the free movement of labor, in keeping with their stalwart adherence to Manchesterian principles of free trade. Conversely, as the neomercantilist movement away from free trade and toward imperial preference gained ground, it provided a rationale for restricting the free entry of people as well.

Finally enacted by the Conservative majority in 1905 as the first immigration control measure since the era of the Napoleonic Wars, the Aliens Act merely restricted the landing of poor immigrants who might constitute a public burden; but the context makes it quite clear that this was designed principally to reduce the ongoing flow of Russian Jews. Although the incoming Liberal government decided not to apply it systematically, the measure appears to have served as an effective deterrent, as indicated by the immediate decline of recorded immigration from 12,481 in 1906 to 3,626 in 1911, a period of rising immigration elsewhere.[68] Immigration was further restricted at the outbreak of World War I and again in the 1920s, when Britain experienced a protracted period of slow economic stagnation and unemployment. Consequently, around 1930, Britain had the lowest proportion of foreign-born of any industrial democracy.[69] It is thus appropriate to view Britain as the first industrialized country to achieve a "zero-baseline" immigration policy. However, it should be noted that it did not entail any sort of sacrifice on the part of Britain's employers, since Ireland continued to provide a plentiful supply of migrant labor, as it does indeed to this day.

As noted, in Germany the "immigration crisis" was precipitated by the influx of both Jews and non-Jewish Polish agricultural workers from Czarist Russia and the Austro-Hungarian Empire.[70] In 1885, Bismarck dealt with the problem on an ad hoc basis by a massive expulsion; but the Prussian landlords were adamant and subsequently resumed their recruitment. Following the denunciation of these practices by Max Weber and his associates as contrary to the national interest, the German authorities devised a system combining the recruitment of temporary workers with draconian controls on border-crossings and on their stay in Germany, which anticipated twentieth-century guest worker programs.

Against this general background, France emerges as an intriguing deviant case. Immigration, which was well under way by the 1880s, continued to grow with the encouragement of the state until World War I; the number of foreign-born doubled further in the decade after World War I, and as of 1931, there were 2.7 million foreigners as well as nearly 0.4 million naturalized citizens, constituting together approximately 7.3 percent of the total population. Initially the largest groups were Belgians and Italians, with smaller numbers of Spaniards and Swiss, neighboring groups somewhat equivalent to the Irish in Britain, Poles in Germany and Mexicans and Quebecers in the United States; however, from the 1880s onward France also began to receive Jews from Eastern Europe.[71] Xenophobic prejudices were at least as widespread among the general public and among the elite as in other Western countries, and nativists were well organized politically; yet, although some fifty mostly restrictionist bills were proposed between 1883 and 1914, most of them failed because of the strong resistance of employers and of the state.[72]

Although cultural nationalists in France as elsewhere warned against the detrimental consequences of *métissage* (miscegenation), applied here to the nation as a whole, under France's demographic conditions a nationalist argument could also be made on behalf of immigration as a vital source of military manpower. Accordingly, France adopted a highly assimilationist stance and facilitated the acquisition of French nationality by way of naturalization or birth. Unable to impose the restrictions they advocated throughout the life of the Third Republic, the French nativists got their revenge after its demise: Vichy deprived recent immigrant Jews who had become naturalized of their citizenship and turned them over, with all the foreign Jews they could trap, to the Nazis for disposal.[73]

Conclusion

The erection of a global network of barriers that successfully confined most of the world's population in their countries of birth, precisely at a time when social and economic forces disposed them to expand the domain of their movements and endowed them with an enhanced capacity for doing so, constitutes a remarkable example of the contradictory character of historical change and an even more remarkable demonstration of how apparently irresistible historical trends can be contradicted—for better or for worse—by concerted human action.

Even as worldwide movement multiplied opportunities for the cultural and biological mixing of groups hitherto separated and thereby enhanced the unity of humankind, the retrenchment of nations behind their self-made walls helped foster a cultural construction of "societies" as self-contained population entities with a common and homogeneous ancestry, growing by way of natural reproduction alone. In relation to these endogenous entities, immigration came to be regarded as a pathogenic source of otherness. It was the first episode in the protracted confrontation of the world's paramount "imagined communities" with the realities of globalization.[74]

Notes

1. However, this did not preclude tightly regulated and often largely involuntary relocation of populations to serve colonial needs, sometimes to another colony altogether.

2. For restrictions on exit, see Alan Dowty, *Closed Borders: The Contemporary Assault on Freedom of Movement* (New Haven: Yale University Press, 1987). It is worth noting that the policies of colonial governments regarding international movement have hardly been examined.

3. This point was emphasized by Hannah Arendt in *The Origins of Totalitarianism* (New York: Harcourt, Brace, Jovanovich, 1973), 269–290. For a fuller discussion, see Aristide R. Zolberg, "The Formation of New States as a Refugee-Generating Process," *Annals of the American Academy of Political and Social Science* 467 (May 1983): 27–31.

4. See, for example, tables 8 and 9 in Paul Bairoch, "International Industrialization Levels from 1750 to 1980," *Journal of European Economic History* 11 (1982): 35–74.

5. For a good overview, see Eric Hobsbawm, *The Age of Empire, 1875–1914* (New York: Vintage Books, 1987).

6. This analysis, which contests the conventional notion whereby greater liberalism is assumed to entail lesser state power, is founded on Michael Mann's distinction between "despotic" and "infrastructural" power. See Michael Mann, "The Autonomous Power of the State: Its Origins, Mechanisms, and Results," *European Archives of Sociology* 25 (1984):185–213.

7. Geoffrey Barraclough, *An Introduction to Contemporary History* (Harmondsworth, Engl.: Penguin, 1967), 65.

8. E. A. Wrigley, *Population and History* (New York: McGraw-Hill, 1969), 205.

9. Michael S. Teitelbaum and Jay M. Winter, *Fear of Population Decline* (New York: Academic Press, 1985). The role of population in relation to international power was emphasized by the "geopolitical school" of international relations that flourished around the turn of the century and was revived in the United States (in opposition to "Wilsonian idealism") after World War II. See, for example, early editions of Hans Morgenthau's foundational text book, *Politics Among Nations* (New York: Alfred A. Knopf, 1948).

10. Barraclough, *Contemporary History,* 80–81.

11. E. G. Ravenstein, "The Laws of Migration," *Journal of the Royal Statistical Society* 48:2 1885:167–235; and 52:2 1889:241–305.

12. B. R. Mitchell, *European Historical Statistics 1750–1970* (New York: Columbia University Press, 1976), table G1, 583–584.

13. Jean Heffer, *Le Port de New York et le commerce extérieur américain, 1860–1900* (Paris: Publications de la Sorbonne, 1986), 48, 160.

14. Walter Nugent, *Crossings: The Great Transatlantic Migrations, 1870–1914* (Bloomington: Indiana University Press, 1992), 31.

15. Nugent, *Crossings,* 41, 85.

16. Nugent, *Crossings,* 98, 101.

17. Heffer, *Le Port,* graph 19, 169; Nugent, *Crossings,* 51.

18. Nugent, *Crossings,* 59.

19. Karl Polanyi, *The Great Transformation* (Boston: Beacon Press, 1957).

20. Leslie Page Moch, *Moving Europeans: Migration in Western Europe Since 1650* (Bloomington: Indiana University Press, 1992), 104–160. For the process of transformation more generally, see the classic work by Karl Polanyi, *The Great Transformation.*

21. For the historical background, see Aristide R. Zolberg, "International Migration Policies in a Changing World System," in William McNeill and Ruth Adams, eds., *Human Migration* (Bloomington: Indiana University Press, 1978), 241–286.

22. The now vast literature on the subject is rooted in Marx and Engels's analysis of the use of the Irish in Britain. For a brief discussion of recent theoretical developments, see Aristide R. Zolberg, "The Next Waves: Migration Theory for a Changing World," *International Migration Review* 23:87 (Fall 1989):403–430.

23. Nugent, *Crossings,* 103.

24. Computed from Nugent, *Crossings,* table 1, p. 12 (based on B. R. Mitchell, *European Historical Statistics*). Actual figures were undoubtedly somewhat higher because the table in question omits some of the lesser European contributors (notably Belgium and the Netherlands, Greece, and others in the Balkans).

25. Nugent, *Crossings,* table 9, p. 43 (based on Ferenczi and Wilcox).

26. Sidney Mintz, *Sweetness and Power: The Place of Sugar in Modern History* (Baltimore: Penguin, 1986).

27. On the persistence of "unfree labor" and its relationship to migration, see Robin Cohen, *The New Helots: Migrants in the International Division of Labour* (Aldershot: Gower, 1987).

28. Eric Wolf, *Peasant Wars of the Twentieth Century* (Boston: Beacon Press, 1969), 371.

29. Hugh Tinker, *A New System of Slavery: The Export of Indian Labour Overseas, 1830–1920* (London: Oxford University Press).

30. Wolf, *Peasant Wars,* 371.

31. Sucheng Chan, "European and Asian Immigration into the United States," in Virginia Yans-McLaughlin, ed., *Immigration Reconsidered* (New York: Oxford University Press, 1990).

32. Chan, "European and Asian Immigration," 43; Farley M. Foster, "The Chinese Coolie Trade, 1845–1875," *Journal of Asian and African Studies* 3:3–4 (July and October 1968):257–270.

33. Marianne Bastid-Bruguière, "Currents of Social Change," in Denis Twitchett and John K. Fairbank, eds., *The Cambridge History of China,* II, Part 2 (London: Cambridge University Press, 1980), 582–586, 591–593.

34. Chan, "European and Asian Immigration," 44.

35. Curtis T. Henson, Jr., *Commissioners and Commodores: The East India Squadron and American Diplomacy in China* (Tuscaloosa: University of Alabama Press, 1982), 83.

36. Lucy Cohen, *Chinese in the Post–Civil War South: A People Without a History* (Baton Rouge: Louisiana University Press, 1984), 35.

37. Cohen, *Chinese in Post–Civil War South,* 50.

38. The treaty was signed on behalf of the emperor by Anson Burlingame, the former U.S. Ambassador to China, but now in Washington as head of a *Chinese* mission, despite any specific mandate to that effect and without consulting the Chinese government. I. Hsu, "Late Ch'ing Foreign Relations, 1866–1905," in Twitchett and Fairbank, *The Cambridge History of China,* II, Part 2, 73–74; Davids, 1973: I, xxiii–xxiv, 49.

39. William Armstrong, "Godkin and Chinese Labor: A Paradox in Nineteenth-Century Liberalism," *American Journal of Economics and Sociology* 21 (1962):93.

40. Cohen, *Chinese in the Post–Civil War South,* 45.

41. Cohen, *Chinese in the Post–Civil War South,* 107.

42. Guenther Barth, *Bitter Strength: A History of the Chinese in the United States, 1850–1870* (Cambridge, Mass.: Harvard University Press, 1964), 203–207.

43. *Historical Statistics of the United States,* 1961, C 88–114, pp. 58–59.

44. Sucheng Chan, "European and Asian Immigration," 38.

45. Alexander Saxton, *The Indispensable Enemy: Labor and the Anti-Chinese Movement in California* (Berkeley: University of California Press, 1971), 10.

46. Wolf, *Peasant Wars,* 175.

47. Sucheng Chan, "European and Asian Immigration," 50.

48. Philip Curtin, "Migration in the Tropical World," in Virginia Yans-McLaughlin, *Immigration Reconsidered,* 21–36.

49. Eric R. Wolf, *Europe and the People Without History* (Berkeley: University of California Press, 1982), 361–379; and Robin Cohen, *The New Helots: Migrants in the*

International Division of Labor (Aldershot, Engl.: Gower, 1982), 73–110. For a further elaboration, with emphasis on the international dimension of the system and its consequences for the contemporary period, see Aristide R. Zolberg, Astri Suhrke, and Sergio Aguayo, *Escape from Violence: Conflict and the Refugee Crisis in the Developing World* (New York: Oxford University Press, 1989), 72–89.

50. See Vernon K. Dibble, "Social Science and Political Commitments in the Young Max Weber," *European Journal of Sociology* (1968):95–109.

51. Because it required overhead capital, the use of Chinese labor gave larger industry an edge over small operations; and because Chinese entrepreneurs were more efficient than U.S. entrepreneurs in exploiting their countrymen within the confines of the enclave economy, they competed successfully in certain mass-production sectors, particularly cigar-making and garment-manufacturing.

52. Mary Coolidge, *Chinese Immigration* (New York: Henry Holt, 1909), 384.

53. Miller, 1969, 151, 159.

54. Chan, "European and Asian Immigration," 62.

55. Coolidge, *Chinese Immigration*, 384.

56. Friedrich Katz, *The Secret War in Mexico: Europe, the United States, and the Mexican Revolution* (Chicago: University of Chicago Press, 1981), 7.

57. The classic source on the subject remains John Higham, *Strangers in the Land* (New York: Atheneum, 1970).

58. Edward George Hartmann, *The Movement to Americanize the Immigrant* (New York: Columbia University Press, 1948).

59. Ever since the early part of nineteenth century, state and local authorities availed themselves of these elements to secure the cooperation of shippers in keeping out paupers and the like, by way of holding them financially liable for landing prohibited persons; but the shippers generally got around the regulations by ignoring them altogether, or making a market in the required bonds, or yet challenging them in the courts as unconstitutional impediments to commerce. Following the nationalization of immigration regulation, and as the categories of prohibited persons proliferated around the turn of the twentieth century, the authorities made some headway in integrating shippers into the border control apparatus by requiring them to return those rejected.

60. Although Canada was considered independent for this purpose, the British West Indian colonies came under the United Kingdom quota, which was the largest, and usually unfilled.

61. Freda Hawkins, *Canada and Immigration: Public Policy and Public Concern*, Second Edition (Kingston, Ont.: McGill-Queen's University Press, 1988).

62. Chan, "European and Asian Immigration," 55.

63. C. A. Price, "Australia," in D. Kubat, ed., *The Politics of Migration Policies* (New York: Center for Migration Studies, 1979), 3–18; J. Zubrzycki, "International Migration in Australia and the South Pacific," in M. Kritz, C. Keely, and S. Tomasi, eds., *Global Trends in Migration* (New York: Center for Migration Studies, 1981), 158–180.

64. Although the number of Chinese in Britain remained in the hundreds, responses to their presence were conditioned by negative reports on the situation in the empire; hostility to Chinese labor in the Transvaal became an issue in the 1906 general election campaign, and five years later a mob destroyed all of Cardiff's thirty-odd Chinese laundries (J. P. May, "The Chinese in Britain, 1860–1914," in

Immigrants and Minorities in British Society, 111). The alarm was sounded also by Kaiser Wilhelm at the time of the Boxer uprising (Barraclough, *Contemporary History,* 81).

65. Bernard Gainer, *The Alien Invasion* (London: Heinemann Educational Books, 1972), 112.

66. Cholera irrupted from Eastern Europe in 1865–1868; 737 died in Atlantic crossings or in quarantine in 1866, mainly from Hamburg; the following year another 133, again mainly from Hamburg. There were severe outbreaks in 1873 and 1887 among passengers embarking in Marseille, and again in 1892, 132 deaths were recorded among passengers emabarking in Hamburg, mainly Jews (Nugent, *Crossings,* 175). For the association of Chinese with disease, see Guenther Barth; on the more general theme, see Alan M. Kraut, *Silent Travelers: Germs, Genes, and the "Immigrant Menace"* (New York: Basic Books, 1994).

67. See, in addition to Gainer, Jack Wertheimer, *Unwelcome Strangers: East European Jews in Imperial Germany* (New York: Oxford University Press, 1987); Peter G. J. Pulzer, *The Rise of Political Anti-Semitism in Germany and Austria* (New York: Wiley, 1964); David A. Gerber, ed., *Anti-Semitism in American History* (Urbana: University of Illinois Press, 1986).

68. Gainer, *The Alien Invasion* 211.

69. Dudley Kirk, *Europe's Population in the Inter-War Years* (Princeton: Princeton University Press, 1946), 222.

70. Ulrich Herbert, *A History of Foreign Labor in Germany, 1880–1980: Seasonal Workers/Forced Laborers/Guest Workers* (Ann Arbor: University of Michigan Press, 1990); Knuth Dohse, *Ausländische Arbeiter und bürglerlicher Staat* (Könngsten, 1981); Wertheimer, *Unwelcome Strangers.*

71. André Armengaud, *La population française au XXe siècle* (Paris, Presses Universitaires de France, 1973), 43–57, 62–66; Yves Lequin, ed., *La mosaïque France: Histoire des étrangers et de l'immigration en France* (Paris: Larousse, 1988), 323–428.

72. The theme of undesirable immigrants, particularly Jews, was prominent among nationalist movements. See particularly Raoul Giardet, *Le Nationalisme français, 1871–1914* (Paris: Armand Colin, 1966); Eugen Weber, *Action Française* (Stanford: Stanford University Press, 1962); and Dominique Schnapper, "Le Juif errant," in Lequin, *La mosaïque France,* 373–388.

73. Michael Marrus and Robert Paxton, *Vichy and the Jews* (New York: Basic Books, 1981).

74. Benedict Anderson, *Imagined Communities: Reflections on the Origin and Spread of Nationalism,* rev. ed. (London: Verso, 1991).

About the Book and Editor

Humans have been on the move for millennia. They have done so slowly as well as quickly, sometimes involuntarily, sometimes transported by force, often relocated at great cost in lives, but they have always moved. Over the centuries, improved transportation has eased the movement, even in the face of man-made or natural obstacles. But in modern times, migration has accelerated and its reach has become truly global.

Whether it is Turkish *gastarbeiter* in Germany, Japanese *Nisei* in Seattle, Filipinos in Kuwait, or Haitians in Brooklyn, the costs and benefits of human mobility on such a wide and rapid scale are hotly debated. *Global History and Migrations,* the second volume of the *Global History Series,* explores the historical background of this issue by focusing on recent history, a time when human movements have been at their most dynamic. This book provides a rich, cross-cultural foundation for a more enlightened understanding of migration and its role in the unfolding shape of global history.

Wang Gungwu is the vice chancellor of the University of Hong Kong.

DATE DUE
